E. M. FORSTER: THE CRITICAL HERITAGE

THE CRITICAL HERITAGE SERIES

GENERAL EDITOR: B. C. SOUTHAM, M.A., B. LITT. (OXON.)
Formerly Department of English, Westfield College, University of London

---

For a list of books in the series see the back end paper

E. M. FORSTER

THE CRITICAL HERITAGE

Edited by
PHILIP GARDNER
Associate Professor of English
Memorial University of Newfoundland

ROUTLEDGE & KEGAN PAUL: LONDON AND BOSTON

First published in 1973
By Routledge & Kegan Paul Ltd
Broadway House, 68–74 Carter Lane,
London EC4V 5EL and
9 Park Street,
Boston, Mass. 02108, U.S.A.

ISBN 0 7100 7641 X
Library of Congress Catalog Card No. 73–77562

Printed in Great Britain by
Butler and Tanner Ltd
Frome and London

General Editor's Preface

The reception given to a writer by his contemporaries and near-contemporaries is evidence of considerable value to the student of literature. On one side we learn a great deal about the state of criticism at large and in particular about the development of critical attitudes towards a single writer; at the same time, through private comments in letters, journals or marginalia, we gain an insight upon the tastes and literary thought of individual readers of the period. Evidence of this kind helps us to understand the writer's historical situation, the nature of his immediate reading-public, and his response to these pressures.

The separate volumes in the *Critical Heritage Series* present a record of this early criticism. Clearly, for many of the highly productive and lengthily reviewed nineteenth- and twentieth-century writers, there exists an enormous body of material; and in these cases the volume editors have made a selection of the most important views, significant for their intrinsic critical worth or for their representative quality – perhaps even registering incomprehension!

For earlier writers, notably pre-eighteenth century, the materials are much scarcer and the historical period has been extended, sometimes far beyond the writer's lifetime, in order to show the inception and growth of critical views which were initially slow to appear.

In each volume the documents are headed by an Introduction, discussing the material assembled and relating the early stages of the author's reception to what we have come to identify as the critical tradition. The volumes will make available much material which would otherwise be difficult of access and it is hoped that the modern reader will be thereby helped towards an informed understanding of the ways in which literature has been read and judged.

B.C.S.

To

Averil

Contents

A Passage to India (1924)

Four Views of Forster (1927)

Aspects of the Novel (1927)

The Hill of Devi (1953)

Marianne Thornton (1956)

Maurice (first version, 1914)

Maurice (1971)

Two Valedictory Reviews

Preface

Writing of E. M. Forster in 1934 Peter Burra made the interesting statement: 'Probably the writing of novels has not been the most important element in his life'. Forster's literary career was indeed long and diversified, and after 1924 he turned exclusively to non-fiction, to articles, essays and broadcasts, and to remembrance of things past in the form of biography and the publication of his own letters home from India. He was also, for many, a 'good influence' and a living symbol of liberal values. It may be said that, because of this, his reputation is greater than the sum of its parts.

Nevertheless, my choice of material for inclusion in this book is based on the assumption that Forster is known to the reading-public, and to critics, primarily as a writer of fiction, and that his reputation —however it ramifies—is planted on his six novels and two books of short stories. When one considers that he made his appearance in 1904 as the author of 'The Story of a Panic', and his posthumous farewell in 1971 as the author of *Maurice*, he may reasonably be called, if not first and foremost, then certainly first and last a writer of fiction. There are thus in this book few reviews of his non-fiction. I have, on the whole, confined my selection in this area to reviews written by distinguished fellow-practitioners, to reviews which in some way reflect on his career as a novelist, and in certain cases to reviews which counteract the widespread worship which was made to him as a man in his later years. Reviews of his biography *Goldsworthy Lowes Dickinson* (1934) are entirely omitted, since I have discovered none which relate cogently either to Forster the novelist or to Forster the man.

With a literary career as long as Forster's (which began in 1905 with *Where Angels Fear to Tread* and ended in 1956 with *Marianne Thornton*), and a life even longer, which ended as recently as 1970, it has been peculiarly difficult to fix a 'cut-off' date for the material presented here. The position is further complicated by the publication of *Maurice*, reviews of which had obviously to be included, in 1971. My main concentration has been on the period from 1905 to 1928, when Forster retrieved and published as his last book of fiction, *The*

Eternal Moment, six stories mostly dating from before the First World War. A second, overlapping, series of critical articles and comments covers more thinly the period from 1927 to 1938, when the first book on Forster appeared in England, and on to 1943, when Lionel Trilling's more penetrating critical study was published in America and inaugurated a 'Forster revival'. Since that time articles and, more recently, books on Forster have appeared with increasing regularity. 1943 may thus be regarded as the 'cut-off' date for this book, though the fact is blurred by the necessary inclusion of a few reviews of Forster's later non-fiction and a larger number of reviews of *Maurice*.

Because the focus of this book is Forster's fiction, and because the quantity of this is more limited than its quality, I have taken the opportunity to include as many kinds of response to it as possible: not only reviews in important metropolitan newspapers and journals, but also reviews in provincial publications; not only perceptive reviews, but also crass ones; not only public pronouncements on Forster, but also letters to him from his friends. Such a broad selection sets Forster, I hope, more squarely in his time—and by this I mean the earlier time in which he was a practising novelist as well as the later time in which he had ceased to be one; but in addition it implies that a writer's 'reputation' is more than what the best-known critics have chosen to bestow on him.

The order in which the material is presented is essentially chronological, with the following exceptions. Forster's fiction did not begin to be published in America until 1911, and in a different sequence from the English one at that (at least until 1924). I have chosen to place American reviews in order of book-publication in England, rather than incur what seemed the greater evil of letting the reader encounter, say, American reviews of *The Longest Journey* just before reviews of *A Passage to India*. The second exception is similar: comments on books made sometimes well after their publication (as for instance Nos 35 and 75) are added to the section relating to the book's original publication rather than isolated between sections devoted to later books. The third exception is minor: within a set of reviews and comments on one book, individual items have sometimes been transposed to bring out a significant relationship to each other which a chronological order would blur (as with Nos 97 and 98 and Nos 115 and 116).

Acknowledgments

I wish to acknowledge with gratitude the generous help I have received from the following people and institutions:

The Trustees of E. M. Forster's Estate, the late Professor W. J. H. Sprott, Dr Donald Parry and Mr George Rylands (Vice-Provost and Fellow, respectively, of King's College, Cambridge), who released for my consultation and use many letters to E. M. Forster in the possession of the College; Mr P. N. Furbank, whose kind waiving of his own prior claims as Forster's official biographer made my consultation of these letters possible; Mr Furbank and Mr Michael Holroyd, who identified for me the three people referred to in Lytton Strachey's letter (No. 168); Miss Elizabeth Ellem, who placed at my disposal lists of Forster reviews which she had collected; Dr Patrick Parrinder; Dr A. N. L. Munby, Librarian of King's College, Cambridge, and his staff; Dr Rabindranath Majumdar of Calcutta, who supplied me with a number of Indian reviews; Dr Walter Redfern, who checked and improved my translations of French reviews; the staffs of the Cambridge University Library, the British Museum Newspaper Library, and the British Museum Reading Room; the Periodicals Division of Memorial University of Newfoundland Library; the North American Inter-Library Loan Service and its many co-operating libraries in Canada and the United States; Professor Alastair MacDonald; Professor S. P. Rosenbaum.

In common with many students of Forster I am indebted to the lists made of material relating to Forster by Professor F. P. W. MacDowell; and to the invaluable *Bibliography* of Miss B. J. Kirkpatrick.

In addition to acknowledgments made in individual headnotes, I am grateful to the following for allowing me to reprint material within their copyright or other control:

The Trustees of the E. M. Forster Estate for Nos 20, 35, 68, 74, 91, 95, 113, 127, 140, 167, 168; Laurence Pollinger Ltd, the Estate of the late Mrs Frieda Lawrence and the Viking Press for Nos 35, 74, 88, 91, 109, 123; A. P. Watt & Son and Magdalene College, Cambridge for Nos 68 and 95; George Allen & Unwin Ltd for Nos 113 and 167;

Times Newspapers for permission to reprint Nos 94, 142, 172, 173, 184, originally published in *The Times, The Times Literary Supplement* and *The Times Educational Supplement*; the *Guardian* for Nos 100, 144, 154, 160, 171; the *Sunday Times* for Nos 158 and 178; the *Observer* for Nos 99 and 179; *Time and Tide* for Nos 102 and 162; *Springfield Union and Sunday Republican* for Nos 13, 37, 78, 126; *Saturday Review of Literature* for Nos 117 and 118; the *New York Herald Tribune* for Nos 124 and 145; the *Statesman* (Calcutta) for Nos 114 and 121; the *New Statesman* for Nos 99, 130, 138, 148, 104, 115, 116, 141, 165, 174; the *Spectator* for Nos 105, 135, 137, 143, 155, 161, 163, 176; the *Daily Telegraph* for Nos 170 and 180. It has proved difficult in certain cases to locate the proprietors of copyright. However, all possible care has been taken to trace ownership of the selections included and to make full acknowledgment for their use.

Finally I am grateful to the Canada Council for their generous provision of research grants which enabled me to work on this book in England in the summers of 1971 and 1972; and to my wife and colleague Averil Gardner, for her advice and encouragement over the past two years.

Work on this book was begun shortly before E. M. Forster died late in 1970. As one of the many undergraduates to whom he had extended kindness during the years when he was a Fellow of King's College, Cambridge, I had hoped to be able to consult him about it and thus reduce the likelihood of error or false emphasis. This proved impossible. I can only trust that the material I have collected here depicts the growth of his critical reputation in sufficient breadth to avoid incurring the charge (in Forster's own phrase) of 'pseudo-scholarship'.

Introduction

I

It is no more than a statement of the obvious to say that by now, in the nineteen-seventies, E. M. Forster is one of the fixed stars of the century's literary firmament. Opinions may differ as to his precise magnitude, but he is to be observed shining alongside such other fixed stars as Lawrence, Joyce and Virginia Woolf. Like them he is studied in universities, like theirs his novels are widely available both in hardback and in paperback editions. Thus Forster is no remote literary figure, of canonised but ignored importance; he is read, and his present-day readers, like their predecessors, may be assumed to be forming opinions of their own about him.

Nevertheless, it is hardly possible for all Forster's present-day readers to form those opinions in a critical vacuum; many of them are likely to turn to what has been written about Forster in order to see his novels and short stories in some sort of perspective. As this perspective is most conveniently furnished by books, and as most of the books on Forster have appeared in the last decade, they are likely in some degree to be the victims of a species of critical imbalance that is peculiar to Forster's reputation and that it is a part of the purpose of this volume to correct.

The imbalance involved here is a result of the large space of time which separates Forster's last novel, *A Passage to India*, published in 1924, from the main concentration of books about him—fourteen critical studies which appeared between 1960 and 1970. The gap is not narrowed by taking into account the publication dates of either *The Eternal Moment* (1928) or *Maurice* (1971), since both these books were written before the First World War. Forster's literary reputation, considered since 1924 and in terms of the number of *books* about him (and this is how it is likely to be considered by more recent readers of his work), takes the shape of an inverted pyramid, with all the weight at the top. As one goes backwards, the pyramid narrows drastically: only two books on Forster (James McConkey's and Rex Warner's) appeared in the nineteen-fifties, only one (Lionel Trilling's) in the nineteen-forties. The base of the pyramid of critical books is Rose Macaulay's *The Writings of E. M. Forster*, published in 1938, already fourteen years after Forster ceased to practise as a novelist and, indeed, as a writer of fiction. Thus, in historical terms, the pyramid appears not even to teeter top-heavily on the work with which it deals, but actually to hover, Laputa-like, above it.

The metaphor, as can be seen, goes too far. Just as, in *Aspects of the Novel*, Forster preferred to see his group of novelists, widely separated in time, writing simultaneously in the Reading Room of the British Museum, so Forster's critics of the last decade may claim an equal right to consider his novels despite the long lapse of time since they were written. Much has been added by their doing so. It is no denigration of this, however, to suggest that, considering the period spanned by Forster's career as a novelist—from 1905 to 1924—the perspective needs widening, to take into account not only a view of Forster which brackets him with Lawrence, Joyce and Virginia Woolf, but also one which brackets him with his earlier contemporaries, Wells, Galsworthy, Arnold Bennett, and many others now almost totally forgotten.

Forster has had much to offer, both as a novelist and as a 'liberal humanist', with the result that, though his message of the importance of personal relationships and of the need to 'connect' has never gone unnoticed, he has been seen differently, if not remade, by each generation that has come to his work: one notes the words of Lionel Trilling who said, in 1943, that 'a consideration of Forster's work is, I think, useful in time of war'. But one needs also to remember the words of Virginia Woolf, who said in 1927: 'Mr. Forster is a novelist . . . who sees his people in close contact with their surroundings. And therefore the colour and constitution of the year 1905 affect him far more than any year in the calendar could affect the romantic Meredith or the poetic Hardy'. It should never be forgotten that Forster was born in the Victorian age and wrote most of his novels in the Edwardian. His career as a novelist (and this includes his abandoned novel *Arctic Summer* and his long-unpublished *Maurice*) was virtually over when *Sons and Lovers* and *Dubliners* were published, and before Virginia Woolf made her début as a novelist with *The Voyage Out* in 1915. *A Passage to India*, published in 1924, is a novel only of the British in India, not in England, whose life after the First World War Forster never described in fiction.

There seems therefore good reason for agreeing with the contention, expressed by Frederick C. Crews in 1962, that Forster was a novelist the 'real centre' of whose career 'lies in the first decade of the twentieth century'. Much of the material in this book provides a reminder of how Forster appeared to his contemporaries of that decade and of the next two. The reminder is only fair, since those whose society his novels in part mirrored should be given their opportunity of commenting on the accuracy of their literary reflections; it is also necessary, to balance the more easily accessible recent views of Forster's contribution and present the fullest possible perspective on his reputation. The reminder may also be a salutary one, in suggesting that the understanding of Forster by his earlier contemporaries was no worse, if no better, than that demonstrated by his later.

II

The generally accepted verdict that *A Passage to India* is Forster's best book is confirmed both by the volume and by the almost complete unanimity of the response when it was published in 1924. It seems reasonable to claim that the contemporary reader's awareness of its importance is what prompts him to look more closely at Forster's work as a whole, and indeed this is likely to have been so for a long time, since *A Passage to India* was much the earliest of Forster's books to appear as a Penguin, in 1936. But the response to *A Passage to India* in 1924 was no new thing in itself, despite Forster's absence from the literary scene for almost fourteen years; it was rather the culmination of an awareness, steadily increasing ever since his first book appeared in 1905, that Forster was a novelist of startling originality (No. 3). It was *Howards End* that moved one reviewer (*Daily Telegraph*, No. 58) to call Forster 'one of our assets, and . . . likely to become one of our glories', that phrase seen over and over again on the back cover of Penguin editions of Forster's novels. It was also *Howards End* that provoked the *Morning Leader* (No. 56) to assert that 'if he never writes another line, his niche should be secure'.

The gradual and steady rise in Forster's reputation from 1905 and 1924 is shown not only by the amount and tenor of the reviews of his work, but by the waxing faith of his publishers that increased numbers of his books would sell. *Where Angels Fear to Tread* was published by William Blackwood in October 1905 in an edition of

1050 copies, swelled by a further 526 the following January, no doubt as a result of reviews so favourable that the worst the only dissenting journal (No. 5) could point to was 'a not particularly interesting story'. Blackwood's took the modest risk in 1907 of publishing 1587 copies of *The Longest Journey*. There were more reviews of this than of *Where Angels Fear to Tread*, but though the majority of reviewers treated the book with respect they did not always know what to make of it, Forster's often remarked predilection for 'sudden death' being not the least of their problems. Later critics of what Forster called in 1960 the novel he was 'most glad to have written'[1] have usually found it 'puzzling', like the reviewer of the *World* (No. 29), but they have not displayed the uninhibited petulance of the reviewer of the *Outlook* (No. 33), who roundly declared it to be 'the most impossible book we have read for many years'.

In October 1908 Edward Arnold (who were to publish Forster's remaining novels) brought out *A Room with a View* in an edition of 2000 copies. This was well received, except, again, by the *Outlook* (No. 48), whose reviewer felt that, to have written this story 'about people who never act or talk quite sanely', Forster must have had 'an exceptionally curious experience of modern society'; and by the *Birmingham Daily Post*, which thought the story too light to merit serious attention. The novel was accorded this, however, in a long and interesting review (No. 38) by R. A. Scott-James, and in an equally interesting and even more unequivocally favourable one (No. 46) by the Liberal Member of Parliament C. F. G. Masterman, who had already written two favourable reviews of Forster's earlier novels.

The tendency thus far demonstrated for Forster's novels to be issued in enlarging editions was maintained by *Howards End*, 2500 copies of which were published in October 1910. This novel so consolidated Forster's reputation that another 7500 copies had been printed by the end of the year. It was called by Scott-James, already a well-disposed critic, 'the year's best novel', and by Archibald Marshall 'the season's great novel'. Marshall also described it as 'a general subject of talk in literary circles' (No. 63), and Arnold Bennett reinforced this picture of its impact, saying that 'it has been mightily argued about during the repasts of the *élite*' (No. 71)—repasts, and arguments, in which he had no doubt participated. *Howards End* was the first of Forster's novels to appear in America, but interestingly enough only 1500 copies were published, by Putnam's in January

1911. And whereas English strictures had been on the whole minor, though significant, one American reviewer (No. 73) confessed himself 'a trifle puzzled and a trifle bored', and the *New York Times* (No. 72) compared Forster unfavourably with Galsworthy. The lack of general knowledge of Forster in America at this time is amusingly evidenced by the certainty of the *Review of Reviews* (vol. 43, 1911) that E. M. Forster was a 'nom-de-plume', and by the strong impression formed by a reviewer in the Chicago *Tribune* that Forster was a woman. Oddly enough, and less excusably, this thought had already been whispered in passing in a review (No. 18), published in the *Evening Standard & St James's Gazette*, of *The Longest Journey*.

Despite the increasing sales of Forster's novels, only 1000 copies of *The Celestial Omnibus* were published, by Sidgwick and Jackson, in May 1911, though the warm enough response to these short stories encouraged the issue of a further 500 copies in February 1912. His other book of short stories, *The Eternal Moment*, published by Sidgwick and Jackson in 1928, similarly broke the pattern: despite the great critical and popular success of *A Passage to India*, only a comparatively small edition of 3720 copies of Forster's last work of fiction was published, though the response—accompanied by a slightly distorting element of retrospect and valediction—was generally favourable.

In his Introduction to *Maurice* (1971), P. N. Furbank speaks of the 'disturbing effect' which the success of *Howards End* had on Forster, who became afraid that he might dry up as a writer. To all public appearances (*Arctic Summer* and *Maurice*, written between 1911 and 1914, were, respectively, abandoned and apparently unpublishable) Forster did dry up, but during the fourteen-year period before *A Passage to India* brought his reputation back in triumph American readers had a chance of catching up with him, as, in editions of never less than 2000 copies, *A Room with a View* appeared in 1911, *Where Angels Fear to Tread* in 1920, *The Longest Journey* in 1922, and *The Celestial Omnibus* in 1923. In addition to these novels, which had a rather mixed reception (*The Longest Journey* being thought 'a story of dreary pessimism'), *Howards End* was reissued by Knopf in 1921, to far greater understanding and approval than had greeted its original appearance in America in 1911.

The response to *A Passage to India*, in England, America and India itself, was almost overwhelmingly enthusiastic. By the end of 1924, 18,000 copies had been published in England, and no fewer than 34,000 in America. Clearly Forster was now a name as potent for the general reader as *Howards End* had made him for the intelligentsia: the *Observer* prophesied (No. 99) that he 'might well become a popular novelist on the strength of his power as a story-teller', and though Leonard Woolf (No. 97) and H. W. Massingham (No. 98) might disagree on whether critical emphasis should be placed on form or content, they agreed on the novel's excellence. Even the *Outlook*, previously unpersuaded by Forster, changed its mind, feeling that 'Politics . . . give this novel at least half its value' (No. 96). There seems little doubt that, coming only a few years after the still hotly-debated Amritsar massacre, Forster's novel had a topical relevance and an excitement that increased its acceptability to the more general reader of the time, and it is likely that the response of Americans was the stronger for not being confined within what previously seemed to some of them exclusively English horizons. It should not be thought, however, that reviewers in England or America failed to notice the book's more enduring human and literary qualities.

Brief references to Forster had already been made between 1918 and 1922 in a number of general works on the English novel, but little of consequence was said, and the best early appreciations of Forster's strengths and weaknesses are to be found in reviews of particular novels and in the comments of Forster's friends and literary colleagues. The effects of the success of *A Passage to India*, however, made themselves felt in a number of long essays on his work as a whole published in the later nineteen-twenties, by Virginia Woolf, I. A. Richards and others. Forster's work had penetrated to Europe as early as 1907, when Téodor de Wyzewa had written on *The Longest Journey* (No. 34), but the translation of *A Passage to India* into French, in 1927, by Forster's friend Charles Mauron, was paralleled by a much fuller article by Jacques Heurgon (No. 133) which tried to trace an over-all pattern and preoccupation in his work. One may point out here that in so far as Forster's reputation abroad has been based on translations of his work, it is *A Passage to India* which is his most widely-known book: between a translation into Swedish in 1925 and one into Turkish in 1961 there have been sixteen translations, seven of these before 1939. The next novel to be translated, *A Room with a View*, did not appear until 1947, in a French version again by Charles Mauron; and there are more translations of *A Passage to India* than of all the other novels put together.

More articles on Forster's work appeared, at intervals, during the nineteen-thirties, most notably the first long American article, by

Howard N. Doughty, Jr (No. 151), the first Canadian article, by E. K. Brown (No. 153), and two articles now disowned by their authors, Montgomery Belgion and F. R. Leavis. The first book on Forster, by Rose Macaulay, was published in 1938. Lionel Trilling's, published in America five years later in 1943, was the cause of a 'Forster revival' there, yet it was not followed by another book until 1957. Nor did many articles on Forster appear after the short-lived 'revival' died down, but since 1957 both articles and books have proliferated. One is back to the inverted pyramid mentioned at the beginning, but an examination of its contents, often excellent but inevitably separated from the milieu in which Forster's novels were first published, must be postponed awhile to allow a return to that heyday when Forster, not yet a figure in literary history, was a practitioner of fiction.

III

THE FIRST THREE NOVELS (1905–1908)

The literary world in which Forster made his first appearance was evoked, and its faded names reburnished, with such verve by Rose Macaulay that her description deserves to be quoted at length:[2]

> Mr. Forster arrived as a story-writer into a world twinkling with the earlier coruscations of H. G. Wells, ruddy with the sinking but still flashing imperial torch of Mr. Kipling, sturdily muscled, manned and midlandized by Enoch Arnold Bennett, decorated by the elegant gaieties of Max Beerbohm, Saki, Henry Harland, Anatole France, and the left-overs from the *Yellow Book* and the *Savoy*, entertained by the Benson family, sustained by Hardy, James and Meredith as its grand old men, interested in the experiments of Mallarmé and Gide, excited by Huysmans, wearying of Zola and naturalism, of Pierre Loti and romance, of Paul Bourget and religiousness, just awakening to the Russian excitement of the uneventful hour, yet still rich in plots and passions, with windows that open every now and then on to some uncanny land of ghosts, centaurs or magic. There was a rich and exciting choice of field for the young rider into fiction.

Forster was twenty-one at the turn of the century, and only a young man of twenty-six when his first novel, *Where Angels Fear to Tread*, was published in 1905. One wonders whether the title's implication was one of Forster's earliest ironies, directed not merely at his Sawston characters but at himself, for riding into the field of fiction with so little practice (technical inexperience was certainly a charge laid against his second novel, and he had only begun to publish his short stories in 1903). But though 'amusing facility' and 'amusing cleverness' (No. 2) were listed among its qualities, Forster's control of his novel struck nearly all his reviewers. C. F. G. Masterman (No. 10) was particularly impressed by what he called 'this brilliant novel' which, for the work of a new writer, was so rare in 'directly conveying the impression of power and an easy mastery of material'.

Though many of the reviewers, naturally enough, spent some time in abbreviating the novel's story for their readers (and even how a story is retold reveals each reviewer's slightly different angle of vision), they did not miss either the broad contrast it provided between 'English principles and prejudices' (No. 8) and 'the glare of the vertical Italian sun' (No. 9), or the 'main issues of life' (No. 2) lurking beneath what might superficially appear its 'grotesque incidents, vulgar details, and coarse caricature' (No. 8). The novel was seen as 'a protest against the worship of conventionalities' (No. 3) in its material, and as an original statement of that protest—the words 'original' and 'originality' occur in a number of the reviews, though the name of Meredith is invoked in No. 3 in an attempt to define the sense in which the book could be called 'a piece of comedy'. What later came to be thought, by Lionel Trilling, one of Forster's most striking, and even disconcerting, characteristics, his mixture of serious matter and comic manner, was remarked early, when the London *Bookman* (No. 2) pointed out the co-existence in *Where Angels Fear to Tread* of 'an appearance of jocularity which is very engaging and a truthfulness which is, by contrast, often startling'.

Some extra-literary prejudices, not especially of the day perhaps, are also given an airing. The mixed character of Gino is generally grasped, and his various elements given their due value, but the reviewer of the *Glasgow Herald* (No. 4) betrays a vicarious pleasure in describing him as one of the 'easy-going, cynical, coolly-tyrannical, decidedly and blatantly masculine specimens that unspoiled Italy can still boast of'. Equally revealing, in a different way, is the slightly-pained reluctance of the *Speaker* (No. 9) to believe in Caroline Abbott's preference of Gino to Philip Herriton, and the moral repugnance aroused by that preference in the *Birmingham Daily Post*.

Many reviewers saw *Where Angels Fear to Tread* as a comedy, C. F. G. Masterman indeed speaking of its 'radiant atmosphere of humour' (No. 10). Others, however, felt that 'the persons depicted are a shade too unpleasing' (No. 7), and that the book was 'pervaded by an atmosphere of snobbishness and vulgarity' (No. 11). Forster's 'comedy' was certainly of a disturbing kind, and a plea was entered by the *Manchester Guardian* (No. 3) that he might try in future to be 'a little more charitable'. For the very gloomy reviewer of the *Spectator* (No. 12), who found the novel 'exceedingly clever but decidedly painful', the violence of Gino was less upsetting than the colder vices of some of the English characters. His approach to the book is one-sided, but it has the merit of recognising in Forster a quality of 'disillusionment' that was to deepen in later novels, and thus partly frustrate his hope that 'so original and searching a talent may yet give us a story in which the fallibility of goodness and the callousness of respectability are less uncompromisingly insisted upon'.

The Longest Journey, published in 1907, was more widely and more lengthily reviewed than its predecessor; but its reception was more mixed. Downright hostility was demonstrated in only one review (No. 33); bewilderment and varying degrees of disappointment in three others (Nos 22, 23, 29), the first of which felt that Forster had 'attempted things beyond his powers' and as a result produced a 'forced and hysterical' book. Even C. F. G. Masterman (No. 19) and the reviewer of the *Nation* (No. 17), both of whom thought highly of the novel, described it as 'elusive'. The consensus of opinion is fairly enough expressed by the reviewer of *Black and White* (No. 24): for him it was 'a book that grips' but 'not a well-constructed novel'. The *Cambridge Review* (No. 27), whose acknowledgment that Forster had translated the quality of undergraduate discussion 'unerringly . . . into words' carries particular weight, thought that he had lived up to the expectations aroused by his first novel; nevertheless, it felt obliged to add that 'the design falls short of the excellence which marks the book in other respects'.

Some specific objections are worth recording. The most widespread of these concerns Forster's habit of dealing out 'death . . . on the slightest provocation' (No. 25). The *Athenaeum* concludes its pompously-rolling, if kindly, periods with the Olympian remark: 'too brusquely, at least, this god descends from the machine'. Though praising Forster (in effect) for daring to present 'a study of an amiable failure', the *Tribune* (No. 15) deplores his tendency 'to make the general grey too monotonous'; indeed the *Spectator* (No. 32) accuses Forster of wantonly inflicting on the reader a 'glut of disagreeableness', and finds an element of the 'abnormal' in his characters' behaviour. Whatever one thinks of his view here (and other reviewers felt that Forster lacked a proper sympathy for his characters), his opinion that the scene in which Ansell violently denounces Rickie in front of a roomful of schoolboys is 'preposterous' certainly anticipates later reservations about it. Later critics have also experienced difficulties with the character of Stephen Wonham not very different from those experienced in 1907. The *Morning Post's* fairly representative view was that 'it is not certain that Mr. Forster has not attempted the impossible in endeavouring to make intelligible and attractive the blend of pagan god and modern hooligan which goes to make Stephen Wonham'.

The total impression created by the reviews, however, is of a novel that forced people to take it seriously, whatever reservations they might have about individual, and often different, points. The *Morning Post* (No. 21), having mentioned a number of objections, went so far as to discard them from its summing-up, conceding that 'it would be altogether out of place to quarrel with a writer of Mr Forster's performance and promise about formal unities or small points'. Some of the book's positive qualities which shifted the emphasis so favourably are suggested by a review in the *Liverpool Daily Post* (No. 30): 'It isn't that it is life-like. Such an attribute is an insult. With all its questionings, its openings for speculative perusal, its demands on our rational faculties as well as our power of mere reading, it is rather an experience of life itself, miles away from the ordinary novel of the day. We feel that these people all live'. The *Manchester Guardian* (No. 26) was especially impressed with Forster's portrait of the schoolmaster Herbert Pembroke, 'this personification of unreality', thinking him the best character Forster had yet drawn. But perhaps the very praise of the *Liverpool Daily Post*, with its emphasis on the novel's demand for more than 'mere reading', only reinforces C. F. G. Masterman's conclusion that *The Longest Journey* was 'a book (it is to be feared) only for the few'. It was in fact the last of Forster's fictional works to appear in a Penguin edition, as recently as 1960.

The anonymous reviewer of the *Spectator* (the same man, apparently, as the one whose approval of Forster's first two novels was tinged with gloom) was so pleasantly surprised by *A Room with a View*, published in 1908, that he pronounced it 'much the best of the three' (No. 50). He found in Forster's third novel 'a kindlier tolerance' for, and 'greater sympathy' with, his characters, and was reassured that Forster had not found it necessary to kill any of them off. His review, which appeared at the beginning of 1909, sums up quite well the attitudes variously stated in the autumn and winter of 1908. Masterman (No. 46), who had already shown himself such a devoted follower of Forster's career, was particularly appreciative of the contrasting values presented in *A Room with a View* and symbolised in its title: for him the book's excellence lay in its harmonising of social observation with the revelation of the workings of the 'hidden life' on its way to fulfilment.

Most reviewers liked Forster's characters, the *Pall Mall Gazette* (No. 43) finding them 'admirably drawn' and absolutely lifelike, and were able to see their function as a thematic as well as a narrative one. The *Outlook*, however, continued to be obtuse, though its travesty of Lucy's search for her true self is unintentionally very funny: 'She is kissed on all possible occasions, and without provocation, by the uncouth George Emerson, and these osculatory overtures as often unsettle her intentions' (No. 48). The insensitivity revealed here certainly makes one feel that this paper's puzzlement over *The Longest Journey* was largely self-inflicted. The need, demonstrated by this example, to assess the value of reviews by reference to other reviews of Forster in the same paper (if it seems, as here, that they are by the same man), is more disconcertingly pointed up by considering the case of the *Evening Standard & St James's Gazette*. In 1907 this paper had found 'a touch of genius' in *The Longest Journey*. In 1908 it found far less of this in *A Room with a View* (though its review, No. 49, was nonetheless glowing), but it undermined its comparison by casually mentioning—and with apparent seriousness—that Forster's 'genius' in the earlier book resided most 'triumphantly' in his managing of the death of Gerald—one of the least likely of Forster's sudden 'literary homicides'. If hostility can sometimes be discounted, so, unfortunately, can praise.

Perhaps the two most interesting reviews of *A Room with a View* are that in *The Times Literary Supplement* (No. 39), which is attributed by Professor Frederick MacDowell to Virginia Woolf, and that in the *Daily News* (No. 38), by R. A. Scott-James, who was to pronounce *Howards End* the best novel of 1910. The reviews are interesting separately, in that each combines a sensitive awareness of Forster's virtues with an equally sensitive (though in the case of Virginia Woolf—if it is she—a more obscurely-phrased) account of its possible drawbacks: Scott-James is noteworthy in being the first critic to object to Forster's 'instruction' of the reader, especially where that instruction was devoted to 'moral mannerisms' which had, in his opinion, already become obsolete. But the reviews are even more interesting taken together, for they reveal completely opposite feelings about the same thing. Virginia Woolf finds the ending of *A Room with a View* disappointing (and in this the *Pall Mall Gazette* agrees with her); Scott-James finds it 'humanly absorbing'. That even so relatively uncomplicated a book as *A Room with a View* could produce in two intelligent readers such different reactions suggests that the 'elusive' element remarked earlier in Forster was still present—an element which partly accounts for the difficulty experienced by many critics since in assigning him his precise 'magnitude'.

Howards End (1910)

Only two periodicals dissented from the solid vote of confidence in Forster's talents provoked by the publication of *Howards End* in 1910. One, it seems by now inevitable, was the *Outlook* (5 November) which, though managing not to miss some of the book's virtues, was irritated to find it 'rather fatiguingly elusive and allusive'. The other was the *Western Mail* (No. 69), which admired the dialogue but not the 'wilderness of eccentrics' that spoke it: 'The Schlegels, Wilcoxes, and Basts will take a deal of beating for oddity. Few people would care for them as neighbours, except, perhaps, to study as psychological curiosities'.

Not in Cardiff in 1910, perhaps; but other sections of the provinces and certainly the metropolis, were neither hampered by a sense of unfamiliarity with the characters nor blind to the theme they embodied. The *World* (No. 70), though it went on to point out 'grave faults', recorded the effect *Howards End* had produced on the majority of reviewers: it was 'one of the sensations of the autumn season'. For many the book had an essential solidity and coherence which had been lacking in the first three novels. *The Times Literary Supplement* (No. 54) recapitulated the shortcomings previously noted in them with reasonable accuracy, though with a faulty syntax surprising in so august a journal: 'Neither of its three clever, imperfect, slightly baffling predecessors was quite at unity with itself. In each case there was an uncertainty of attack and a want of harmony in the method which prevented an exceptionally fine sense of character from making its proper effect'. *Howards End* had completely overcome these problems, and Forster's 'method' was now so 'under control' that a description of his peculiar 'gift' could now be attempted: 'It is in the first place securely founded . . . upon a power of generalization which holds the tightly-handled plot compactly together. But Mr. Forster works from the centre outwards, and reaches the graces and humours of the surface of his story with a mind quite clear as to the structure beneath'.

Although the common denominator of all critical reaction to *Howards End* could be summed up in the *Pall Mall Gazette's* phrase 'a work that should count' (No. 55), the critics by no means agreed about every aspect of the book. The *Standard* (No. 57) emphasised and approved the all-pervading importance of Howards End, the house itself, in providing a touchstone of value in all the characters' actions, whereas Forster's Cambridge friend A. C. Benson (No. 68) felt its appeal was 'a little strained'. Similarly, the *Standard* had high praise for the drawing of Mrs Wilcox, whereas the *Westminster Gazette* (No. 65) judged that her evolution into 'a sort of over-soul' had been inadequately prepared for by Forster's treatment of her 'in the flesh'. One recalls here critical disagreement in 1907 over the presentation of Mrs Failing in *The Longest Journey*. A number of reviewers concurred with the *Saturday Review* (26 November 1910) in not feeling sure that Forster 'knows the Leonard Basts of this world', and there was widespread reluctance (for a mixture, one suspects, of aesthetic and moral reasons) to credit Leonard Bast's 'seduction' of Helen Schlegel. The *Observer* (No. 60) found her 'fall' 'disagreeable'; the *Spectator* (No. 59), more flattering to her female autonomy, saw it as 'an extraordinary act of self-sacrifice'. No-one, however, approached the waspishness of Katherine Mansfield in 1917 (No. 75) in attributing Helen's pregnancy not to the agency of Leonard himself but to that of his 'fatal forgotten umbrella'.

The objections voiced here to one specific incident hard to accept were damagingly generalised by the *Morning Post* (No. 66), which thought that Forster 'always shirks the description of objective events', and by the *Morning Leader* (No. 56), which felt him unable to treat 'strong passions powerfully'. Later critics have frequently encountered such problems of artistic verisimilitude, and they are stated in advance by the reviewer of the *World* (No. 70): 'Mr. Forster has yet to become more supple in his use of incident. Any given circumstance or action is possible in real life, but mere possibility is only an excuse for the amateur. The master must aim at probability'.

The reviewer of *The Times Literary Supplement* had also realised this flaw (which involved Forster's over-use of coincidence) in *Howards End*, but he was not alone in regarding it as a 'subsidiary defect' (No. 62), and even more than in the case of *The Longest Journey* one is brought up against the reviewers' final consensus that Forster's strengths outweighed his weaknesses: 'We are dealing with a very remarkable and original book, and we will not linger over faults which do not touch its central virtue' (No. 54). Forster's first three novels had been thought to possess affinities with Meredith; *Howards End* was compared very favourably with Galsworthy's *The Man of Property*, and indeed Forster's method was described by R. A. Scott-James (No. 61) as a 'sort of bridge' between Galsworthy and Conrad. But none of these comparisons was intended to diminish the originality of Forster's own contribution, for which, in the words of the *Saturday Review*, 'the word Forsterian is already demanded'. *Howards End* shows the reputation of Forster consolidated and given clearer definition than before. Not only was the word 'Forsterian' first used in connection with it, but it inspired, in the reviewer of the *Manchester Guardian* (No. 53), the use of another term which was to become permanent in the vocabulary of Forster criticism: the adjective 'humane'.

The Celestial Omnibus (1911)

Before his first novel appeared in 1905 Forster had written a number of short stories, the first of which, 'The Story of a Panic', dates from 1902. His stories were published from 1903 onwards in the *Independent Review*, two members of whose editorial board were Goldsworthy Lowes Dickinson and Nathaniel Wedd—Fellows of King's College, Cambridge and mentors of Forster the undergraduate who had first encouraged him to write. His stories had gained Forster a small public, particularly in Cambridge, before his novels widened his audience. In 1911 Forster gathered six of them together in *The Celestial Omnibus*, and their generally warm reception indicates that they retained their original appeal. The *Cambridge Review* (No. 86) went so far as to record the opinion that 'The Story of a Panic' was superior to Forster's first novel, and that *The Celestial Omnibus* itself, 'for pure imaginative writing', surpassed his second—which, nevertheless, it had reviewed with great approval (No. 27). The *Athenaeum* (No. 85) was considerably less happy: it recognised, as it could hardly fail to do, the 'smack of the fantastically supernatural' in all the stories, but was unsure whether they came off. Nor does this particular reviewer seem to have known of their earlier publication, though his crass final comment at least senses that they belonged to a more youthful period of Forster's life: 'They might, one concludes ultimately, have been written as a spirited "lark" by a young writer'. The *Athenaeum*, one concludes ultimately, rather missed Forster's point; so that it is reassuring to find that the *Nation* did not: 'Mr. Forster's literary arrows are sharp and shining, and they wing his quarry none the less effectually because they are feathered with magic plumage'.

The Times Literary Supplement (No. 84) was too charmed by the stories to wish to break a butterfly on a wheel, though it permitted itself to hint that the 'slippery little allegories' might not 'bear sustained pressure'. Despite this, the interweaving of prosaic and supernatural, and the counterpointing of the obtuseness of some characters to 'nature and poetry and the finer sentiments' with others' sensitivity to them, were largely successful. The *Daily Telegraph* (No. 80) was just a little concerned lest an element of preciosity might be creeping in.

The co-existence of fantasy and realism (their ratio varying from book to book) has sometimes been a stumbling-block for critics of Forster. On the whole the reception of *The Celestial Omnibus* suggests that early reviewers were unworried by any need to weigh scrupulously Forster's success with each element; nor did most of them feel an evaluation of short story *versus* novel was called for. The *Daily Telegraph's* remark that 'The Celestial Omnibus' 'shows Mr. Forster in a very different mood from the acute reality of his *Howards End*' does not sound a loaded one. The exception was Dixon Scott, in an amusingly pugnacious (and perhaps attention-seeking) review in the *Manchester Guardian* (No. 82). For Scott, Forster's stories 'do not convince', because they are too explicit, and 'Pan' has been reduced to 'Puck', a lesser immortal altogether. Scott's review is the first example in Forster criticism of the 'debunking' approach, and it might well be compared with Pete Hamill's review of *Two Cheers for Democracy* in 1965 (No. 166). As with Hamill's, however, Scott's debunking makes a *volte-face* halfway through, and in what may now seem a very surprising direction. Forster's stories are 'rare and delicious', and far from wishing him to diminish the 'heavenly' in them Scott would have him increase it: the Wellses and the Bennetts can be left to 'earthly meanings' while Forster, uniquely able to do so, takes the reader 'over a rainbow'. Such a hope, Scott realised, unfortunately ran counter to Forster's development, and his last words offer a wistful minority comment on the success of *Howards End* the year before: 'What is the use of these weak entreaties? Too late, too late. *Howards End* is already on our shelves. Like all the rest of them, Mr Forster has taken up life'.

FORSTER AND SOME LITERARY CONTEMPORARIES, 1911–C.1924

Between 1911 and 1924 the reading public might well have concluded that 'life' had not taken up Forster. His work up to 1914 on *Arctic Summer* and *Maurice* was known only to a few friends, and his fictional silence was broken by no more than the publication in 1920 of *The Story of the Siren*—a volume slim to the point of emaciation. But the reviews of Katherine Mansfield and Rebecca West (Nos 89 and 90), disproportionate in terms of length, indicate how far from forgotten he had become in the intervening years, years of war though they had been.

Thomas Sturge Moore's wish (No. 79) to nominate 'young Forster' to the Royal Society of Literature, especially since it was expressed only two weeks after the Society first met in 1911, is glowing evidence of the position he had attained to with his first four novels. The proposal of a man of thirty-two to membership of a body whose Academic Committee included such established reputations as A. C. Bradley, Robert Bridges, Edmund Gosse, Gilbert Murray, G. M. Trevelyan, Conrad, Hardy and Henry James could hardly be bettered as a sign of the esteem in which Forster was held by at least one of his senior contemporaries; the more so because the only other writer Sturge Moore wished to have elected was George Bernard Shaw.

Sturge Moore's feeling that Forster's election might well show 'foresight' was echoed by the novelist Hugh Walpole, five years Forster's junior, when he mentioned him in passing in a book he published on Conrad in 1917. Walpole had used the term 'Romantic-Realism' to describe the work of Conrad, and he went on to place Forster not only in the same category but also on much the same level of eminence: 'Mr E. M. Forster is a romantic-realist of most curious originality, whose *Longest Journey* and *Howard's End* [*sic*] may possibly provide the historian of English literature with dates as important as the publication of *Almayer's Folly* in 1895'.[3] The excitement of reading Forster for the first time was testified to by Elizabeth Bowen, who recalled, in 1969, her first impressions of his work in the second decade of the century.[4] Between 1918 and 1922 Forster's work was touched on, though not very interestingly, in a number of unremembered surveys of the modern English novel.[5] More important is the testimonial passed on by Florence Hardy, who said in a letter written to Forster in January 1924 that her husband Thomas Hardy had 'the *greatest admiration*' for his work.

Hardy's admiration was not shared by all Forster's fellow-writers, however. Katherine Mansfield confided to her Journal in 1917 that *Howards End* was one of her 'weakest books' (No. 75); Forster came no nearer to providing the nourishment she expected from fiction than 'warming the teapot'. She expressed this pervasive sense of dissatisfaction with a more urbane moderation when she reviewed *The Story of the Siren* in 1920: 'In *Howards End*, though less than elsewhere, we are teased by the feeling, difficult to define, that he has by no means exerted the whole of his imaginative power to create [his] world for his readers . . . How is it that the writer is content to do less than explore his own delectable country?'

Some such feeling that Forster dealt only in half-measures seems to have been at the root of D. H. Lawrence's attitude towards him. After Lawrence's death in 1930, Forster flustered Bloomsbury (with which Lawrence had had an unsatisfactory encounter) by calling him 'the greatest imaginative novelist of our generation'.[6] Lawrence could also speak well of Forster: despite the rather grudging praise of *A Passage to India* expressed in letters to Martin Secker and John Middleton Murry (Nos 109 and 123), he wrote in August 1924 to the Italian critic Carlo Linati drawing his attention to Forster, whom he called 'about the best of my contemporaries in England'.[7] These mutual compliments, however, do not fully represent the uneasy relationship of two major figures who were so alike and yet so different.

Early in the February of 1915 Forster spent three days with the Lawrences at their borrowed cottage in Sussex. Judging from Lawrence's subsequent letter to Bertrand Russell (No. 88) the visit was a tense one, 'on the edge of a fierce quarrel all the time'. Forster later recounted to Angus Wilson that Lawrence had 'spent one whole afternoon condemning my work'.[8] Lawrence's exhortations of a man some years his senior cannot have been too easy to tolerate: one infers from his letter to Russell that Forster had not simply been put to the question as a writer but also as a human being. Lawrence, with naïve arrogance, saw himself as trying to draw out someone who had not realised his full potential; Forster, more inhibited, felt that he was being made a fool of. In a letter to Forster of about the same period as this visit Lawrence had called *Howards End* 'a beautiful book', but had added the unsuitably headmaster-like encouragement 'now you must go further'. How far Lawrence had understood *Howards End* one is not sure, since the only detailed remark he recorded about it was made in 1922 in another letter to Forster (No. 91): the tolerance extended by the book to the Wilcoxes had been seen by him as no subtler than 'glorifying those *business* people'. According to Forster the only good thing Lawrence conceded to the book in 1915 was the 'courageous' portraying of Leonard Bast.[9]

One can only infer from the evidence available that Lawrence first cast Forster in the role of an unwitting disciple, or perhaps potential ally, who needed more bringing along. Little wonder, then, that he could mention to Lady Ottoline Morrell in 1929 that he had received from Forster 'such a silly, funny little letter . . . telling me *à propos* of nothing that he admires me but doesn't read me'.[10] For Lawrence, it would seem, Forster did not 'go further', and his own consequent turning-away was intimated in a letter to S. S. Koteliansky in November 1927: 'Judging from the notice of Forster's last book [presumably *Aspects of the Novel*], he must be rather a piffler just now. And I read the *Celestial Omnibus* again—and found it rather rubbish. Those things don't wear'.[11]

FORSTER'S RECEPTION IN AMERICA, 1911–1924

Forster's pre-war novels were published in America in a different order from that in which they first appeared in England, and it was not until early in 1911 that he was introduced to the American reading public. American reviewers were not always at home with his work, and their comments often lack the sense of perspective available to English critics who had had the advantage of following Forster's career from the beginning. For some of them the novels existed separately, each in a vacuum, and *Howards End*, seeming the first Forster novel to those who had not already heard the whisper of his name from across the Atlantic, arrived in America like a boy transferring to a new school, where his previous exploits and talents go at first unrecognised.

Howards End was published in America in January 1911. The reactions sampled by *Current Opinion* (No. 73) were not particularly favourable, and a certain isolationism seems implied in that of the New York *Globe*: though the characters were 'broadly human', this conclusion was reached 'although [they] are British'. The *Independent* of Boston (10 April 1911) made a neat distinction between Wilcoxes and Schlegels, describing the former as 'like their diamonds, hard and cold and clear', and the latter as 'opaline, shifting and changing with circumstance'. But its comment on the house itself seems oddly out of focus: 'its singular dominance and triumph at the end are sinister peculiarities of a very original book'. How far one can safely extrapolate from this eccentric judgement is uncertain, but it at least suggests that the premisses on which early American views of Forster were based differed from English ones. The *New York Times* (No. 72) saw Forster's attempt at tolerant 'connection' as mere fence-sitting, and deplored the 'fatuous placidity' of the book's conclusion. Though Forster was granted a talent for 'conventional comedy', anything more was an unwise strain on powers inferior not only to Galsworthy's but even to those of May Sinclair.

A Room with a View appeared a few months later in the same year. The *New York Times* (No. 52) found it easier to praise because, this time, Forster's 'pretty comedy gift' was 'undimmed by any over-serious intention'. The influence of Meredith on his comic attitude was pointed out, but Forster's entirely unimitative style freed him from any charge of slavishness. The New York *Outlook* (10 June 1911) found a 'rare quality' in the book, whose 'subtle suggestion rivets one's attention from the first'. The Chicago *Inter-Ocean*, however, accused it of being 'hard to read' and clever-clever (No. 51). *Where Angels Fear to Tread*, published in America in 1920, was briefly noted in a number of journals; those which treated it at greater length, including the *New York Times* (11 April), found it appealing and original and had little of significance to say against it, though the *Springfield Sunday Republican* (No. 13) was not sure that Forster had been altogether wise in adding deeper overtones to his 'comedy'. A review in the New York *Bookman* (May 1920) is interesting for revealing the writer's ignorance, even at this late date, of Forster's previous career, which he had needed to look up in *Who's Who*.

In 1921 *Howards End*, whose first American edition had long been out of print, was reissued by Knopf. This time the reaction was both favourable and marked by a critical approach which could encompass more than the comic segment of Forster's spectrum. A possible reason for this change of attitude was hinted at by Elinor Wylie in her later review of *A Passage to India* (No. 124): a 'rather young' world had since 1910 caught up with *Howards End* and 'the conclusions and . . . the wisdom of the book are now admittedly foregone and bitterly acquired'. Certainly the *New Republic* thought the characters in no way dated by the subsequent war, even though, for the *Dial* (No. 77), the book's conclusion was still not 'lifelike' and Forster's 'symbolism' and 'spiritual values' 'blur in the too sharp light of melodrama'.

The Longest Journey appeared in 1922. If one were to believe the reviewer of the *Boston Evening Transcript* (No. 36), Forster's novels were even at this time 'still practically unknown to America' because he possessed a 'point of view . . . so intensely English as to be incomprehensible to an American'. Certainly this particular novel could hardly have been comprehensible to any reviewer who could simplistically reduce Stephen Wonham to 'a horrible illegitimate step-brother'. For this one the style of the book was 'harsh and contorted' and there was no likely future in America for 'the depression of its philosophy'. Luckily other reviewers disagreed, the *New York Times* (14 May 1922) calling it 'a most distinguished rendering of the unfortunate career of Rickie Elliott', and the *Springfield Sunday Republican* complimenting it by a comparison with *One of Ours*, the latest novel of Willa Cather.

The Celestial Omnibus, published in 1923, was uniformly welcomed, and Forster did not suffer by the many parallels drawn—to the 'master' Arthur Machen (New York *World*, 29 July 1923), to Walter de la Mare, and to the Irish poet and short story writer James Stephens (*Nation*, 5 September). By this time Forster's work was fully available in America, and his arrival in the American literary consciousness was celebrated in a long review by Hamish Miles (No. 92), published just a month before *A Passage to India* appeared. Miles's style is over-elaborate and his picture of Forster's English ambience too much that of a fanciful tourist with an eye for the quaint, but he is sensitive to Forster's books, seeing in all of them a 'peculiarly civilized quality'. Although 'no giant, no innovator, no seer', Forster was 'unmistakably unique'. Miles's testimonial was weightily endorsed in 1930, when Forster wrote to congratulate Sinclair Lewis on his being awarded the Nobel Prize for Literature. Sinclair Lewis said in reply that he particularly valued Forster's good wishes, since 'you happen to be one of the few authors in the world for whom I have an immeasurable admiration'.

A Passage to India (1924)

In the *New York Times* for 4 February 1923, Henry James Forman concluded a long review of an American reissue of *A Room with a*

View with these words: '[Forster] has written little, but that little is capital. And, though his audiences in both England and America are still limited, it is very obvious that soon they will be widespread. For when a writer so true and sincere, so rich in knowledge, gives us the best of himself, it becomes very soon impossible to resist him'. The same month, in a letter from London dated 1 December 1922, 'Simon Pure' of the New York *Bookman* informed the American literary world that 'at last Forster is engaged in writing a novel. No further news of it is available, but even the news that such a work is in progress is excellent . . . there can be no question about its welcome by all who care for good writing, for outstanding intelligence'.[12]

These two predictions, that of Forman even more solidly based than he realised, were fulfilled by the publication of *A Passage to India* in the summer of 1924. It was reviewed more extensively than any of its predecessors, and hardly a dissonant voice marred the equally extensive acclamation. The fear which Rebecca West, remembering no doubt Forster's earlier mixed reception in America, felt bound to utter in the *Saturday Review of Literature* (No. 117)—that American readers might 'fail to appreciate' this 'study of a certain problem of the British Empire'—proved to be groundless. To say the least of an enthusiastic American reception, it included a pleasant reversal of the inferiority of Forster to Galsworthy pointed out in 1911: now, according to *Current Opinion* (lxxvii, October 1924), Forster was granted to possess 'the intellectual detachment of a John Galsworthy'.

British reviewers warmly greeted Forster's return to the company of writers of fiction. The *Manchester Guardian* (No. 100) asserted that it was 'the first duty of any reviewer to welcome Mr. Forster's reappearance as a novelist', and the welcome extended by J. B. Priestley (No. 106) makes it clear that Forster was not only a novelist superior to most possible rivals but also a symbol of sanity and civilisation: 'now that he has come back, as a novelist, to a world that is even more insane and even more in need of his clear-sighted exquisite charity, than the world he stopped writing about so many years ago, now that he has returned we should celebrate the event'.

The detached and tolerant attitude which Forster brought to his material was widely and favourably remarked on, and even Edwin Muir, who commented bitingly that 'the intellect is not exercised to its utmost in going halfway in all directions' (No. 125), gave his approval to the 'writing', which was 'a continuous delight'. A special characteristic of much of the response to *A Passage to India* was, indeed, the admiration expressed for Forster's style, for the beauty of his English. Forster was also generally praised for his creation of Aziz, who struck both Leonard Woolf and the *Birmingham Post* as 'the most absolutely "real" Indian to be found in fiction' (No. 101). Mrs Moore created problems, Leonard Woolf seeing her as 'a superb character', I. P. Fassett describing her in the *Criterion* as 'that sinister obscure, horrible woman' (No. 122). Fassett was disturbed by the air of mystery, and of 'psychic influences', with which Forster had surrounded her, and A. C. Benson, though thinking her 'charming up to a point', was puzzled by 'her sudden lapse into peevish exhaustion' (No. 95). Certain aspects of the book only later critics were fully to explore: not only the function of Mrs Moore, but also the 'nameless horror' of the Marabar Caves, which Ralph Wright (No. 104) found it impossible to believe in, and the full significance of the 'Temple' section, which Edwin Muir thought 'the only feeble part of the novel', and whose ungrasped relationship to what preceded it left Arnold Bennett puzzled as to what the novel as a whole was really 'about' (No. 129).

Much of the interest which *A Passage to India* aroused stemmed from its subject—or rather that part of its subject which was inevitably emphasised at the time: the problem of India and the British. Leonard Woolf, without whose 'encouragement' Forster might not have finished the book,[13] reviewed it (No. 97) in terms of its artistic merit and its ability to suggest the infinite recession of one 'subject' into another and yet another even more significant and comprehensive: this despite the fact that he had himself been a Colonial official in Ceylon early in the century and might have been expected to speak of its Indian subject-matter. H. W. Massingham, however, took Woolf to task for so concentrating on the book's aesthetic aspects that he appeared totally to ignore the fact that Forster had 'something extremely pointed to say about India' (No. 98). *The Times Literary Supplement* (No. 94) expressed its view that *A Passage to India* differed from Forster's previous novels by calling it 'essentially a definite picture rather than a creative imagining', and R. Ellis Roberts (No. 107) believed that in it Forster 'deals with a world larger and more significant than any he has dealt with'. Henry Nevinson felt that *A Passage to India* had appeared at 'the psychological moment' (No. 118), coming as it did not so long after the much-discussed Amritsar massacre. His testimony to the novel's worthiness of its important subject—the testimony of a man who had travelled widely in India—

is far from valueless: 'I have never known so accurate, so penetrating, and so sympathetic an account of these divergent lives and characters as this'. Though the moving-on of history may have enabled later critics to amplify the approach favoured by Leonard Woolf, it would be foolishly sophisticated to set aside the more topical reactions of reviewers who felt, with H. C. Harwood, that 'Politics . . . give this novel at least half its value' (No. 96); especially as it was precisely Forster's second visit to India in 1921 that almost prevented him from finishing the book: 'as soon as [the opening chapters] were confronted with the country they purported to describe, they seemed to wilt and go dead and I could do nothing with them. I used to look at them of an evening in my room at Dewas, and felt only distaste and despair'.[14]

Given the 'public' nature of so much of the material of *A Passage to India*, it seems only reasonable to agree with a reviewer in India itself that the writer of such a novel, in so far as he might influence his audience's feelings and opinions, bore a special responsibility to be as accurate as possible in his use of facts: 'the picture should be drawn from intimate and expert knowledge' (No. 121). The conviction which *A Passage to India* carried for most of its Western critics certainly indicates its possession of the necessary artistic verisimilitude—they were made to feel that 'this is surely how things must be'; but it may be questioned how many of these critics possessed the personal knowledge to assert also 'this is how things actually are'. An Anglo-Indian, who did have it, pointed out with some fairness that 'a knowledge of Cambridge and the suburbs of London, while it may equip [English literary critics] to appraise Mr Forster's earlier novels, is scarcely sufficient for the appraisement (apart from the purely literary merits of the work, to which they have done full justice) of this latest one' (No. 115). Rose Macaulay was perhaps implying agreement with such an opinion when she concluded her own review (No. 93) with the words: 'I should very much like to know what Anglo-Indians will think of it'.

One reaction, apocryphal possibly, was embodied in 'stories of civil servants, outward bound for India, who bought the novel as suitable reading for their voyage, only to throw their copies overboard angrily when they discovered the contents'.[15] No such rage-empurpled response inspired two letters sent by Anglo-Indians to the editor of the *New Statesman* in 1924, but the letters made it plain that Forster's picture of India was far from accurate in all its details. E. A. Horne, who had spent fourteen years in the Indian Education

Service, felt that, while Forster's Indians were lovingly observed, his Anglo-Indians 'are not even good caricatures . . . they are puppets' (No. 115). Turton, Callendar and McBryde he described as 'preposterous', not so much because they were shown behaving badly as because their bad behaviour was not the kind their living equivalents would be guilty of. S. K. Ratcliffe, who had edited an Indian newspaper in the first decade of the century, took a more literary approach in that he felt Forster's total depiction of Anglo-India rang true 'in the essentials of character and attitude' (No. 116). Nevertheless he not only confirmed Horne's individual criticisms (criticisms he thought many Anglo-Indians would wish to make) but even added to them, finding the trial scene—exciting to most Western critics—utterly incorrect in its described procedure: 'Mr Forster's externals are continuously wrong'.

The feeling that Forster had not bothered to be accurate about, and hence fairer to, the Anglo-Indian community was shared by journals in India like the *Englishman* of Calcutta (No. 121); the *Statesman* of the same city thought the trial scene 'so full of technical error' as to be 'a serious blemish' on a book which in other ways was 'almost photographic in [its] accuracy' (No. 114). The *Times of India*, however, believed *A Passage to India* to be a 'genuine contribution' to the study of a 'luckless country' which was 'at the moment decidedly overwritten' (No. 111), and the Indian journalist St Nihal Singh welcomed the exposure of Anglo-Indian behaviour (Forster's depiction of which he apparently accepted) despite its being partly counterbalanced by a presentation of Indians who were not *quite* typical of the best the country could offer. The generally favourable Indian view of the book was summed up in 1934 by Professor Bhupal Singh, who praised the 'candour, sincerity, fairness and art' of Forster's treatment of a theme which 'bristles with difficulties' (No. 131).

In reviewing the novel with which Forster had broken his long fictional silence, the *Birmingham Post* spoke somewhat naïvely of 'the admirable self-restraint by which [he] has limited his output' (No. 101)—a remark which Forster himself might well have read with a wryly-sad smile, considering his abortive efforts on *Arctic Summer*, the non-literary 'self-restraint' which had obliged him not to publish *Maurice*, and the long-delayed completion of *A Passage to India* itself. A. C. Benson said in a letter to Forster that he did not 'grasp the significance of the echo' (No. 95). John Middleton Murry, who did (and its meaning might be expressed as that 'possible futility of all life' which the American Clarence H. Gaines saw as 'the background' of Forster's thought), was wiser than to attribute Forster's long silence to an act of artistic choice. For Murry, the 'miracle' of *A Passage to India* was not that Forster 'should have taken fourteen years to write it, but that he should have written it at all' (No. 110). Murry was perhaps the acutest critic of *A Passage to India* in 1924, seeing beneath the dramatic if partly distorted surface of story and character an emptiness into which Forster had stared and found no reassurance. Alone among critics who hoped that *A Passage to India* would be a new fictional beginning for Forster, Murry saw the novel as a terminus and Forster's earlier silence as one unlikely to be 'interrupted again'.

The Eternal Moment (1928)

On the last day of 1926 Arnold Bennett, then a quarter of the way through his novel *Accident*, begun only five weeks before, lunched with E. M. Forster at a friend's house. Bennett, who had never really understood why Forster had not quickly 'followed-up' the success of *Howards End* with more books, found the encounter frustrating. Forster 'said that he had not begun a new novel, and hadn't got any ideas for one. So I cursed him and urged him to get on with a novel: but of course I knew it would be no good'.[16]

In later years Forster was often asked why he had stopped writing novels. His answer was usually 'I hadn't any more I wanted to say' (to which one must obviously add the rider, 'in fiction'). On one occasion,[17] at least, he modified his answer, saying that the world had changed too much for his imagination to feel at home in it. Fiction in such circumstances would have been forced and unreal. The alternative—to keep on writing about a period more and more remote from his readers—would have meant little more than becoming a historical novelist, and this was equally unacceptable.

Whatever Forster's reasons, the fact is that he wrote no new fiction after 1924. His last work of fiction, *The Eternal Moment*, published in 1928, collected together six more short stories of pre-war vintage, the title-story having originally appeared as early as 1905. The valedictory note of Forster's introduction to the book was echoed in the regrets of a number of its reviewers, particularly those who, like Edwin Muir (No. 148), thought that Forster's talents showed to better advantage in his short stories than in his novels. Despite this general preference of Muir's, however, he found a number of the stories 'unconvincing', particularly 'The Machine Stops', in which

Forster was writing of the future. Edward Shanks (in the *London Mercury* for May 1928) thought this fantasy decidedly inferior to the early work of H. G. Wells, and his general view was the opposite of Muir's: 'As a rule, Mr Forster requires more time and room than the short story allows him'. The *Springfield Sunday Union and Republican* (20 May 1928), in similar vein, preferred those 'passages that remind us of E. M. Forster, the novelist—a person whom the reviewer distinctly prefers to E. M. Forster, the short story writer'. The *Manchester Guardian* (No. 144) saw most of the stories as 'calculated rather than conceived', and was obviously glad that Forster had passed on to subjects better 'adapted to the human scale' in being concerned primarily with man rather than with abstract conceptions of a possible future.

Edith Sitwell (No. 140) was far more enthusiastic, and Cyril Connolly (No. 141) conceded 'merit' to all the stories, though he found them 'slight'. The London *Bookman* (No. 147) felt that they had hardly 'dated', but even this statement shows the reviewers' awareness that they were dealing with an earlier (and for some of them an outgrown) phase in Forster's career: L. P. Hartley even described criticism of them as, more properly, 'an exhumation' (No. 146). Taken as a whole, the reviews are rather equivocal; certainly they lack the simpler response found in reviews of *The Celestial Omnibus*. The praise of *The Times Literary Supplement* (No. 142) has a kind of ambivalence absent from reviews of Forster's earlier books. The sentence 'because it was Mr. Forster who wrote these six stories they are all interesting' is oddly reversed in its logic, the author's name determining the value of his work and not the work making his name. That he had reached the point where this could be implied is evidence of Forster's established reputation by 1928, but there is an ominous whiff of the literary mortuary about it.

CRITICAL APPROACHES 1927–1938

Long articles on Forster's novels as a whole began to appear in 1927, in England, France and America. The authors of the two essays published in America in that year were English, however, and one receives the impression that American readers were thought to need an explanation of Forster's career from critics who were more intimately acquainted than their own with his milieu. I. A. Richards's article, 'A Passage to Forster', published in the New York *Forum*, was accompanied by an editorial note which talked rather oddly of Forster's 'meteoric' rise and the puzzle this had been for Americans. Richards's article was offered as a partial solution to the puzzle.

The fairly frequent occurrence of the word 'elusive' in earlier reviews has already been noted. The critical essays published between 1927 and the start of the Second World War can be roughly divided into those which assume Forster's mastery of his medium and try to decide what his essential theme or bias is, and those which are puzzled by something unsatisfactory in his treatment and try, in explaining what this 'something' is, to pin down the reasons why Forster's novels are not, for them, completely successful. Even in this latter group, however, the assumption is usually made that Forster is a novelist of more than ordinary importance.

The young French critic Jacques Heurgon saw Forster's central theme as expressed in the question 'What is reality?'. His long essay (No. 133), which coincided with the serialisation, in the *Revue de Paris*, of *A Passage to India*, is sometimes obscure and often unfamiliarly rhetorical, but it is not without insight, particularly into the fluctuating relationship between mysticism and acceptance of reality to be found in the various novels. Heurgon is notable as seeing Forster as an heir of symbolism who reaches, in *A Passage to India*, a perfect harmony between the seen and the unseen, so that there is no sense of strain or need for any underlining of a philosophic 'message'. The same general conclusion emerges from Edward Shanks's more down-to-earth pursuit of Forster's trail (No. 134): 'he is carried away into an understanding beyond explanation, into the poetic state of mere wonder, and he carries the reader with him'.

The title of I. A. Richards's article, 'A Passage to Forster', is misleading, as he stops short of Forster's last novel and concentrates his attention on *Howards End*. For Richards, Forster is 'on the whole the most puzzling figure in contemporary English letters',[18] since there exists a discrepancy in his work both between an apparent realism and a sometimes 'wanton disregard' for 'vivisimilitude', and between an 'urbane manner' and á 'discomforting vision' which expresses 'less satisfaction with human existence as he sees it than . . . the work of any other living writer I can call to mind'. But the discomfort occasioned Richards by elements hard for him to reconcile does not prevent him from making acute statements about the novels in which they exist. Indeed his view that *Where Angels Fear to Tread* 'is . . . far nearer in spirit to a mystery play than to a comedy of manners' might strike many as solving one of the very problems he himself is bothered by.

Richards was not inhibited by his sense of Forster's flawed or mixed method from discerning a theme which, for him, 'more than any other haunts [Forster's] work'. He was the first to notice in it 'a special preoccupation, almost an obsession, with the continuance of life, from parent to child, with the quality of life in the sense of blood or race, with the preservation of certain strains and the disappearance of others'. *Howards End* most fully embodied this theme, though it was not always fused with the more obvious 'subject' of that novel, namely the relationships of different classes and different attitudes to life: 'the few passages which awaken . . . discomfort in the reader are, I believe, all consequences of the mixing of the two aims of the book, the half mystical preoccupation with survival overforcing the emotion in scenes which have apparently only to do with the sociological thesis'.

In view of the incredulity inspired in earlier reviewers by Leonard Bast, it is striking to find Richards reserving his strongest praise for Forster's treatment of him: 'The presentation of Leonard Bast, in its economy and completeness and adequacy to the context, would be enough by itself to give any novelist a claim to enduring memory'. Richards was especially impressed by Forster's description, in Chapter VI, of Leonard and his wife Jacky at home: 'It is only ten pages long, but what other novelist, though taking a whole volume, has said as much on this theme or said it so clearly'. Forster, one feels, would have been very gratified by this: he once said in an interview that this passage was written without the benefit of any sort of personal knowledge, and he thought it had come off.

Virginia Woolf, like Richards, was not altogether happy with Forster's mixing of methods. For her 'there is something baffling and evasive in the very nature of his gifts' (No. 136), for these gifts—poetry and realism, artistic detachment and an urge to didacticism—were difficult to combine in that 'single vision' which in her view was essential to a masterpiece. Nevertheless, though for her even *A Passage to India* did not quite fuse these various gifts into a compelling unity, the drive and vivacity of her essay on Forster is in part attributable to a response generated by its subject. Certainly her final question 'What will he write next?' contains less dissatisfaction than keen expectation, aroused by a novelist who had 'almost achieved the great feat of animating this dense, compact body of observation with a spiritual light'.

When, five years later, Howard N. Doughty (No. 151) took up Virginia Woolf's criticisms, he was able to see Forster's admitted 'lack of integration' in a more positive way: it sprang from a refusal to be 'impressive' at the expense of being truthful, and it equipped him to write more interestingly than Virginia Woolf. In itself, Doughty's essay is very perceptive, and it offers one of the earliest comparisons between Forster and D. H. Lawrence—a comparison which was not, as frequently later, to Forster's disadvantage. Yet Doughty's rhetorical *volte-face*, conceding Virginia Woolf's point but in effect setting it aside, seems to involve a misunderstanding of her general drift. Where Doughty sees her as wishing Forster to concentrate on comedy and leave alone the 'problem of the universe', a reading of her own essay suggests that she herself wishes him not to choose any one thing but to unify his many strands more convincingly than, for her, he does. One may perhaps feel that, if Forster succeeds for Doughty, he does so at a lower level than Virginia Woolf assumes his talents capable of attaining.

Writing in *Aspects of the Novel* (1927) about what he called 'Fantasy', Forster said that it asked the reader to 'pay something extra'. If 'fantasy', as used of Forster's own work, may be allowed to include the expansion of the mundane into the mystical, and the distortion of the expected called 'absence of verisimilitude', then one of the most important problems confronting critics of his work has consisted in how much extra they were prepared to pay. It may be that Forster's degree of success in fusing disparate elements determines critical generosity; but it may also be that their predisposition to be 'carried with him' determines the critics' views of his success. Put more simply, some critics have seemed to find Forster's supra-mundane side easier to accept than others.

One such critic is E. K. Brown, who in 1934 pronounced Forster 'the greatest master of the contemplative novel in our time' (No. 153). Brown saw Forster's essential theme as the contrast 'between the world of actions and the world of being', the latter not only superior in itself but presented in his novels—particularly through the characters of Mrs Wilcox and Mrs Moore—by means of a 'change of focus' which left the reader no time to question mere matters of prosaic likelihood: 'the novel is momentarily thrown off its course amid general confusion and doubt whether the methods and standards of this world of actions are quite so valid as we had supposed'. Ten years later,[19] Brown was to spend more time considering the charges of 'unrealism' that could be made against Forster, and he stressed that, whatever else it is, a novel 'must be realistic' and 'is not saved by a great theme'. In this view Brown does not essentially differ from Virginia Woolf, who expected both levels of existence to convince, equally and simultaneously. But that Brown's emphasis was still on Forster's relative success in transcending the objections of verisimilitude is clear from a comment about Somerset Maugham, who found Forster's sudden changes of focus hard to follow: 'What Mr Maugham objects to, I am sure, is the soaring . . . Probably he has been too devoted a reader of Anatole France to accept the plane to which Mrs Wilcox soars as a part of life'.

Peter Burra, who also wrote on Forster in 1934,[20] similarly had no trouble with Forster's 'soaring'. He was puzzled only by Forster's reasons for taking up the novel at all, considering his views of its short-comings, its need to tell a story, its assumption 'that life is a neat, well-patterned affair'. Logically, such a view should have led Forster to music, but, Burra decided, 'he has ideas which need a more distinct articulation than music or abstraction can make'. Thus what he evolved was a 'compromise' form, set somewhere between the symbolic tale and the novel of ideas and opinions. Burra admits the 'monstrous improbabilities' of Forster's stories, but believes that these are intended to 'bounce' the reader (to use Forster's own term) into accepting what he says. Burra's argument underlines, I think, the subjectivity of different critical responses, since Forster's 'improbabilities' might as easily stop some readers from accepting what he says (and for some critics it does). But Burra's view is that the stories are true within their own frame of reference: they have something for which he invents the illuminating phrase 'operatic truth', so that even Ansell's denunciation of Rickie in *The Longest Journey* (objected to by a number of reviewers, and by F. R. Leavis in 1938) is carried off by sheer intensity of presentation. In Burra's term 'operatic truth' can be seen as an obvious parallel to Richards's view of *Where Angels Fear to Tread* as a 'mystery play', the vital difference being that Burra's term is intended to resolve an apparent contradiction, Richards's to state it.

Lest it be thought, however, that Burra's opinion of Forster's success in bringing off his effects is dangerously subjective, it should be added that he reinforces his views by argument both painstaking and cogent to prove that Forster's 'surprises' are often prepared for by many careful but easily-overlooked touches—'hence a full appreciation of his novels depends absolutely on a second reading'. The greatest contribution made by Burra's essay is in fact this recognition of Forster's concern for small details, and particularly of his use of recurrent leitmotifs which with unobtrusive force build up over a whole novel a symbolic significance.

A further article on Forster was published in 1934, by Montgomery Belgion. This had the provocative title 'The Diabolism of E. M. Forster',[21] and though it touches on Forster's characterisation (Leonard Bast is hard to credit, many of Forster's characters 'are megaphones rather than people'), its emphasis is not technical but ideological. Belgion felt unsure of what Forster 'stands for', and one becomes aware while trying to follow his attempts at investigation of one of the divisions in the nineteen-thirties, that between Liberal agnosticism and Christian commitment. To a casual observer, Forster might seem to stand for such 'sound' attitudes as not interfering with other peoples' lives, but, in Belgion's view, at a closer look 'one begins to feel a little uneasy'.

The values Belgion discovered in *Howards End*, 'the novel in which Mr Forster rises as high as he can reach', were based on the importance of personal relationships, following one's instincts, and connecting the 'prose' with 'the passion and the poetry'. This latter accomplishment, Belgion felt, few could manage, and he accused Forster of 'sneering' at 'that great mass of unfortunates who can't'. The logic of following one's instincts should imply that those who follow them to a different end from Forster's are as good as he is; but instead Forster's books give the impression that only his instincts and those of his friends are right. Forster's attitude, Belgion concluded, was one of hostile mockery towards those outside his privileged group; the combination of his considerable talent and his 'pernicious' values 'may be diabolical'.

Earlier reviewers had commented on a certain ruthlessness in Forster's fictional judgements, but Belgion's views went outside literary criticism into crypto-Christian polemics: it would seem that if 'instinct' were replaced by dogma, no-one would be able to 'sneer' at anyone, but the logic of the essay's overall argument is as obscure as the process by which Belgion discovered Forster's apparently sound values to be so deeply tainted with quasi-aristocratic disdain. Belgion's article stands rather eccentrically aside from the main path of Forster criticism, and with its stress on the need for some organising dogma[22] it is interesting to compare Derek Traversi's statement early in his article on Forster (No. 157) published in 1937: 'The root of great art is an honesty by the side of which works like *Murder in the Cathedral* and Auden's plays are seen to be marred by something partial and parochial in them'.

The first book on Forster, by Rose Macaulay, was published in 1938. It prompted an article by F. R. Leavis in *Scrutiny*[23] which summarised many of the attitudes expressed by those earlier writers who granted, as Leavis did, Forster's 'real and very fine distinction' while finding in it an 'oddly limited and uncertain quality'. Leavis thought *Where Angels Fear to Tread* 'the most successful of the pre-war novels', but elsewhere, though Forster's gift for comedy was undeniable, his 'poetic communication about life' was 'almost unbelievably crude and weak'. Leavis illustrated this 'weakness' by a passage from *Howards End* already quoted by Richards, the last paragraph of Chapter XIX which describes Helen and Margaret watching the tide flow into Poole Harbour.[24] Richards had seen in this an attempt by Forster to 'put it over' on the reader by 'charging his sentences with a mysterious nervous shiver'. For Leavis it demonstrated a 'vagueness of vision' which Forster was 'inadequate and immature' in thinking a virtue (if indeed he did think it one).[25] Despite the fact that *A Passage to India* was 'a truly memorable work of literature', and that Forster's 'radical dissatisfaction with civilization' prompted comparison with 'D. H. Lawrence rather than Jane Austen', Forster was found to lack 'vitality'.

Clearly the world, so near a second time to war, had moved on from the days when what Forster's novels stood for needed little comment. Seen from Leavis's vantage point of 1938, they now constituted 'an explicit recognition' that 'liberal culture . . . has of its very nature grave weaknesses'. Yet just as W. H. Auden, writing in China 'where the bombs are real and dangerous', could recall Forster's promise that 'the inner life will pay', so Leavis could concede that even Bloomsbury liberalism was 'the indispensable transmitter of something that humanity cannot afford to lose', and that 'Mr Forster's is a name that, in these days, we should peculiarly honour'.

IV

In 1943 Lionel Trilling published in America his study *E. M. Forster*, which for more than a decade was to be for critically-minded readers the main avenue to a fuller understanding of Forster's fiction. It was issued in England in 1944, and apart from Rex Warner's brief pamphlet of 1950 it had no British successor until John Beer published *The Achievement of E. M. Forster* in 1962.

Trilling's over-riding emphasis was on Forster's 'liberal imagination' (not the cliché it has come to sound, but for Trilling a fruitful tension of opposites), and on the struggle in his work between sensitivity and personal integrity on the one hand and convention and the 'undeveloped heart' on the other. For him Forster's masterpiece was *Howards End*, but he also shed valuable light on Forster's 'most brilliant, most dramatic and most passionate novel', *The Longest Journey*, whose technical imperfections had kept it for long only partially understood. Furthermore, the insight revealed in his lapidary précis of Forster's mixed method did much to increase recognition of the genuine complexity (rather than the muddledness) of Forster's approach to life: 'The fierce plots move forward to grand simplicities but the comic manner confuses the issue, forcing upon us the difficulties of the moral fact . . . "Wash ye, make yourselves clean", says the plot, and the manner murmurs, "If you can find the soap" '.[26] Trilling incidentally scouted the view of Forster 'canonized' in *The Concise Cambridge History of English Literature*—Forster the 'shy, unworldly writer'. Where this notion had sprung from one can hardly guess; certainly not, I think, from the majority of early reviews collected in this book.[27]

Trilling's study, together with the reissue of a number of Forster's novels in America, inspired a transient 'Forster revival', marked by articles in American journals by such critics as Clifton Fadiman, Newton Arvin and Morton Dauwen Zabel. In his essay 'The Revival of E. M. Forster' (1944), E. K. Brown felt able to say that Forster 'stands in this country as the greatest living English master of the novel', and a few years later Stephen Spender said much the same thing in England, in his autobiography *World Within World*. 'We may delight', Brown added, 'in any movement to make the works more widely read and the man more deeply honoured'.

The honour in which Forster the man has been held, as a quiet champion of the value and freedom of the individual, may be felt to have been demonstrated, in distorted fashion, by his inclusion in the list drawn up by the S.S. of people to be arrested in the event of a successful German invasion of England. It was also demonstrated, in Forster's later years, by a fulsome degree of encomium and sanctification which Cyril Connolly unkindly summarised in 1971 in his phrase 'the Sacred Maiden Aunt of English Letters' (No. 178), and against which Pete Hamill, brashly but not incomprehensibly, felt driven to protest in 1965 (No. 166). The full weight of literary criticism was not brought to bear on Forster's work until 1957, when James McConkey's *The Novels of E. M. Forster* appeared, also in America. Between that year and Forster's death in 1970 fourteen studies of his work were published: one in Australia, one in India, four in England, and eight in America.

Many of these critical books, though paying altogether proper respect to Lionel Trilling's earlier interpretation of Forster's work, felt that it left out much of what gave Forster's novels their richness and density. McConkey, like so many earlier reviewers, found something 'elusive' in Forster which did not yield to Trilling's method, displaying as it did a tendency 'to turn feeling into idea in order to convey meaning, and to dismiss what cannot be so converted'.[28] McConkey attempted to trap this elusiveness by straining it through various sieves devised by Forster himself in *Aspects of the Novel*. He examined all Forster's novels in terms of People, Fantasy and Prophecy, and Rhythm, and concluded that Forster's vision was most fully expressed in *A Passage to India*, in which 'for the first time in all the novels, the voice is compatible with the theme'.[29]

Frederick C. Crews, in 1962, also found Forster's last novel to be his best, but for a different reason. In Crews's view (as to a lesser extent in Trilling's) Forster's novels showed an awareness of the limitations of the old-fashioned liberal outlook. But whereas Trilling had seen Forster as simply adding to the values of liberalism the equally necessary values of imagination, Crews saw him as reluctantly proceeding, and increasing in stature as he did so, from liberalism's 'candle in the dark' to his final 'solid masterpiece of pessimism' which 'passes beyond humanistic morality to a basically metaphysical critique of man's fate'.[30]

George H. Thomson's study of Forster (1967) rejected the assumptions of both Trilling and Crews, which he believed to be founded upon the fallacy that Forster's works 'belong in the realistic tradition'. Like McConkey, who had considered Forster mainly in terms of Fantasy, Prophecy and Rhythm, Thomson was willing to 'pay something extra'. His examination of Forster's reliance on myth, archetype and symbol is based on the view that 'Forster wrote romances and that the realistic elements of his fiction are used for other than realistic ends'.[31]

Such critical approaches, representative of shades on a spectrum ranging from intellect to intuition, from the social to the other-worldly, demonstrate how much Forster's novels had to offer to different people. Some felt the need to stress one end of the spectrum at the expense of the other. John Beer, exploring Forster's 'achievement' in 1962, was content to suggest that Forster called for an 'uncommon reader' who could so steep himself in the fiction that 'the modes jar against each other less and less, as one becomes steadily more aware of the personality behind, which reconciles them'.[32] In Wilfred Stone's monumental study of Forster, *The Cave and the Mountain* (1966), one finds such a reader, one not only steeped in the fiction but more steeped in Forster's life and personality than any previous Forster scholar. His volume, combining detailed scrutiny of Forster's intellectual origins and development with sensitive analysis of all his work (fiction and non-fiction) in such a way that life and work illuminate each other, has been the most comprehensively valuable study of Forster to appear up to the present.

'The present revival', E. K. Brown wrote in 1944, 'will doubtless fail to make of Mr. Forster a major figure in fiction'. It was a strange thing for so well-disposed a critic to predict, but the prediction indicates a sense of uncertainty about Forster's precise stature which has persisted, however faintly at times, throughout his career, and which made itself heard as late as 1966 in one review of Wilfred Stone's study: the eight years' work it had involved was surely too much time to spend on Forster? Still, at Forster's death in 1970 books about him not only existed in sufficient volume as to imply his likely permanence in literary history, they also gave the impression of defining the various gifts which entitled him to that permanence.

Then, in 1971, with a promptitude which almost suggested a prior wish not to slip into that temporary oblivion that has overtaken so many writers soon after their obituaries, Forster's novel *Maurice* was published. It would be too much to say that the laboriously erected edifice of Forster criticism collapsed, but the haste of many reviewers to re-examine earlier assessments was the result of a tremor strong enough at least to shake out some of its bricks. Only two reviewers, C. P. Snow and Walter Allen, felt able to say that *Maurice* would not affect the general view of Forster's work.

Maurice was finished in 1914, but its theme—the possibility of a satisfactory homosexual relationship—prevented Forster from publishing it at a time when the fate of Oscar Wilde was still remembered and a bishop visiting Cambridge could preach a sermon inveighing darkly against the secret sins of undergraduates. Later on, doubts about its successful treatment of its subject, and family compunction, inhibited Forster from publishing it in his lifetime. At various times, however, he made alterations to it and showed it to his friends, including, in 1927, T. E. Lawrence, who appears to have liked it.[33]

Edward Carpenter, at whose farm the book had been conceived, and Lytton Strachey both praised it, though they differed about the acceptability of the happy ending. The reviewers of 1971 were divided into two almost equal camps about the book's merit, and their views about the relative success of various parts of it also disagreed sharply, David Craig and V. S. Pritchett finding the real life of the book in the relationship between Maurice and Alec, many others valuing more highly the depiction of Maurice's early development and his friendship with Clive. For Craig, the Forster of *Maurice* was a 'brave' but inadequate precursor of D. H. Lawrence; for Nigel Dennis, *Maurice* was 'writing' and *Lady Chatterley's Lover* 'rubbish'. Cyril Connolly felt that *Maurice* showed 'the quality of a novelist at the height of his powers'; but the dating inseparable from its late publication inevitably spoiled its proper effect.

Such diversity of opinion makes it clear that *Maurice* is not a book to be disregarded. Its posthumous publication has had the effect of confronting Forster's audience with what was for them a 'new' novel, and so of producing as vital, if as mixed, a response as Forster's work elicited between 1905 and 1928. Thus the material in this book comes round in virtually a full circle, proceeding through the 'instant criticism' of reviews to the more distant and more pondered judgements of critical studies, and back again to reviews which enable one to compare the insights and errors of 1971 with the insights and errors of 1905. From 'the old man at King's', established and explained, Forster has almost changed back into 'the young rider into fiction'.

What place *Maurice* will eventually find in the Forster canon it is too early to say, as it is too early to say what alteration in our view of the scope and nature of that canon the presence of *Maurice* will bring about. Many reviewers in 1971, like Colin Wilson, John Cronin and the reviewer of *The Times Literary Supplement*, believed that *Maurice* reinterpreted to some degree Forster's other novels and the mystery of his fictional silence since 1924. One thinks of many aspects of Forster to which it may furnish the missing clue: his hostility, first noted by I. A. Richards in 1927, towards such representatives of authority as school teachers, doctors and clergymen; his opposition to censorship and his defence of such books as Radclyffe Hall's *The Well of Loneliness*; his cherishing of personal freedom; perhaps even his failure convincingly to render passion between man and woman.

Certainly at least one more critical work on Forster, which bears *Maurice* in mind,[34] will need to be written; though before P. N. Furbank has published his biography of Forster it would be unwise for anyone to attempt it. Until such a book is written, and perhaps even after, E. M. Forster himself will have the last word.

NOTES

1 E. M. Forster, 'Aspect of a Novel', *Bookseller*, 10 September 1960, 1230. Quoted in Wilfred Stone, *The Cave and the Mountain* (1966), 185.
2 Rose Macaulay, *The Writings of E. M. Forster* (1938), 19.
3 Hugh Walpole, *Joseph Conrad* [1917], 117.
4 Elizabeth Bowen, in *Aspects of E. M. Forster*, ed. Oliver Stallybrass (1969).
5 E. L. George, *A Novelist on Novels* (1918), 86–7; Harold Williams, *Modern English Writers, being a study of Imaginative Literature 1890–1914* (1918), 1925 edition, 402–3; Abel Chevalley, *Le Roman Anglais de Notre Temps* (London, 1921), 128–202; S. P. B. Mais, *Why We Should Read* (1921), 152–6; R. Brimley Johnson, *Some Contemporary Novelists (Men)* (1922), 173–80.
6 E. M. Forster, 'D. H. Lawrence', *Nation & Athenaeum*, xlvi, 1930, 888.
7 D. H. Lawrence, letter to Carlo Linati, *The Collected Letters of D. H. Lawrence*, ed. Harry T. Moore (1962), ii, 800.
8 Quoted in Wilfred Stone, *op. cit.*, 380, footnote.
9 Quoted in Stone, *op. cit.*, 381, footnote.
10 *The Collected Letters of D. H. Lawrence* (1962), ii, 1124.
11 *Ibid.*, ii, 1024.
12 'The Londoner', *Bookman* (New York), lvi, February 1923, 738.
13 E. M. Forster, *The Hill of Devi* (1953), 155.
14 *Ibid.*
15 J. B. Beer, *The Achievement of E. M. Forster* (1962), 133.
16 *The Journals of Arnold Bennett* (1933), iii, 1921–1928, 177.
17 In the mid-fifties, in conversation with the present writer.
18 I. A. Richards, 'A Passage to Forster: Reflections on a Novelist', *Forum* (New York), lxxviii, December 1927, 914–20.
19 In E. K. Brown, 'The Revival of E. M. Forster', *Yale Review*, xxxiii, June 1944, 668–81.
20 Peter Burra, 'The Novels of E. M. Forster', *Nineteenth Century and After*, cxvi, November 1934, 581–94. Reprinted as the Introduction to *A Passage*

to India (Everyman Edition, 1942). The 1957 reprint of the Everyman *A Passage to India* contains this comment by Forster on Burra's article: 'I have re-read it with pleasure and pride, for Burra saw exactly what I was trying to do; it is a great privilege for an author to be analysed so penetratingly, and a rare one. One grows accustomed to being praised, or being blamed, or being advised, but it is unusual to be understood.'

21 Montgomery Belgion, 'The Diabolism of E. M. Forster', *Criterion*, xiv, October 1934, 54–73. Mr Belgion was unwilling to allow this article to be reprinted, as he has since changed his views on Forster.

22 For a more penetrating, and a more sympathetic, Christian view of the effect on Forster's work of his lack of dogma, see Peter Ault, 'Aspects of E. M. Forster', *Dublin Review*, ccxix, October 1946, 109–34.

23 F. R. Leavis, 'E. M. Forster', *Scrutiny*, vii, September 1938, 185–202. Dr Leavis's views on Forster have become less favourable in recent years, and thus he did not wish his essay to be reprinted in this volume.

24 Leavis was so convinced of the faults of this passage that he was still using it as an example of weak writing in his Practical Criticism lectures at Cambridge in the mid-1950s.

25 Cf. No. 153. Also Beer, *op. cit.*, 187–91.

26 Lionel Trilling, *E. M. Forster* (London, 1944), 13.

27 The view raises its head again, however, in Harry T. Moore: *E. M. Forster* (Columbia Essays on Modern Writers, 1965).

28 James McConkey, *The Novels of E. M. Forster* (1957), 2.

29 *Ibid.*, 160.

30 Frederick C. Crews, *E. M. Forster: The Perils of Humanism* (1962), 178–9.

31 George H. Thomson, *The Fiction of E. M. Forster* (1967), 16.

32 Beer, *op. cit.*, 201.

33 See Stone, *op. cit.*, 347, footnote.

34 Such a work will also need to take into account the posthumous collection of Forster's short stories, *The Life to Come*, published late in 1972 after this book was finished. The collection, edited by Oliver Stallybrass, contains five short stories which Forster omitted from *The Celestial Omnibus* and *The Eternal Moment*. These date from Forster's earlier years, one of them being his first published short story, 'Albergo Empedocle', which appeared in *Temple Bar* in 1903. In the view of *The Times Literary Supplement* (Review, 13 October 1972), they 'resemble the other work . . . in subject and treatment' but are less successful. The rest of *The Life to Come* consists of eight stories, concerned with homosexual relationships, written between 1922 and 1958. The existence of these stories, which Forster felt unable to publish but compelled to write, seems to confirm Colin Wilson's conjecture (No. 176) about the reasons for Forster's fictional silence after 1924: in the words of the *T.L.S.* reviewer quoted above, the 'acceptance of his own nature as his only subject'. In his opinion, however, Forster 'couldn't

write well about it, even in private', only 'Doctor Woolacott' even approaching the quality of his published stories. This reviewer's conclusion is that 'the private fantasies remain private; they will help Forster's admirers to understand his nature and his limitations, but they will not add anything to Forster's stature as an artist'. One may immediately agree that these stories increase awareness of Forster as a man, but on such short acquaintance it is premature to dismiss their claim to literary value.

Note on the Text

The material brought together in this volume is reproduced in almost all details exactly as it originally appeared, even to the retention, for instance, of the incorrect apostrophe 's' which made its occasional quaint appearance in early references to *Howards End*. For convenience, however, comments which in letters to Forster were added as footnotes have been relocated (in parentheses) in their appropriate positions in the letters concerned. Reviewers' section headings have sometimes been silently omitted, but the omission of quotations not essential to a reviewer's argument is indicated in the text. The titles which are attached to some reviews are those employed by the reviewers themselves.

WHERE ANGELS FEAR TO TREAD

1905

1. Unsigned notice, *The Times Literary Supplement*

no. 194, 29 September 1905, 319

Here we have a young and flighty widow who shocks her respectable relatives by marrying, abroad, the son of an Italian dentist. She dies and leaves a baby, and the relatives organize an expedition to recover it—some of the incidents indeed are so original as to be almost farcical. There is in fact an odd kind of individuality about the book and its characters which is worth exploring; moreover the writing of it is good and sometimes witty.

2. Unsigned review, *Bookman* (London)

xxix, October 1905, 40–1

This is a book which one begins with pleased interest and gradually finds to be astonishing. Its amusing facility becomes amusing cleverness, and then, almost without realising the development, we find that the cleverness is of a larger style than we thought, and the main issues of life are confronting us where we looked for trivialities. The author takes half-a-dozen or so apparently commonplace people, picks out their little tremors and foibles with a finger which just escapes being cruel; and then, with no greater events than a visit to Monteriano, a wrong marriage, a brown baby, and a few little happenings, he depicts greatness, and Italy, and the point where humanity touches divinity; the whole thing being done with an appearance of jocularity which is very engaging and a truthfulness which is, by contrast, almost startling. The apparently commonplace people are none of them commonplace in Mr. Forster's hands. Mrs. Herriton, the mother-in-law; Harriet, her solid, serious daughter; Philip, her artistic, clever, ineffective son; Lilia, her vulgar, widowed daughter-in-law who—to keep her out of mischief and to give her culture—is sent travelling with the respectable but surprising Caroline Abbot; and Gino, the impossible Italian with whom Lilia falls in love—they are all distinct, and amusing, and fillipic in effect. The story is like the characters, the characters are like the story—at first clever, attractive, and seemingly with no heart, then swept almost into tragedy while scarcely knowing it. The book stands out as unusual and convincing, with its uniqueness and its persuasion accomplished in an unexpectedly fresh manner.

3. 'V', review, *Manchester Guardian*

4 October 1905, 5

Where Angels Fear to Tread is not at all the kind of book that its title suggests. It is not mawkish or sentimental or commonplace. The motive of the story, the contest over the possession of a child between the parent who survives and the relatives of a parent who is dead, is familiar and ordinary enough, but the setting and the treatment of this motive are almost startlingly original. 'E. M. Forster' writes in a persistent vein of cynicism which is apt to repel, but the cynicism is not deepseated. It is a protest against the worship of conventionalities, and especially against the conventionalities of 'refinement' and 'respectability'; it takes the form of a sordid comedy culminating, unexpectedly and with a real dramatic force, in a grotesque tragedy. There are half-a-dozen characters in the book which count, and two of them—Mrs. Herriton, the incarnation of spotless insincerity, and Harriet, purblind, heartless, and wholly bereft of the faculty of sympathy—are altogether repellent and hence not altogether real. The other four, whatever else they may be—and they are all more or less unpleasant—are undeniably and convincingly real. It is a trick of Fortune in her most freakish mood that brings about the union of Lilia, the vulgar, shallow Englishwoman, and Gino, the courteous, shallow, amd discreditable Italian. The results of the trick are at once fantastic and inevitable. The whole is a piece of comedy, as comedy is understood by George Meredith. We wonder whether 'E. M. Forster' could be a little more charitable without losing in force and originality. An experiment might be worth trying.

4. Unsigned notice, *Glasgow Herald*

5 October 1905

There is something so fresh and convincing about this book that we are certain it is the result of first-hand knowledge, indeed we should be surprised if every character in the book has not been copied with fair exactitude from an actual original. The means by which the contrast between the English and Italian natures is shown are both ingenious and effective. A widow of 33, of vulgar instincts but of fairly attractive appearance, escapes from the cultured thraldom of her late husband's family, and goes to spend a year in Italy. Soon after her relations are horrified to hear that she is married. Her prim brother-in-law sets off for the south with a faint hope that it may be a gentleman she has chosen, but is horrified beyond expression to find himself face to face with a handsome child of nature who spits on the floor, wears dirty linen, and is a chum of custom-house officers and stationmasters, his only claim (a dubious one) to respectability being that his father is a dentist. The brother-in-law returns to England, leaving his sister-in-law to discover by degrees the remarkable difference between the submissive, hen-pecked, de-sexed husband of England, and the easy-going, cynical, coolly-tyrannical, decidedly and blatantly masculine specimens that unspoiled Italy can still boast of. Her spirit is thoroughly broken, and she dies when her baby is born. The rest of the story centres round this baby, for whom his Italian and English relations fight like Greeks and Trojans. The poor mite, kidnapped by the prim brother-in-law's sister, gets killed in a carriage accident, and there is a frightful scene between the prim one and the father, who has loved the child with frantic fondness. The prim one is within an ace of being murdered; but he, like everyone else, has fallen in love with the handsome, child-like ruffian, and forgives him; and the climax of absurdity is reached when, on their journey home, the prim one's declaration of love to his lady-companion is anticipated by the latter's passionate cry of love for the bereaved father, who is weeping grimy tears amid the debris, called by courtesy furniture, of the filthy house at Monteriano. The most enjoyable book we have read for many a day.

5. Unsigned notice, *Pall Mall Gazette*

7 October 1905, 9

A not particularly interesting story of the adventures of one Lilio in Italy, including her marriage and death, with an extension of the book giving particulars of some of the devices of her widower, a picturesque but disreputable Italian.

6. Unsigned notice, *Birmingham Daily Post*

13 October 1905

An empty-headed foolish little widow, Lilia Herriton, after having troubled her austere and eminently respectable mother-in-law and family for some years by her irresponsible vagaries, goes to Italy and marries one Gino Carella. She endures much misery at the hands of this Italian, and dies, leaving behind her a baby boy. Her first husband's family, for purely selfish reasons, are now desirous of possessing the child of the Italian marriage, and are convinced that the father is a vagabond without natural affection. Their journey to Italy and encounter with Gino result in a tragedy, and the book closes with a wail at the futility of all earthly things. There is much that is good about the story, but the latter part of it is unconvincing. It taxes our credulity overmuch to believe that after the misconduct of the Italian has brought his wife to an early grave his fascinations should be so great that her dearest friend should 'worship every inch of him.' The characters are all clearly defined, and the descriptions of Italian places and scenery very good.

7. Unsigned notice, *Manchester Courier*

13 October 1905

Where Angels Fear to Tread by E. N. Forster, is apparently a first novel, and as such deserves a hearty commendation. Not that there is any sign in the book of a 'prentice hand, except, possibly, that the writer handles his creations a little too savagely, thus destroying partly the true artistic impression of aloofness. But what distinguishes the work from the great majority of modern novels is its originality of conception and attitude. The characters, strongly marked and distinctive, give an impression of reality which is shared by the incidents of the narrative, whose motive is a study of national temperaments in conflict. The light tone of the opening chapters soon gives place to ironical tragedy, centring about so small a thing as the care of a dead Englishwoman's child by her second marriage with a low-born Italian husband. On the whole, the persons depicted are a shade too unpleasing: Harriet, a type unfortunately common in daily life, is, as the author will have it, detestable! But the book is a notable one, in spite of its unpleasantnesses.

8. Unsigned notice, *Guardian*

no. 3124, 18 October 1905, 1763

The *Guardian* (subtitled 'The Church Newspaper') was founded in 1846.

At a superficial glance, *Where Angels Fear to Tread* seems a farrago of nonsense, with its grotesque incidents, vulgar details, and coarse caricature. But really read it reveals power in characterisation—the revelation of suppressed qualities beneath conventional exteriors, as in Philip Herriton, the passion for Italy beneath the cold, critical English nature: the vein of sentimentality in the decorous Churchworker, Caroline Abbott; and hot, red blood in flippant Lilia. In 'Gino' we have a real Italian type, a nature easygoing and amiable, affectionate and unfaithful, swept by gusts of sudden temper. His love for his son is true to the half-womanly tenderness, half-animal passion of the average Italian towards his child. The atmosphere of Italy is well suggested, as is also its relaxing power on English principles and prejudices.

9. Unsigned review, *Speaker*

28 October 1905, 90

Mr. E. M. Forster has accomplished something quite out of the common in *Where Angels Fear to Tread*, a novel in which the terrible Mrs. Herriton, of Sawston, her daughter Harriet, drably Protestant and rigidly English, and Philip Herriton, the priggish anti-Philistine æsthete, unite to suppress the sloppy Lilia and prevent her from marrying

Signor Gino Carella, the mercenary son of an Italian dentist at Monteriano. Lilia is the widow of the late lamented Charles Herriton and her austere mother-in-law puts the family attitude in a nutshell when she says: 'If Lilia marries him she insults the memory of Charles, she insults Irene, she insults us.' For many years the luckless Lilia had been 'continually subject to the refining influence of her late husband's family,' but on a visit to Yorkshire she had shown alarming signs of breaking out and marrying a certain Mr. Kingcroft, whereupon Mrs. Herriton had intervened decisively, and, in the end, the family had agreed with Philip that the sweet influences of Florence, Gubbio, Pienza, and San Gemignano might open Lilia's purblind eyes and improve her moral tone. Lilia, accompanied by Miss Caroline Abbott as chaperone, was accordingly sent to Italy, and all went well till Sawston was bouleversed by a telegram—*Lilia engaged to Italian nobility. Writing. Abbott.* The unscrupulous Signor Carella and the wretched Lilia, in fact, were already married before the mendacious telegram was despatched, and so Philip, who came post-haste to Monteriano to bribe the dentist's son to break the engagement in consideration of 1,000 lire, had his journey from Sawston for nothing.

What Mr. Forster has done with a refreshing and brilliantly original touch in his novel is so to expose Sawston's ideals and ways of life in the glare of the vertical Italian sun, that the comedy of north meeting south has for us English delicious significance. Middle-class-England-in-little is really represented by the Herriton family circle, so cleverly has the author chosen his types. Mrs. Herriton, resourceful, masterful, tactful, and hard as nails; Harriet, as rigidly unbending in her principles and as raspingly precise as a charity institution; Philip, cultured and advanced in his ideas and painfully prudent and conservative in his life; Lilia, bouncing and impulsive and hopelessly uncritical; and Miss Abbott, full of refined intuitions and romantic emotions; these five people are admirably set off in national temperament against the figure of the subtle, graceful, materialistic, and full-natured Italian, Signor Gino Carella. The English people are so stiffly conscientious, so self-conscious, so earnest in their aims and ideas, the Italian so flexible and so sympathetic in his graceful self-seeking. It would be easy to exaggerate the serious intentions of Mr. Forster underlying this light and delicate satire of his exceedingly clever sketch, but he has undoubtedly caught the essential tone of the modern English mind so justly and finely that we shall be curious to see whether the novel before us will prove to be the first of a series of quiet, refined, satirical studies. His manner of making his points is quite his own, neatly incisive, with a slight tendency now and then to accentuate his criticism. The story carries us along with an easy swimming sense of the author's mastery of his subject, even when we pass unexpectedly from comedy into tragedy, in the last chapter, in which Miss Caroline Abbott confesses her secret passion for Gino. We do not quite believe in this scene, not that we question Miss Abbott's sincerity, but we look in vain for the author's criticism of the romantic fervour of her idealism. This romantic fervour is one of the finest things in the English soul, but if the north can in moments meet and touch hands with the south, are there not temperamental qualities still stronger which would soon have drawn Miss Abbott to Philip? Philip is deliciously English in his halting and hesitating attitude to Caroline Abbott. He does not discover she is beautiful till the Italian has pointed it out to him! and he waits and waits, with his clever head on one side, watching her, till his chance as a lover has gone. We must own to be profoundly interested in the relations between this priggish clever young man and this refined young English lady, and while we urge *The Speaker's* readers to send forthwith for *Where Angels Fear to Tread*, we beg the author to give us the sequel and describe Philip's experiences on his return to the bosom of Sawston.

10. C. F. G. Masterman, review, *Daily News*

8 November 1905, 4

C. F. G. Masterman (1873–1927), Literary Editor of the *Daily News*, was a Liberal MP from 1906 to 1914, and Under-Secretary of State, Home Department, from 1909 to 1912. Like Forster he was a member of the Reform Club. His publications include *F. D. Maurice* (1907) and *The New Liberalism* (1920). He also reviewed *The Longest Journey* and *A Room with a View* (cf. Nos 19 and 46).

Where Angels Fear to Tread is a remarkable book. Not often has the reviewer to welcome a new writer and a new novel so directly conveying the impression of power and an easy mastery of material. Here there are qualities of style and thought which awaken a sense of satisfaction and delight; a taste in the selection of words; a keen insight into the humour (and not merely the humours) of life; and a challenge to its accepted courses.

Sawston and San Gemignano

On the surface are the commonplace outward scenes: Sawston, with its suburban existence; the queer life of the Italian bourgeoisie encamped in the incongruous surroundings of an ancient, crumbling, walled city; and the journeys between one and the other. These scenes are peopled with apparently commonplace persons, a suburban family, the child of an Italian dentist. The conversations are carried on in the departure of the train from Victoria or the railway carriage crawling up the St. Gothard out of Italy. Yet from such material Mr. Forster can weave a vision of life which is at once an approval and a criticism; with the clash of diverse racial characteristics, and the sudden upheaval, both in Italian and English natures, of forces scarcely noticed in the world of every day.

'When the spring came,' says one of the characters, 'I wanted to fight against the things I hated, mediocrity and dulness, and spitefulness and society. I didn't see that all these things are invincible, and that if we go against them they will break us to pieces.' This triumph of the ordered conventional world over the revolt of incongruous, queer, and passionate desires is one of the motifs of the tale. The story, as far as outward scenes are concerned, is of the simplest possible description. Lilia, a girl of humble origin, is persuaded to wander in Italy by the family of her first husband, of secure wealth and respectability. She falls in love in her widowhood with Gino, the little son, scarcely of age, of an Italian dentist. She marries him, and settles down within the crumbling walls of Monteriano, under which title Mr. Forster describes the astonishing little city, San Gemignano. The mother dies on the birth of a child; and the English family at Sawston plan the rescue of the infant from the unspeakable husband and all the corrupt influences of the South. Direct bribery and persuasion having failed, an attempt is made to kidnap the child, who perishes in a scene which mingles a kind of wild laughter and tears. The father, after one outburst of insane ferocity, settles down into acquiescence, and the story ends with the return of the expedition, which had failed so woefully, from the magic of the South into the rational air of England.

'A Country Behind Him'

Into such a simple narrative Mr. Forster has crowded not only pieces of sharp description which give to the whole affair a convincing air of reality, but also those challenges of ultimate things which are rarely faced in the even flow of an orderly world. Sawston is challenged by Monteriano. The routine of the suburban life appears intolerable to one half of the mind, longing with a kind of physical hunger for the sun and enchantment of Italy. But in the midst of the ruins and unaccountable courses the other half turns to the security of the recognised ways—'to Sawston after the summer holidays, bicycle gymkanas, and the annual bazaar in the garden for the C.M.S. It seemed impossible that such a happy life could exist.' Gino at first appears unspeakable; unclean, vulgarly dressed, coarsely eating his food, brutal with animals, idle, unfaithful to his wife. But there is the other side also; boundless good temper and good fellowship; the fierce and passionate devotion of the father for his child, which is utterly incomprehensible to the colder Northern nature; and something mysterious and terrible, congruous with the hot night and magic of the hills and valleys, and all the enchantment of a land where the intellect is paralysed by the emotions. 'He has got a country behind him,' is the verdict, 'that's upset people from the beginning of the world.' The country itself, with its vast slopes of olives and vineyards and little towns outlined against the cloudless sky, has 'scarcely a touch of wildness in it.' 'But it was terrible and mysterious all the same.' The collegiate church of Santa Deodata, with the frescoes of its child saints, confronts with a kind of dumb challenge all the respectabilities and good works of the English suburb.

The Challenge of Italy

The struggle between Gino and Lilia is national. 'Generations of ancestors, good, bad, or indifferent, forbade the Latin man to be chivalrous to the Northern woman; the Northern woman to forgive the Latin man.' The poverty-haunted people of the little forgotten town assemble with great joy in the theatre to applaud Donizetti's 'Lucia di Lammermoor.' Outside the window of the hotel is evidence of the fighting of 1338. 'It reaches up to Heaven,' is the summary of it all, 'and down to the other place.' The idiot who, in another country, would have been shut up is here accepted as an institution and part of Nature's scheme. 'He understands everything, but can explain nothing,' is the verdict of the landlady. 'And he has visions of the saints,' is the corroboration of 'the man who drove the cab.'

Mr. Forster makes here none of the conventional attacks against conventional evils. He gives the picture of the one and the other: Italy and suburban England, worldly success against complete worldly failure, idleness in the sunlight against a beaver-like industry under grey skies, material comfort contrasted with indifference to life's minor luxuries, life lived for the future contrasted with life living on the past. He stands aside, with the detachment of the artist, presenting no verdict of judgment, preaching no obvious gospel; as dispassionate in his vision of those who are driven by ennui into good works in the middle classes of England who are successful as in those who enjoy their lives and disappear like the midge in the middle classes of Italy who have failed. He knows the indignation of the tourist as he (or she) drifts through the heat and dust, blinking wearily at historical monuments, and continually exasperated by the futile good temper of the aborigines. He knows also that this acquiescence amongst dead things means an abandonment of material advance and progress. The conquering Briton has gained the whole world; perhaps the Italian, amongst the ruins of populous cities, has preserved his own soul.

'Life was greater than he had supposed,' is the verdict rescued from it all. 'But it was even less complete. He had seen the need for strenuous work and for righteousness, and now he saw what a very little way these things would go.' Always such conceptions can be disturbed by that magic accent of the South; the laughter in the theatre; the silvery stars in the purple sky; the violets of a departing spring. Outwardly, after this plunge into another universe, life will continue in its courses. Sawston will maintain its activities in the 'service of the corpulent poor,' the book club, the debating society, progressive whist, the bazaars. Far away on its southern hillside the people of Monteriano will collect in the sunshine, discourse in the cafés, drift on in their destined and quiet ways. But in the momentary clash between the two something unaccountable, almost elfish and fantastic, has been revealed of the queer, irrational material of the soul of woman and of man; and the world is the richer for such a revelation.

Such is the theme of this brilliant novel. It is told with a deftness, a lightness, a grace of touch, and a radiant atmosphere of humour, which mark a strength and capacity giving large promise for the future.

11. Unsigned notice, *Yorkshire Post*

6 December 1905, 5

Where Angels Fear to Tread, by E. M. Forster, treats of an English middle-class family affair. The best part of the action is laid in Italy, where, while on tour, a light-hearted widow, much to the disgust of her late husband's snobbish relatives, contracts marriage with a native holding no higher social position than that of a dentist's son. And 'even in England,' the author explains, 'a dentist is a troublesome creature whom careful people find difficult to class.' The story, though not unskilfully told, is pervaded by an atmosphere of snobbishness and vulgarity. Of all the characters, only the despised Italian dentist's son seems to merit sympathy. And, judging by the title of the book, this would almost appear to be the author's own feeling.

12. Unsigned review, *Spectator*

no. 4043, 23 December 1905, 1089–90

Mr. Forster, who is, to the best of our belief, a newcomer in the field of fiction, has at once revealed himself as a writer to be reckoned with in his exceedingly clever but decidedly painful story. When, however, we say 'painful,' the epithet needs reserves and explanations. *Where Angels Fear to Tread* is not a story written with the deliberate aim of challenging attention by giving offence, nor is it disfigured by the wanton intrusion of disagreeable or repulsive details. On the contrary, in handling a difficult theme the author has shown in the main remarkable tact and reticence, while the chief practical lessons of the story —the dangers of international marriages, the need of domestic tolerance, and the futility of ill-considered rebellion against convention— are unimpeachable in their strong if indirect confirmation of orthodox views. All this we cordially admit; but though Mr. Forster is neither cruel nor anarchical in his attitude, he deals largely with those elements in modern society which make for domestic disintegration rather than solidarity. Above all, the story is steeped in disillusionment. Steele, giving a new lease of life to a famous Greek maxim, said in reference to a good woman that 'to love her was a liberal education.' Mr. Forster, on the other hand, has shown how the love felt by a good woman, so far from exerting an educational influence, may be a relapse to a primitive and barbaric instinct, a mark of degradation rather than elevation.

The personages concerned in Mr. Forster's story are in no case of a truly or consistently heroic cast,—indeed, there is only one who is in any way capable of rising to the occasion, and in her case the disillusionment excited in the reader is in some ways the keenest. As for the plot, it centres in the unfortunate remarriage of Lilia Herriton, a young widow, a good-natured, impulsive, but second-rate woman, who has lived with her husband's people after his death, and has at every turn been made to feel her intellectual and social shortcomings by her mother-, brother-, and sister-in-law. When, therefore, she thinks of having a *Wanderjahr* in Italy, they encourage the plan, and a companion is found in Caroline Abbott, an excellent young lady who is apparently devoted to good works, district visiting and the like, but in reality is just as anxious as Lilia to escape from her dull surroundings and see something of real life. They are both intoxicated by the sense of freedom and the charm of Italy, and Lilia, without protest from her companion, falls in love with a handsome young Italian, the son of a dentist, half Faun, half Satyr. The Herritons are horrified at the news, and Lilia's brother-in-law Philip—an ineffectual aesthete whose strong critical faculty and sense of humour are not backed by any force of character—is despatched in hot haste by his mother to break off the match, but arrives to find that the lovers are already secretly married, and returns in disgust with Miss Abbott, leaving Lilia to her fate. Alternately cowed and neglected by her husband, who had only married her for her money, which he squanders on dissipation, and disowned by her relatives and connections, Lilia, in spite of her vulgarity, attains to a tragic pitch of desolation and misery before she dies in giving birth to a son. The only person, indeed, who feels the slightest compunction is Caroline Abbott, who, smitten with remorse at her lack of foresight in encouraging the match and her cowardice in deserting her friend, resolves to rescue the child from its surroundings. Mrs. Herriton, insensible to the call of natural affection, is at once roused from her indifference to the fate of the 'beastly Italian baby' by wounded pride, and a second rescue party is organised, in which Philip's sister, a narrow-minded religious fanatic, takes a leading and disastrous part. There is only one bright spot in the squalid tragedy of this episode, the courage and tact shown by Caroline Abbott, who saves the situation when it had become well-nigh desperate, awakens Philip to a sense of his worthlessness, and inspires him with the resolve to abandon the rôle of the cynical onlooker. But Caroline, having placed herself on a pedestal, abruptly shatters her claims to reverence by the humiliating confession that she too had been fascinated by the Faun-Satyr, though fully conscious of his cruelty and baseness, and was only prevented from declaring her feelings by the fact that he regarded her as a being on a wholly higher plane.

A rough outline such as the foregoing, while it gives what we hope is not an inaccurate sketch of the contents of the book, must inevitably fail to convey any impression of the persuasive skill with which Mr. Forster has contrived to lend an engrossing interest to a disconcerting, and even distressing, study of contemporary civilisation. As we have said at the outset, one can read half-a-dozen excellent orthodox morals into the story, but the dominant impression left on the mind of the present writer is that under the stress of opportunity primitive instincts reassert themselves in the most carefully educated and studiously repressed natures. The cruelty and callousness of old Mrs. Herriton is even more sinister, because more unexpected, than the frank inhumanity, tempered with graceful animalism, of the young Italian. Mr. Forster has succeeded, with a cleverness that is almost uncanny, in illustrating the tragic possibilities that reside in insignificant and unimportant characters when they seek to emancipate themselves from the bondage of convention, or to control those who are dominated by a wholly different set of traditions. He has done this in a manner which is void of offence, but is none the less painful and disquieting. Let us hope that so original and searching a talent may yet give us a story in which the fallibility of goodness and the callousness of respectability are less uncompromisingly insisted upon.

WHERE ANGELS FEAR TO TREAD

(American edition) 1920

13. Unsigned review, *Springfield Sunday Republican*

(Springfield, Massachusetts) 21 March 1920, 11a

Those whose business or pastime it has been to follow the development of English fiction have known for fully 10 years that E. M. Foster was an artist of distinction, although they may seldom have felt complete satisfaction in his work. *Where Angels Fear to Tread* has the subtle comprehension, the subdued irony, the charm of temperament and the delicacy of style that have been found in all his books; and it presents that same merger of comedy and tragedy which was attempted in *Howard's End.* In the accomplishment of this change of purpose, there is a trace of the far-fetched, even the fantastic, yet nowhere is there a stroke which is not evolved out of the writer's artistic consciousness.

The story is founded on Mr. Foster's acute perception of certain contrasted human qualities—culture versus vulgarity, spontaneity versus convention, the naturalness and emotion of the South versus the calculation and suppression of Anglo-Saxon minds. But Mr. Foster makes his characters no arbitrary embodiments of values that are congenial to him or the reverse. His irony—even his vein of poetry—plays impartially over all. And the brightness, the suppleness, the alacrity of the style are those of a person who at least masters his material, chapter by chapter, as he writes, even if his architecture, as a whole, is a good deal short of perfection.

The story is about Lilia, a cheerful young widow, and the scandal that she causes her dead husband's family because she marries a good-for-nothing son of a dentist in an Italian town. Her extremely 'correct' mother-in-law treats her with kindly disdain, knows her to be 'impossible,' but means to do what duty requires for her and her daughter, who is left behind, when she makes the journey in the course of which she so suddenly and unaccountably marries. Lilia's brother-in-law is the quiet young Englishman of artistic tastes, who is sufficiently a man of the world to make the practical arrangements demanded by an emergency; who probably likes his sister-in-law—as, indeed, all men do—yet who is amusedly conscious of her amiable and innocent vulgarity; who adores Italy, and yet sees the imperfections of the uncultivated native character.

Here is the best of material for a comedy. And it is as comedy that Mr. Foster presents his material up to a certain point. Some may think that he would have done better had he decided to preserve that vein to the end. But Mr. Foster seems determined that the emotions or the deep sense of duties of his people must have full recompense in the final adjustment of values. Lilia has a child and dies. Her husband's family decide that they must obtain possession of the second child in order to 'bring it up properly.' (The motive here is slender and strained.) They try persuasion but that fails. An attempted kidnapping, in which Lilia's highly unpleasant and unsympathetic sister-in-law takes an important part, terminates in an accident, in which the baby is killed. The shiftless father, grieved and enraged by the loss of his offspring, almost kills Lilia's brother-in-law in a struggle. But the Englishman is rescued by the interposition of Miss Abbott, a charitable-minded young woman, who at first accompanied Lilia to Italy, and who has flitted back to the romantic scene.

Miss Abbott, in the midst of her village charities, seemed at first destined for spinsterhood. But Italy has been enkindling, and from under her reserve emotion breaks forth. Lilia's brother-in-law, at first skeptical about Miss Abbott as about most of the conventional figures of his family and his mother's 'set,' falls in love with her and asks her to marry him. But she refuses him. And we learn that she has been in love with the good-for-nothing Italian from her first days in Italy. He, of course, has interested himself in other women soon after Lilia's death.

There is undoubtedly a good deal to criticize adversely in the structure of the story. But Mr. Foster has a power of winning, even of persuading, the reader.

14. Unsigned article, *Bookman* (London)

xxxii, June 1907, 81–2

A full-page article (with photograph) in 'The Bookman' Gallery.

We have fallen into such an easy habit of mis-using words that every writer of fiction who is publishing his first book is automatically described as a new novelist, when as a rule we mean no more than that he is a young one. I find a popular novelist telling us in her latest work that America produces a genius a day and doesn't know it; and if one out of each week's supply is a literary genius, nobody else knows it either. A new novelist is really so much of a rarity that if we get three or four in a decade we may account ourselves uncommonly fortunate. Most of those who are catalogued as new have nothing new about them but their bindings. That the story they tell has, superficially speaking, all been told before is of little or no importance; what matters is that they have obviously gathered their knowledge of life from the books of others, they have no personal experience to draw upon, no individual outlook; their thoughts are not coloured by their own thinking, and their style is a mere echo of somebody else's.

Therefore, when you do amongst the annual output of fiction come across a novel that is authentically new, you are not slow to offer up thanks for it and keep an eye open for the next book with the same author's name on it. When *Where Angels Fear to Tread* made its appearance about a year ago most critics of any discernment made haste to put Mr. E. M. Forster into their limited list of new novelists who are really new, and the publication of *The Longest Journey* this spring has amply justified them in doing so.

It is not safe to make sure of your new novelist on the strength of a first book only; nine out of every ten men who delight us with a more than ordinarily good first book never do another that will bear comparison with it; but Mr. Forster is not one of these, for his second story, both in breadth of design and treatment, and in the strength and subtle charm of its style, touches a higher level than was reached by the first.

Happily, Mr. Forster is a young novelist as well as a new one, but though these are his first novels, they are not his only nor his earliest work in literature. He has from the first been a contributor to the *Independent Review* (which has lately changed its name to the *Albany*), and considers that he owes very largely to its encouragement his introduction to the public. Some of the short stories he contributed there are similar in aim to the imaginative, unappreciated stories which he makes 'Rickie' write in *The Longest Road*—stories that get into touch with nature as the Greeks were in touch with it, so that the trees and coppices and summer fields are alive with a life that is half human and half godlike. A fondness for Latin literature has led Mr. Forster to edit the *Æneid* for Messrs. Dent; but outside the writing of fiction his chief interest is in history, particularly the history of the Italian Renaissance, on which he is hoping presently to publish some studies.

He does not hamper himself with any artistic formula, and his ideas on the respective merits of good and bad endings for novels are courageously and emphatically illustrated in his own books. Nothing could be worse than the happy ending at any price; and nothing could be better than the bad or sad ending that is the true, the evident, the inevitable result of all that has gone before it. The fact is there is no such thing as a gloomy ending of a novel that counts for anything. I know of nothing that is fuller of heartbreak than is the close of *Jude the Obscure*. The very memory of it haunted me like a personal sorrow for a week after I had read it, but the sheer joy one has in the stern truth and exquisite art of it is a finer, more elevating pleasure than any to be won from the most gracefully, artfully, artificially cheerful conclusion that the novelist with no conscience will fashion for the pleasure of the crowd.

Neither of Mr. Forster's stories finishes with the cheap conventional smile under a heaven from which all clouds have been swept, presumably for ever; but there is nothing forced or aggressive in the end to which they do come. The sudden confession of Miss Abbott to Philip, in the last chapter of *Where Angels Fear to Tread*, surprises him more than it should surprise the reader, though even the reader, who has by this been cleverly lured into forgetting things, is for the moment taken aback; but their final parting, handled with a shrewd and delicate irony, is the right and satisfying thing, after all.

Some of Mr. Forster's opinions of men and things are very healthily irritating, and I have been glad to find myself resenting or dissenting from many of them. He has wit and humour, and a good gift of irony;

his characters are living and human, with an ingrained flesh-and-blood humanity; he writes imaginatively, with spiritual insight, and an underlying sense of the beauty, and sordidness, and pathos of mortal life.

He has travelled a great deal in Germany, Greece, France, but, more than all, in Italy; the latter country supplies certain of the most memorable scenes of his first novel, and in Gino, frank, joyous, irresponsible, shallow, not over cleanly, 'a boy of medium height with a pretty face, the son of a dentist at Monteriano,' a sunny fellow whom all women fall in love with, and one, an English widow, his senior and social superior, makes the mistake of marrying, he has given a brilliant and sympathetic study of Italian character. Gino is easy-going and impressionable, as ready to fall in love as to be fallen in love with; he is more than willing to marry the charming widow, Lilia Herriton; he is fond of her, but is not blind to the fact that she has money; and after their marriage he masters her, despite his happy carelessness and his apparently boundless good-nature, and despite the other fact that she is nearing forty, and he is little more than twenty. It is round this marriage really that the whole story revolves. Since her son's death, Mrs. Herriton, senr., has taken possession of his wife and small daughter, and, being herself of a wonderfully orthodox and exclusive middle-class respectability, sets herself to see that the child is strictly brought up, and that the widow maintains a social dignity and decorum worthy of the respectable traditions of her husband's family. From a cryptic message of Miss Abbott's, who is in Italy with Lilia, she gathers news of Lilia's engagement to Gino, and in a state of horrified alarm sends her younger son Philip out at once to stop the marriage. But, with the connivance and approval of the romantic Miss Abbott, the marriage has been solemnised before he can get there. Later, when Lilia is dead, it comes to pass that, solely for the sake of appearances, Mrs. Herriton finds herself constrained to undertake the maintenance and upbringing of her baby, but to her amazement Gino declines to part with it. His opposition piques her to a firmer resolve; she sends her son and daughter out to obtain the infant at all costs, and Miss Abbott, remorseful for the share she had in her dead friend's marriage and yearning to atone as far as possible, goes out also. Gino's natural love for his small son is very subtly and beautifully developed, and the bootless negotiations and intriguings of the three English visitors have one tragic and more than one unlooked-for result.

It is a very striking and original piece of work, and in following it as he has done with his even stronger and more ambitious book, *The Longest Journey*, Mr. Forster has not only fulfilled the highest expectations of his readers, he has convinced them that he has not yet touched the limit of his powers, and that they may confidently expect still better things of him.

THE LONGEST JOURNEY

1907

15. Unsigned review, *Tribune*

22 April 1907, 2

One of the points in which Fiction is most at loggerheads with Fate lies in its admiration of the successful. It always devotes its keenest sympathies to those who succeed—whether in love, in honour, in ethical or material prosperity. In real life, of course, seventy-five out of every hundred people—to be on the optimistic side—are doomed, almost from their birth, to be failures—and most of them know it. Which is doubtless why they like, in Fiction, to be transported into a happier world, where success is the rule rather than the exception. And that was why, when a great man, half a century ago, wrote a novel without a hero, such was in itself a sufficiently remarkable fact to differentiate from all its fellows. That, again, is why not one out of ten novels of to-day deserves a similar sub-heading—however it may be with heroines.

Mr. E. M. Forster, having already earned the right to do so by one clever novel, *Where Angels Fear to Tread*, now dares to give us a study of an amiable failure, which he might well, had he so chosen, have christened with the other half of the proverb, 'Fools Rush In.' For Rickie Elliot is a fool of the nobler type that is not far removed from genius, and he moves in a world of fools, less admirable than himself. Therein, be it said, lies the weak point of an undeniably clever book. We may live in a world of fools, but some of us, without being geniuses, are not unadmirable. And just as it is false to Art and Nature to paint all humanity as very white or very black, so is it to make the general grey too monotonous—if, chasing our several worthless baubles, we present one universal monotone of foolishness, there are at least lights and shades in other aspects of our characters. The greatest writer, too, is he who sympathizes with us, even while he smiles—and sympathizes with all alike, even the black sheep.

Mr. Forster sympathizes, contemptuously though, with Rickie Elliot; he has very few tears to shed for Agnes his wife, or Mr. Pembroke her brother. He draws their selfishness, their lack of understanding; he even shows us how they slowly harden into stone; he quite realizes their tragedies, but he will neither sympathize nor allow his reader to sympathize with them at all. It is a pity, for *The Longest Journey* is, be it said again, a very clever novel—that might have been, had not its author determined otherwise, a great one. It contains some very striking character drawing—especially in the case of Agnes—the uninspired wife and her uninspired brother. So again the contrast between Rickie, the lame, neurotic visionary, and Stephen, his fleshly, inebriate half-brother, for whose safety he ultimately lays down his life, is well done—though Rickie is drawn with too much care, his broader tendencies obscured by too many minor touches to be altogether convincing. This lack of absolute conviction may be due in some measure, it is only fair to add, to the fact that he is drawn as being so different from other men that he is not quite comprehensible to the plain, ordinary man. We are expected always to bear the circumstances of his parentage in mind as clearly as do he and his creator, which is more than is to be expected of the average reader—to remember exactly how they might be expected to influence his behaviour in love and marriage, his attitude towards his illegitimate half-brother, his general outlook upon life. In the case of the half-brother, Stephen, this is less insisted upon, though not the less necessary, and Stephen is accordingly more easily to be assimilated. As is not infrequently the case, some of the best characters are those of the minor personages introduced, many of which, as, for example, the Ansell family—of the prosperous provincial draper type—stand out with considerable vividness.

Intermixed with the human interest are many excellent little sketches of Cambridge life, of a large school, of farm life in Wiltshire, all showing marked ability in descriptive penmanship. *The Longest Journey* is emphatically a novel to be noted. But Mr. Forster would be wise to cultivate more sympathy with his characters—which is to say, with the world he endeavours to reproduce.

16. Unsigned review, *The Times Literary Supplement*

no. 276, 26 April 1907, 134

Readers who remember *Where Angels Fear to Tread* remember some hours of lively entertainment, and the question at the end, 'What will the next book be?' Now that the next book, *The Longest Journey*, is before us the question seems only transferred once more, and to the credit of Mr. Forster's power of entertainment we ask it as curiously as ever. For *The Longest Journey*, although it is entirely free from shyness, has still much of the character of a young book; it is so very clever and so very well pleased with its own ingenuity. Mr. Forster fastens himself again, like some sharp wholesome insect, upon the life of the suburbs and the ideals of those who dwell in red brick villas and in the form rooms of public schools. And in the art of stinging these good people to exhibit their antics in a natural manner he is undoubtedly an expert; Sawston is certainly alive. His hero, Rickie Elliott, is born under the influence; 'he had opened his eyes to filmy heavens and taken his first walk on asphalt. He had seen civilisation as a row of semi-detached villas and society as a state in which men do not know the men who live next door'. But, inconveniently enough, he manages to preserve the power of seeing something beyond, and cannot acquiesce. At Cambridge, of course, he meets people who have nothing to do with the suburbs and can sit discussing the existence of objects and drawing circles within squares. 'Are they real?' 'The inside one is—the one in the middle of everything, that there's never room enough to draw'. But certain visions obscured Rickie's view of the true circle, and he is married by a suburban lady, Miss Agnes Pembroke, the sister of a master at Sawston school. Then he must give up his dell, somewhere near Cambridge, where fauns live and a fair woman pursued by suburban love can turn into a tree. But to follow the theory of Rickie's life, so skilfully developed and illustrated in its various stages—Cambridge, Sawston, Wiltshire—is hardly within our scope. It is certainly a very skilful arrangement, and yet it does not afford us so much satisfaction as the dexterity of the writer seems to intend. It is a serious matter, and yet if we are to feel it so the comedy should be a little less shrill. But the jingle which the idols make as they fall, adroitly knocked on the head by a tap of Mr. Forster's pen, destroys the deeper note; there is a sound like the striking of hollow brass. But then, and we return to our 'but', how vivacious and neat-handed it all is! Mr. Forster has mastered his method, and manipulates his facts, his theories, and finally his men and women with a facility that leaves the reader, as may be he is intended to be left, gasping and groping for support. Where are the connexions? Sometimes the short cut succeeds and sometimes it fails; Miss Pembroke is a success, and Mrs. Failing, though pierced again and again, is almost completely missed. The method is clearly dangerous. And yet we have a sense of some larger background, where there are Greeks, if they are only there as a contradiction to Sawston; just as Rickie's vision is always shot by a pellet of suburban mud. But it is interesting and living and amusing, and we still ask, 'What will be the next?'

17. Unsigned review, *Nation*

i, no. 9, 27 April 1907, 357–8

In a passage in this elusive novel, *The Longest Journey*, Agnes, the hero's wife, says to him: 'Couldn't you make your stories more obvious? I don't see any harm in that. Uncle Willie floundered hopelessly. I had to explain, and then he was delighted.' But Rickie, the lame and weakly hero, can only reply to this, dubiously, 'You see ——.' He got no further than 'you see.'

In truth it is not easy to explain the subtle quality of Mr. Forster's brilliant novel to Uncle Willie and his kinsfolk. The book is one that sounds the depths of character and conduct, that discloses the finest shades of spiritual meaning, that is as elusive, as actual, as ordinary withal as a wind that sways the tree tops. It is a novel of witty surfaces, and growing surprises, with scores of fine delicate thoughts gleaming in the current of the story. The style and method of our author are as original as his outlook on life. They are as uncommon as the stuff of this fabric of life is common and everyday. All lies in the telling, and how can the art of telling, this network woven of a succession of tiny touches be brought home to Uncle Willie? The critic can only indicate the artistic quality of *The Longest Journey*, by saying that there are some faces whose character lies in the smoothness of their contours, and the almost imperceptible movements of the lips and eyes. In the first third of the book the reader may be dubious as to what it is he is gathering; in the last half he will, if he is intelligent, be visited with a baffling sense of the strangeness of life, of its commonplace complexity, of the unresting forces, of its movement and energy, of its puzzling meaninglessness, with its sudden upheavals of immense meaning. Let us, however, not exaggerate the merits of *The Longest Journey*. Let us only say that its quality is quite unusual, and that it holds within it a criticism of ordinary life which is both philosophical and witty, spiritual and full of humorous by-play.

The inner meaning of the story may be roughly defined as a shadowing of that spiritual gulf which lies between two classes of minds, viz., of the minority who have the instinct to think for themselves, and so arrive in some degree at spiritual and mental honesty, and the majority whose valuations, dictated by stupidity, worldly prudence, social pressure and the like, are, in short, those conventional soulless valuations, which in Ibsen's *Peer Gynt*, go into the melting-pot and receive no mercy from the Button Moulder.

Rickie Elliot, the hero, whose struggle to be himself is the book's centre, is the lame and weakly son of parents who have never loved one another, and who have come to live apart. His mother, who is 'beautiful both within and without,' has married as a girl a Mr. Elliot, a barrister, whose voice 'was very suave with a fine command of cynical intonation. By altering it ever so little he could make people wince, especially if they were simple or poor.' As a man, Mr. Elliot 'never did or said or thought one single thing that had the slightest beauty or value.' He has means, and a set of rooms in town, and sees little of his son, whom he dubs 'Rickie,' because of his deformity, which he takes pleasure in alluding to. Both parents die when Rickie is fifteen, and the lad, who has had a solitary and unhappy childhood, passes 'cold and friendless and ignorant' through a great public school to Cambridge, which 'takes and soothes and warms and laughs at him, telling him not to be tragic.' At Cambridge we are introduced to Miss

Agnes Pembroke (to whom Rickie, after a couple of years of idealising her, becomes engaged), and to her brother, Mr. Pembroke, a master in the great public school at Sawston. The Pembrokes are inimitably drawn, and the sly precision of touch which defines their bright and banal insincerity of spirit, their cultured Philistinism, is quite masterly.

[Long quotation follows]

Rickie, who is only an idealistic boy, marries the handsome and practical Agnes Pembroke, who 'warms up' for him her old feeling for her dead lover Gerald. The unhappy Rickie, by this marriage, is taken over and run henceforward by the bland and smug forces of Sawston—a provincial Philistia. The spiritual gulf between Rickie and Agnes is adroitly indicated. 'He valued emotion—not for itself, but because it is the only final path to intimacy. She, ever robust and practical, always discouraged him. She was not cold: she would willingly embrace him. But she hated being upset. . . .' What an immense class of marriages, spiritual mismatings, this phrase 'she hated being upset' hits off. Rickie is boyishly weak before Mr. Pembroke, and allows himself to be 'fitted into' the position of assistant master at Sawston School. 'Above all,' thought Mr. Pembroke, 'it will be something regular for him to do . . . A schoolmaster has wonderful opportunities of doing good; one mustn't forget that.' So Rickie loses his independence, and Mr. Pembroke gets him as his assistant master to do his dirty work for him, while Agnes fits in nicely into Dunwood House as the housekeeper. Soon Rickie perceives that he is deteriorating. He is forced to recognise that Agnes will never get nearer to him, that she is content with the daily round, the common task performed indifferently, that she regards him as a dreamer, and doesn't respect him, and that he is ceasing to love her, and that their life must be stale and stupid together. Their ideals are totally different. The Pembrokes, in fact, are the children of this world, who are wiser in their generation than the children of light. 'They live together without love. They work without conviction. They seek money without requiring it. They die, and nothing will have happened either for themselves or for others.' The crisis comes when his half-brother, the illegitimate Stephen Warham, quarrels with his aunt, Mrs. Failing, and turns up at Dunwood House expecting to be helped. Agnes has intrigued against Stephen in order that Rickie shall inherit Mrs. Failing's money, and she has succeeded before this, for conventional reasons, in getting Rickie not to avow his relationship, of which Stephen is then ignorant.

Rickie is now guilty of the meanness of turning his back on his half-brother, while Agnes treats him as a blackmailer and interviews him cheque-book in hand. But Stephen has not come for money, he has come for sympathy. There is fine analysis of the Pembrokes' outlook when Stephen turns carelessly away from the door, spits in the gutter, and sums up the position as a 'take in.' He is hungry and penniless, and disappointed, the Elliots seem to him simply 'dirty people, not his sort.' But Rickie learns by accident a few minutes later that Stephen is not his half-brother by his detested father, but by the mother he reveres! She has loved another man, and his aunt, Mrs. Failing, has kept her secret. Rickie then breaks away from the grip of the Pembrokes' gods for good.

The character studies of the bitter and malicious old woman, Mrs. Failing, and of the rough, manly, and frank-hearted Stephen, whom the respectable world conspires to boycott, are admirably done. Many of the pages that describe the country life at Cadover have the rough vigour and something of the flavour of Meredith, to whose spiritual example our author is perhaps a little indebted. A quiet hatred of shams has inspired Mr. Forster to one of the subtlest exposures of the modern Pharisee that we can recall in fiction. Bit by bit he gently peels off the respectable casings that enwrap his Philistines' souls.

The only criticism that we have to point against our author is that he uses the accident of sudden death too frequently in his artistic scheme. We resent Rickie's death at the close, though we cannot but admit that the squabble between Mr. Pembroke and Stephen over Rickie's literary remains is too good to wish away. We may add that the vision of *The Longest Journey* is the vision of a poet doubled by a humourist, and this it is that explains the freshness and depth of this original book.

18. Unsigned notice, *Evening Standard & St James's Gazette*

30 April 1907, 5

About *The Longest Journey*, by E. M. Forster, it is surely not too much to say that it has a touch of genius. The outlook, the ideas and similes, the dialogue, and the development are original, and yet not eccentric; there is a living core to the book, and it has flashes of wit that make the reader feel like clapping his hands. If the author will follow no popular school, and will keep his (her?) restraint over extravagance, there is a literary future for him. Of course, there are many drawbacks and some crudities. The trick of introducing some startling tragedy with hardly so much as a new paragraph becomes irritating. To interest one in a character for hours, and then casually remark, 'He died that night,' has all the effect intended the first time it is tried. After that one has an annoying feeling of insecurity. Moreover, the commonplace people in the book suffer from their author's hatred in some cases. The disastrous heroine is not allowed the qualities of her defects. Stephen is too spasmodic and contradictory, behaving one moment like one possessed of more than ordinary vision and the next as a delightfully primeval being, a lovable brute. The author shows him now as not degraded by his animalism, because it is the simple expression of his nature, and then again as lofty of soul beyond all material degradation. His letter to the unwholesome schoolboy is sheerly delightful, as is very much in the book. It is easily the most striking novel published lately.

19. C. F. G. Masterman, 'The soul in suburbia', *Daily News*

3 May 1907, 4

He 'watched his clever friend draw within the square a circle, and within the circle a square, and inside that another circle. "Are they real?" "The inside one is the one in the middle of everything, that there's never room enough to draw!" ' This is human life as seen by the author of this amazingly clever book. It continues, always, at Cambridge, when men discuss metaphysics, and hope later to encounter reality; at Sawston, in the stifling miasma of the suburb, and the more stifling miasma of the English public school; at Wiltshire, challenged by the night and the wide sky. It is born by the coming of sudden death, and the incidents of change. It is confronted, sometimes perturbed, by the life of the earth. 'I say once more,' is the warning of one of the characters, 'beware of the earth.' We are conventional people, and conventions—if you will but see it—are majestic in their way, and will claim us in the end. It lives under no illusion. ' "So it goes on for ever," she cried excitedly. He replied, "Not for ever. In time the fire at the centre will cool, and nothing can go on then." ' But here it abides—circle within square, and square within circle, with the only one that is real, the one there is never room enough to draw. 'I see the respectable mansion,' is the confession of one. 'I see the smug fortress of culture. The doors are shut. The windows are shut. But on the roof the children go dancing for ever.'

The promise of *Where Angels Fear to Tread* is more than fulfilled in this volume. It is difficult, elusive, exasperating: with something of the cleverness of the young in it, and something of the cruelty. The influence of Meredith is there, especially of such a work as *Rhoda Fleming*, with the strong acknowledgment in both of the strange impalpable influences which the earth exercises over her children. There is little story: when Mr. Forster wishes to get rid of his characters he murders them ruthlessly with sudden death on a railway crossing or in the football field. There is a cold satire upon the normal respectable life, the revolt against convention and routine, and the hypocrisies which make up the world of every day, combined with a kind of quality of elusiveness and suggestion which opens the vision of far horizons even in the suburban street or the school playing-field. *The Longest Journey* is not a great novel; but it has embedded in it many of the ingredients of greatness. Its author will go far.

The Contest

'Rickie' Elliot, a cripple, clever, a teller of stories, in which the natural world is alive, and the old gods suddenly return, is passing through Cambridge, through marriage to a dreary, conventional pretty woman, to a respectable career as a house master in a suburban public school. This is one force, pulling him always into the accepted ways. The other is that of his illegitimate brother, the child of romance and passion, reared in the Wiltshire Downs: to the outward eye a rather crude rustic, with an unnatural thirst for drink, and half formed doubts concerning religion and the conventions. But he has great allies: the Downs themselves, huge and impressive under the quiet sky; all the natural impulse of the world of out-of-doors; all the interpretations which make the real life seem unreal.

The contest is undecided. The end is cut short by death; but the night before the tragedy Rickie had nearly surrendered, knowing (a disquieting revelation) that the earth is round, and 'the day is straight below, shining through other windows into other homes'; stimulated by remembrance of the lighted paper flames which they had sent sailing down the dark tunnel towards the sea.

They played as boys who continued the nonsense of the railway carriage. The paper caught fire from the match, and spread into a rose of flame. 'Now gently with me,' said Stephen, and they laid it flower-like on the stream. Gravel and tremulous weeds leapt into sight, and then the flower sailed into deep water, and up leapt the two arches of a bridge. 'It'll strike!' they cried; 'no, it won't; it's chosen the left,' and one arch became a fairy tunnel, dropping diamonds. Then it vanished for Rickie; but Stephen, who knelt in the water, declared that it was still afloat, far through the arch, burning as if it would burn for ever.

The Ascendant Force

Rickie had been raised in the heart of it all. 'He had opened his eyes to filmy heavens, and taken his first walk on asphalt. He had seen civilization as a row of semi-detached villas, and society as a state in which men do not know the men who live next door. He had himself become part of the grey monotony that surrounds all cities.' Later his half-brother, driven by revolt into the morass of London, was to feel something of the horror of the earth-born for this quick, populous life, and is comforted by the knowledge that 'there's no such thing as a Londoner. He's only a country man on the road to devilry.'

After a few crowded hours of glorious life at Cambridge, the whole dead weight of these dead things rolls back upon him again. He is enmeshed in the net of the public school: choked in the existence of the House Master, with his little ineffectual aphorisms of dignity and honour, and effort to steer the young of the new generation into similar conventional ways. It is an atmosphere of dust and futility; with his brother-in-law, the skilled 'organizer' and type of it all; and every chink or crevice closed which might admit fresh air or a vision of the Infinite beyond.

> His technical position was that of master to a form low down on the Modern Side. But his work lay elsewhere. He organized. If no organization existed, he would create one. If one did exist, he would modify it. 'An organization,' he would say, 'is after all not an end in itself. It must contribute to a movement.' When one good custom seemed likely to corrupt the school he was ready with another; he believed that without innumerable customs there was no safety, either for boys or men. Perhaps he is right, and always will be right. Perhaps each of us would go to ruin if for one short hour we acted as we thought fit, and attempted the service of perfect freedom. The school caps, with their elaborate symbolism, were his; his the many-tinted bathing-drawers, that showed how far a boy could swim; his the hierarchy of jerseys and blazers. It was he who instituted Bounds, and Call, and the two sorts of exercise paper, and the three sorts of caning, and 'The Sawstonian,' a bi-terminal magazine. His plump finger was in every pie. The dome of his skull, mild but impressive, shone at every master's meeting. He was generally acknowledged to be the coming man.

It is all harmonised to the same chromatically spectral life: with the 'decent water colours in the drawing room' and 'Madonnas of acknowledged merit on the stairs,' and 'the strip of brown holland that led diagonally from the front door to the door of Herbert's study,' and the Master asking blandly, 'What does philosophy do? I fancy that in the long run Herbert Spencer will get no further than the rest of us;' and the woman who can never understand—who never could understand—why Rickie loved her, and why he left her, and why he would never come back to her again.

Outside on the open road is this crude, simple figure, with his absurd doubts and absurd assertions: a child of impulse, living, not comprehending; not desiring to comprehend. 'One of those sixpenny books tells Podge that he's made of hard little black things; another that he's made of brown things, large and squashy. There seems a discrepancy; but anything is better for a thoughtful youth than to be made in the Garden of Eden.'

A book (it is to be feared) only for the few, but full of suggestion, of insight, of astonishing cleverness: the work of one who is determined to face the world of real things.

20. Elizabeth von Arnim, letter to E. M. Forster

5 May 1907

Elizabeth Mary Annette Beauchamp (Mary Annette, Countess Russell) (1866–1941) was born of British parents in Australia. She married Count Henning August Arnim and went to live at the von Arnim estate at Nassenheide, Pomerania (just north of Berlin). Here she wrote her best-known book, *Elizabeth and Her German Garden* (1898), and others including *The Adventures of Elizabeth on Ruegen* (1904) and *Fräulein Schmidt and Mr Anstruther* (1907). After her husband's death in 1910, she married the Second Earl Russell (brother of Bertrand Russell) in 1916. In spring 1905 Forster spent some time as a tutor on her staff at Nassenheide; in a letter to him of 11 March 1905 she said that it was 'the very place for the writing of books, which is what you are apparently going to do'. Forster's own impressions, by no means unmixed, of his stay at Nassenheide are recorded in Leslie de Charms, *Elizabeth of the German Garden* (1958), 101–4.

Countess Russell was the aunt of Sidney Waterlow (cf. No. 168) and a cousin of Katherine Mansfield (cf. No. 75). The review referred to in her letter is No. 16.

In 1923 Countess Russell re-read *Howards End*, and commented deflatingly in her Journal (22 June): 'Disliked first part—disliked his women all through—I think it can justly be described as full of promise. He has a curious effect of sidling up to one with his whimsies—then suddenly real power' (de Charms, *op. cit.*, 257).

Published by permission of Mrs Corwin Butterworth.

It's a wonderful book, and I thank you herewith solemnly for the day you gave me with it. That, of course, is a little thing, but it's not at all a little thing to have written that book. I thought the *Times* review good till I'd read the book, then, strange to say, I discovered it fitted excellently to the *Angels* but not in the least to this one. How can they talk of your tapping the people neatly with your pen on the head at the end and it all crumbles away—it was something like that—I don't quite remember—never was anything deeper (?true)[. . .]—no irresponsible pen-tappings would send those people off into nothingness—and, what the timid *Angels* hadn't got, it has lovable people in it—Rickie is absolutely dear—and there is Ansell, and the young animal—but don't ever marry an Agnes, will you, for if you did your future is certain—there it is in your book prophetically set forth. Well, I can't tell you how truly beautiful I think it, and if I could it would only make you shrug your shoulders, for what does it matter what the foolish and the illiterate think? But I think you must be very happy—you've got very near to the 'words of eternal life'.

21. Unsigned review, *Morning Post*

6 May 1907, 2

Those who like to confine their acquaintance to really nice or happy people should avoid reading *The Longest Journey*. They will thus miss more entertainment than it is perhaps kind to tell them about. A set of people from whom as neighbours or relations we should all pray to be delivered proves absorbing company with Mr. Forster as merciless showman. Rickie Elliott, of unhappy childhood and inherited lameness, having 'crept cold and friendless and ignorant out of a great public school, preparing for a silent and solitary journey and praying as a highest favour that he might be let alone,' finds his prayer unanswered at Cambridge, and during a few magic years makes friends and the nearest approach to rational happiness accorded to any of the prominent characters in the book. Unfortunately he is taken in marriage at the age of twenty-three. His motive is clear and his side of the transaction admirably related. He had seen Agnes Pembroke in the arms of a previous lover—Gerald Dawes, with the figure of a Greek athlete and the face of an English one, so that 'just where he began to be beautiful the clothes started'—and she is transfigured for him by the memory of that moment and of one other when that lover lay in her arms—dying of football injuries. Her motive is perhaps less clear. She recognises the possibility of greatness in Rickie and snatches for herself a treasure which she cannot understand, and so destroys. Deserted by his Cambridge friends and giving up unconvincing short stories about Dryads for schoolmastering, Rickie is soon swallowed up in the 'beneficent machine' of his brother-in-law's boarding-house at a gimcrack Eton, and acts the lies and conventionalities without which he learns that the machine would not be beneficent. From this he escapes—or rather is dragged out—for a moment, but dies, gone bankrupt once more, and admitting with his last breath the rightness of his aunt's view that 'the important things in life are little things and that people are not important at all.' Then the events of the last chapter suggest that after all he had been right and his aunt wrong. Mr. Forster pillories his characters with diabolic humour. Agnes, the mock unconventional, who got over the birth and death of her horrible child as she got over everything; Rickie's aunt, first introduced as the possibly influential lady who never pushed anyone because she found them always rebound and crush her, and exposed more fully later as a person who had laughed so much that she had forgotten what people were like; Rickie's father, who by laughing at the wrong time sent his wife off almost against her will with another man (again an extraordinarily clever and convincing episode); Mr. Pembroke the organiser, phrase-maker, and bland tactician; Rickie himself, under the primal curse of 'knowledge of good-and-evil'—one after another are found wanting. One character escapes this criticism, yet it is not certain that Mr. Forster has not attempted the impossible in endeavouring to make intelligible and attractive the blend of pagan god and modern hooligan which goes to make Stephen Wonham. Mr. Forster, however, can be tenderly imaginative as well as mordant. He can show qualities yet more remarkable when now and again in some subtly-horrifying episode he lets the natural and animal rise to the surface through the iridescent scum of the conventional. The book as a whole is more provocative than satisfying. Formal criticism might say that it does not hang together enough, that there is a want of balance between the various ingredients, that there are too many bolts from heaven to give unity of character a chance, but too few to make a fine melodramatic thunderstorm. The sudden death-rate among the significant characters, exclusive of two children, one of whom is done to death quite wantonly on the railway, is 44 per cent. The method of Rickie's appointment as a schoolmaster is more diverting than absolutely convincing. But it would be altogether out of place to quarrel with a writer of Mr. Forster's performance and promise about formal unities or small points. It is better to be thankful for what he has already given us and to await the next book—as all who read this and his first one will do—with eager anticipation.

22. 'St Barbe', notice, *Queen*

cxxi, 11 May 1907, 880

Mr. E. M. Forster's new book, *The Longest Journey*, does not bear out the promise of his earlier work, *Where Angels Fear to Tread*. He has lost himself in a labyrinth of characterisation. He attempts things beyond his powers, and the result is forced and hysterical. The book is divided into three portions—Cambridge, Sawston, Wiltshire. In each the almost daily doings of two or three groups of people are carefully followed, but the plot, hard to discover, is lamentably devoid of climax or climaxes. Rickie, the hero, was lame. He had been nicknamed Rickie by his father because he was rickety. Mr. Elliot was a disagreeable person, who 'took pleasure in alluding to his son's deformity, and was sorry that it was not more serious than his own'. His wife was unhappy and lonely. So was Rickie. He loved Agnes, the *fiancée* of a strong man called Gerald, who one day gets killed. By and by Rickie marries her, and their child, a daughter, is even more deformed than her father. Sawston School provides work and a home for them. Further complications, not all to do with Rickie, are introduced, but the lack of straightforwardness makes the interest in the book meagre.

23. Unsigned notice, *Pall Mall Gazette*

11 May 1907, 4

Mr. Forster is a sensitive and well-equipped writer, handicapped by a certain poverty of dramatic feeling. The result is that Rickie Elliot, the self-conscious student, is presented to us in the light of a 'case' rather than as a fragment of real humanity. His experiences of life, ambition, idealism, and matrimony are developed with much consistency, and we pause every now and then to admire the author's perception; but the whole subject leaves us cold, and we are not particularly anxious to remember it. Our old friend 'human interest' seems to be the missing link between Mr. Forster and artistic success, and we doubt not that an author of so many genuine endowments will eventually discover the means of forging it.

24. 'R. W. L.', notice, *Black and White*

xxxiii, no. 849, 11 May 1907, 658

The latest talent to set people talking is that of Mr. E. M. Forster, the author of *The Longest Journey*. This is not a satisfactory novel; it is not a well-constructed novel. It opens, however, with brilliant promise, and the closing chapters are at least strong enough and original enough to keep alive one's interest. Personally, I do not see that very much is gained by making Stephen Wonham turn out to be the illegitimate son, not of Rickie's father, but of his mother. The catastrophe could surely have been brought about without that. The whole story of Stephen and the curious, cranky people who surround him on the Utopian estate leaves a rather confused impression on the imagination.

The real matter of interest in the book is the gradual degradation of Rickie, the charming, quiet, dreaming Cambridge graduate, who pays in his maimed body and otherwise for his father's sins. Perhaps I ought to say 'undergraduate,' for some of the scenes that are most instinct with life and dramatic interest take place while Rickie and his friends are still at the University. A scene, for instance, like the following—by no means a wonderful or critical scene—has real vitality and grip.

'I maintain,' said Rickie, . . . 'I maintain that one can like many more people than one supposes.'

'And I maintain that you hate many more people than you pretend.'

'I hate no one,' he exclaimed with extraordinary vehemence; and the dell re-echoed that it hated no one.

'We are obliged to believe you,' said Widdrington, smiling a little; 'but we are sorry about it.'

'Not even your father?' asked Ansell.

Rickie was silent.

'Not even your father?'

The cloud above extended a great promontory across the sun. It only lay there for a moment, yet that was enough to summon the lurking coldness from the earth.

'Does he hate his father?' said Widdrington, who had not known. 'Oh, good!'

'But his father's dead. He will say it doesn't count.'

'Still it's something. Do you hate yours?'

Ansell did not reply. Rickie said: 'I say, I wonder whether we ought to talk like this?'

'About hating dead people?'

'Yes——'

'Did you hate your mother?' asked Widdrington.

Rickie turned crimson.

'I don't see Hornblower's such a rotter,' remarked the other man, whose name was James.

'James, you are diplomatic,' said Ansell. 'You are trying to tide over an awkward moment. You can go.'

Widdrington was crimson too. In his wish to be sprightly, he had used words without thinking of their meanings. Suddenly he realised that 'father' and 'mother' really meant father and mother—people whom he had himself at home. He was very uncomfortable.

The Longest Journey, indeed, is a book that grips. Rickie, as he marries Agnes and comes under her thumb, and when he becomes a colleague and pedantic pedagogue of his clerical brother-in-law and comes under his thumb, is one of the most vital and sympathetic character-studies we have had in recent fiction. Only, somehow, one does not believe that he caved in so easily. If Mr. Forster continues to take his art seriously he ought to produce some really good work.

25. Unsigned notice, *Standard*

14 May 1907, 5

The Longest Journey is a clever, almost pitiless, dissection of a lonely and deformed boy who goes up to Cambridge, makes some uncommonly talkative friends, and finally falls in love with a commonplace and rather obvious kind of girl who takes pity on him, and marries him, and the sequel is—mutual unhappiness. Mr. Forster, who incidentally deals out death to any one of his characters on the slightest provocation, would probably tell us that an introspective, moody, and romantic kind of boy like Rickie was born to unhappiness as the sparks fly upward. That is probably true, but in Mr. Forster's realism there is a curiously repulsive note. Now and again he lets daylight into a man's or a woman's soul with merely a phrase; but unfortunately that phrase sticks, and the consequence, to our minds, is not a feeling of wonder or awe, but rather of disgust, for the sunshine suddenly vanishes, and we are conscious of a place of desolation and of a breeze stirring some dead bones. At times the atmosphere of the story becomes peculiarly hot, acrid, and oppressive, and strangely reminiscent sometimes of George Meredith, occasionally of a writer who called himself Benjamin Swift, and a few years ago made a reputation with *Nancy Noon.*

26. 'V', review, *Manchester Guardian*

15 May 1907, 5

Mr. E. M. Forster has written a second novel which possesses all the characteristics which made his first remarkable. In *The Longest Journey* Mr. Forster is as brilliant, as incoherent, as original, and as pessimistic as he was in *Where Angels Fear to Tread*. His hero, Rickie Elliott, is endowed with an abnormally sensitive temperament, aggravated by a lonely childhood and unhappy schooldays. He is intellectual but not clever, and he first really 'finds himself' in the congenial society of a small set of reading and thinking men at Cambridge. Then he proceeds to lose the self which he had found in marriage with a woman whom he only fancies that he loves, and whose 'spiritual apathy' is gradually and irrevocably revealed to him when it is too late. His marriage is only a part of the tragedy of his existence. Not less destructive to the vitality of his real self is the occupation of assistant to his brother-in-law, a schoolmaster with a genius for organising away personality and systematising life into convention. Rickie's awakening is achieved through the instrumentality of an illegitimate brother, a being conceived by Mr. Forster as almost wholly animal but unmistakably real. Rickie forsakes his wife and abandons his profession, and devotes himself to writing and to taking charge of his irresponsible brother, in saving whose life he is shortly afterwards killed. The book is full of strong and vivid writing, and also of studied eccentricities and abruptnesses which subject the reader to a continuous succession of shocks. Mr. Forster (like the erratic philosopher Ansell, who plays a wholly incredible part in his story) seems to be intent on preaching the gospel of reality, in opposition to the convention, organised make-believe, and etiquette which he sees as ruling nine-tenths of civilised life. He writes in a spirit of revolt, which breeds sincerity and conviction, but which perhaps leads him to identify the real to an unnecessary extent with the grotesque and the eccentric. But his studies of the unreal are exceedingly good. Best of all is Herbert Pembroke, who devotes himself to the task of converting a suburban grammar school into an imitation Eton, prepares himself to be ready to enter holy orders when the prospect of scholastic promotion renders it expedient, and proposes marriage at two days' notice when the possession of a wife seems a necessary qualification for becoming a house master. This personification of unreality is the most real character that Mr. Forster has yet drawn.

27. Unsigned notice, *Cambridge Review*

16 May 1907, 408

The *Independent Review*, a liberal journal, was founded in 1903 by, among others, Goldsworthy Lowes Dickinson, a Fellow of King's College, Cambridge (Forster's own college). Dickinson and another Fellow of King's, Nathaniel Wedd, were members of its editorial board. Dickinson and, more particularly, Wedd influenced Forster greatly during his time at Cambridge. Between 1903 and 1906 Forster published some ten stories and articles in the *Independent Review*, together with one more piece in 1908, when it had changed its name to the *Albany Review*.

Cf. No. 86 and No. 14.

If Mr. Forster had written nothing but *Where Angels fear to tread* we should have thankfully admired him: and now that he has *The Longest Journey* to his credit our sentiments are only more pronounced. Mr. Forster has a future; not that he will write very much better books, though even that may happen, but the public, when he has written more, will realise that it has been entertaining a genius unawares, and will behave as it does on those occasions. The scene of his new novel is laid for the most part in Cambridge. There is no 'local colour,' no description of the May Races, but the mental atmosphere of a small group of undergraduates in a certain College has been caught and unerringly put into words. We watch *Rickie* from his University days to his death some ten years later, gradually altering the views of life which he once held so easily: and we watch *Ansell* steadily holding to his own, and becoming an almost diabolical young fool who thinks that because he uttered a principle of life in his College rooms it is his duty to stand to it afterwards at the expense of his friend's happiness. *Agnes*, who marries *Rickie*, and nearly pulls him down to her level, is the ideal woman of a misogynist, *banal*, scheming, unprincipled without the excuse of being immoral; she has the distinction of having Mr Pembroke to her brother, and he draws forth from Mr Forster's pen a brilliant analysis of character. He is introduced to us in the first chapter as being 'not in orders, but on the verge of them'—a delightful phrase. *Gerald*, the boorish athlete, who was engaged to *Agnes*, and whose 'clothes hide him where he begins to be beautiful,' dies with a horrible suddenness, which marks all the very numerous deaths in this story. *Stephen Wonham*, a glorious pagan, is the most interesting character in the book after *Rickie*. He turns out to be his half-brother, and seems to be a kind of complement to him. The book is so admirably written, so full of brilliant things, that it is difficult to decide whether the design is as good as the workmanship. Personally, we think that the design falls short of the excellence which marks the book in other respects. Whether this is so or not, it remains a very remarkable novel. May we hope, in conclusion, that Mr Forster will collect his short stories from the *Independent Review*, and publish them as soon as may be.

28. Unsigned review, *Athenaeum*

18 May 1907, 600–1

The Longest Journey may be described as a careful study of an impassioned idealist who is forced, by dint of time and circumstance, to shed most of his ideals on the way, or perhaps, rather, to witness their gradual disintegration and partial reconstruction. A number of half-gods go, while the gods that eventually succeed in arriving are avid of sacrifice. The story opens at Cambridge with a light glimpse of undergraduate life, and later the scene is laid mainly in the turbid shallows of a large scholastic establishment not impenetrably veiled under the name of 'Sawston', where the hero's last illusions are put finally to flight. To elucidate this somewhat elaborate process would be unfair to the reader, for the hero's adventures are mainly emotional, and the manipulation, rather than the bare plot, is interesting throughout. Skilful in a far higher degree are the portraits of the pragmatic managing schoolmaster—breezy in manner, utterly and unconsciously commercial in spirit—and his equally specious sister, who begins as Pallas Athene, and ends perilously like a highly respectable and commonplace Medea. It seems a pity that so decidedly clever a writer should have given 'Rickie', his central figure, such an anaemic personality, for all his really noble intent. Neither in his falling away nor in his precipitate regeneration, nor even in his final immolation, does he truly convince us; nor does the splendid savage Stephen Wonham, who, we shrewdly suspect, was evolved from the author's love of abrupt contrast. We should like to believe in them both, especially in Stephen, but the task is difficult. The cynical aunt, however, is brilliantly done, and the small galaxy of minor characters drawn with a sure and vivid touch. The construction inclines to laxity, while the introduction of Death, as a factor, is too catastrophic for art; too brusquely, at least, this god descends from the machine.

29. Unsigned notice, *World*

21 May 1907, 924

The Longest Journey, by E. M. Forster, is a puzzling book. From first to last it is elusive—in its short sentences, in its scrappy indications of who's who, in its abruptness. It is as uncomfortable as a portrait without shade, staring like Queen Elizabeth's in the jewelled gown and no perspective. There are good things in it, choice bits here and there; but it jerks and slides and slips about in a fatiguing fashion. The narrative which we fail to follow, having honestly tried, has no consecutiveness. It begins with a group of persons—unconventional in manners to a degree which we prefer to regard as impossible—in Rickie's rooms at Cambridge (he is politely called 'Rickie' because there is something wrong with one of his feet). They say odd things with startling abruptness. A Mr. Pemberton said: ' "Life without an ideal—" and then stopped, for his mouth was full of coffee-grounds. The same affliction had overtaken Agnes.' Previously Mr. Pembroke has failed to reply to something said by Rickie—firstly, 'because the meringue was, after all, Rickie's; and secondly, because it was gluey and stuck his jaws together.' After some talk about an 'uncrushable Aunt Emily,' Mr. Pembroke's teeth were clear of meringue, and he could refrain no longer 'from talking to Rickie, concerning whom our only sentiment is that he really ought to have been saved by somebody from his friends.' Agnes has presumably enjoyed a neglected education, for she is made to *think* 'What a snob the boy (Rickie) is getting!' We suppose there is some subtlety in the book and some stupidity in ourselves which combine to bewilder us; but it is a fact that we cannot enlighten our readers as to the purpose of this curious work, and so must only beg their pardon and refer them to the pronouncement of the slip-cover that *The Longest Journey* 'has been looked forward to with the highest anticipations, and these will not be disappointed.'

30. Unsigned notice, *Liverpool Daily Post*

22 May 1907, 8

To read *The Longest Journey*, by E. M. Foster, is to co-operate with the brilliant author, for all is so subtle, the inferences are so vaguely indicated, that it is a constant mental effort to grasp what precisely is intended. It is not, in the ordinary sense, a novel. Rather is it a bundle of wonderful studies in human psychology. It is a study of abnormalities in the normal; of eccentricities in the commonplace. Rickie, the hero, is brought before us at Cambridge, where he meets Miss Pembroke and her brother. Rickie might be said to have a great future before him, but he ends in being under-master in a school where Mr. Pembroke is the organising, dominant spirit—organisation being his fetish. Rickie marries Miss Pembroke, and this marriage, with all its possibilities, with its hideous failure, is the focus-point of the story. The result is a grim tragedy; in fact, the tragic close is the one blemish on the work, for Rickie had capacities for re-organising himself, just as his wife had capacities for re-forming their marriage. Yet, who can deny that the characters reveal precisely that in them which makes for catastrophe? Possibly psychological fiction will never become popular. The world prefers the sword-thrusts of Mr. Stanley Weyman to the intellectual pin-prickings of Mr. Henry James. Yet it is a rare delight to pass through a phase of life with such a guide as the author of this book. It isn't that it is life-like. Such an attribute is an insult. With all its questionings, its openings for speculative perusal, its demands on our rational faculties as well as our power of mere reading, it is rather an experience of life itself, miles away from the ordinary novel of the day. We feel that these people all live. We feel that we know far more of them than the writer has told us—and that is the profoundest compliment. They are persons, not puppets; the difference is that in persons there is an area for mental exploration, while puppets merely require a label. Possibly the method is carried to an extreme, but it is a rare achievement to show us the hardest of life's ironies with such intense conviction.

31. Unsigned notice, *Birmingham Daily Post*

24 May 1907, 4

Mr. Forster's book is for the adult reader who has learned patience and has no objection to an occasional riddle. His opening chapter seems specially designed to provoke and mystify almost to the point of exasperation. The philosophic mind, however, smiles at the discussion in its first pages, and the ordinary one skips it and gets into the story. Mr. Forster's method is somewhat peculiar. He tells the story of a man physically unsound, with exalted aims and generous impulses. In order that his hero shall be properly understood, it is necessary that his early home life shall be depicted. The story of his childhood is given as it appeared from the point of view of an affectionate, well-disposed, but somewhat feeble boy. As his history unfolds itself he is presented as embarking upon the utterly uncongenial career of a schoolmaster at the instigation of the woman he has persuaded himself he may marry. From this moment his life presents an aspect of failure and perpetual conflict. He is stricken down when he discovers he has a half-brother as unlike himself as it is possible for a man to be. This man is represented as physically sound, utterly uncontrolled and rebellious, a very pagan. A little less reticence than the writer has displayed would have converted this especially strong character into a monster rather than a man. Again, the reader is taken back over a period of years to learn of other episodes in the lives of the parents of the two men. Such a method makes the story somewhat difficult to follow. It is not until the end of the book is almost reached that it becomes possible to pick up the head and limbs of the novel and stick them on to the torso. Mr. Forster may be proud of the heroic proportions of this figure of his imagination. It stands to represent life in its truest form without the wrappings of conventionality or the shackles of ignorance. It is hard to sympathise altogether with so emotional and neurotic a hero; it is harder still to avoid feelings of positive disgust at some of the performances of his drunken and boorish half-brother, until one recognises that each man represents in his own life a definite teaching. Mr. Forster is particularly interesting in those pages where he deals with boy life at public schools. His ideas with regard to boys and home life as opposed to the boarding-house system in vogue at so many public schools are thoroughly sound. He does not say in so many words that all young boys are little Cains, but he recognises how little notion they have of real good fellowship, a virtue that rarely develops till after adolescence. His formalist schoolmaster, with a passion for organising, is a hard, cold personality. But his sister Agnes, who is the subject of what little love-making there is in the story, is a complete surprise. Beautiful, affectionate, and intellectual, she is nevertheless, in her human relationships, almost ghastly, and an example of the mischief one woman can do when embarking upon a course of deceit.

32. Unsigned review, *Spectator*

xcix, no. 4123, 6 July 1907

We confess to preferring agreeable to disagreeable people in books as well as in life. A few disagreeable persons, to be sure, may serve the useful purpose of intensifying our sense of the amiability of the others, but when nearly all are disagreeable we ask the author to show some reason for offering us this glut of disagreeableness. There may be very good reasons, of course. The author may have made a faithful transcript from life, and it would be wrong, even disastrous, to shut out from art the results of industrious observation merely because they are disagreeable. But if the author does not make us feel quite sure that, like a Hebrew prophet, he is telling the truth, or that which has the value of truth, for our good, then we suspect him of perversity. We have a right to condemn his judgment in selection even before we can test the trustworthiness of his evidence. The word 'abnormal' is used often in this story, and it might be justly applied to the behaviour of most of the characters. A few grains of geniality would have saved them nearly all their crises. This is a pity, because Mr. Forster has genuine and unusual talents. He invents excellent phrases without labouring them. He is capable of humour, too, as one sees sometimes when it is not overlaid with an 'abnormal,' almost brutal, cynicism. The study of the rival factions in the prosperous school which is gradually turning itself from a commercial foundation drawing its strength from day-boys into an ordinary public-school with a majority of boarders and *esprit de corps* and everything else handsome about it is really first-rate.

Rickie Elliot, the hero of the story, is one of a clique of Cambridge undergraduates who spend their afternoons going long 'grinds' in the country instead of playing games. They talk philosophy and despise the Philistines. Mr. Forster very nearly gives a new illumination to that old relation of youth,—the athlete and the 'prig,' or, to put it more in the words of the schoolboy, the bully and the 'smug.' Rickie is a congenital cripple (his agreeable father, who was also a cripple, called him Rickie because he was rickety!), and he had a miserable time at school. At Cambridge he is conscious of a rehabilitation. He is given a new chance; he finds that he need not be good at games to command some respect; he makes friends, and is extremely happy. Perhaps the pride of spirit of the philosophy-talking clique and their contempt for stupid physical robustness is somewhere near a truth which is not often expressed. At all events, an examination of the outlook on University life of a lame philosopher would be welcome to a world rather wearied by the snobbery of 'muscular Christianity.' The author, however, sheers off from this subject. The philosophers are not nearly so clever as they think they are, and we cannot help feeling that if culture necessarily led to the superfluous crises which blight so many lives in this story, the urbane Matthew Arnold would turn in his grave; and for ourselves, we should seriously consider whether a Pass degree and a severe course on the river would not be the most salubrious curriculum for our sons. While Rickie is still at Cambridge he falls in love with Agnes Pembroke, a young woman who seems quite amiable till Mr. Forster's mordant cynicism gets to work on her character. She is already engaged to be married to an athletic young soldier who is a Greek god in appearance, but not exactly Hellenic in intellect. Mr. Forster, who is not afraid of risking ridicule, kills off this god-like creature by an accident in a suburban football match. We are not sorry to lose him, as we cannot easily believe in his character. No British officer, we hope, would be vulgar and, as it were, unsportsmanlike enough to fume with rage at the awkward but well-meaning cripple who 'insults' him by generously offering him money so that he may be married without delay. When death has cleared the way for Rickie, he very abnormally sets up the figures of the deceased Dawes and Agnes in his mind as images made radiant and consecrated by the greatest event in Agnes's life. He rubs salt into her wounds. 'You've got to mind it,' he says, if she shows signs of letting time do its work of consolation. Even after he himself has surrendered to circumstances and become engaged to Agnes, though he had vowed that he would never tell his love, he deplores her insensibility to the past. As for his clever friends, they are rude and awkward beyond belief in the presence of Agnes. Rickie fails as an author, soon learns to despise the worldliness of his wife, and abandoning literature, accepts the offer of her pompous schoolmaster brother to become his junior house master. The best part of the book follows. We quote a passage from a conversation between Rickie and his wife:—

'There's very little bullying here,' said Agnes.—'There was very little bullying at my school. There was simply the atmosphere of unkindness, which no discipline can dispel. It's not what people do to you, but what they mean, that hurts.'—'I don't understand.'—'Physical pain doesn't hurt—at least not what I call hurt—if a man hits you by accident or in play. But just a little tap, when you know it comes from hatred, is too terrible. Boys do hate each other: I remember it, and see it again. They can make strong isolated friendships, but of general good-fellowship they haven't a notion.'—'All I know is there's very little bullying here.'—'You see, the notion of good-fellowship develops late: you can just see its beginning here among the prefects: up at Cambridge it flourishes amazingly. That's why I pity people who don't go up to Cambridge: not because a University is smart, but because those are the magic years, and—with luck—you see up there what you couldn't see before and mayn't ever see again.'

The estrangement of Rickie from his wife, and also from his friends, grows complete over the affair of his half-brother. All his life he has not suspected the nature of his relationship to Stephen Wonham—a kind of Tony Lumpkin not without his good points in an uncouth way—and when the truth is revealed to him he is induced by his wife to conceal it. There is no more reason for doing this than there used to be for similar acts in the old-fashioned 'three-decker' novels; but we must say that the author graduates and accumulates very skilfully the prevarications, which are little more than acts of convenience at the moment, yet lead up to a wrong of real magnitude. Even then we cannot believe that the man who had been Rickie's greatest friend at Cambridge would have come, when the wrong was exposed, and denounced Rickie in a preposterous scene before a roomful of schoolboys without having made the least attempt to help him or warn him beforehand. Rickie, at all events, is left to atone for much injustice to his half-brother. How he pays for his fault is the *dénoûment* of the story, and we shall not disclose it. This novel is worth consideration, not for what it is, but for what it nearly is. It is a token of what Mr. Forster may yet do,—unless, unhappily, the 'abnormality' of his invention is constitutional and ineradicable.

33. Unsigned notice, *Outlook*

13 July 1907, 55

Those who saw in Mr. Forster's previous work the promise of an original writer, cannot fail to be disappointed with his latest effort. *The Longest Journey* is frankly the most impossible book we have read for many years. Throughout the three hundred odd pages we have striven to discover one solitary gleam of Nature, and have wasted our labour. We feel inclined to give the author the advice bestowed upon his hero by the editor: 'See life, Mr. Elliot, and then send us another story.' We do not propose to discuss the plot, although a synopsis might be of service to the novel-reader who has not the patience to seek a plain meaning in what would seem to be deliberately obscure verbiage. To describe the action of the narrative without a detailed explanation of the characters which develop it, would be to make the book seem even more fantastic than it is.

34. 'A newcomer', *Revue des Deux Mondes*

xlii, no. 4, 15 December 1907, 916–17

Translated from T. de Wyzewa, 'Le roman anglais en 1907: II, Les nouveaux venus'.

Téodor de Wyzewa (1862–1917) was a prolific Polish writer and critic, who spent most of his life in France. His career is described in Elga Liverman Duval, *Téodor de Wyzewa: Critic without a Country* (Geneva and Paris, 1961).

Forster had heard of Wyzewa's review, but seems not to have been able to obtain a copy. He was, however, greatly encouraged by a letter Wyzewa later wrote him, and in his reply (3 November 1910) said: 'I like [*The Longest Journey*] myself—in the peculiar way in which one does like one's own work—but feared that it was provincial rather than intimate, and would only interest the limited circle of my friends. Leaving aside the high authority of the *Revue des Deux Mondes*, it does touch me very much that a reader, not an Englishman, should care for my book more at a second reading than at a first, and should detect in it a few of the qualities that I prize myself in the books of others.'

I hope also soon to have the opportunity of speaking at more leisure about Mr. E. M. Forster, author of a very curious novel entitled *The Longest Journey*. Mr. Forster tells us, on the title-page of his book, that he has already published another novel, *Where Angels Fear to Tread*; but I cannot help imagining that he is a very young man, resolved to correct numerous faults which he still displays in *The Longest Journey*. I have rarely read a story told so unskilfully, showing so complete an ignorance of the usual techniques of the novel. Mr. Forster seems to have no idea, for example, of the advantage there would be, for him, in preparing and highlighting the important scenes in a dramatic action: he spreads out all his scenes on the same level, or even takes time off for purely episodic conversations, while he hurries in a few pages through events which we should like to see in all their detail. Along with this goes a curiosity no less childish about familiar incidents in university life: so much so that we think we are listening to a Cambridge student who is under the impression that the whole world is as interested as he is in the syllabus, in the technicalities of examinations, in the prowess of football players or oarsmen. The first part of his novel, called 'Cambridge', should, instead of taking up half the book, have been compressed into about twenty pages; similarly, we could easily have done without whole chapters given up to the description of daily life in a boarding school, where Mr. Forster's hero, after leaving Cambridge, is employed obscurely as an assistant master.

These are weaknesses one would not dream of pointing out, let alone deploring, in a run-of-the-mill novel; but the pity is that here they risk spoiling the charm of a work full of observation and of poetry: for this former Cambridge student, this obscure teacher, whose story Mr. Forster tells us, is certainly one of the pleasantest figures I have met in the whole series of new English novels that have come to my notice. He has a soul of an unparalleled sensitivity and purity, which accepts the cruellest blows of fate with a sweetly-resigned smile, and which always transforms into beautiful full-blown dreams the sadness or ugliness of reality. He is gauche, timid, incurably naive and, to cap it all, lame; his young wife despises him, his friends refuse to take him seriously, and a brother for whom he tries to show his affection fails to respond, being unable in his own vigour of body and spirit to understand the desires and pains of this sick heart. He continues, still, on his 'journey', looking at the world with a kind and startled gaze, and even death does not alter the melancholy serenity of his dreaming. Certainly we are correct to expect much of a writer who has been able to imagine and execute this poetic portrait; not to mention the fact that, around his charming hero, the author has sketched several other figures no less alive and original in the supporting roles he has given them.

[Wyzewa goes on to call John Galsworthy, 'in complete contrast' to Forster, 'perhaps the most skilful new novelist in his country'.]

35. Frieda Lawrence, letter to E. M. Forster

Undated, probably 1915

Frieda Lawrence (born Frieda von Richthofen) married D. H. Lawrence after her divorce from Ernest Weekley in 1914. This letter was written to Forster from Greatham (near Pulborough) in Sussex, where the Lawrences stayed from January to July 1915 (cf. Nos 74 and 88).

I love the *longest journey*. It touched me on the quick—and the quick responded joyfully. Rickie of course isn't a bit dead, it's only one of those many healthful deaths one dies—Also, as you can understand, the question of man-to-man love instead of bloodrelationship made me happy in the book because of my children—I suppose as a mother I have failed them: now for the man-to-man—This sounds bold, more sound than truth—Your women I don't understand, *you* seem to dislike them *much*! Rickie was a very domineering young man in spirit! I would have argued with him—

[. . . . .]

THE LONGEST JOURNEY

(American edition) 1922

36. Unsigned notice, *Boston Evening Transcript*

19 April 1922

Probably because his point of view is so intensely English as to be almost incomprehensible to an American, Mr. Forster's novels are still practically unknown to America. The plot of this one is very slight and the theme an insistence on a return to the Greek ideal of beauty as a panacea for the ills of modern life. The hero is a student at Cambridge, deformed by hereditary lameness and with no definite capacity beyond an inclination to write and a 'desire for beauty that leads him astray if he is not careful.' His parents had died and 'he had crept cold and ignorant and friendless out of a great public school, preparing for a silent and solitary journey, but Cambridge had taken and soothed him and warmed him and had laughed at him a little, saying that he must not be so tragic yet awhile, for his boyhood has been but a dusty corridor that led to the spacious halls of youth.'

The friendships at the University and his enjoyment of his chums with their philosophical discussions are the only bright spots in the book. His only relatives are a disagreeable aunt and a horrible illegitimate step-brother. He marries a girl who has previously given her entire soul to a lover who has died. 'Later he found light neither in work for which he was unfitted nor in a woman who had ceased to respect him and whom he was ceasing to love.' A lame daughter was born to them, who dies. The hero himself dies rescuing his drunken brother, who had fallen on the railroad track. Altogether it is a story of dreary pessimism. Rebecca West calls Mr. Forster's novels 'wildly and tragically beautiful,' but the harsh and obscure style and the depression of its philosophy will hardly make this one widely read in America.

37. Unsigned review, *Springfield Sunday Republican*

(Springfield, Massachusetts) 29 October 1922, 7a

Similar in theme to Miss Cather's impressive American novel [Willa Cather's *One of Ours*, reviewed on the same page] is E. M. Forster's *The Longest Journey*, an English work presenting the same tragedy of sensibility, imaginativeness and a delicate sense of honor thwarted by the world. The tone of the work is more consciously literary; the prose richer in shading and more assured—also more impregnated with Meredithian subtlety. Rickie, a Cambridge graduate, handicapped by lameness and somewhat afflicted with morbidity as a consequence, lives in and for his enthusiasms—disinterested emotions, generous friendships, intellectual intercourse, imaginings, literary aspirations. Like the American hero, he marries a woman who does not sympathize with him, though she at least understands her husband, while association between the ill-mated American pair hardly gets as far as the understanding of mutual dislike. Rickie, and his friends, scorn the world: but it is his fortune to be set down in the rigid, soulless environment of a preparatory school conducted for profit.

Fantastic events like bolts out of the blue bring out the tragedy of this sensitive spirit beating its wings in vain. An illegitimate half-brother comes out of nowhere to plague him, not directly, for he wishes to acknowledge and care for his unfortunate relative, but through his scheming wife, solicitous for money and social position. He has his little day of moral courage and dies.

The work subtly contrasts the spiritual heritage of man—a heritage having its background in Nature—with his small realization of it in his 'short day of frost and sun.'

No one reading the book can question the imaginative possibilities of the modern novel. Mr. Forster combines in high degree irony and poetry.

'There is . . . another coinage that bears on it not man's image but God's. It is incorruptible, and the soul may trust it safely; it will serve her beyond the stars. But it cannot give us friends, or the embrace of a lover, or the touch of children, for with our fellow-mortals it has no concern. It cannot even give the joys we call trivial—fine weather, the pleasures of meat and drink, bathing and the hot sand afterwards, running, dreamless sleep. Have we learnt the true discipline of a bankruptcy if we turn to such coinage as this? Will it really profit us so much if we save our souls and lose the whole world?'

There is no questioning or resisting the charm of Mr. Forster. It is itself a fine companionship. This novel steadily attains beauty. The only drawback is that in its setting forth of spiritual realities it sometimes becomes fancifully attenuated.

A ROOM WITH A VIEW

1908

38. R. A. Scott-James, 'A novel of character', *Daily News*

20 October 1908, 4

R. A. Scott-James (1878–1959), journalist and author, was Literary Editor of the *Daily News* from 1906 to 1912 (cf. C. F. G. Masterman, Nos 10 and 19). He also, at various times, worked for the *Daily Chronicle*, was Assistant Editor of the *Spectator*, and was Editor of the *London Mercury*. He published *Fifty Years of English Literature: 1900 to 1950* in 1951.

There is just enough that is right in Mr. Forster to triumph over the mass of him that seems to us to be wrong. There is no use denying that he begins by irritating us exceedingly. He is full of views; what is worse, he is full of subtlety, a subtlety that rises up and assails you in pregnant epigram or paraded restraint. He insists on assuming—with that blind faith in unrealities which only the 'intellectual' is capable of—that Early Victorian rules of propriety are the rules of today, and he flagellates these extinct, or, at least, dying, moral mannerisms with caustic, but belated, satire.

The truths with which he is concerned are sometimes of so subtle a character that he forgets, if he has ever known, some of the elementary ones. For instance, he is so intent on showing that all that is 'British' is hypocritical and hollow that he forgets that an English young lady, travelling in Italy, is not so strictly chaperoned as an Italian young lady, and that even the prim inhabitants of an English pension do not regard it as indecent for a lady who has fainted at the sight of a murder in the streets to be escorted home by an acquaintance who has the ill-breeding to be a man. Or, again, while we may admit, with Mr. Forster and the two Messrs. Emerson, that springtime and love are admirable things, and that 'we have no rights' over a cabman's soul, we still think it was reasonable for the occupants of a hired carriage to object when their driver, not content with taking his sweetheart on the box, loaded her with embraces. It was just as reasonable to object as it is unreasonable to bring in the moral problem of the 'proprieties.' If Mr. Forster would be more intent on story-telling and less intent on instruction he would save the strength which he spends in tilting at windmills.

In Florence

And yet this is a brilliant novel, a novel which begins by being brilliantly dull and ends by being humanly absorbing. The author gradually gets into his stride, and comes to know his own characters, and make us know them. Dull and trivial as they may seem, they learn to be natural, and the prim, the semi-suburban, the conventional is suddenly brought into contrast with the primitive earnestness of flesh and blood and feeling. Lucy has been through her Italy, and has endured the constraint of Miss Bartlett's foolish chaperonage. She has walked, Baedeker in hand, through the streets and churches of Florence; she has endured and, indeed, accepted the chatter of a pension; she has talked to the kindly parson, Mr. Beebe, listened to the spiteful parson, Mr. Eager, and been submerged beneath the ungoverned outpourings of Miss Lavish, the local-colour novelist. She has been forced to talk to Mr. Emerson, père, and Mr. George Emerson, fils, whom the pension will not tolerate; by the latter she has been rescued at the fateful moment when an Italian, bleeding from a death wound, seems to speak to her as the blood spirts from his mouth. Startled into reality by this literal 'call of the blood' she has conversed with a live man almost with freedom; and, again, she has come upon him suddenly among the 'cataracts' of violets, when without hesitation the crude man has 'stepped quickly forward and kissed her'; and she has been whisked away by the prim Miss Bartlett, and engaged to that cultured gentleman, Mr. Cecil Vyse.

The Man of Culture

Then it is that the story begins to move with a more powerful irony and a more real effect of passion. Lucy is at home now at Windy Corner. Her kind, querulous, solicitous mother is in the house; so is her noisy, brainless, healthy brother, Freddy. Cecil Vyse begins to pervade the scene. From his intellectual throne in a corner of London, where he is surrounded by ideas in the shape of books and the Philistinism of metropolitan culture, he ventures to descend to the unsophisticated circle of Windy Corner. He had known Lucy for years, but Italy had 'worked some marvel in her. It gave her light, and—which he held more precious—it gave her shadow. Soon he detected in her a wonderful reticence. She was like a woman of Leonardo da Vinci's, whom we love not so much for herself as for the things she will not tell us.' He looks for 'charm' in her; he would be shocked by any positive assertion of character. He likes to speak to her of books, and poetry, and pictures, and to be heard; and once, under the appropriate influence of the fields and trees, he even submits himself to the 'momentary cult of the fresh air' and the delight at her simplicity. And so he explains his newly-acquired feeling for pathways:

> 'I had got an idea—I daresay wrongly—that you feel more at home with me in a room.'
>
> 'A room?' she echoed, hopelessly bewildered.
>
> 'Yes. Or, at the most, in a garden, or on a road. Never in the real country like this.'
>
> 'Oh, Cecil, whatever do you mean? I have never felt anything of the sort. You talk as if I was a kind of poetess sort of person.'
>
> 'I don't know that you aren't. I connect you with a view—a certain type of view. Why shouldn't you connect me with a room?'
>
> She reflected a moment, and then said, laughing:
>
> 'Do you know that you're right? I do. I must be a poetess after all. When I think of you it's always as in a room. How funny!'
>
> To her surprise, he seemed annoyed.
>
> 'A drawing-room, pray? With no view?'
>
> 'Yes, with no view, I fancy. Why not?'
>
> 'I'd rather,' he said reproachfully, 'that you connected me with the open air.'
>
> She said again, 'Oh, Cecil, whatever do you mean?'

The Man of Fact

'Views are really crowds—crowds of trees and houses and hills—and are bound to resemble each other, like human crowds—and . . . the power they have over us is something supernatural, for the same reason. . . . For a crowd is more than the people who make it up. Something gets added to it—no one knows how—just as something has got added to those hills.' It is not Cecil who teaches Lucy that; it is George Emerson, the man who had kissed her when she came through the cataracts of violets, who kisses her again when she is another man's fiancée, who teaches her that Cecil is 'the type who's kept Europe back for a thousand years,' who has been 'playing tricks on people, on the most sacred form of life that he can find.'

Mr. Forster breaks through the bonds of his own art; the very lessons he began laboriously to teach crumble beneath the central human facts which at the last hold his and our attention. The fine, primitive, deep things which do not deny the flesh, even if they are not 'of it,' are dear to him, so that he forgets his horrible artificialities, and becomes genuine. The book grows on the reader, and, if he reads with care, he will have cause to be grateful to Mr. Forster.

39. Unsigned review, *The Times Literary Supplement*

no. 354, 22 October 1908, 362

This review is attributed by Professor F. P. W. MacDowell, the American Forster scholar, to Virginia Woolf.

Mr. E. M. Forster's title *A Room with a View* is symbolical, of course; and to explain the sense which he conveys by it will introduce our comment also. Lucy Honeychurch and her elderly cousin Charlotte go to stay at a pension in Florence; their rooms, they grumble, have no view. A gentleman promptly exclaims, 'I have a view; I have a view', and proceeds to offer them his room and the room of his son George. They are outraged, but they consent; and when cousin Charlotte has insisted that she shall occupy the young man's apartment, because he is a bachelor, she discovers, pinned over the washstand, 'an enormous note of interrogation'. 'What does it mean? she thought. . . . Meaningless at first, it gradually became menacing, obnoxious, portentous with evil'. But if we are not cousin Charlotte, in age or temper, if, moreover, we have read what Mr. Forster has written in the past, we are amused rather than bewildered. We are more than amused, indeed, for we recognise that odd sense of freedom which books give us when they seem to represent the world as we see it. We are on the side, of course, of Mr. Emerson and his son George, who say exactly what they mean. We care very much that Lucy should give up trying to feel what other people feel, and we long for the moment when, inspired by Italy and the Emersons, she shall burst out in all the splendour of her own beliefs. To be able to make one thus a partisan is so much an achievement, the sense that one sees truth from falsehood is so inspiriting, that it would be right to recommend people to read Mr. Forster's book on these accounts alone. If we are honest, we must go on to say that we are not so confident by the time the book is at an end. The story runs simply enough. Lucy is kissed by George Emerson, and the ladies fly to Rome. In Rome they meet Mr. Cecil Vyse, a young man who feels of his own accord what other people feel, both about art and about life. When Lucy is back again in her ugly home in Surrey she agrees to marry Mr. Vyse, but happily the Emersons take the villa over the way, and Lucy is made to own that she can tell the true from the false before it is too late. To compress the motive of the book into this compass is, of course, to simplify it absurdly, for nothing is said of the cleverness, the sheer fun, and the occasional beauty of the surrounding parts. We sketch the story thus, however, because we believe that it was meant to take this line, and we are conscious of some disappointment when for one reason or another it goes a different way, and the view is smaller than we expected. The disappointment is not due to any change of scene, but to some belittlement, which seems to cramp the souls of the actors. Lucy's conversion becomes a thing of trifling moment, and the views of George and his father no longer spring from the original fountain. But should we complain when we have originality and observation, and a book as clever as the other books that Mr. Forster has written already?

40. Unsigned notice, *Morning Leader*

30 October 1908, 3

Though *A Window with a View* is not consistently vivacious, and has not quite the brilliance of *Where Angels Fear to Tread*, it is still one of the best novels of the season. Perhaps it may be called the truest. Mr. Forster has one aim only: he sets out to make clear the limitations of the cultured middle-class. He achieves it perfectly. The class writhes at the point of his pen in the most lifelike and diverting manner. His humor is indescribably penetrating. He makes his characters reveal themselves with complete naturalness and complete self-condemnation: yet they all show their virtues as well as their follies. And in his caustic asides he is absolutely inimitable. We have enjoyed this book as much as anything written in the last decade.

41. Unsigned notice, *Daily Mail*

31 October 1908, 8

This is one of the cleverest and most entertaining novels we have read for some time. We meet Miss Lucy Honeychurch and her cousin and chaperon, Miss Bartlett, at a pension in Florence, where Mr. Emerson and his son George give up to them, each, a room with a view. Afterwards Lucy, who has been going to marry a prig, is once more rescued by George Emerson, and again given a room with a view, a room in life, in which no doubt she will be happy.

The characters are as clear and salient as a portrait by Sargent, and there are many of them. One is continually moved to appreciative smiles by clever little touches of description and enlightenment. The story, too, is interesting and real, although we do not quite understand the attitude of the delightful clergyman, Mr. Beebe, in face of the last development of Lucy's career. Mr. Forster is to be welcomed into the company of the novelists who count for something.

42. 'F', review, *Manchester Guardian*

4 November 1908, 5

When Lucy, the heroine of *A Room with a View*, by E. M. Forster, found herself at the Pension Bartolini in a room without a view, it was to the Emersons, father and son, that she owed the change which gave her a sight of the busy life of Florence and of Fiesole across the city's towers. And it was George Emerson who afterwards made a window in her being to let in the light. [rest of paragraph gives a sympathetic summary of the book's story, bringing out its theme clearly] . . .

Such is an inadequate account of a very clever book. Mr. Forster is a humourist who has looked on many aspects of human life with kindly and discerning eyes. Underneath his satire and his mockery of the shows of life there lies a very real belief in the things which really count—in the joy of the sun and the free air, in sincerity of soul, and in passion. He is an optimist in spite of his irony, for there is no hint of the obstacles which chance and circumstance may throw in the way of the disciple of nature, nor can we divine how he would have had his heroine behave if George Emerson had convinced her of sin after instead of before her union with Cecil. We have left ourselves no space to pass in review the characters which fill this admirable comedy. They are not described, but display themselves in action. They are all typical and at the same time clearly individualised. Here and there, as in the ways and speech of Cecil, we catch echoes of Mr. Bernard Shaw and our author has in many respects a kindred spirit to Meredith, but he owes no debt to one writer or the other. He has his own humour and his own philosophy and his own admirable style. But he should beware of farce, in which he is unlikely to excel.

43. Unsigned notice, *Pall Mall Gazette*

6 November 1908, 4

This odd title suggests a story rather out of the common, and it does not prove in the least misleading. The book is both original and delightful, presenting scenes of everyday life almost commonplace sometimes in their fidelity to nature, but chronicled in such a happy vein of quiet humour and with such penetrating observation as makes each little incident and dialogue a source of sheer joy to the reader. The characters are admirably drawn. We have met them all in real life—that is to say, we have met Lucy, the engaging heroine, and her pleasant mother and brother, her unpleasant elderly cousin, and her supercilious fiancée, but George Emerson and his father are new and welcome acquaintances. This couple, chiefly owing to the old man's disconcerting habit of speaking the truth, have a most upsetting effect in both the places in which we meet them, first in the Pension Bertolini at Florence, where they encounter the newly-arrived heroine and her cousin and embarrass them by offering to give up their own 'room with a view' for their benefit; and again to 'Windy Corner', Lucy's country home in England, where they finally succeed in opening her eyes and changing the whole current of her life. The book might be considered as a sermon on Dr. Johnson's text, 'Clear your minds of cant', and we feel a satisfactory sense of principle rightly-applied when Lucy at last gives up trying to feel as others expect her to feel, and 'lets out the whole length of the reins' and faces the consequences bravely. But somehow the last chapter falls a little flat after the high level of the rest of this book of delightful 'unexpectedness'.

44. 'A young woman in a muddle', *Observer*

8 November 1908, 4

An unsigned notice.

A Room with a View, by E. M. Forster, might also have been called 'A Young Woman in a Muddle.' It is a remarkably clever study of the hopeless confusion existing in the mind of an ordinary English girl of the middle classes. Lucy Honeychurch is an average specimen of her kind—unoriginal, pretty and 'nice', with second-hand opinions and borrowed enthusiasms. Unconscious of mistake, she blunders into an engagement with an irritating young prig, but, when she does at least learn what she wants, has the courage to break free from the tangle. Possibly this book may not appeal to all tastes, but to some it will prove an undiluted joy. It is full of humour and delightful, commonplace people. Mr. Forster's gift for sighting the comedy of ordinary social intercourse amounts to genius, the more so as it is entirely unforced and free from exaggeration.

45. 'A clever novel', *Morning Post*

23 November 1908, 2

An unsigned review.

There is much that is strong and admirable in *A Room with a View*, and we must congratulate Mr. E. M. Forster on having added considerably to his reputation. His satire is clever and biting, but his sense of humour and the occasional ridiculousness of his situations save his satire from being ill-natured. In the first part of the book the scene is laid in Florence, and is mostly taken up with discussions and dialogues and witticisms, but the characters are introduced in an original manner, which argues well for further acquaintance with them. The real human interest begins in Part II, at Windy Corner, overlooking the Sussex Weald, the bourgeois home of Lucy and Freddy and their amusing mother Mrs. Honeychurch. The threads of life had combined together to weave Lucy into a fresh, natural, adorable creature; but art, in the shape of a lover, with the additional aid of a chaperon had conspired to print a conventional stamped pattern on the original pure homespun. Lucy gets engaged to Cecil, a distinguished sensitive person, who despises the world and thinks this method a test of refinement. Windy Corner was not perfect, but it had a way of getting the 'grittiness out of life,' and Cecil was not altogether at home in this atmosphere. Much family merriment is expended over the announcement of the engagement, and even Anne, the maid, seemed to put down each plate at the table as 'if it were already a wedding present.' Cecil tries to improve Lucy, and, according to *Punch*, people do not want to be improved except in their worldly circumstances. Anyway, George Emerson accepted honesty as a natural birthright, and believed it 'grew heavenwards like the flowers,' also he could love passionately, and Cecil was at heart an ascetic. It is all very well told, for it requires ingenuity and originality to conceive a character like George Emerson and touch him with a magic wand so that his love episodes appear spontaneous and sincere instead of vulgar and uncontrolled, as they might have done with a less skilful pen. There is such a thing as the genius of love, and this man had it, and it is the function of such genius that it bursts all bonds and sees the naked truth by the light of its own inner force. Mr. Beebe, a family friend, had said of Lucy that one day the 'water-tight compartments in her will break down, and music and life will mingle.' So these two bright, brave natures face life together, and Cecil retires, a wiser man. Truth to say, his renunciation of Lucy makes us almost like him, 'for nothing in his love became him like the leaving of it.'

46. 'The half-hidden life', *Nation*

iv, no. 9, 28 November 1908, 352–4

An unsigned review by C. F. G. Masterman.

In a letter to Forster (1 December 1908) Masterman said: 'I wrote some obscure stuff about your book in the *Nation*: which only very inadequately represented the pleasure which I obtained from it.'

Mr. Forster has earned the right to serious criticism. His work—limited to three novels and some shorter stories and sketches—has revealed individuality, distinction, and a power of suggestion which opens large issues. *A Room with a View*, the title of his latest book, might stand for a title of all his work. He reveals in minute and exact detail the 'room' and its contents: the patterned paper on the walls, the sofas and antimacassars, the elaborate, grotesque, or stuffy artifice of conventional construction. And beyond, he shows the 'view': outside man's handiwork, judging, sometimes condemning, always disturbing, the contented occupants of the artificial arena. Dawn flares through the blinds, the sunset casts haunting shadows on the carpets and cushions, outside is the sound of tempest or the challenging silence of the night. And the conflict amongst all his characters—set in the moment where two eternities meet, which is always a moment of supreme choice—arises just from the fact that although their natural and accepted habit approves of the orderly comfort of the 'room,' there is within all of them some wild or exultant element which responds to the high calling of the 'view'.

The 'room' may take many shapes and forms. In that fascinating and tragic farce, *Where Angels Fear to Tread*, it is found (for one nation) in the spreading securities of suburban London, for another in the crumbling dead streets of a little Tuscan city. In *The Longest Journey*, it varied from the traditional decencies of the older Universities—with their secret for the fashioning of the completed English gentleman—to the traditional decencies of the English countryside, the English gentleman, completed, pursuing his ordered and tranquil existence in that station of life to which he has been called. In his latest novel the scene also changes; from the English pension at Florence, with its enthusiasm for the work of Karl Baedekker and John Ruskin, to the spreading suburbs of Surrey, in those regions where the new rich and the emigrant clerk are making desolate the hills which look southward to the sea. Both of these are outposts of man's civilisation: both, therefore, places of especial danger. The *pension* has high bulwarks in the atmosphere of breezy clergymen and maiden ladies, in the advantage which can be given by such outside aids in the city as joint excursions of British tourists, English afternoon tea shops, and the 'cultured English community' resident in Florence. But in the immediate background is a nation with a thousand centuries behind it: passion in the city square leading to sudden death: Phaethon and Persephone, who will drive the blithe and unsuspecting party up the hillside to Fiesole, disguised as an Italian coachman and his 'sister': with (at the summit) a field blue with violets and the vision of 'fifty miles of Italian spring.' And the little semi-urban village of the Surrey hillside, although linked firmly to the city by the South Eastern Railway, and stuffed with all the material of contemporary life—illustrated papers, and tennis courts, and clever conversation—has also below it deep pinewoods with a lake in the heart of them, and a wide southern plain leading beyond to one grey glimpse of sea. Here are things which own no allegiance to convention, fit habitation for those which still survive of all the older gods. And to Mr. Forster, as to Heine and others, the older gods have not perished: they but remain, abiding in patience, until the tyranny of denial be overpast. In one of his sketches in the *Independent Review* (not yet republished), 'A Panic Fear,' in a party on picnic in a valley of Greece, Pan appears for a moment, and asserts his supremacy: in a gust or tumult, suddenly coming and going, no man knowing whether in external Nature or the mind of man. And it is Pan who here appears, in the hills above Florence first, and later in the well-trimmed garden of an English suburban residence in the neighbourhood of Dorking: when George Emerson kisses Lucy Honeychurch, first in violation of all standards of conventional respectability, and later in violation of all standards of conventional honor.

It is this hidden life—secure and silent, and often, through a lifetime, undisturbed—that Mr. Forster sets himself to reveal in the characters of the working world. It is a current flowing, mysterious, elusive, behind the motives and desires which make the web of conscious apprehension. The efforts to explore it are like occasional soundings swung into an unfathomed deep: adventures upon an uncharted shore. The normal activity of existence flows on, men are getting and spending, enjoying bodily exercise, discussing their surface politics, philosophies, and religions: women are 'falling in love' with conventional figures, and (for the most part) accepting with satisfaction the affection and the convention. But beyond and behind it all, are tides and oceans which may at any time surge up into the sheltered ports and harbors, and sweep the little craft which have found shelter there far out to sea. The tiny, intelligent life is outraged and defiant: it protests and it weeps, it refuses to face realities, it lies heartily and continuously to the outside world and to itself. Sometimes it triumphs in the re-establishment of order: the ship has regained the shelter again, and its occupants, wasted by the struggle, anchor more firmly in the shadows, and declare that they will never more put out to sea: sometimes the upheaval is permanent: the land drops behind the horizon, and the vessel rides buoyantly over the waste of waters, rejoicing in the challenge of its vast and incalculable tides. And all these spiritual conflicts the author can set—with a quiet and detached vision, more ironical than any deliberate interference or exposition—amid the dust and dead flowers of a tourist-haunted Italian city, or between the tennis-court and the drawing-room of an English suburban villa.

From the beginning of this story of the spiritual adventure of

George Emerson and Lucy Honeychurch, the chief protagonists have some advantage denied to their contemporaries; weak places (as it were) in the wrappings of convention, which may wear thin through the influence of circumstance, and leave them exposed to naked reality. George—from start to finish a rather shadowy, indefinite figure—is the son of a father who has refused to accept the recognised standards, just because they are the standards which are recognised. His revolt, indeed, is as much on the surface as the standards themselves: it is not a revolt from the depth: and his protests of emancipation come in the end to exhibit themselves as ridiculous, and as tedious as the normal praises of imprisonment. But he has been teaching his son. 'He has the merit,' is the explanation of the clergyman, 'of saying exactly what he means. He no more thought of putting you under an obligation than he thought of being a bore. It is so difficult—at least I find it difficult—to understand people who speak the truth.' 'A type,' is the summary, 'one disagrees with rather than deplores.' Lucy finds him willing to act as guide in Santa Croce. 'I hope you have not been put to any great inconvenience,' she declares. 'My dear,' the old man answers, 'I think that you have been repeating what you have heard older people say. You are pretending to be touchy. But you are not, really. Stop being so tiresome.' His loud and incredulous comments in the Peruzzi Chapel drive forth in silent indignation a congregation and lecturer 'directing them how to worship Giotto, not by tactile valuations, but by the standards of the spirit.' 'My father has that effect on everyone,' explains George, ruefully, 'he will try to be kind.' 'I hope we all try,' said she, smiling nervously. 'Because we think it improves our characters,' he answers; 'but he is kind to people because he loves them: and they find it out, and are offended or frightened.'

And Lucy, though springing from and encompassed by convention, has radiant youth on her side, and music, with a reaction also, intensifying in bitterness, against her cousin and companion Miss Bartlett, a spinster too obviously dedicated to the worship of false gods. In her playing, 'passion was there, but it could not be easily labelled: it slipped between love and hatred and jealousy; and all the furniture of the pictorial style. And she was tragical only in the sense that she was great, for she loved to play on the side of Victory.' And she is not unmoved also by the general spirit of revolt and vague disturbance: which has come to one who 'reigned in many an Early Victorian castle, and was queen of much Early Victorian song.'

In her heart, also, there are springing up strange desires. She, too, is enamoured by heavy winds, and vast panoramas, and green expanses of the sea. She has marked the kingdom of this world, how full it is of wealth and beauty and war—a radiant crust, built around the central fires, spinning towards the receding heavens. Men, declaring that she inspires them to it, move joyfully over the surface, having the most delightful meetings with other men; happy, not because they are masculine, but because they are alive. Before the show breaks up, she would like to drop the august title of the Eternal Woman, and go there as her transitory self.

Given these persons, the machinery of Chance or Natural Design effects the rest. The unrestful challenge of old things in Florence is stimulated by the emotional experience of a murder in the Square; then a spring expedition to the hills, and a chance encounter there, when Pan had scattered the excursionists, breaks through the recognised barriers. In a vision of the earth's exuberance, violets appearing as beauty gushing out to water the earth, he, a man, sees her, a woman; nothing else but the approving earth under a limitless sky. From that moment the thing works itself out to inevitable conclusion. There is the spirit of high comedy in it. Mr. Forster can describe with sure touch the queer satisfactions and still queerer repugnances which make up the strange region of modern things. Had this element been there alone, the book would have been merely an excellent satirical judgment of manners and conventions. Had the other element stood alone—the revelation of the hidden life—it would have been mystical, intangible, illusory. By the fusion of the one with the other, he is able to present work humorous and arresting, with a curious element in it of compelling strength and emotion.

47. Unsigned notice, *Athenaeum*

no. 4234, 19 December 1908, 784

This story of the love-affairs of a commonplace young lady and her two commonplace lovers is too flat for sustained enjoyment. The dialogue is amateurish, and the author, who takes pains to make some of the characters revolt against 'conventionality', nevertheless thinks an elderly and esteemed acquaintance and his son 'abominably impertinent' for offering their services to two young ladies as guides over an Italian Church. Occasional passages such as that describing an English tourist's Italian form a welcome relief.

48. Unsigned notice, *Outlook*

xxii, no. 569, 26 December 1908, 906

This is an irresponsible sort of story about people who never act or talk quite sanely. The author has a gift for quaint dialogue, but he indulges it overmuch. It would be better assimilated with a leaven of common-sense. The heroine is one of those uncomfortable girls who cannot make up their minds. She is kissed on all possible occasions, and without provocation, by the uncouth George Emerson, and these osculatory overtures as often unsettle her intentions. We do not share the disquiet of her family when at last she decides to marry George; indeed we are grateful to the young man for taking her off their hands. Judging by the types he has collected together, Mr. Forster would appear to have had an exceptionally curious experience of modern society, or else his mental focus of human nature is all wrong.

49. Unsigned notice, *Evening Standard & St James's Gazette*

30 December 1908, 5

A Room with a View, by E. M. Forster, may not have in it anything so triumphantly of genius as the death of Gerald in *The Longest Journey*. But it quite does away with any fear that Mr. Forster's gift is a flash in the pan. It is packed with wonderful impressions and radiant sayings. Its point of view is new, not in the sense of bewildering one with its perversity; it is more as though another little window had been knocked out in one's mind, giving upon a landscape of truth. The glimpse of George, 'with beautiful things behind him unexpectedly,' the wonderful bathing scene of the three men, and, most wonderful of all, the scene in the Italian square that first draws the lovers together—all these are unique, probably faultless in psychology, and certainly most delicate in impressionist art. Some of the opinions of George's father might have been spared, though here and there an inspired thing is given him to say. Miss Bartlett is delightful, and Mr. Beebe. In short, it is rather hard not to gush when one is smothered in ordinary fiction and then comes across this.

50. Unsigned review, *Spectator*

cii, no. 4201, 2 January 1909, 23–4

Mr. Forster's new novel is not only much the best of the three he has written, but it clearly admits him to the limited class of writers who stand above and apart from the manufacturers, conscientious or otherwise, of contemporary fiction. To note improvements first, one finds in *A Room with a View* greater sympathy with and interest in his own *dramatis personae*. In *The Longest Journey*, for example, Mr. Forster's detachment at times reached the verge of callousness, and personages were suddenly killed off in a manner suggesting that he had got bored with them and wanted to make a fresh start. In the novel before us the characters are treated more patiently, sympathetically, and with greater consistency, and the author's attitude not only leads to a greater continuity, but is far more effective in securing and riveting the interest of the reader. Again, the freakish and somewhat cynical humour which disfigured his earlier work is here replaced by a kindlier tolerance. In short, Mr. Forster, while retaining all the freshness and unconventionality of his outlook, has come to regard the human comedy with greater respect and sanity. When the story opens, Lucy Honeychurch, an attractive young English girl chaperoned by a middle-aged cousin, Charlotte Bartlett, has just arrived at the Pension Bertolini in Florence. The proposal of two Englishmen, father and son, to exchange their rooms with those allotted to Lucy and her cousin, clumsily offered and reluctantly accepted, forms the 'take off' of the ensuing romance. The Emersons are looked at somewhat askance on social and other grounds by the other visitors in the *pension*, including two elderly spinsters of the Mrs. Nickleby type, and a strong-minded novelist; but Lucy is on her *Wanderjahr*, temporarily emancipated from the shackles of villadom, and athirst for adventure. George Emerson, the son, happens to be at hand when Lucy is the unwilling witness of a painful street tragedy, his timely support begets mutual confidence, and in a moment of expansion, though not without provocation, he so far forgets himself as to kiss her at a picnic. Lucy is really angry; she has no difficulty in persuading herself that she cares nothing for young Emerson, and Charlotte sweeps her away from the danger zone to Rome, where they join forces with their friends the Vyses. Thus when the action is resumed in Surrey Lucy has just become engaged to Cecil Vyse, a highly presentable and altogether blameless prig. But by a coincidence of which Mr. Forster is so far aware that he is at pains to account for it with considerable ingenuity, the Emersons become the tenants of a neighbouring villa, and renewed propinquity forces on Lucy the need of reconsidering her position, with results that may be readily forecasted when the characters of her two suitors are taken into account. The conclusion, however, is not easily arrived at, for Lucy, with all her charm and intelligence, belongs to that not inconsiderable tribe of people who habitually misinterpret their genuine instincts. She is not a *femme incomprise* so much as a girl who cannot understand herself. Periods of rebellion alternate with periods of abject slavery. To make matters worse, she relies, at a critical period in her development, on the judgment of her cousin, who is an excruciatingly conscientious prude. The gradual emancipation of Lucy from Charlotte's influence, and that of other representatives of narrow-minded conventionality, is illustrated with great subtlety and humour, and it is much to the credit of Mr. Forster that, while enlisting the sympathies of his readers on the side of Lucy in her struggles towards self-assertion, he by no means fails to render justice to those who thwart and resist her. Charlotte, though exasperating and ridiculous, is not altogether contemptible; indeed, one parts from her with a certain compassion for this angular poor relation, incapable of exciting affection, and always conscious of her obligations. Excellent also is the portrait of Cecil Vyse, the blameless and cultured young man who was perfectly at his ease with books and pictures, but incapable of reading the hearts of men and women. With a touch of fantastic humour, more surprising than convincing, Mr. Forster discovers in Cecil an element of nobility in the hour of his defeat; while Mr. Beebe, the witty, tolerant, and conciliatory clergyman, develops a vein of inhumanity at the close for which we are not sufficiently prepared.

Mr. Forster's novel lends itself readily to quotation, but we must content ourselves with only a few extracts. Thus Mrs. Honeychurch's crudely practical point of view is happily illustrated by her explanation of her son's hostility to his prospective brother-in-law:—'You are jealous of Cecil because he may stop Lucy knitting you silk ties.'

On the other hand, Cecil's aesthetic interest in Lucy is defined by the phrase: 'She was like a woman of Leonardo da Vinci's, whom we love not so much for herself as for the things that she will not tell us'; while his failure to rise to a great occasion suggests the comment: 'Passion should believe itself irresistible. . . . Above all, it should never ask for leave when there is a right of way.' We get a vivid picture of Lucy's neighbours in Surrey by the reference to 'their kindly affluence, their inexplosive religion, their dislike of paper-bags, orange-peel, and broken bottles.' Mrs. Vyse's pretensions to culture are well hit off in the account of her dinner-party 'consisting entirely of the grandchildren of famous people. The food was poor, but the talk had a witty weariness that impressed Lucy.' And again: 'Mrs. Vyse was a nice woman, but her personality, like many another's, had been swamped by London, for it needs a strong head to live among many people. The too vast orb of her fate had crushed her; she had seen too many seasons, too many cities, too many men for her abilities, and even with Cecil she was mechanical, and behaved as if he was not one son, but, so to speak, a filial crowd.' Lastly, Charlotte's failure in life is almost explained in the exaggerated deference of her appeal: 'Dearest Lucia, may I trespass upon you for a pin?'

There are no remarkable or heroic people in the book, but Mr. Forster has the happy knack of making stupid people interesting and tiresome people amusing. And he has a gift for dialogue which should stand him in excellent stead if he ever turns his attention to the stage.

A ROOM WITH A VIEW

(American edition) 1911

51. Unsigned notice, *Inter-Ocean* (Chicago)

20 May 1911, 5

This novel by the author of *Howard's End* is extremely hard to read, because of its author's irritating self-consciousness and his equally irritating desire to be clever in a different way—both of which obsessions are made evident continually. The book is therefore not what one could call a sincere, real, living work at all. It is a would-be difficult and would-be novel trick in the gymnastics of psychology.

52. Unsigned notice, *New York Times*

xvi, 30 July 1911, 472

This review was entitled 'The candid, innocent seriousness of father and son'.

In *Howards End*, which reached American readers earlier in the season, Mr. E. Morgan Forster evinced a very pretty comedy gift obscured by a somewhat foggy social philosophy. In *A Room with a View* the same gift appears undimmed by any overserious intention, and all the philosophy is of that ingenuous youthful sort which urges an honest reckoning with nature as the prime essential. Shockable people, pretentious people, sticklers for propriety and all such as mistrust and deny their natural impulses—with these Mr. Forster has very good fun, continually picturing them discomfited by some unconscious display.

As the chief instruments of his derisive designs he employs two characters, father and son, who take themselves and their feelings with a candid and innocent seriousness. These work havoc to conventional decorum among the middle class English folk at a pension in Florence, and later in an 'exclusive' London suburb. The 'room with a view,' which the older man, unintroduced, forced upon Lucy Honeywell and her embarrassed chaperon; the unconsidered kiss with which the young man saluted her on the violet-grown Italian hillside, and her final rescue from a merely 'suitable' match with a supercilious young prig—these make a story of unusual originality and freshness.

There is, to be sure, a little preachment at the end on the 'deliberate return to nature,' the attainment of simplicity 'by many conquests,' and, above all, the avoidance of the 'muddles' in which pretense involves its victims: but any individual scene in which truth routs hypocrisy is worth all of the moralizing.

In this book the quality of Mr. Forster's mirth plainly shows the influence of Meredith, and more than one phrase makes the explicit acknowledgment. The light touch with which the ironic possibilities of certain situations are developed could scarcely have been learned from any other master. Happily Mr. Forster has not fallen into imitative practices in the matter of style: he says his say often pointedly, and always clearly and simply.

HOWARDS END

1910

53. A. N. Monkhouse, initialled review, *Manchester Guardian*

26 October 1910, 5

Allan Noble Monkhouse (1858–1936), journalist, novelist and playwright, was on the editorial staff of the *Manchester Guardian* from 1902 to 1932. His many plays (including *Mary Broome*, 1911) were performed at repertory theatres in Liverpool, Manchester and Birmingham, and in America. He was a close friend and great encourager of W. Dixon Scott (cf. No. 82).

Howards End . . . is a novel of high quality written with what appears to be a feminine brilliance of perception. The facts of the story are sometimes very difficult to reconcile with the people, but we are to remember that 'all over the world men and women are worrying because they cannot develop as they are supposed to develop'. So it is with the two sisters Margaret and Helen, who know the best, or at least a pretty good, London, and manage, it seems, to be thoroughly alive in it, but Margaret marries Henry Wilcox, and the unwary reader will be revolted by it, as Helen was. Henry is not at all in the front of civilisation, but rather at the base of it; he is elderly, prosaic, competent, and everything that romance is not. He has not the least comprehension of what we may call his wife's spiritual portion; he does bad things, such as filching public lands and trading unscrupulously, which she abhors; and there is even conjured up, to his momentary confusion, a battered mistress who proves him to have been unfaithful to his first wife, a woman after Margaret's own heart. And Margaret, who is twenty years his junior, loves him; she does not develop as the romantic conventions would have her, but according to profound instincts and fundamental good sense. It is all very surprising, and it is a remarkable stroke of art that makes the younger sister, Helen, approach the hard masters of the world first. She had fallen in love with the Wilcox family, and incidentally with a boy of it; she 'had vowed to be less polite to servants in the future', and had perceived the charms of downrightness and brutality, of 'the life of anger and telegrams'. The reaction carried her far, and she bitterly resented Margaret's defection. We rebel against it with Helen; we cannot accept this triumph of nature without seeming to love something infinitely precious; life is a compromise, but the spirit cannot be content with mere solidities. The impulsive Helen comes terribly to grief, the happenings are bold and original, but the conclusion leaves one fairly safe with the conviction that 'personal relations are the real life', that the sisters 'have built up something real, because it is purely spiritual', and that 'it is the vice of a vulgar mind to be thrilled by bigness, to think that a thousand square miles are a thousand times more wonderful than one square mile, and that a million square miles are almost the same as heaven'.

The problems that are evoked and the general criticism of life must not obscure what is most memorable in a novel that is witty and penetrating, too. We may not like 'Unworthiness stimulates woman. It brings out her deeper nature, for good or for evil'; indeed, it strikes one as pointing to development as women are supposed to develop or even as a variant of the old calumny that women love a rake; but the sisters are extraordinarily vivid and true; there are two scenes between them—the one where Margaret tells Helen of her intended marriage and the other, even more beautiful, when in spite of confusions and estrangements they determine to spend a night alone together in the house that is full of associations—which are nobly human. The first Mrs. Wilcox, too, who met the clever London set at lunch and 'twice deplored the weather, twice criticised the train service on the Great Northern Railway', has the kind of originality that belongs to a perfectly sane and simple person. There is an immense liberality in the book, a sympathy that is so little eclectic that it seems indulgent. It is always a humane presentment of real men and women even when their doings surprise us into some kind of protest.

54. Unsigned review, *The Times Literary Supplement*

no. 459, 27 October 1910, 412

Mr. E. M. Forster has now done what critical admirers of his foregoing novels have confidently looked for—he has written a book in which his highly original talent has found full and ripe expression. Neither of its three clever, imperfect, slightly baffling predecessors was quite at unity with itself. In each case there was an uncertainty of attack and a want of harmony in the method which prevented an exceptionally fine sense of character from making its proper effect. All this is put right in *Howard's End*. Here Mr. Forster has finally got his method under control, and has seized his idea in a grasp that completely encircles it; so that the peculiar freshness and individuality of his gift can now be properly seen and understood. It is in the first place securely founded, this gift, upon a power of generalization which holds the tightly-handled plot compactly together. But Mr. Forster works from the centre outwards, and reaches the graces and humours of the surface of his story with a mind quite clear as to the structure beneath. His generalization starts from the everlasting opposition of the two types which between them hold civilized life together, the people who are not interested in 'personal relations' but who alone make the world practically habitable for the other type, the people who are not interested in the thing done but only in the human beings who do it. The Wilcox family stand for the first, English, honest, unimaginative, exasperating, and the Schlegel family for the second, of mixed blood and restless brains and hampering imaginations, certainly not less exasperating, the Wilcoxes being those who deal in realities without understanding them, the Schlegels those who understand realities without dealing in them. The Schlegels, indeed, must do all the understanding, and the question is whether they can understand enough for both and so effect an alliance with the Wilcoxes, instead of standing aside and making fun of them. Margaret Schlegel makes the attempt and dares a compromise: 'More and more', she says, 'do I refuse to draw my income and sneer at those who guarantee it'. Helen, her sister, is *intransigeante*, and faces the disaster to which her consistency brings her. Mr. Forster seizes the very essence of the contrast, and again and again pierces his material, with the sharpest needles, at the exact psychological point. It is another question whether the actual incidents of the story, apart from the perfect justice of the psychology, are well invented and disposed; and here we could make some criticisms. But we are dealing with a very remarkable and original book, and we will not linger over faults which do not touch its central virtue. Nor need more be said of the character drawing than that it has all the light shrewdness we have seen before in this writer's work, with the added clarity of practice. What gives Mr. Forster's writing its quite unique flavour is something more than this. It is the odd charming vein of poetry which slips delicately in and out of his story, showing itself for a moment in the description of a place or a person, and vanishing the instant it has said enough to suggest something rare and romantic and intangible about the person or the place. It is a refinement which belongs to realism, not romance, for it is simply due justice done to an element in life too momentary and swift for most realism, so called, to overtake. But where quick-fingered lightness and deftness are demanded there Mr. Forster never fails; and he has caught in this book a sensitive reflection of life on which he is very heartily to be congratulated.

55. Unsigned notice, *Pall Mall Gazette*

28 October 1910 (illustrated literary supplement, 8)

The tame and, indeed, somewhat absurd opening of *Howard's End* may tempt the reader to skip, if not to lay down, the book. But in either case he would be unwise, for, with a little patience and plodding, he will find the searching analysis of motive and the clever 'filling-in' of character both skilful and artistic. There is too much conversation that leads to nothing; the treatment of episode is altogether too matter-of-fact and colourless; but the presentment of the conventional Wilcoxes and the wholly unconventional Helen, is as striking in its truth as in its contrast; and especially good, ringing true in every line, is the chapter in which it is vainly pointed out to the respectable head of the respectable Wilcox clan that his sin in keeping a mistress while his wife was living was greater than that of his sister-in-law in yielding her honour, while yet unmarried, to a lover in distress. The author is certainly among the writers whose work counts for something.

56. 'The part and the whole', *Morning Leader*

28 October 1910, 3

An unsigned notice.

You cannot indict a class, any more than a nation. But Mr. Forster goes very near it in *Howard's End*. He shows us the well-to-do, cultured middle-class in the persons of a bare half-dozen people. His caustic humor and keen observation make his characters representative as well as individual. But in the end he has to come down to particular events to finish the book. We are rather sorry he does so, because the events are not representative, and are rather melodramatic. One of two delightful half-German girls becomes engaged to a rich financier, who in his younger days had seduced a lady who cannot have been a very unwilling victim. When his fiancée, Margaret, tries to help this woman's latest lover, she discovers the truth, but forgives him. Meanwhile her sister Helen has herself been seduced; and the engaged man is in the position of being asked to forgive the same kind of wrong as he himself had been forgiven. It is too artificial a situation to be quite convincing, and Mr. Forster has not in any marked degree the gift of treating strong passions powerfully. In subtle, incisive analysis of class distinctions, manners, and conventions, he is simply inimitable. In many ways *Howard's End* shows a broader, more discursive outlook than his earlier works, and we, therefore, regret the narrower elements in it. But whatever he writes, he is an author of distinction and exceptional ability.

57. Unsigned notice, *Standard*

28 October 1910, 5

Mr. Forster's work—*Howard's End* is Mr. Forster's fourth novel—occupies a niche entirely by itself in the house of contemporary fiction. It is not like anything else that is being done, and everything that he writes develops his original statement consistently and clearly. The secret of his original statement may be found in the title of his last novel, *The Room with a View*, in the motto to his new story 'Only Connect . . .,' and in the name of a delightful short story that he wrote some time ago, *The Celestial Omnibus*. There is a Room—a Room described with minuteness, accuracy, and a remarkable feeling for the salient things in it; but it is 'a Room with a View.' . . . There is an Omnibus, with all its everyday complement of absurd persons, wisps of straw from the stables, and the daily paper in the hands of its passengers; but the Omnibus is Celestial. Most novelists would have us to understand that we reach heaven by getting as far from earth as possible. Mr. Forster's philosophy is that heaven is all about us and the vision of it is granted only to those who will catch up their piece of earth in both their hands and go bravely forward. It is this doctrine of courage and common sense that gives Mr. Forster's book so compelling a fascination, and he has never before vindicated both his message and his method so ably as in his new novel. In its broadest outline the subject of *Howard's End* is the all-pervading influence of Place, and it is curious to note that this has been the subject of several recent novels. But Mr. Forster develops his theme beyond its ordinary range. In his other novels—especially in *The Longest Journey*—the influence of place has been felt, but now it is the faith, the creed, the gospel of the persons of his story. Every one is tested by the walls, the chimneys, the garden of *Howard's End*. Do they see, do they understand, can they connect? The Willcox family has the house in its possession. Mrs. Willcox (the most arresting and subtle character in all Mr. Forster's gallery) does understand and dies, leaving the place to the one person who shares her knowledge. But the Willcoxes—good, honest, stubborn, blind—cling to their possession, and during the rest of the book we see the house quietly, subtly, actively, setting to work to deliver itself into the hands of its proper possessor. When the book is closed the reader glances apprehensively about him—regards his tables and chairs with alarm, invests the meanest lodging with terribly secret activity.

One can fancy only too easily the way that such a theme would have been treated by other writers. There would be great slabs of scenery, the house would be drawn again and again, every actor in the comedy would have passed sniffing about the garden and exclaiming in emphatic asides that he always felt so odd in that part of the country and he really did not know what was happening to him. Mr. Forster emphasises nothing; he draws the house in several sharp, startling lines, and then leaves it to his readers. He makes no statement, and he flings his characters from place to place, from incident to incident, from life to death, from death to immortality with an apparent indifference. It seems possible, as we read, that anything may happen to any one, and that there are no rules or laws at all—and then, at the end, 'Only Connect . . .' Mr. Forster whispers, and everything falls into its place and the ordinary certainty of life is revealed.

There are a great many other things in the book. The characters of Margaret and Helen, Mrs. Willcox, Mr. Willcox, and Leonard, are wonderfully rendered, and there are scenes—the coming of Margaret to Howard's End, Leonard's death, Margaret's motor drive through the country—that are unforgettable. Mr. Forster's humour, too, is quite unlike anyone else's humour, and it is always surprising and unforeseen. With this book he seems to us to have arrived, and, if he never writes another line, his niche should be secure.

58. Unsigned review, *Daily Telegraph*

2 November 1910, 14

There is no doubt about it whatever. Mr. E. M. Forster is one of the great novelists. His stories are not about life. They are life. His plots are absorbing because his characters are real; he does not create them, but observes them. While he has not the grand manner nor the supreme wit and uncanny humour of Meredith, the humour of the man looking down from a height above the rest of his fellows, he has in an unusual degree the intelligence which probes the actions of human beings, and, above all, the spirit, as he himself would say, which connects. We are concerned here chiefly with two families—the Schlegels, two sisters, Margaret and Helen, and their brother Tibby, together with one or two relations, and the Wilcoxes. The Schlegels, of Anglo-German parentage, are intellectuals, and never has an intellectual atmosphere been better transferred to paper. They are interested in all the 'movements' of the day; their outlook is independent, and their spirits are fierce and vigorous. The Wilcoxes are an ordinary English bourgeois family, with the qualities and defects of such families. The two sets are mixed up together by fate, and in the clash is the comedy. From the beginning the ideas of the girls arrest us, from the moment that Margaret says to her philosopher father, 'To me one of two things is very clear. Either God does not know His own mind about England and Germany, or else men do not know the mind of God.' Later on she remarks, 'It seems silly to speak about "the Continent," but really it is all more like itself than any part of it is like England. England is unique. The Continent, for good or for evil, is interested in ideas. Its literature and art have what one might call the kink of the unseen about them. People will there discuss with humility questions that we here think ourselves too good to touch with tongs.'

Margaret is a remarkable girl, and, like such girls, singularly pure-minded and proud of thought. Henry Wilcox, the middle-aged head of his family, is quite different. He has no pride of thought, his conduct is not above reproach, but he is eminently respectable, a good and useful citizen. The other members of the two families are proper pendants to and variations of them. Margaret and Henry fall in love, and a great part of the book is the history of their courtship and marriage and its effect on them and their belongings. Howards End, the Wilcoxes' country house, furnishes the leit motif throughout. The excellences of the variations cannot be more than hinted at here. And now we come to a character who plays an important part in the story, though really outside it, a character on whom the author has bestowed some of his best work, in connection with whom there are scenes which betray the veritable genius of the writer. It is Leonard Bart, the little clerk, with a longing for higher things. We venture to say, though it may be our limitation rather than the author's, that Bart, the most fascinating of all the characters, does not ring true. Would such a man have had the pluck to commence life as he did? Surely he was too nervous, too suspicious, to have formed the connection with 'Jacky' which led to marriage. And again, we submit, as they say in the law courts, that Leonard Bart's seduction of Helen Schlegel is an unlikely incident. At any rate, it strikes a false note such as is never struck, for instance, in Meredith's novels. We do not feel that it is inevitable, but that it is the author's will, and that he is doing violence to his characters in bringing it about. There are one or two other blemishes, as they seem to us, though less important, and we remark them because the author is so intensely interesting, so full of the real stuff, so considerable a novelist. Other readers may not agree with these strictures; in any case the author will be indifferent to their opinion no doubt, for he must have a very settled mind. But all will agree as to the value of the book, as to its absorbing interest, the art and power with which it is put together, and they will feel with us that it is a book quite out of the common by a writer who is one of our assets, and is likely to be one of our glories.

59. Unsigned review, *Spectator*

cv, no. 4297, 5 November 1910, 757

There is no novelist living on whom one can more confidently rely for unexpected developments than Mr. Forster. Surprise, whether consciously or unconsciously administered, is of the essence of his method. The expert reader can usually predict the course of events after reading the first fifty pages of an average novel; but it would need clairvoyance of the highest order to forecast the ultimate issue of Helen Schlegel's visit to Howards End, and of the premature revelation of her attachment to Paul Wilcox. Mr. Forster's story may be roughly described as a set of free variations on the old theme of *amantium irae*. In this case the plot is entirely concerned with the relations of two families, the Schlegels and the Wilcoxes, and the more they fall out the closer they are drawn together. Anything more radically dissimilar than the two households it would be difficult to imagine. The Schlegel girls—the brother is a negligible and contemptible youth who counts for little in the story, though his pedantic egotism has an amusing side—are orphans, the daughters of a German idealist who settled in England, but without a trace of Teutonic stolidity. They are adventurous amateurs of culture, brilliant inconsequent talkers, deeply interested in music and literature, in the poetry and romance of life. On the other hand, Mr. Wilcox is a very prosperous, capable, somewhat cynical man of the world. He and his sons and daughters have all of them 'got their hands on the ropes.' They own motor-cars and country places; their houses are splendidly and solidly equipped; they appreciate comforts, taboo sentiment, and, with one exception, face emergencies without emotion or nerves. The Schlegels are partly attracted by qualities which they do not possess; but the real link is Mrs. Wilcox, a graceful, kindly, distinguished, inarticulate, but sympathetic woman, who has a genuine, and even passionate, affection for the country place which gives its name to the story. The acquaintance begins with a chance meeting on the Continent. Helen Schlegel, the more attractive, impulsive, and undisciplined of the two sisters, is invited to stay with the Wilcoxes, and in an expansive mood tumbles into love with one of the sons. But Paul Wilcox is a weakling, uncertain of himself, and afraid of his father, and the attachment is abruptly and violently ended before it has reached the stage of an engagement. Helen's lack of reticence leads to a *contretemps* which provokes an unpleasant family quarrel, and relations are broken off. Relations are resumed, however, when the Wilcoxes, by one of the convenient coincidences of which Mr. Forster so liberally avails himself, take a flat within a stone's-throw of the Schlegels' house in town. This time it is Margaret, the elder, plainer, but much more interesting sister, who is impressed by the Wilcoxes, and, after a false start, strikes up a close friendship with Mrs. Wilcox. At this point Mr. Forster resorts to a favourite device of his to develop his plot,—that of abruptly killing off one of the characters. Mrs. Wilcox, who is the victim of this habit of literary homicide, dies suddenly, leaving written instructions to her husband to present Howards End—her own property—to Margaret Schlegel. These instructions he deliberately disregards as fanciful and disloyal, and his family are disposed to harbour renewed resentment against the Schlegels. But in spite of himself he is convinced that Margaret's affection for his wife was disinterested, and a fresh *rapprochement* is brought about, which proceeds by leaps and bounds until Margaret consents to become his wife. Now the Schlegels, in their forthcoming, expansive way, had taken up and encouraged a half-baked young clerk with literary aspirations whom they first met at a concert. Leonard Bast is married to an undesirable wife with a past; his manners are uncouth and his character lamentably weak. But he has a romantic side to him, and the kindly, if injudicious, patronage of the Schlegels brings a ray of sunshine into his sordid life. This friendly interest, however, brings the Basts into contact with the Wilcoxes, and on the eve of Margaret's marriage leads to a painful disclosure of the previous relations between Mrs. Bast and Mr. Wilcox, and to an extraordinary act of self-sacrifice on the part of Helen Schlegel. The sequel is concerned with the unflinching way in which Margaret, belying the 'sloppiness' of her early career, uses the weapon of her knowledge to conquer her husband and rescue her sister from social outlawry. The situation is not a pleasant one; but it is impossible to deny the extreme cleverness with which Mr. Forster has utilised the lapse of Henry Wilcox to balance that of his sister-in-law, though we cannot bring ourselves to regard the latter as probable. Again, the sudden elimination of the wretched Leonard Bast is grotesquely contrived. The handling of incident is perhaps Mr. Forster's weakest point: it is often forced, artificial, and violent. There is no inevitable march in the progress of his story; it moves by jerks, though in between the jerks the movement is natural enough. He is at no pains to practise self-effacement, and reveals his prejudices at every turn. But if his defects are exasperating, his qualities are remarkable,—vivid characterisation, a happy command of dialogue, and a freakish humour. The clash of modern culture and modern materialism has seldom found a more vivid interpreter. There are many scenes in this story that will abide in the memory, but the best of all is the description of a performance of Beethoven's C minor Symphony in Queen's Hall.

60. Unsigned notice, *Observer*

6 November 1910, 8

Mr. E. M. Forster is astonishingly clever, but if he is acquiring a wider range and a greater subtlety of method, it is at the expense of much of the humour that made his first novels so delightful. He works on somewhat the same lines as Mr. Galsworthy, and an analogy might be traced between this book and *A Man of Property*. *Howard's End* is the history of the Wilcoxes and the Schlegels, people with fundamentally different habits of mind, whose destinies are inextricably mingled. The Wilcox family, practical, unimaginative, business-like, typically English, stand for the outer life of efficiency; the Schlegels, Margaret and Helen, for the intellectual and inner life. Margaret becomes the second wife of middle-aged Henry Wilcox; it is she who invades and breaks up the great Wilcox tradition. Her affection bridges the gulf between two irreconcilable points of view. A succession of small events, seemingly unimportant, but sketched with an infinity of pains, leads in a leisurely manner up to the moment when husband and wife are confronted with a definite moral issue, and then the catastrophe is precipitated in a scene of consummate mastery and incisiveness. The story of Helen's fall is disagreeable; perhaps it was necessary for the purpose, but it introduces a jarring note. None the less, Mr. Forster is a writer who stands head and shoulders above the ruck of his fellows; his observation and sense of character are remarkable, his art is undeniable.

61. R. A. Scott-James, 'The year's best novel', *Daily News*

7 November 1910, 4

'Only connect . . .' is Mr. Forster's motto. It is because he has taken this motto not only for his book but also for his method of work that he has achieved the most significant novel of the year. Those who seek to express a philosophic view of life in fiction generally strain their characters till they are puppets of their philosophy. Those, on the other hand, who are content to trace individual characters realistically are in danger at all times of losing the scheme and purpose of their work. It is because they do not 'connect'; because to write a novel near to nature on the one hand, and true to the larger vision on the other requires tremendous labour of thought making perception and wisdom fruitful; the fitting of the perception of little things with the perception of universal things; consistency, totality, *connection*. Mr. Forster has written a *connected* novel.

Mr. Forster's method is a sort of bridge between that of Mr. Conrad and that of Mr. Galsworthy. The former, I am told, starts the making of a story with an incident which impressed itself on his imagination, and round this primary situation the story is hinged; the latter, starting with a generalisation, selects facts which illustrate it. Both methods are legitimate, and the one by Mr. Conrad, the other by Mr. Galsworthy, have been successfully used. But who could say of *Howard's End* that the one method or the other had been adopted?

The novel rises like a piece of architecture full-grown before us. It is all bricks and timber, but it is mystery, idealism, a far-reaching symbol.

House and Home

And as it happens Howard's End, from which the title is taken, is itself a house. Though the scene is only occasionally placed in this old house, with its wych-elm, its garden, and its Hertfordshire environment, Howard's End is always the background of the story. It is always there as a soft refrain which comes back and back amid a hundred new situations. This house itself is a sort of symbol of everything in England, old and new, changeless, yet amid flux. It connects in itself two ideas which seem to be sundered as the Poles. First of all it is a *home*. To Mrs. Wilcox, who was born there, it stands for everything personal, intimate, cherished; not merely 'bricks and mortar,' but a 'Holy of Holies into which Howard's End had been transfigured.' But in the second place it is property; it is bricks and mortar simply; it is exchangeable for money; it is part of the economic order of things, and has no sacred connection save that which attaches to the 'rights of property.' For Henry Wilcox, and for Charles, his son, it is no home; it is only a house. 'To them Howard's End was a house: they could not know that to her it had been a spirit, for which she sought a spiritual heir.'

For Mrs. Wilcox thought she had found a spiritual heir to her home in Margaret Schlegel; and she had indicated her wishes in a little pencil note which the Wilcoxes ignored.

> May they not have decided even better than they supposed? Is it credible that the possessions of the spirit can be bequeathed at all? Has the soul offspring? A wych-elm tree, a vine, a wisp of hay with dew on it—can passion for such things be transmitted where there is no bond of blood? No, the Wilcoxes are not to be blamed. The problem is too terrific, and they could not even perceive a problem.

If Margaret Schlegel stands for the refinement which has survived culture, the personal force which combines intellect, perception, and charm, her sister Helen is more truly the antithesis to the Wilcoxes, or, to be precise, the eldest son Charles Wilcox. Helen is all that which is known as 'temperament.' With what vivacity Mr. Forster makes her talk, with what high spirits and impulsive generosity she always acts! She does not see so clearly as Margaret does the danger of the Schlegel life, which is all ideas, enlightenment, and fineness, the danger that it may become 'sloppy.' For a moment Helen had responded to the lure of the Wilcox energy, the pushful, practical, masterful makers of the world, the people who lived 'the outer life of "telegrams and anger."' She had responded, in her impulsive, slightly hysterical way, at the touch of a younger Wilcox, but she shrank away again to a settled hostility against it; whereas to Margaret this life—the life of 'telegrams and anger'—'was to remain a real force. She could not despise it, as Helen and Tibby affected to do. It fostered such virtues as neatness, decision, and obedience, virtues of the second rank, no doubt, but they have formed our civilization. They form character, too; Margaret could not doubt it: they keep the soul from becoming sloppy. How dare Schlegels despise Wilcoxes, when it takes all sorts to make a world?'

Poetry and the Economic Basis

For Mr. Forster does not let us forget that even Helen Schlegel, with all her indifference to material things, with her recklessness, her generosity, her habit of taking not thought, has a secured income of six hundred a year. And that is the great difference between her and Mr. Bart, the miserable little clerk, who yearned after the infinite, but was by pressure of poverty and social pretensions compelled to yearn even more after his lost umbrella. Helen is willing to do anything for the squalid Mr. Bart, because he is unfortunate, and because he has ideals. But Margaret is more practical without suffering loss on the finer side.

'The imagination (she says) ought to play upon money and realise it vividly, for it's the—the second most important thing in the world. It is so slurred over and hushed up, there is so little clear thinking—oh, political economy, of course, but so few of us think clearly about our own private incomes, and admit that independent thoughts are in nine cases out of ten the result of independent means. Money: Give Mr. Bart money, and don't bother about his ideals. He'll pick up those for himself.'

Margaret, then, does not give rein to her bias. It is Helen who is the *extreme* of the spiritual life, plunging into it like a gambler, seeing the moment but not seeing whither it leads. And her antithesis is the brutal Charles, who stands equally recklessly on his right of property —on the speed of his motor-cars, the decisiveness of his actions, the effectiveness of his anger and his telegrams. He is all prose, and goes to prison; Helen is all passion, and has a bastard child. But Margaret has her feet at least firmly planted on the earth, and she is able to make a success of marriage with Henry Wilcox.

> Only connect! That was the whole of her sermon. Only connect the prose and the passion, and both will be exalted, and human love will be seen at its height. Live in fragments no longer. Only connect, and the beast and the monk, robbed of the isolation that is life to either, will die.

In thus drawing together one or two of the threads with which the story supplies us, I may seem to have emphasised too much the theoretical or philosophical side of this novel. A philosophical novel it is, but its fineness as philosophy is just that which would have delighted the late William James. At all points it is life itself, experience itself, which is the touchstone and the fabric of Mr. Forster's theory. No cut-and-dried view of life, no summary of society, but a consciousness of the infinitely variable thing that is human nature, obedient to no laws but the laws of personality. If personality dwindles into a piece of mechanism in Charles Wilcox and diffuses itself into a lost aspiration in Mr. Bast, it is even so the product, albeit a wrecked product, of the millions of personal forces that have made England. Each of these persons whom he shows to us is pathetically individual—pathetically, because it is hardly possible to be otherwise when you expose a limited human soul in the naked light of the whole universe; and it is for this reason that Mr. Forster, vainly holding up before us an ethical ideal with hopeful intention, is often depressing to a bewildering extent. Yet the persons are too human to affect us long in this way. Charles is real enough to be hateful. Which of us has not known a Tibby, self-possessed, unbiassed in his narrow intellectual freedom, unaware of the world, and scornful of it? Mrs. Munt, the fussy aunt, is an admirable intrusion of comedy. Poor, squalid Mr. Bast, with his drunken 'Jacky,' his poverty, his democratic gentility, and his one romance in life, is an exquisite piece of diabolical character-drawing. And there is Evie, and Dolly, and the sweet Miss Avery; and permeating the book, like Howard's end itself, is the simple, dignified, homely figure of Mrs. Wilcox, whose personality haunts us even as the genius of the house seems to take wings of fancy in Mr. Forster's hands, and put us among fantastic, other-worldly things. 'Couldn't you and I camp out in this house for the night?' cries Helen, inflamed with fancies which its owners, who hated her, could never have understood.

'Because my plans ——'

'——Which you change in a moment.'

'Then because my life is great, and theirs are little,' said Helen, taking fire. 'I know of things they can't know of, and so do you. We *know* that there's poetry. They can only take them on hearsay. We know this is our house, because it feels ours. Oh, they may take the title deeds and the doorkeys, but for this one night we are at home.'

'It would be lovely to have you once more alone,' said Margaret. 'It may be a chance in a thousand.'

'Yes, and we could talk.' She dropped her voice. 'It won't be a very glorious story. But under that wych-elm ——'

There is life, imagination, and the very flame of action giving quality to this novel over and above the technique with which it is built up and the wisdom with which it is informed.

62. 'Villadom', unsigned review, *Nation*

viii, no. 7, 12 November 1910, 282–4

The habit of orthodox criticism is to be stiff or condescending to a new author when he first appears with an original book, and to increase the measure of praise according to his repeated successes. Mr. E. M. Forster has now given us four novels, and his last, *Howard's End*, will probably receive compound interest on whatever sum of approval was bestowed on *The Longest Journey*. It is as well. *Howard's End*, by its far-sighted criticism of middle-class ideas, is a book that says most effectively those very things that the intelligent minority feel, but rarely arrive at formulating.

The story is built out of the intercourse of the sisters, Margaret and Helen Schlegel, with the Wilcoxes, a typically prosperous British family. Helen and Margaret are neither 'English to the backbone' nor 'Germans of the dreadful sort.' They are children of an idealistic German father, who, after a life of variegated interests, had settled down in England and married a rich Englishwoman. The girls, who think for themselves, and are 'emancipated' in their ideas, naturally live the surface life of 'culture,' Continental travel, visiting friends, attending concerts, picture galleries, &c., which in general suffices to keep the woman of independent means from showing too consciously that she wants something better. The Schlegels have made the acquaintance of the Wilcoxes in a Continental hotel, and Helen is on a visit to Howard's End, Mrs. Wilcox's modest, old-fashioned house in Herts, when Paul, the youngest son, kisses her on the lawn by starlight, and an absurd squabble between Helen's aunt, Mrs. Munt, and Charles Wilcox, leads to the two families breaking off relations. Helen, at the outset, had been under the spell of the Wilcoxes. 'She had liked giving in to Mr. Wilcox, or Evie, or Charles; she had liked being told that her notions of life were sheltered or academic, that Equality was nonsense, Votes for Women nonsense, Socialism nonsense, Art and Literature, except when conducive to strengthening the character, nonsense. One by one the Schlegel fetiches had been overthown, and, though professing to defend them, she had rejoiced.' But when, the morning after the love passage, Paul comes down to breakfast looking frightened lest she should give him away, Helen 'feels for a moment that the whole Wilcox family is a fraud, just a wall of newspapers, and motor-cars, and golf-clubs, and that if it fell she should find nothing behind it but panic and emptiness.' Margaret defends the Wilcoxes. They represent to her 'the great outer life, which, though obviously horrid, often seems the real one.' But Helen knows that the Wilcoxes, once bereft of this 'outer life,' have nothing to fall back on. They 'dodge emotion.' They hold it of little importance, or if they recognise it they are afraid of it. On the other hand, it is true that the Wilcoxes have their hands on all the ropes. Their 'outer life' fosters such virtues as neatness, decision and obedience—virtues of the second rank, no doubt, but they have formed our civilisation. They form character, too; they keep the soul from becoming 'sloppy.' It seems destined that no further occasion will be given the two families of criticising one another, but fate has it otherwise. The Wilcoxes take one of the expensive new flats that shut out the light from the Schlegels' old house in Wickham Place, and soon Margaret finds herself on intimate terms with the sweet and retiring mother, Mrs. Wilcox, who, from the point of view of her over-energetic family, is as much behind the times as is the honest, unpretentious old house, Howard's End.

The artistic setting of the novel certainly owes much to the spiritual background, which is symbolised by the old-world atmosphere of Howard's End. We require something by which we can measure Mr. Wilcox, busy with his company promoting and his new fortune, made out of oil and rubber, his sound Imperialism, his motoring, his shooting, and his energy in local politics. Mrs. Wilcox and Howard's End both have spiritual grace, and the old house reflects the unobtrusive charm and settled standards which the pushing husband, the self-assertive son, Charles, and the athletic daughter, Evie, despise. But Mrs. Wilcox, who understands her family, is stricken suddenly and dies in a nursing home, leaving a scribbled message for her husband, 'I should like Miss Schlegel (Margaret) to have Howard's End.' This dying request, after being carefully debated by the Wilcoxes, is dismissed as 'unbusinesslike' and 'unlike mother,' the whim of an invalid, in fact, and the family, being destitute of imagination, are incapable of realising that Howard's End, which to them is merely a saleable property of bricks and mortar and a large garden, was a spiritual sanctuary to the dead woman. Several years pass, and when the Schlegels and the Wilcoxes come together again, Mr. Wilcox has grown tired of being left to his own devices by his married children, and Margaret feels solitary and old-maidish. She is thrilled by the idea of this elderly man turning to her for companionship, and when he offers her his hand and heart, she accepts gladly, despite Helen's bitter opposition.

In the working out of the fortunes of the two families, now united by marriage, Mr. Forster shows to great advantage his rare gift of philosophic criticism. His characters are real enough, but their importance as individuals is less than their significance as contemporary signposts. It is the ideas behind them, the code of manners and morals, and the web of forces, material and mental, that are woven before our eyes in the life of London, that Mr. Forster is deeply concerned with, and from the standpoint of the interested looker-on we can only admire the dexterity with which the disaster that overtakes the Wilcoxes is bound up with the fate of the insignificant clerk, Leonard Bast, and his disreputable wife, Jacky. Briefly, the Basts are befriended by the passionate Helen, and accidentally the disclosure is forced upon Margaret of an unsavory episode in Mr. Wilcox's past life. Margaret condones the past offence; but a little later, when Helen, who has taken refuge in Germany, discloses that the child she is going to bear will be illegitimate, Mr. Wilcox plays the part of the outraged moralist and the stern *père de famille*. Leonard Bast is, in fact, the father of Helen's child, and in a scuffle with him the bullying George commits what is technically manslaughter, and is sent to prison for three years. The shock of the tragedy of Leonard's death crumbles down Mr. Wilcox's philistine defences, and the novel ends with a retrospective chapter, in which a humbled Helen, a calm Margaret, and a broken-spirited Mr. Wilcox are shown living together peacefully in the tranquil atmosphere of the old house, Howard's End. We say that one must admire the ingenuity with which the fabric of the plot is woven out of the fortuitous yarn of the meetings and the accidental relations of the three sets of characters; but in closing the book, we perceive that Mr. Forster has sacrificed the inflexibility of artistic truth to the exigencies of his philosophical moral. There is too much ingenious dove-tailing of incidents, too much of accidental happenings, too much twisting and stretching and straining of human material for *Howard's End* to rank high as a work of art. The individuality of each figure is made obedient to the convenience of the author's purpose, and, though great pains are taken to make the whole story and all its parts probable, at critical junctures Helen's action or Mr. Wilcox's attitude are perceptibly strained to produce a dramatic situation. Not grossly strained, be it remarked, but perceptibly; but it is just this clever ingenuity that robs the work of artistic inevitability. It would, however, be doing both the author and our readers poor service to make much of a subsidiary defect in the author's accomplished method. The novel's original value, which is great, rests primarily on the acute analysis of the middle-class British code of ideas and standards, typified by the rise and progress of the Wilcoxes. Mr. Forster understands the outlook of Villadom perhaps better than the fourscore of writers who speak from the 'vantage ground of its bulwarks. He is no partisan, but renders justice in a manner that may well bring those he paints to sue for mercy.

63. 'The season's great novel', *Daily Mail*

17 November 1910

This review was signed 'M' and was by Archibald Marshall (1866–1934), prolific minor novelist, author of *Peter Binney, Undergraduate* (1899), *The House of Merrilees* (1905), *Exton Manor* (1907), etc.

Mr. E. M. Forster is not a new novelist in the sense of coming before the public with a first book. *Howard's End*, which has become a general subject of talk in literary circles, is his fourth novel, but with it he may be said to have arrived, as the phrase goes. He showed much of his power in his last book, *A Room with a View*, but *Howard's End* is a riper work altogether, and raises its author to a place among contemporary novelists which few even of those whose earlier work shows promise succeed in attaining to.

Howard's End is the name of a house, a little, old, rather inconvenient country house, not so very far from London. It belongs to the Wilcoxes, capable, business-like people, all clear and sane and effective on the outside, all muddled and wrong about the deeper things that really matter—matter at least to people like the Schlegels, who are contrasted with them throughout the story. The house also plays its part throughout. Mrs. Wilcox, to whom it actually belongs, and who loves it, dies suddenly, and leaves a pencilled note to say that she should like it to go to Margaret Schlegel, the elder of the two orphan sisters, knowing that she will cherish it as a possession, and feeling perhaps that her own bustling family will never value it beyond its appropriateness or otherwise as the sort of house they want to live in. But Mr. Wilcox tears up the paper, and Margaret hears nothing of the bequest until at the very end of the story, when she is married to Mr. Wilcox as his second wife and many other things have happened between them.

The contrast of character

The Schlegels, always on the look-out for originality, come across a pathetic, ineffective little clerk with leanings towards adventure both of the mind and body. He is married to a woman of no intelligence at all, who has entrapped him in his youth, and there is a breathless scene when Helen Schlegel rushes the pair of them down to Shropshire, where Mr. Wilcox is marrying off his daughter, and the startling fact bursts upon Margaret, whose own marriage is about to take place, that Mr. Wilcox during the lifetime of his first wife has had relations with the unspeakable and irresponsible 'Jacky.'

Helen also discovers the fact, and her piercing sympathy with the troubles of the poor little clerk brings about her sudden undoing. The way in which the truth, when it comes out, forms the pivot of the final struggle between Margaret's essential rightness of mind and her husband's crude and illogical want of principle is realised in a masterly way.

In the end there is happiness between the warring factions. Love and reason have triumphed. Unfortunately it is just here that Mr. Forster, having elaborated his theme at great length throughout the book, hastily takes leave of us with a very slight gathering up of the threads, and we are left wondering exactly how the happiness we are assured has descended once more upon Howard's End can have come about. We are not quite satisfied with his sketched-in explanation, and Mr. Wilcox's conversion somehow recalls that of Mr. Dombey.

But the faults of this book are as nothing compared to its merits. The way in which the characters—even those minor ones who have not been mentioned above—are made to live before us is of the essence of all great fiction. *Howard's End* is essentially a novel of character, but where it differs from a good deal of clever modern work done more or less upon the same lines is that Mr. Forster has gone back to the old canons of fiction and exhibited his characters in action. That is to say, he has made it his business to tell us a story about them. Things are always happening in *Howard's End*, and although there is a great deal of talk, and very good talk, both from the characters themselves and also from the author, it is not all talk. That is why *Howard's End* will be widely read. There will be many who will read it for the story alone, and they will be right to do so, for the best novels have always contained the best stories.

When Margaret Schlegel was looking out for a new house in London Mr. Wilcox suggested that his unoccupied house in Ducie-street might suit her. When she was engaged to him they looked over the house with the idea of living in it, and he told her that Ducie-street had huge drawbacks. 'There's a mews behind.'

Margaret could not help laughing. It was the first she had heard of the mews behind Ducie-street. When she was a possible tenant it had suppressed itself, not consciously, but automatically. The breezy Wilcox manner, though genuine, lacked the clearness of vision that is imperative for truth. When Henry lived in Ducie-street he remembered the mews; when he tried to let he forgot it; and if anyone had remarked that the mews must be either there or not, he would have felt annoyed, and afterwards have found some opportunity of stigmatising the speaker as academic. So does my grocer stigmatise me when I complain of the quality of his sultanas, and he answers in one breath that they are the best sultanas, and how can I expect the best sultanas at that price? It is a flaw inherent in the business mind, and Margaret may do well to be tender to it, considering all that the business mind has done for England.

This little passage is typical of Mr. Forster's method. He takes infinite trouble to devise little episodes and illustrations to show up his characters, instead of telling us what they are like. It is, of course, the method of the old, good novelists, but the clever moderns are apt to forget it. Invention means trouble, and it is much easier to write pages of analysis; only they are not so easy to read.

Mr. Forster's worldly philosophy

Another short quotation may serve to show the author presenting ideas, of which throughout the book he is delightfully prodigal.

Death destroys a man; the idea of Death saves him. Behind the coffins and the skeletons that stay the vulgar mind lies something so immense that all that is great in us responds to it. Men of the world may recoil from the charnel-house that they will one day enter, but Love knows better. Death is his foe, but his peer, and in their age-long struggle the thews of Love have been strengthened, and his vision cleared, until there is no one who can stand against him.

Howard's End is packed full of good things. It stands out head and shoulders above the great mass of fiction now claiming a hearing. The autumn season has brought us some good novels, but this is, so far, the best of them.

64. 'A fine novel', *Daily Graphic*

19 November 1910, 4

An unsigned notice.

Howard's End is a novel of high talent—the highest. That is praise which the reviewer reserves, or ought to reserve, for the work of an author whose future seems to him as certain as his present or his past. In the case of E. M. Forster's work there is no room for uncertainty. It is uneven; here and there, in this story as in *The Longest Journey*, which preceded it, there is a kind of formlessness, or rather, perhaps, an attempt to fill out or connect some masterly drawings of character, temperament, and of the way in which events mould or affect character and temperament—by the crude mechanism of ordinary fiction.

For example, the main theme of the novel is the conflict of temperament between people to whom thought, culture, art, and a noble spirit are the real things in life, and people to whom action, business, work, are supremely important. A French philosopher has indicated the outcome of the conflict in the phrase that all the things that matter take place in the realm of human thought. Such is E. M. Forster's opinion; and the two sisters who are his heroines, and neither of whom makes a success of her life according to the usual standards, are left triumphant over the practical Wilcoxes with whom they are placed in antithesis. But the ending is brought about, or at any rate is accompanied, by incidents which, in any other juxtaposition, we should call sensational; and which in their sober surroundings have a disturbing crudity. Perhaps that is E. M. Forster's intention; but, to use a phrase of the author's own, these incidents do not 'connect'; and, by raising a doubt in the mind as to their probability, give an air of unreality to the closing chapters of a book which, in its descriptive and reflective power, is, as we begun by saying, of the highest talent.

65. Unsigned review, *Westminster Gazette*

19 November 1910, 16

In *Howards End* Mr. E. M. Forster has written a very remarkable book, though he has hardly achieved an altogether satisfactory novel. It is in his treatment of the 'personal relations' that he excels—those factors in human life which stood for 'the real' in the lives of Margaret and Helen Schlegel as against the mere externals of intercourse which in their strange elliptic parlance they sum up in the two symbols 'telegrams and anger.' Symbols mean far more to those two women than the actual facts of life; they are a curious complex pair, living in a world of dreams and ideals, yet with a far-sighted common-sense sometimes materialising, contradictory traits of which we see the germ both in parentage and education. Mr. Forster has handled these two women with an intimacy which is little short of amazing. Perhaps Helen is not always quite convincing, especially at the supreme crisis of her life; but his analysis of the almost more complex Margaret, who can step down from the clouds to make a commonplace marriage with a middle-aged unimaginative gentleman, whom she can love well if not passionately, is quite extraordinary. He gets inside the very soul of the woman, and touches with an equally sure hand the trivial things of every day and the great moments of her development. It is almost with surprise that we realise that the author, who can show such very unusual insight into the rarefied atmosphere of the idealist's inner life, can at the same time appreciate all that goes to the making of the more conventional types. His delineation of the Wilcoxes, who stand for the contradiction of everything which the Schlegels have taught themselves to cherish, is no less admirable than his treatment of the two women and their very individual brother, one of the most lifelike and remarkable portraits in the book. To give an outline of the story would be to give no idea of the value of the book, which is dependent on the 'personal relations' of those involved, in the contrast and balance of character. Mr. Forster has little sense of form; his book has no constructive harmony. But he is something of a seer, something of a mystic, though his mysticism is somewhat intangible, and he can hardly put it into shape. The strange influence of Howards End, realised by the Schlegels rather than by the Wilcoxes, to whom it belonged; the curious personality of Miss Avery, who makes, as it were, a connecting-link between the Schlegels and Howards End, are suggested rather than insisted on. But with Mrs. Wilcox, the real owner of Howards End, who recognised Margaret as her spiritual heir, and who, in leaving her Howards End, felt that she was conveying an atmosphere to one who could appreciate it, Mr. Forster is more definite. 'I feel,' says Margaret to her sister after Mrs. Wilcox's death, 'that you and I and Henry are only fragments of that woman's mind. She knows everything; she is everything. She is the house and the tree that leans over it. People have their own deaths as well as their own lives; and, even if there is nothing beyond death, we shall differ in our nothingness. I cannot believe that knowledge such as hers will perish with knowledge such as mine. She knew about realities. She knew when people were in love, though she was not in the room. I don't doubt she knew when Henry deceived her.' Mrs. Wilcox thus represents a sort of over-soul. But for this development we had been quite unprepared, and herein lies the real weakness of Mr. Forster's book. He has given us no cause to expect this evolution. He has evidently a strong impression which he wishes to produce, but he fails to produce it because of his treatment of Mrs. Wilcox in the flesh. Spiritualists would doubtless tell us that manifestation on this material plane has but little relation to a higher one. Mr. Forster is working in a particular medium, and he must use that medium to get his effect. He fails with Mrs. Wilcox, perhaps because he takes too much for granted on the part of his reader. And his book suffers in consequence. Nevertheless it remains quite one of the most remarkable novels of the year.

66. Unsigned review, *Morning Post*

24 November 1910, 16

'Only connect.' It was clever of Mr. E. M. Forster to put this cryptic injunction on the title-page of his new novel, *Howards End*, for it aroused our curiosity. If only we could be quite sure what these words meant we felt that the acute and illuminating analysis of the two families of Schlegel and Wilcox with which the early part of the book was concerned would find a place in some larger philosophy of life, and while we played with the freakish idea that the words were addressed to a dilatory municipal department that refused the benefits of electricity to a house that was wired and waiting we possessed our souls more or less, in patience. In Chapter XXII we were rewarded. The explanation was to be found in the lesson that Margaret Schlegel was to teach her husband, the excellent and courtly Mr. Wilcox. Only connect! That was the whole of her sermon. 'Only connect the prose and the passion and both will be exalted, and human love will be seen at its height. Live in fragments no longer, only connect, and the beast and the monk, robbed of the isolation that is life to either, will die.' This is only one aspect of Mr. Forster's philosophy of 'connecting'; it is not merely concerned with linking into a harmonious whole the sensual instincts and the ascetic revulsions of the individual. It has a wider sweep than that; by it, we take it, philanthropy is not to be allowed to sink into a system, nor business into an excuse for breaking all the teachings of morality. The harmony so lacking in our modern life is to be found in it somehow or other. To explain this panacea is the ambitious object of *Howards End*, and if it is not altogether achieved the attempt is certainly justified by an able and profoundly interesting piece of work.

Readers of Mr. E. M. Forster's previous novels, particularly *A Room with a View*, do not need to be reminded that he is a writer with a highly sensitised imagination and real intellectual ability. His previous books have shown what the schoolmaster calls 'steady progress,' and *Howards End* is undoubtedly the best piece of work he has yet produced, and ranks as one of the really significant features of the present publishing season. Probably the reason for this is that Mr. Forster is true to his own philosophy. He is not content to give merely haphazard fragments of life: he 'connects,' moving steadily and industriously to a comprehensive view. He has yet some way to go. He still writes chiefly as a student who has not yet quite connected the meaning of life with life itself; thus the outstanding incidents of his book, such as Helen's love affair and Leonard's death, strike us as unreal, or only half real, and it is clear that Mr. Forster always shirks the description of objective events. Nearly everything that 'happens' in his book takes place off the stage, as in Greek tragedy; and there is not even a messenger to tell us clearly what has happened, only a principal actor in the incident to be affected psychologically. Obviously the main intention of Mr. Forster in giving his book the title *Howards End*, and in then linking the fortunes of his characters to a typical old English house in the country is to show the importance of the connection of the past and the present, and to give to the 'back to the land' cry a new and deeper meaning. Perhaps in a later book he will arrive at the point of connecting the objective and the subjective (if this odious jargon may pass for once) and so produce a really great novel.

It must not be imagined from the manner of our criticism that Mr. Forster is in any way dull. His novel at the worst may be regarded as a series of brilliantly sustained table-talks engaged in by people as alive, perhaps to most of us more alive, than the majority of people we meet in everyday life. From the first chapter, which contains Helen Schlegel's letter to her sister Margaret describing her visit to the Wilcoxes, to the last chapter, when the Wilcox family submits as gracefully as is possible to people whose eyes are fixed entirely on material ends, to the triumph of the hated German family there is a continual crackle of good things—quaint and suggestive descriptions of persons and things, lively contrasts of different points of view, clever examples of the art of pure conversation, and occasional bits of satire happily expressed.

[The rest of the review is taken up by illustrative examples.]

67. Unsigned review, *Athenaeum*

ii, no. 4336, 3 December 1910, 696

This novel, taken with its three predecessors, assures its author a place amongst the handful of living writers who count. It is the story of a conflict between points of view. The Schlegels are clever, sensitive, refined; they have a feeling for beauty and truth, a sense of justice and of proportion; they stand for what is best in modern civilization: the Wilcoxes are vulgar, blatant, and brutal; such time as they can spare from money-making they devote to motors and bridge and suburban society; they stand for all that is worst. The two families are thrown together. The younger Miss Schlegel, Helen, is uncompromising; one cannot touch pitch without being soiled, she feels; the elder, Margaret, who refuses 'to draw my income and sneer at those who guarantee it', marries Mr. Wilcox. Helen and the reader have to watch Margaret's fine edges grow blunt, till at last, by one of those *dei ex machinis* of which Mr. Forster is too fond, the irreconcilables are reconciled, and some of them live happily ever after.

The defects of this novel are that the protagonists are points of view rather than characters; that the two chief events—Margaret's marriage and Helen's seduction—are unconvincing; and that, in our judgment, the moral is wrong. We do not object to didacticism; but we cannot admit that what is bad ought to be loved, or that the finer feelings are not too high a price even for enlarged sympathies. The great thing in the book is the sisters' affection for each other; personal relationships, except those between lovers, have never, we venture to say, been made more beautiful or more real. But, from beginning to end, it is full of brilliant and delicate strokes, which reveal, with surprising clearness, those subtle states of mind and elusive but significant traits that are apt to escape even the most acute observation.

68. A. C. Benson, letter to E. M. Forster

9 December 1910

Arthur Christopher Benson (1862–1925), the son of Archbishop Benson of Canterbury, was a Scholar of King's College, Cambridge, and Master of Magdalene College, Cambridge from 1915 until his death. He was a poet and a writer on literary subjects, contributing volumes on Rossetti (1905), Fitzgerald (1905) and Pater (1906) to the *English Men of Letters* series.

You will think me very discourteous or very perverse not to have written to you before about your book. But I wanted my mother to read it and tell me what she thought, because I look upon her as a remarkable instance of a very feminine woman and at the same time a highly intellectual one. She is Henry Sidgwick's[1] sister, and has much of his power [. . . .] She says 'Might not the drift of H.E. be called Pragmatism? What chiefly seems to me to emerge is that, so to say, situations make their own ethics: that instead of having a fixed code of morals, a better thing is to be led by desire and impulse, and to find in the situations this leads to the true moral of fact. And that this leads to great general misunderstanding of other people and their lives, and to an absence of all "being shocked". To this is to be added "connect, connect", by which I suppose the author means that it finds and also establishes hitherto unthought-of connections in the one life, and with all the others who share in the problem. . . . This is most inadequate, and please let us talk about it. It interested me enormously, and one will never forget it. It certainly hits the want of elasticity in some codes, and accounts for the general mellowing in all good lives; but it also has tremendous dangers?'

I think this criticism which I copy down just as it was written will interest you. My own feeling about the book—which stirred me

[1] Henry Sidgwick (whose sister was Benson's mother, and whose wife became Principal of Newnham) lived from 1838 to 1900 and was Professor of Moral Philosophy at Cambridge from 1883. He wrote a number of books on ethics and political economy.

very much—was much the same; but being partly a determinist and partly a pragmatist I didn't feel the emphasis as my mother does. (I felt it to be poetical rather than philosophical.) My own belief is that people *do* act by desire and impulse, almost invariably, and that moral codes are mere names of psychological genera and species, without any particular inspiration or power of restriction. I took the book rather to be a study of the immense strength of sturdy and conventional humanity, just as the sparrow farcs best among the birds—and the contrast between Margaret and Helen seemed to me to be another point—the emotional and intellectual nature, with and without moral force.

I felt throughout that the appeal of the *house* was a little strained—I should rather have expected the *conventionalists* to have felt that than the idealists. . . . But I must not go on—the book interested me very greatly, and gave me the beautiful sensation of a sudden *uplifting* of thought every now and then, like a mountain breaking out of a cloud!

69. 'A story of remarkably queer people', *Western Mail* (Cardiff)

10 December 1910, 9

An unsigned notice.

Seldom have we read a really good story with queerer people in it than *Howard's End*, by E. M. Forster. The Schlegels, Wilcoxes, and Basts will take a deal of beating for oddity. Few people would care for them as neighbours, except, perhaps, to study as psychological curiosities. The Schlegels are half English, half German, but with few German characteristics that we can see. The sisters Helen and Margaret are cast in no ordinary mould, and their brother —though more normal—has his own peculiarities. Mr. Wilcox is a study in himself: but his son Charles and his young wife are fairly natural, and as such shine like a green oasis in this wilderness of eccentrics. When Mrs. Wilcox dies and Margaret Schlegel marries the widower we look out naturally for squalls, and we get them. Nevertheless, the Mr. Wilcox of the second marriage has toned down considerably, and it is a surprise to us when we learn that even such as he should have committed himself with the female Bast earlier in his career. Yet so it was, and it set up a stumbling block between him and Margaret, whilst another came when Helen compromised herself with the male Bast, who was afterwards to pay for his romantic imprudence with his life. At the close of the book all seem to have made up their minds to become a bit more normal—and so we leave them. There is a bit of the sex problem in this book, and a lot about social questions, and the dialogue is perhaps the best part of it, being managed with great skill throughout. Nevertheless, very few of the dramatis personae have a real human ring about them: they are for the most part marionettes, and we say good-bye to the lot without any particular feeling of sorrow.

70. Unsigned review, *World*

20 December 1910, 943

There is no doubt that this novel has been one of the sensations of the autumn season, and, in that respect, it has been made—not wisely—to overshadow Mr. Arnold Bennett's *Clayhanger*, which is a much greater book. Nevertheless, we must congratulate Mr. Forster upon the tremendous strides which he has made since *The Room with a View*: he has really found himself this time. *Howard's End* is a work of the highest talent. The author has not merely thought of a plot and expanded it, but he has imagined people—real people—and logically worked out their reactions upon one another under given circumstances. The Wilcoxes and the Schlegels—the one family British, unromantic, businesslike, banal, but essentially men of action; the other of a mixed race, full of ideals gleaned from art and literature, steeped in the poetry of life but blunderers in its prose—impulsive, yet dreamers—are the two opposing tendencies which clash throughout. We shall not attempt to tell Mr. Forster's story: it is full of surprises, which must come upon the reader unprepared. In fact, there are too many surprises. Mr. Forster has yet to become more supple in his use of incident. Any given circumstance or action is possible in real life, but mere possibility is only an excuse for the amateur. The master must aim at probability. The climax of this novel, which begins with what passed between Helen Schlegel and Leonard Bast at the inn, is not probable. To say it is horrible is beside the point, for so is the story of Electra: but that Helen and Leonard, given what we are told about them, would have so acted is a serious violation of probability, especially as we think that the latter character is too shadowy. We learn much of his mind, but too little of his will. Mr. Forster's book has grave faults, but it is very good in spite of all. He has abundantly that delightful sense of humour, based on a delicate sense of incongruity in things usually accepted, which is so typical of to-day, especially at the Universities: he has great power of description, shown particularly in his passage on the view from the Purbeck Hills; and he has sympathy, without which he could not have drawn Mrs. Wilcox, the only pleasant member of the family. However, Mr. Forster, in company with all the modern school of Wells, Galsworthy, and Bennett, is one-sided in his sympathies. These writers cannot bring themselves to present fairly, as Henry James and George Meredith do, the side of English life supposed here to be represented by the Wilcoxes. Thousands of Wilcoxes did not die to make England, it was something far better. The modern intellectual will not see this, for his sympathies are Radical. The type of Sir Philip Sidney is the real type, and it still exists in plenty, but not obviously, like the Wilcoxes.

71. 'Jacob Tonson' (Arnold Bennett), notice, *New Age*

n.s. viii, no. 11, 12 January 1911, 257

Arnold Bennett (1867–1931), author of many novels including *The Old Wives' Tale* (1908), lived in Paris from 1902 to 1912. His novel *Clayhanger* was published, like *Howards End*, in 1910 (cf. No. 70).

Now I am in a position to state that no novel for very many years has been so discussed by the *élite* as Mr. Forster's *Howard's End*. The ordinary library reader knows that it has been a very considerable popular success; persons of genuine taste know that it is a very considerable literary achievement; but its triumph is that it has been mightily argued about during the repasts of the *élite*. I need scarcely say that it is not Mr. Forster's best book; no author's best book is ever the best received—this is a rule practically without exception. A more curious point about it is that it contains a lot of very straight criticism of the *élite*, or at any rate of the first census of the *élite*. And yet this point is not very curious either. For the *élite* have no objection whatever to being criticised. They rather like it, as the alligator likes being tickled with peas out of a pea-shooter. Their hides are superbly impenetrable. And I know not which to admire the more, the American's sensitiveness to pea-shooting, or the truly correct Englishman's indestructible indifference to it. Mr. Forster is a young man. I believe he is still under thirty, if not under twenty-nine. If he continues to write one book a year regularly, to be discreet and mysterious, to refrain absolutely from certain themes, and to avoid a too marked tendency to humour, he will be the most fashionable novelist in England in ten years time. His worldly prospects are very brilliant indeed. If, on the other hand, he writes solely to please himself, forgetting utterly the existence of the *élite*, he may produce some first-class literature. The responsibilities lying upon him at this crisis of his career are terrific. And he so young too!

HOWARDS END

(American edition) 1911

72. Unsigned review, *New York Times*

xvi, 19 February 1911

This review was entitled 'A novel that suggests the work of Galsworthy but lacks the Galsworthian strength'.

The note of fatuous placidity on which *Howards End* concludes recalls Charles Godfrey Leland's excellent quatrain:

'De gustibus', 't is stated,
'Non disputandum est'.
Which means, when 't is translated,
That all is for the best.

As a social philosopher, evidently, Mr. Edward M. Forster has not yet arrived at any very positive convictions. Having deferentially inclined a trifle toward each of the prevalent opinions, he gracefully recovers his balance on the fence: no combatant, he.

Yet *Howards End* is fashioned in the likeness of the sociological-psychological novel. Its three families are evidently designed to epitomize three distinct social strata; their intercourse presents some possible phases of the relationship between these classes, and each individual character consistently maintains his own peculiar 'social attitude'. The three families are the half-German Schlegels, cultured idealists of the leisure class; the all-English Wilcoxes, hard-headed men of affairs, and the also English Basts, unhappy under-dogs of the present social system. Leonard Bast, an ignominious insurance clerk, is a prey to ill-advised yearnings for culture and spiritual adventure. The responsibility for his financial ruin and the moral ruin of his degraded wife belongs to Mr. Wilcox. But Mr. Wilcox, who exemplifies the dextrous practicality, the intellectual sophistry, and the taint of sensuality characteristic of the money-making type, is equally conscienceless—on both charges, being constitutionally averse to all soft notions of 'personal responsibility'.

Helen Schlegel, who insists upon personal relations as the only things of value in life, and upon personal responsibility as the only remedy for social injustice, undertakes, with impressive generosity, to help Mr. Wilcox's victims, only to be herself drawn into a liaison with the wretched Leonard. It remains for her sister Margaret to exhibit wiser idealism, sensibly tempered by an appreciation of practical values. Her specialty is 'seeing life whole and seeing it steadily'. As Mr. Wilcox's second wife her tolerance and sympathy enable her to pardon the excesses of both her husband and her sister, to reconcile them, and as far as possible to retrieve their errors. After the violent death of Leonard, the consequent imprisonment of Mr. Wilcox's son, and the birth of Helen's illegitimate child—circumstances which Mr. Forster rises to contemplate from mystical heights, intoning, 'Let Squalor be turned into Tragedy, whose eyes are the stars and whose hands hold the sunset and the dawn'. Howards End, the house which Mr. Wilcox's first wife had loved and with prophetic intentions desired to leave to Margaret Schlegel, is awarded to her, in the terms of her husband's will, as a sort of reward of merit, and the story ends with entire cheerfulness on the part of the author. 'All is for the best'.

Among its multiplicity of 'motifs' the reader of *Howards End* will distinguish the shadowing counterparts of certain themes which have been handled with greater vigor and discrimination by Mr. Galsworthy in *The Country House*, *The Man of Property*, and *The Fraternity*, and by Miss Sinclair in *The Divine Fire*. Mr. Forster's métier would seem to be conventional comedy. To that his sense of character values is entirely adequate, while there his blithe manner and journalistic wittiness of phrase serve him well. But he evinces neither power nor inclination to come to grips with any vital human problem.

73. An American summing-up, *Current Opinion* (USA)

l, April 1911, 454

An unsigned review.

England has hailed *Howard's End* with enthusiasm. We are a trifle puzzled and a trifle bored. The author's name is new to us, but it seems to have graced the title pages of more books than one. The *Daily Mail* (London) indorses the work as the great novel of the season. The book takes its name from a house, a little, old, rather inconvenient country house, not so very far from London. This house belongs to the Wilcoxes, capable business-like people, all clear and sane and effective on the outside, all muddled and wrong about the deeper things that really matter—matter at least to people like the two sisters, Margaret and Helen Schlegel, who are contrasted with them throughout the book. Altho the types described are British, they are, on the whole, thinks the *Globe* (New York), broadly human. As literature, the writer goes on to say, the story reaches a very high mark and ranks with the best that has been done by Galsworthy, Wells, or Arnold Bennett. The book, remarks the Brooklyn *Eagle*, with considerably less enthusiasm, 'seems to be an arraignment of our industrial civilization for killing the spiritual element in life and for weakening the sense of personal responsibility for the black spots of our social system. But the arraignment is by no means clear, the author does not suggest a remedy, and in the end the most spiritually-minded girl in the book makes a wreck of her life in a distressing way, for which neither the industrial situation nor anything else except a set of unhappily disordered nerves is responsible. You write about the book as a social study, because its characters lack the strength which compels you to think about them as individuals.'

[Quotes the *New York Times* review (No. 72).]

The astute literary editor of the Boston *Transcript* regards the novel as 'a scrap book into which Mr. Forster has gathered, without form or coherence, his ideas concerning human actions and the human mind.' Like the authors of the two other books discussed by us this month, Forster attempts to delineate life, not to tell a story. Like Wells, if his philosophy is obscure, his wit at least is incisive. Elia W. Peattie, of the Chicago *Tribune*, insists that the author must be a woman. She writes:

In feeling the book is feminine; but it is not to be gainsaid that a number of the strongest masculine writers of our times have been able to represent the feminine mind, with its irrational yet dramatic succession of moods, better than any woman can do it. It may be that E. M. Forster is one of these, but my impression is that the writer is a woman of a quality of mind comparable to that of the Findlater sisters or to May Sinclair.[1]

The particular allure of these writers is almost as different to define as personality itself. Their methods are so fine and high that to make mere ingenuity one of their aids is superfluous indeed. Plot is an artificial contrivance which they do not require to strengthen the purport or increase the interest of their tales. Character, approached from the psychological avenue, is their specialty, and however scientifically accurate they may be, they transcend mere science by their art, their imagination and their subtlety, and produce a result of great vividness and considerable perpetuity.

[1] May Sinclair (1865–1946) was an English novelist better known in America than in England, her most famous work perhaps being *The Divine Fire* (1904). She was a keen psychologist in her view of her characters, and has been described as 'almost a major novelist, who had the misfortune to be born too early for her destined public'.

74. D. H. Lawrence, letter to E. M. Forster

Undated, probably 1915

The letter was sent from Greatham in Sussex, where the Lawrences stayed in 1915 in a cottage lent them by the novelist and poet Viola Meynell.

Thank you for *Howard's End*—It got hold of me and not being a critical person I thank the Lord for it, and what he gives me. Only perhaps the end—broken Henry's remain Henry's as I know to my cost—It's a beautiful book, but now you must go further—

. . . .

75. Katherine Mansfield's Journal

May 1917

Katherine Mansfield (1888–1923), the short story writer, was born in New Zealand and came to London in 1908. Her best-known books are *In a German Pension* (1911) and *The Garden Party* (1922). She married John Middleton Murry in 1918.

Reprinted from *The Journal of Katherine Mansfield* (Constable, 1954), 120, by permission of The Society of Authors as the literary representative of the Estate of Katherine Mansfield, and by permission of Alfred A. Knopf, Inc.

Putting my weakest books to the wall last night I came across a copy of *Howard's End* and had a look into it. But it's not good enough. E. M. Forster never gets any further than warming the teapot. He's a rare fine hand at that. Feel this teapot. Is it not beautifully warm? Yes, but there ain't going to be no tea.

And I can never be perfectly certain whether Helen was got with child by Leonard Bast or by his fatal forgotten umbrella. All things considered, I think it must have been the umbrella.

HOWARDS END

(American edition) 1921

76. 'R. H.', review, *New Republic*

xxvi, 20 April 1921, 246

Few modern fictionists have revealed so robust a sense of the elusive and intangible as one finds in this novel of E. M. Forster's. And the main reason, one decides, is that the author of *Howards End* has realized the importance of relating even the most tentative conclusion about life as firmly as possible to the whole of life. Many adventures into cryptic borderlands have seemed to detach themselves from other phases of thought and feeling as if unable to bear the touch of a too crass reality. But Forster stands four square to the 'winds and odors of life,' presenting a rich complex of characters and reactions from which to evolve the more delicate nuances of his theme.

'Only to connect!' says Margaret Wilcox, looking deep through the prosaic kindliness and competence of her husband. Connect what? Why the gulls and the stars and the wych-elm and the tender cruelties of love itself with the garage, the motors, the nervous stupidity of Dolly and the middle-aged materialism of Henry Wilcox. To connect ricks of food and over-furnished dining-rooms with a hungry clerk who spends money for concrete and walks alone all night in the country. To see abyss and plains and mountain peaks clearly enough to recognize the common elements of all. This is of course an ancient task, ancient and possibly eternal, but in the story of *Howards End* it is essayed with rare insight and originality. Neither is it as serious as all this sounds. The book is entrancingly human with much of that deep-running humor that bubbles up from the heart of things.

The time is about ten years ago when Pan-Germanism and English Imperialism were being discussed discreetly, but in the same breath. The novel is a reprint, having been published at this earlier date and since then long out of print. An evidence of soundness is the fact that one reads it without any feeling of its having been bowled over by the war. The people are alive. The dialogue is apt and revealing. Margaret and Helen Schlegel are two wealthy and spirited young women living in London with their younger brother. With only Aunt Juley to visit them and remonstrate occasionally, the sisters lead an alert, independent existence, concerned a bit consciously over Art and Thought, but fearless and unusually clear-eyed.

'Some ladies do without hotels. Are you aware that Helen and I have walked alone over the Apennines with our luggage on our backs?'

'I wasn't aware, and if I can manage it, you will never do such a thing again.'

These two remarks suggest the respective mental attitudes of Margaret and her elderly husband. But if anyone could connect a Henry Wilcox with a subtler and more far-reaching world than he had known it would be such a person as Margaret Schlegel. In spite of her impetuosity she has a sustaining simplicity and patience. She is affectionately tolerant except when she denounces Henry in one splendid outburst at his hypocritical judgment of her sister. The same poise which has kept her indulgent of his blindness supports her condemnation and allows her to spare nothing of the bitter truth. The same intellectual steadiness enables her to pull together the broken threads of life at Howards End. In their helter-skelter eagerness she and Helen had reached a plane of the unseen which transcended the security of the whole Wilcox clan who with all their capability had never really learned to say 'I.'

Dramatic values are expertly managed. The breadth and casualness of the approach forms a specious background for the poignant climax which holds one to the last page.

77. Unsigned notice, *Dial*

lxxi, October 1921, 483

Howards End is a reprint which is new to the United States and should be welcomed here. The author has a keenness of perception of small encounters which is one of the essentials of fine narrative. His people are nervous, sensitive, alive. It is in his effort at symbolism that he fails, and spiritual values blur in the too sharp light of melodrama. Life may be like the end of this book, but the end of this book is not life-like. It is well worth reading for its beginning.

78. George B. Dutton, review, *Springfield Sunday Republican*

(Springfield, Massachusetts) 1 January 1922, 11a

George Burwell Dutton (1881–1930) was educated at Williams College, Massachusetts, and at Harvard University. He taught English at Williams College from 1910, becoming Professor of English in 1921.

One of the most arresting of recent novels is not recent. *Howard End* by E. M. Forster, is a reprint of an English book written over 10 years ago. It is a work of such unusual flavor that one is glad to have it brought to the attention of Americans.

'Only connect . . .' is the inscription on the title page, and in a way that is the theme of the novel—the necessity for establishing relationships, for seeing things in their entirety. The variations upon the theme unfold as in a symphony with exquisite naturalness.

'Only connect . . .'—To connect the prose and the passion of life, to live in fragments no longer, so that 'the beast and the monk, robbed of the isolation that is life to either, will die.' To connect our abstractions with facts, to relate conditions to individual and thus reveal the fallacy of the 'talk of impersonal forces, this cant about God doing what we're too slack to do ourselves.' To connect 'the transitoriness of life with its eternal youth—connect without bitterness until all men are brothers.' To connect oneself with what one condemns, until judgment is tempered by understanding.

'Proportion is the final secret.' 'The business man who assumes that this life is everything, and the mystic who asserts that it is nothing, fail on this side and on that, to hit the truth.' Yet one must not begin by seeking proportion. 'Only prigs do that.' Rather, a sense of proportion must grow out of experience, out of life itself.

It will readily be seen that the novel is in a way one of those adventures among generalizations to which, according to Mr H. G. Wells, the future belongs. Yet the generalizations are not those that Mr Wells most emphasizes and the modern reader of fiction most expects. They are not economic or sociological but rather philosophical in the sense that they involve some of the ultimate questions about personality, its development, and its value.

So unusual is it to get hold of a novel of ideas of this character that perhaps the appraising critic is tempted to stress them overmuch. But to have adventure there must be adventurers, and certainly this perilous journey among generalizations is taken by an interesting and varied and actual set of men and women. The characters, despite the fact that they come into contact with ideas, are not nebulous.

Fundamentally they are divided into two groups, the Schlegels and the Wilcoxes. The Schlegels of the world are they who think personal relations and the truths pertaining to them are the supreme fact in man's universe. The Wilcoxes are not so. They are the practical ones of life, that miss life's essence. Yet Margaret Schlegel, with her beautiful serene honesty can perceive that 'if the Wilcoxes hadn't worked and died in England for thousands of years, you and I couldn't sit here without having out throats cut. . . . Without their spirit life might never have moved out of protoplasm.'

Around Howards End, the old remodeled farmhouse owned by the Wilcoxes, the symbol of those personal relations that Wilcoxes cannot comprehend, the story revolves. There are excursions into the London of glittering and freakish activity, but after the fret of modern civilization, it is Howards End that furnishes calm.

It is at Howards End that Henry Wilcox, assured, truculent, successful when he first meets Margaret Schlegel, finally attains to something of her poise and vision. The stages of that process constitute the main story.

One finds it difficult to convey without the effect of exaggeration an adequate notion of the charm and rich humanity of the book. On the other hand *Howards End* is far from being a perfect novel. The light that plays over its pages is at times rather parching. The story is now and then a trifle shadowy. Personality is occasionally though not often sacrificed to the pursuit of the ideal of personality. The behavior of characters in a crisis is not always satisfying.

But the work is nevertheless one to linger over. It is the sort of book you are impelled to read with your pencil. It is full of wise sayings. It gives one a sense of space, of amplitude, that most new books lack. And it is remarkably sane.

79. T. Sturge Moore, letter to W. B. Yeats

20 April 1911

Thomas Sturge Moore (1870–1944) was a poet and wood engraver. He was also a member of the Academic Committee of the Royal Society of Literature, which first met in April 1911; its function, in the words of Lord Haldane in his inaugural address, being 'to attend to the standard of style in this country. . . . Style means form. Form and matter are never wholly separable'.

The thirty original members of the Academic Committee (one of whom was Yeats) made up a roll-call of the most famous names of the time, creative and academic. Yeats had suggested nominating Hilaire Belloc, Alfred Doughty and Wilfred Scawen Blunt to the R.S.L.; no subsequent letter from him to Sturge Moore took up the latter's counter-proposal of Forster.

Reprinted from *W. B. Yeats and T. Sturge Moore: Their Correspondence 1901–1937*, ed. Ursula Bridge (Routledge & Kegan Paul, 1953).

I think young Forster should be nominated; he at least has always tried for literature and nothing but literature. Each one of his novels has been better worth reading. He is clean. He is young. We shall very likely show foresight in electing him. I would much rather vote for him than Blunt. E. M. Forster, who wrote *Howard's End*, *A Room with a View*, *Where Angels Fear to Tread*. He has quite a following and of the right sort. I have no doubt Binyon and Newbolt would be willing to nominate him.

Why go for people hopelessly prostituted in politics and journalism when one could have a man like that! It is insane! Belloc? No! a thousand times no! It is disgusting. You read *A Room with a View* and see what you think.

THE CELESTIAL OMNIBUS

1911

80. Unsigned notice, *Daily Telegraph*

17 May 1911, 4

Mr. E. M. Forster's exact intention in some of these stories is a little vague and elusive, so that from time to time one has the impression that pleasant though they are to read, they must have been even pleasanter to write. Especially is this so with 'Other Kingdom,' which, we fancy, a good many readers will give up as a bad job somewhere about the middle, but then, let it be added, there are many more who will enjoy it to the end. Of the other five our favourites are the first, 'The Story of a Panic,' and 'The Curate's Friend.' The former is a most poetical and delightful piece of writing, which describes how an English boy of 14, holiday-making with a party of dullish people in Italy, suffers a change, miraculously wrought, from a lethargic, peevish lad into an elfin creature, a spirit of the woods, for whom henceforth life among mortals, cribbed and confined between four walls, is impossible. We leave him escaping into the woods, while the Italian boy, the only one of the party who has understood his secret, falls dead in his effort to aid his escape. It is a fanciful tale, full of charm and power, and shows Mr. Forster in a very different mood from the acute reality of his *Howard's End*, which dissected real people with so much adroitness. *The Celestial Omnibus* is in the same vein, an allegory of the real and unreal, the world of imagination as against the fairyland of commonsense. As we have hinted, Mr. Forster here writes a little too much for himself, and pays hardly enough attention to the readers who may clamber after him in the dark, but there is great charm in the volume, and it will be welcomed by that public which the author has gained for himself. Mr. Forster is always distinguished in his work, but we hope that he will not become 'precious,' because as yet he has not shown that it is necessary for him to do so to get his full effects.

81. 'A book of phantasies', *Daily Mail*

19 May 1911, 11

An unsigned notice.

The six stories of which this little book consists are delightful phantasies in which the old gods of the woods and the fields have dealings with those who are worthy to know them, much to the surprise of those who are not. The intrusion into the lives of ultra-moderns of ancient conceptions of what is good and what is evil gives Mr. Forster opportunities of which he is very capable of making use. His feeling for nature is subtle and inspiring, too, and his Paganism refreshingly wholesome. He has succeeded in expressing his ideas in most readable tales which are quite unlike those written by anybody else.

82. Dixon Scott, 'The pipes of Puck', *Manchester Guardian*

24 May 1911, 7

Walter Dixon Scott (1881–1915) was educated at Liverpool University and contributed many signed reviews to the *Manchester Guardian* and the *Bookman*. Commissioned Lieutenant in the Royal Field Artillery, he died of a particularly severe attack of dysentery at Gallipoli. Many of his literary reviews (though not this one) were published posthumously in *Men of Letters* (1916), which had an affectionate introduction by Max Beerbohm. His letters were published in 1932; Lascelles Abercrombie, introducing them, spoke of his 'genius' and took the view that his early death had cut short a brilliant career as a critic. One of his letters (to Ward Muir, December 1910) relates to *Howards End*, which he had not then read: 'They talk in such a proud way of Forster that one wonders . . . but that's cant. *Good* stuff *is* popular: it's only the would-be-goods that are martyrs for the sake of art. I must get hold of *Howards End*. But I hope it isn't Meredith. Those boots are worn out—as well as several sizes too big for anyone now to be observed.'

Nobody managed to hold out against *Howards End*—and what an escape of gush there was! And since that kind of tap is more difficult to turn off than on, the nonsense is welling out again at the sight of *The Celestial Omnibus* and other stories. 'Has achieved a miracle'—'Has plundered the ancients to get their vital spirit'—'Has brought myth and legend to the service of modern realism': a generous brew. So that it is only natural to feel a deep curmudgeonly desire to take these little stories very calmly—agree that they are pretty, full of promise—but as for being miracles—come, come! And it is easily done. For these, we are sure, are the very stories—'all harping on the ridiculous idea of getting into touch with nature'—which Rickie wrote in *The Longest Journey* and tried vainly to get published. 'I'm sorry', said one very nice publisher, 'but—your stories do not convince. They convince in parts—but they do not convince as a whole'; and he recommended Rickie to try a real good ghost story. We sneered at the publisher at the time—but now it seems that he was really almost right. For Rickie *did* say Dryad. Rickie took Miss Pembroke's advice. The reader of *The Longest Journey* remembers it? 'What I write is too silly', he had been telling her. 'It can't happen. For instance . . .' and then he gives her what may be called an impartial digest of the longest story ['Other Kingdom'] in this very book:

[Quotation from Ch. 7: 'For instance, a stupid vulgar man . . .' to 'Otherwise, with such an original story, people might miss the point'.]

And Rickie did! He used the word Dryad. Not in that particular story indeed—which therefore remains much the best in the book; but in 'The Curate's Friend' and 'The Story of a Panic' the fatal words are uttered, the cloven hoof appears. For the curate's friend, who puts him up to all the secrets of hills and streams and human beings, is frankly and specifically a faun—'of the kind that capers in the Neo-Attic reliefs'—with the orthodox ears and tail. And in 'The Story of a Panic' the untamed power that turns a prim party of tourists mad with terror and transforms a little pale boy into a poet leaves objective hoofprints in the solid earth.

And the result, as the nice publisher said, is that the stories do not convince; and they fail to convince for exactly the reason he had in mind when he urged a real good ghost story—because they are insufficiently fantastic. Nameless terror does not seize us when we spy those hoof-marks in the sod. Rather, we are reassured. The tale becomes a tableau vivant—very charming. Instead of a symbol of the something burning and rebellious in modern life we have modern life meekly reproducing an old symbol. The wild, sweet, untamed element which the figure of the piping goatfoot once perfectly summed up still stamps and cries in our streets of course, as ineradicable as the spring, as much at home in a music-hall as on a mountain-top, the true minister of the affairs he seems to mock; but the old figure expresses it no longer—he expresses rather the prettiness he ought to stamp on: we need another symbol now. For Pan is worse than dead—he is domesticated. He has become a popular pet. He grazes on Hampstead Heath, plays with the children in Kensington Gardens like a little gentleman. He has been christened Peter.

And yet—and yet. Even a curmudgeon must be honest—and we

may as well own up at once that if we had seen *The Celestial Omnibus* before we heard the gush we would have hailed it rapturously. Pan may have petered out, but Puck is still alive in the land, capering uncaptured, and through all these elvish pages he mocks and glimmers and eludes. Not since Henry Harland[1] tossed *Grey Roses* in his face has the English reader been granted a story-book so brimful of perfume and caprice. To open it is like opening a box of butterflies—instantly the air is alive with eddying brightness and elusive wings. It is for ever springing soft surprises—now of the impish, impudent kind that made *Howards End* lead off with a cool 'One may as well begin with Helen's letters'—now of the keen dramatic kind that kills a character with a full stop, as though it were a rifle bullet—and incessantly of the sort that startles us when we see poetry and puns playing hide-and-seek together, or loveliness breaking into laughter, or laughter swaying up into pure song. These are the true Dryad changes. 'Plundered the ancients?' It is as English as Ariel—or an undergraduate. Yes, out of a pinch of myth and a puff of modernity and a spice of original sin Mr. Forster has compounded something so rare and delicious that one is compelled to wind up by weakly surrendering our last and best chance of being chilling. The really superior way of bidding good-bye to the book would be to urge the writer to redeem those petty promises—'to take up life' as Rickie's friends advised—and then some day he will perhaps be able to write a real book, a book like *Howards End*. But we cannot do it. We are with the publisher. We long to see Mr. Forster snip the silken thread that keeps the butterflies captive. These are heavenly stories with an earthly meaning. What fun to drop the earth! *Panem et circenses* then, instead of *pan ovium custos*. Like the celestial 'bus itself, which ran from Sudbury to the Land West of the Moon, this book plies between two planes. Why urge its driver to settle down at the Sudbury terminus? With our Wellses and our Bennetts we have plenty willing enough to do that—to go in for earthly meanings. But there is scarcely another with Mr. Forster's gift for running us over a rainbow. In the midst of their *Sturm und Drang* we pine for an occasional 'Tempest'. But there! What is the use of these weak entreaties? Too late, too late. *Howards End* is already on our shelves. Like all the rest of them, Mr. Forster has taken up life.

[1] Henry Harland (1861–1905) was an American writer whose early novels (about New York Jewish life) were written under the pen-name 'Sidney Luska'. Harland moved to London in 1889, becoming an aesthete and Roman Catholic convert, and editing the *Yellow Book* from 1894–7. *Grey Roses* was published in 1895.

83. Unsigned review, *Nation*

ix, no. 11, 10 June 1911, 410

Mr. E. M. Forster's treatment of the supernatural is a proof that even the oldest pebbles from the brook can be made available by the hand of the cunning slinger who sallies forth bent on the overthrow of Goliath. It is a testimony to Mr. Forster's art that he rarely takes the sword in hand himself, but divides the camp of villadom against itself, and incites the superior inmates to fall on their Philistine brethren and cut off their heads. A particularly neat example is 'The Story of a Panic,' which sets forth how the great God Pan appears at a picnic in a chestnut wood at Rapallo, where the two Miss Robinsons and their nephew Eustace, and the curate Mr. Sandbach, and Mr. Leyland, an artist, and the respectable narrator and his wife have foregathered. The party is incontinently filled with a bestial fear, and takes to mad flight—everybody, that is, except Eustace, who is found, later on, lying on his back, playing with a lizard. Nothing can be got out of him, but that evening Eustace behaves very strangely, talking familiarly to ragged old peasant women, and even throwing his arms round Gennaro, an impertinent fisher-lad, who is acting as waiter at the boarding-house. Eustace behaves still more strangely in the night, escaping from his bedroom and standing in the garden, in his night-shirt, saluting, praising, and blessing the great forces and manifestations of Nature. The boy easily eludes his English relatives and friends who give him chase, but Gennaro is seduced by the promise of a few lire to betray him into their hands. Ultimately the forces of Nature prove too strong for the powers of British respectability, and, in a vivid scene at the close, Eustace is seen leaping down the hillside, laughing and shouting in an inhuman voice, while the perfidious Gennaro breaks his neck by falling from the terrace in a dispute over the payment of the lire. Mr. Forster gets his effects by making his cultured people uneasily self-conscious that these incredible events would be beautiful if read of in the classics, but are to be repressed sternly when they apply, spiritually, to themselves. In 'The Road from Colonus,' we find an admirable burlesque of modern insincerity in the description of the facile enthusiasm of a party of English tourists, who halt at a tiny khan, or country inn, in Messenia. Old Mr. Lucas drinks of the spring, gushing from a hollow tree, and straightway forgets all about his suburban vexations, and determines to remain, lotus-eating, 'in the benedictory shades of the planes.' When his family discover that he is in earnest, they take strong measures to remove him from the dangerous locality. Mr. Lucas has indeed lost all sense of the suburbs by drinking the enchanted water of the spring of eternal youth. But his family is deaf to his appeals, and he is worsted and carried back to his hateful old life. Here, as in 'Other Kingdom,' the things of the spirit are in league with the powers of the supernatural world, and at war with the prosaic pettiness of our daily outlook and environment. The artistic appeal is successful, because the uncanny element symbolises the unforeseen turns of the wheel that fate has in store for every man, and there is a constant appeal made from man-made law to the mysterious workings of Nature. Mr. Forster's literary arrows are sharp and shining, and they wing his quarry none the less effectually because they are feathered with magic plumage.

84. Unsigned review, *The Times Literary Supplement*

no. 493, 22 June 1911, 238

There were not a few readers who used to watch the magazines carefully for Mr. E. M. Forster's Short Stories, before he gathered in a wider public with his novels; and these may turn the pages of *The Celestial Omnibus* with a sense that it is peculiarly theirs, by right of having been first in the field with appreciation. The little volume contains only half-a-dozen of these earlier pieces; and without recalling and regretting certain omissions, let us say that we re-read those we are given with a confirmed admiration of their originality and grace. The difficulty about criticizing them is that they are all so lightly fitted together and airily thrown off that it seems brutal to hold them down and examine them. If we did so we might find that the slippery little allegories which run through them would not always bear sustained pressure, and we should certainly find that some of them are very loosely written. But it is more to the point to notice how neatly the two elements in the contrast which is the subject of them all are made to play in and out of each other. Heavy-handed literalness gets so daintily mocked and flouted in these anecdotes that we hardly dare try to say what the contrast is; but, vulgarly put (it is safer to be vulgar than to be solemn), it is between those who are 'in the know' on the subject of nature and poetry and the finer sentiments, and those who are not. If Mr. Forster were ever capable of being heavy or solemn himself, it would be a dangerous subject. But we cannot catch him out; the people in his stories who understand, who have eyes to see Pan in a chestnut wood and fauns on the Wiltshire Downs, are too agreeable to make us ever feel inclined to side with the stupid ones against them. As for the stupid ones, we know how unerringly and with what elfish sharpness Mr. Forster pins them down in their most unsuspecting moments. If the style, as we hinted, is not always equable, it must be said that in most of the stories Mr. Forster deliberately adopts the difficult method of making one of the stupid people the narrator, so that the revelation of character has to be unconscious —and that, of course, means that to keep the manner consistent with itself needs a highly practised hand. But the lapses of this sort do not affect more than two or three of the stories, and anyhow they are all very entertaining. We cannot think the volume adorned by the somewhat scratchily symbolic 'end-papers'.

85. Unsigned notice, *Athenaeum*

no. 4366, 1 July 1911, 12

There is a certain nexus uniting the stories in *The Celestial Omnibus*, by E. M. Forster: They all have a smack of the fantastically supernatural. Two at least deal with Pan and the ancient earth gods; others are linked with the imaginative realms of faery. We are not sure that the stories can be considered wholly successful, nor are they original in their main design. In treatment, however, the author has his own methods. Occasionally, as in 'The Celestial Omnibus' and 'The Other Side of the Hedge', we are reminded of the whimsical humour which Mr. Barry Pain[1] once scattered over his pages. Sometimes we are frankly beaten in our effort to find a meaning, as in 'Other Kingdom'. It has atmosphere, but what is its significance? The effect of the six stories is somewhat monotonous, and a note of facetiousness is apt to spoil the narratives. They might, one concludes ultimately, have been written as a spirited 'lark' by a young writer. Perhaps they have been.

[1] Barry Pain (1864–1928), hailed in his time as a 'new humourist', edited *Granta* while at Corpus Christi College, Cambridge, later worked for the *Daily Chronicle* and *Black and White*, and succeeded Jerome K. Jerome as Editor of *To-Day*. He published some novels and much humorous writing, including *Eliza* (1900) and *The Diary of a Baby* (1907).

86. Unsigned notice, *Cambridge Review*

xxxiii, no. 813, 19 October 1911, 40

Cf. No. 27.

The best short stories of the day are to be found in Mr. E. M. Forster's *The Celestial Omnibus*. Ever since the first of them, 'The Story of a Panic', appeared in the *Independent Review*, Mr. Forster may claim to have established his right to be heard. There was nothing in his first long novel to touch it, nor did his second novel, for pure imaginative writing, bear comparison with the story which gave its name to the present volume. If there is no story, except perhaps the first, in this volume which can touch the immortal chapter of the Florentine Meadow in *A Room with a View* (a chapter which is equal to anything written by Meredith at his best), the author comes near it in 'Other Kingdom'. But this volume must be read as a whole. The price seems excessive, but the get-up is worthy of the text, and makes an admirable gift book.

THE CELESTIAL OMNIBUS

(American edition) 1923

87. Unsigned notice, *New York Evening Post*

(Literary Review) 29 September 1923, 83

Even the first part of *Pharos and Pharillon* is not, in our opinion, to be compared with the best of these stories which are dedicated 'To the memory of the *Independent Review*.' *Parva sed apta!* You can easily hear great things of *Howards End* or *A Room With a View*, and E. M. Forster is a novelist to be reckoned with—but the title story of this volume, 'Other Kingdom,' and 'The Road From Colonus' must—like certain bargains in real estate—be seen to be appreciated. They are unusual short stories. Panic things and supramundane things are handled in a manner that rivals Algernon Blackwood at his very best, and the mind behind them is more truly sapient. Here is a finished style combined with unusual imaginative invention.

This is one of the few books of short stories of the day that should become a permanency in the library of the judicious book-buyer; here are half a dozen tales that impress themselves deeply upon the sensitive perception. We are far from hailing Mr. Forster as a great writer, but he is certainly a remarkably good writer. He knows his craft, and his mind is most curious and searching. Better than Arthur Machen he knows not only how to create atmosphere, but how to tell a good story with the proper completeness, how to satisfy one's desire for structural unity. His tales are comparatively brief, but they are compressed to their essence without thinning their richness. There is a deal of allegory, if you like, but the stories are stories first of all, convincing in all their improbabilities. To us *The Celestial Omnibus* itself is the gem of the collection, but the others arouse fertile speculation. 'Wildly and strangely beautiful,' Rebecca West has said of Forster's novels. The phrase applies here. Philosophical subtlety, humor, and fantasy are combined in the Forster blend. We have rarely so enjoyed a book of tales.

88. D. H. Lawrence, letter to Bertrand Russell

12 February 1915

D. H. Lawrence (1885–1930) completed *The Rainbow*, originally banned in England and the subject of much controversy, in 1915. This letter is written from Greatham in Sussex, where Forster visited the Lawrences in February. Lawrence described the same visit in a letter (24 February 1915) to Mary Cannan thus: 'We had E. M. Forster here for a day or two. I liked him, but his life is so ridiculously inane, the man is dying of inanition. He was very angry with me for telling him about himself'.

Gilbert Cannan (b. 1884) was educated at King's College, Cambridge, like Forster himself. Though trained as a barrister, he never practised and instead devoted his time to the drama (with John Drinkwater and others he founded the Manchester Repertory Theatre) and to the writing of novels once thought daring. *Young Earnest* was published in 1915.

From *The Collected Letters of D. H. Lawrence*, ed. Harry T. Moore (Heinemann, 1962), I, 316–19.

Dear Mr Russell: We have had E. M. Forster here for three days. There is more in him than ever comes out. But he is not dead yet. I hope to see him pregnant with his own soul. We were on the edge of a fierce quarrel all the time. He went to bed muttering that he was not sure we—my wife and I—weren't just playing round his knees:

he seized a candle and went to bed, neither would he say good night. Which I think is rather nice. He sucks his dummy—you know, those child's comforters—long after his age. But there is something very real in him, if he will not cause it to die. He is *much* more than his dummy-sucking, clever little habits allow him to be.

I write to say to you that we *must* start a solid basis of freedom of actual living—not only of thinking. We *must* provide another standard than the pecuniary standard, to measure *all* daily life by. We must be free of the economic question. Economic life must be the means to actual life. We must make it so at once.

There must be a revolution in the state. It shall begin by the nationalising of all industries and means of communication, and of the land—in one fell blow. Then a man shall have his wages whether he is sick or well or old—if anything prevents his working, he shall have his wages just the same. So we shall not live in fear of the wolf—no man amongst us, and no woman, shall have any fear of the wolf at the door, for all wolves are dead.

Which practically solves the whole economic question for the present. All dispossessed owners shall receive a proportionate income—no capital recompense—for the space of, say fifty years.

Something like this must be done. It is no use saying a man's soul should be free, if his boots hurt him so much he can't walk. All our ideals are cant and hypocrisy till we have burst the fetters of this money. Titan nailed on the rock of the modern industrial capitalistic system, declaring in fine language that his soul is free of the Oceanids that fly away on wings of aspiration, while the bird of carrion desire gluts at his liver, is too shameful. I am ashamed to write any real writing of passionate love to my fellow men. Only satire is decent now. The rest is a lie. Until we act, move, rip ourselves off the rock. So there must be an actual revolution, to set free our bodies. For there never was a free soul in a chained body. That is a lie. There might be a resigned soul. But a resigned soul is not a free soul. A resigned soul has yielded its claim on temporal living. It can only do this because the temporal living is being done for it vicariously. Therefore it is dependent on the vicar, let it say what it will. So Christ, who resigned his life, only resigned it because he knew the others would keep theirs. They would do the living, and would later adapt his method to their living. The freedom of the soul within the denied body is a sheer conceit.

Forster is not poor, but he is bound hand and foot bodily. Why?

Because he does not believe that any beauty or any divine utterance is any good any more. Why? Because the world is suffering from bonds, and birds of foul desire which gnaw its liver. Forster knows, as every thinking man now knows, that all his thinking and his passion for humanity amounts to no more than trying to soothe with poetry a man raging with pain which can be cured. Cure the pain, don't give the poetry. Will all the poetry in the world satisfy the manhood of Forster, when Forster knows that his implicit manhood is to be satisfied by nothing but immediate physical action. He tries to dodge himself—the sight is pitiful.

But why can't he act? Why can't he take a woman and fight clear to his own basic, primal being? Because he knows that self-realisation is not his ultimate desire. His ultimate desire is for the continued action which has been called the social passion—the love for humanity—the desire to work for humanity. That is every man's ultimate desire and need. Now you see the vicious circle. Shall I go to my Prometheus and tell him beautiful tales of the free, whilst the vulture gnaws his liver? I am ashamed. I turn my face aside from my Prometheus, ashamed of my vain, irrelevant, impudent words. I cannot help Prometheus. And this knowledge rots the love of activity.

If I cannot help Prometheus—and I am also Prometheus—how shall I be able to take a woman? For I go to a woman to know myself, and to know her. And I want to know myself, that I may know how to act for humanity. But if I am aware that I cannot act for humanity—? Then I dare not go to a woman.

Because, if I go, I know I shall betray myself and her and everything. It will be a vicious circle. I go to her to know myself, and I know myself—what?—to enjoy myself. That is sensationalism—that I go to a woman to feel myself only. Love is, that I go to a woman to know myself, and knowing myself, to go further, to explore in to the unknown, which is the woman, venture in upon the coasts of the unknown, and open my discovery to all humanity. But if I know that humanity is lame and cannot move, bound and in pain and unable to come along, my offering it discoveries is only a cynicism. Which I know and Forster knows and even Gilbert Cannan knows. 'They can't hear you,' Gilbert Cannan says of the public. 'They turn you into a sensation.' So he panders to the chained Prometheus, tickles him with near sensations—a beastly thing to do. He writes *Young Earnest*.

If I know that humanity is chained to a rock, I cannot set forth to find it new lands to enter upon. If I do pretend to set forth, I am a cheating, false merchant, seeking my *own* ends. And I am ashamed to be that. I will not.

So then, how shall I come to a woman? To know myself first. Well and good. But knowing myself is only preparing myself. What for? For the adventure into the unexplored, the woman, the whatever-it-is I am up against.—Then the actual heart says 'No no—I can't explore. Because an explorer is one sent forth from a great body of people to open out new lands for their occupation. But my people cannot even move—it is chained—paralysed. I am not an explorer. I am a curious, inquisitive man with eyes that can only look for something to take back with him. And what can I take back with me? Not revelation—only curios—titillations. I am a curio hunter.'

Again, I am ashamed.

Well then, I am neither explorer nor curio hunter. What then? For what do I come to a woman? To know myself. But what when I know myself? What do I then embrace her for, hold the unknown against me for? To repeat the experience of self discovery. But I have discovered myself—I am not infinite. Still I can repeat the experience. But it will not be discovery. Still I can repeat the experience.—That is, I can get a sensation. The repeating of a known reaction upon myself is sensationalism. This is what nearly *all* English people now do. When a man takes a woman, he is *merely* repeating a known reaction upon himself, not seeking a new reaction, a discovery. And this is like self-abuse or masterbation [*sic*]. The ordinary Englishman of the educated class goes to a woman now to masterbate himself. Because he is not going for discovery or new connection or progression, but only to repeat upon himself a known reaction.

When this condition arrives, there is always Sodomy. The man goes to the man to repeat this reaction upon himself. It is a nearer form of masterbation. But still it has some *object*—there are still two bodies instead of one. A man of strong soul has too much honour for the other body—man or woman—to use it as a means of masterbation. So he remains neutral, inactive. That is Forster.

THE STORY OF THE SIREN

1920

89. Katherine Mansfield, 'Throw them overboard!', *Athenaeum*

no. 4711, 13 August 1920, 209–10

John Middleton Murry, Katherine Mansfield's husband, was Editor of the *Athenaeum* from 1919 to 1921.

It is interesting to compare Katherine Mansfield's passing references to *Howards End*, here, with her caustic observations in No. 75.

The delightful event of a new story by Mr. E. M. Forster sets us wishing that it had not been so long to wait between his last novel and his new book. He is one of the very few younger English writers whose gifts are of a kind to compel our curiosity as well as our admiration. There is in all his novels a very delicate sense of the value of atmosphere, a fine precision of expression, and his appreciation of the uniqueness of the characters he portrays awakens in him a kind of special humour, half whimsical, half sympathetic. It is in his best-known novel, *Howard's End*, that he is most successful in conveying to the reader the effect of an assurance that he possesses a vision which reigns within; but in *Howard's End*, though less than elsewhere, we are teased by the feeling, difficult to define, that he has by no means exerted the whole of his imaginative power to create that world for his readers. This, indeed, it is which engages our curiosity. How is it that the writer is content to do less than explore his own delectable country?

There is a certain leisureliness which is of the very essence of Mr.

Forster's style—a constant and fastidious choosing of what the unity shall be composed—but while admitting the necessity for this and the charm of it, we cannot deny the danger to the writer of drifting, of finding himself beset with fascinating preoccupations which tempt him to put off or even to turn aside from the difficulties which are outside his easy reach. In the case of Mr. Forster the danger is peculiarly urgent because of his extreme reluctance to—shall we say?—commit himself wholly. By letting himself be borne along, by welcoming any number of diversions, he can still appear to be a stranger, a wanderer, within the boundaries of his own country, and so escape from any declaration of allegiance. To sum this up as a cynical attitude on the part of the author would be, we are convinced, to do him a profound wrong. Might it not be that his conscience is over developed, that he is himself his severest critic, his own reader full of eyes? So aware is he of his sensitiveness, his sense of humour, that they are become two spectators who follow him wherever he goes, and are for ever on the look-out for a display of feeling. . . .

It was the presence of 'my aunt and the chaplain' on the first page of 'The Story of the Siren' which suggested the tentative explanation above. The teller of the story is in a boat outside a little grotto on a great sunlit rock in the Mediterranean. His notebook has dropped over the side.

> 'It is such a pity,' said my aunt, 'that you will not finish your work at the hotel. Then you would have been free to enjoy yourself and this would never have happened.'
>
> 'Nothing of it but will change into something rich and strange,' warbled the chaplain. . . .

It would be extremely unfair to suggest that Mr. Forster's novels are alive with aunts and black with chaplains, and yet those two figures are so extraordinarily familiar, that we caught ourselves unjustifiably wondering why there must always be, on every adventure, an aunt and a warbling chaplain. Why must they always be there in the boat, bright, merciless, clad from head to foot in the armour of efficiency?

It is true that in this particular story the hero escapes from them almost immediately. He and Giuseppe are left on a rock outside the cave, so that the boatman may dive and recover his notebook. But the mischief is done. All through the enchanting story told by Giuseppe after the book is rescued, we seem to hear a ghostly accompaniment. They 'had been left together in a magic world, apart from all the commonplaces that are called reality, a world of blue whose floor was the sea and whose walls and roof of rock trembled with the sea's reflections'; but something has happened there which should not have happened there—so that the radiance is faintly dimmed, and that beautiful trembling blue is somehow just blurred, and the voice of Giuseppe has an edge on it which makes it his voice for the foreigner: the aunt and the chaplain, in fine, are never to be wholly got rid of. By this we do not wish to suggest for one moment that the key of the story should be changed, should be pitched any lower. It is exquisitely right. But we do wish Mr. Forster would believe that his music is too good to need any bush.

90. Rebecca West, review, *New Statesman*

xv, no. 385, 28 August 1920

Rebecca West (1892–), novelist, journalist and critic. Author of *The Return of the Soldier* (1918), *The Judge* (1922), *The Thinking Reed* (1936), *The Meaning of Treason* (1949), etc. She was made D.B.E. in 1959.

There is no one quite like Mr. E. M. Forster except Jack Frost. The patterns drawn on winter windowpanes, icily glistening, yet tracing the soft and fragile forms of lace and plumes, fantastic and filmy yet regular as mathematical diagrams are not unlike his novels, for they are inhuman and yet richly imaginative about people, wildly and strangely beautiful, and yet planned and orderly. He has published nothing for some years, having immersed his talents for the period of the war in educational work with the Army in Egypt, and one looked eagerly in this new publication for an indication what path of development this cold and dreamy talent had followed during this time of silence. This short story shows us that his talent will probably follow no path of development. His mind mirrors a particular phase of the mind of man, a spiritual state which corresponds to the hour before twilight, as one might imagine it up on the Wiltshire downs. The wholesome sun has gone, and the serene light of the stars is not yet, but it is not dark; there is a cold white glare of the dead sunset in the western room, by which things can be seen quite distinctly. One can see everything: the rolling hills chequered with the crops sown by the living. The shoulders of the downs humped here and there with tumuli dug by the dead. Everything looks so beautiful that one beholds it with joy. Nevertheless, something in the quality of this hour afflicts the beholder with a sense of desolation. The living who have sown the crops seem as remote as the dead who dug the tumuli. It seems not worth while following the chalk road where it dips to the village, for that has lost its daylight cheer and it is not dark enough for the windows to send out an orange glow. Mr. Forster's books are always like this hour. He is intensely aware of the present state of the mind of man and its status in antiquity, and beauty is the constant condition of his work. But there is always a similar grey magic of inhumanity about it. In his books people die suddenly and are not grieved for by those who loved them, and women surrender themselves to men who are not their conquerors. And *The Story of the Siren* reveals that his books will always have this character, for it is the expression of something fundamental in him.

The best thing in *The Story of the Siren* is the description at the very beginning of how the writer's book of notes on the Deist controversy, looked when he dropped it overboard and it fell through the blue waters of the Mediterranean. The picture of its behaviour brings the peculiar sense of enrichment that is given by the fixing of a transient form of beauty in phrases perfect enough to be permanent. The rendering of the conversation of the chaplain and the aunt and the chaplain's sister when they watch the accident and notice that the boatman is undressing in order to dive after it ('Tell him another time, dear') is potting at rather small game for the prelude of such lyrical recall of dead gods as this is intended to be, but it is amusing. The story that follows is not only a very good story, but is also a real myth, the adequate symbol of a spiritual adventure. One can read, simply for the sake of the yarn, the tale that the boatman tells the writer of how his brother dived without crossing himself and saw the siren who dwells at the bottom of the grotto, her singing a mere bubbling in the water, because the priests have blessed the earth and the air and she cannot come and sit on the rocks and sing as sirens used to do in the old unredeemed world; of how he came out of the water mad, sceptical of the wisdom of the present order of things and plainly plotting against it; of how he found a bride who had, like him, been driven mad by the sea, and how they were going to have a child who would in the fullness of time bring the siren up from the sea and destroy the power of the Pope and save the world; of how the priests, concerned for the Church, and the hotel-keepers, concerned lest the season should be spoiled by the cataclysm, organised her murder, and the man who had seen the siren wandered off on a hopeless search for another woman who, like him, knew the secret of the sea, and died at last at 'Liverpool, is the district probable?' But the story also expresses that sense, which comes over one when one is brought in contact with the more attractive survivals of savagery, that the pursuit of civilisation involves the sacrifice of many things that are good and pleasing to the soul of man. When, for instance, one sits at a bull-fight and sees the gay excitement of men and women, it is obvious that these people have a certain advantage over one in being exempt from the feeling of pity. Life unshadowed by the consciousness of any pain but one's own must be more brilliant than we know it, more in accordance, too, with the natural order of things, which knows little of altruism. This mood is perfectly expressed in the detached admiration (such as a music-deaf man might give to a singer with a beautiful voice) with which Mr. Forster describes the cruelty of his characters; how, for instance, the man who saw the siren, knocks down his brother, and makes the matter surer by breaking both his wrists, so that he will not be able to go out and murder the wife's murderess since then the man would be involved himself, and unable to take a form of revenge on the Christian community far fiercer than this simple human vengeance. The passage is an adequate symbol of this regret at the sacrifices we have made to be civilised, and yet we feel vaguely, till a single sentence reveals the source of our dissatisfaction, that though it may be adequate it is not entirely apt. When the boatman says contemptuously 'Love is everywhere since the death of Jesus Christ,' one is conscious that this is exactly what the boatman would not have said. Catholic boatmen who hate priests, are less likely to dive into grottos after sirens than to take the much deeper dive into *Das Kapital* after Karl Marx, and they are not likely to feel this resentment at a glut of love and this passion for the recognition of cruelty as a reasonable and liberating force, when their religion perpetually lays emphasis on the sufferings of Christ and the hard bargain of the Atonement driven with a just God. These things are actually more likely to be felt by a Protestant in revolt against the increasing lip-service to love that has spread through his Church ever since the Reformation and has been intensified by succeeding Evangelical movements.

To conclude with a word on Mr. Forster himself. The structure of emotion we have superimposed on the primary necessities of life seems to him Gothic and he is by instinct a classicist. He has not quite the poetic *élan* to lift him to an individual point of view where the general point of view could cease to distress him. So he writes books in which he devises cold variations of human relationships that shall flout the common demand that these should perpetually be close and warm, and tries to bring back paganism to his depicted world which, since that is a religion dead beyond the recall of any genius, gives his work this atmosphere of the ghostly hour before twilight, making it, like *The Story of the Siren*, faintly terrifying.

91. D. H. Lawrence, letter to E. M. Forster

20 September 1922

From *The Letters of D. H. Lawrence*, ed. Aldous Huxley (Heinemann, 1932), 552. Copyright 1932 by the Estate of D. H. Lawrence, 1962 by Angelo Ravagli and C. M. Weekley, Executors of the Estate of Frieda Lawrence Ravagli.

This letter was written from Taos, New Mexico. Cf. Nos 74 and 88.

We got here last week from San Francisco—from Sydney—Found your letter. Yes, I think of you—of your saying to me, on top of the downs in Sussex—'How do you know I'm not dead?' Well, you can't be dead, since here's your script. But I think you *did* make a nearly deadly mistake glorifying those *business* people in *Howards End*. Business is no good.

92. Hamish Miles, *Dial*

lxxvi, May 1924, 452–6

Review article on *Howards End*, *Pharos and Pharillon* (1923) and *The Celestial Omnibus*.

Polite and distinguished is the solitude of Mr. Forster in the clatter of English letters. Within its security he stands alone, no giant prophet in a wilderness, not even a *chef d'école*, but urbanely, tranquilly, unmistakably unique. His solitary figure evokes (does it?) one of those discreetly elegant little houses lingering still on the outward fringes of London, modest country manors hardly a century ago, but encompassed now and forever more by the hosts of, it is said, desirable villas. O and alas! All too obviously are those villas kept in touch with the conveniences of a metropolis by clanging tram-cars and scarlet buses, and, spiritually, by all the communistical apparatus of gramophones and broadcasting and circulating libraries. But somehow, in the general and miserable barbarism, the Forsterian manor remains inviolate, tinged perhaps with the delicately regretful melancholy of the virgin, but self-possessed, integral, and in the best sense familiar. Passing within, one is aware that here at least, behind those curving bay-windows, there live books which will never return strapped and ticketed to the library, and music that is still played (yes) by hand, that it is still possible in summer to take one's tea (China, of course) outside under the Araucaria, and look southward toward Surrey and the Dorking Gap. Here the Times brings its news of the encroaching world and the tiny fluctuations of the more gilt-edged stocks; and although one cannot help being aware of these tram-cars lunging past on the roadway outside, even their roar is held back from a too damaging irruption into the Schumann sonatas, or, when the Rector calls, the tea-table talk of the parish, or the plans for Easter at Assisi, by that lofty wall, topped with sherds of broken glass, which Grandfather so far-sightedly had strengthened and heightened, about the year of the Great Exhibition . . .

But the peculiar and endearing virtue of Mr. Forster is simply this: that he is consummately civilized.

Alarming enigma! So far is this quality to seek among our novelists, that the fact of its existence has confounded half of Mr. Forster's critics, however much it has delighted his inarticulate admirers. Only watch his reviewers: with what anxious enthusiasm they have hastened to heap upon his slightly deprecating figure the very dearest jewels of their little thesaurus: charm, of course, and subtlety and insight, a beauty wild and strange, and wit—and a hundred more have been proffered. In vain. The enigma remains. When we feel that a writer is being adequately served by the bestowal of these amiable, decorative comments, we may wonder whether the bedizened one is anything more than a nine-days' marvel. But when (the case is rarer) their apt profusion leaves him still naked and unexplained, may we not be fairly certain that the content of his writing is of some stuff richer than at first sight appears?

For Mr. Forster's work, I would make that claim. Epithets leave it undescribed. Admittedly: no giant, no innovator, no seer. But the fact remains that somehow—by virtue, I would urge, of the peculiarly civilized quality pervading all his work—Mr. Forster is left standing alone among the English writers of our generation. Observe that none of the superficialities or voguish manners of 'civilized' writing are here in question at all. The virtue of Mr. Forster is no painstaking sophistication of wit or intellect. Nor is it the elaborated urbanity of a Beerbohm. It is neither exotic nor *saugrenu*. It rests never on any glyptic cunning in words: on the contrary, his style is simple and direct with the trim, intuitive precision of Jane Austen. Its roots are deeper, springing from an intrinsic richness of human experience, a delicate sensibility to humane values.

The critical key, I think, is hidden in *Howards End*. Hardly hidden, perhaps; for one guiding phrase stands as motto to that rarely accomplished example of the modern novel. But *Howards End* contains so much of the essential quality of Mr. Forster's work that its own clue is bound, to some extent, to guide one also through his writings as a whole. Recall the phrase in question: Margaret Schlegel is determined to find her way to Henry Wilcox, and make him find her; and 'it was hard-going in the roads of Mr. Wilcox's soul':

'It did not seem so difficult. She need trouble him with no gift of her own. She would only point out the salvation that was latent in his own soul, and in the soul of every man. Only connect! That was the whole of her sermon. Only connect the prose and the passion, and both will be exalted, and human love will be seen at its height. Live in fragments no longer. Only connect, and the beast and the monk, robbed of the isolation that is life to either, will die.

'Nor was the message difficult to give. It need not take the form of a good 'talking'. By quiet indications the bridge would be built and span their lives with beauty'.

Only connect!

It is this idea which alone can produce, out of long conflict of elements, that rare amalgam of inward and outward experience of which the truly integral and civilized life must after all be composed. It is the grand negation of all the cheap, ready-made, 'outlined', standardized 'culture' of our age (recall, in this novel too, the victim of that, the pitiable character of the clerkling, Leonard Bast). And in it lies the secret of that unity of vision and coherence of beauty which mark indubitably the creations of the true artist in writing, which are, as I believe, the assay-marks of Mr. Forster's peculiar virtue, a developed consistency of temper and sensibility.

In other passages too he has brought out its implications. Earlier in *Howards End*, for instance, comes an allied passage which, particularly with regard to another branch of his imaginative work, is illuminating:

'To Margaret this [outer] life was to remain a real force. She could not despise it, as Helen and Tibby affected to do. It fostered such virtues as neatness, decision, and obedience, virtues of the second rank, no doubt, but they had formed our civilization. They form character, too; Margaret could not doubt it: they keep the soul from becoming sloppy. How dare Schlegels despise Wilcoxes, when it takes all sorts to make a world?

' "Don't brood too much", she wrote to Helen, "on the superiority of the unseen to the seen. It's true, but to brood on it is medieval. Our business is not to contrast the two, but to reconcile them" '. And in the half-dozen stories which make up *The Celestial Omnibus*, the seen and the unseen, gentlemen and demigods, are merged with a certainty and cunning of touch that leaves Mr. Forster, with this one volume (*plus* a single story, *The Song of the Siren*, published separately) almost unrivalled in the *genre*. It is needless to comment on them. In themselves, they are complete and self-explanatory. They spring from a rare intimacy with that great pagan emotion which was too suddenly stilled when Thamus the mariner heard, over the Aegean, the false cry that a god was dead. In essence, they are more than the neat triflings of a story-writer with a taste for classical mythology; it would be wrong to be deceived by their air of polite and humorous detachment. 'How suddenly', said Nietzsche, 'the wilderness of our exhausted culture changes when the Dionysian magic touches it! A hurricane seizes all that is decrepit and decaying, collapsed and stunted —wraps it whirling into a red cloud of dust, and carries it like a vulture into the air . . .' And so on, tumultuously. In the sudden clarity of the 'Dionysian magic', Nietzsche found the birth of Tragedy: in the touch of Pan upon the staleness and lethargy of our etiolated modern minds, Mr. Forster has seen a birth of finer life and deeper understanding. Thank God, he is far too agreeable a writer to say so, heavily, there, like that: but the best of his stories slip almost imperceptibly into one's consciousness, like poems, lingering, and evoking greater images than, in their modesty, they ventured to present.

Pharos and Pharillon is an indefinable little book, except in so far as its subject is Alexandria, Ancient and Modern, but unmistakably Forster, a distillation of a tenderly ironic spirit. In one of its all-too fragmentary essays, there comes a sudden enchanting glimpse, at an Alexandrian street-corner, of a 'gentleman in a straw hat, standing absolutely motionless at a slight angle to the universe'. Actually, it is the figure of Mr. C. P. Cavafy, a contemporary Demotic poet of the city, yet somehow—remove that straw hat, and animate (but slightly) that immobility . . . is this not Mr. Forster himself? He likewise has this divine gift of being able to stand at a slight angle to the universe; and from the peculiar perspective which he thus enjoys, emerges this exquisitely amusing series of dissolving views. The inclination varies, ever so slightly, magnetically perhaps in some obscure, incalculable way, but the effect is a delicious foreshortening of the history of Alexandria into an ironic, wrong-end-of-the-telescope miniature of much else. *Pharos* is neither a work of humour nor a work of history, but it indicates a possible form (sketched already, it is true, by Anatole France) invaluable to a charitable comprehension of civilization, its rise and fall. In the mud of Alexandria lies hid so much of the death of the ancient world and the slow parturition of the new, the mingling of West and East, Christian and Moslem and Hebrew, wars of Arianism, Monophysism, Monothelitism, what not. (Two thousand years hence, New York may have taken on the historic significance of Alexandria, the legendary memory of Woolworth or the Statue of Liberty its symbolic Pharos, for ever lost and unexplained.) In such a history, perspective could be found only in the vast rhythms of a

Gibbon, or by abbreviation into that lesser form of proportion styled humour. Writing elsewhere of Alexandria, Mr. Forster quotes the saying of Plotinus, that 'to any vision must be brought an eye adapted to what is to be seen.' Wherein lies the secret of the truly civilized traveller, as indeed of the novelist. Only connect . . . Not to contrast, but to reconcile . . . Mr. Forster is happy in his understanding of sympathetic and coherent vision. Plunged into the peculiar lucidity of his mind, the most dully familiar persons and things must always emerge transformed, admirable, glittering, crystalline, comical and lovely and real, and magical as the *rameau de Saltzbourg*.

A PASSAGE TO INDIA

1924

93. Rose Macaulay, 'Women in the East', *Daily News*

4 June 1924, 8

(Dame) Rose Macaulay (1881–1958), novelist, essayist, author of *Potterism* (1920).

The Anglo-Indian opinions which she wonders about in this review are indicated by Nos 115 and 116.

Mr. E. M. Forster is, to many people, the most attractive and the most exquisite of contemporary novelists (for a contemporary novelist he has, fortunately, now once more become). Further, he is probably the most truthful, both superficially and fundamentally. His delicate character presentation—too organic to be called drawing—his gentle and pervading humour, his sense and conveyal of the beauty, the ridiculousness, and the nightmare strangeness, of all life, his accurate recording of social, intellectual and spiritual shades and reactions, his fine-spun honesty of thought, his poetry and ironic wit—these qualities have made him from the first one of the rather few novelists who can be read with delight.

No one now writing understands so well as he the queer interaction of fantasy and ordinary life, the ghosts that halo common persons and things, the odd, mystic power of moments. Neither does anyone, I think, understand quite so well, or convey with such precision and charm, what ordinary people are really like, the way they actually do think and talk. His people are solid, three-dimensioned, and he sees them both from without and within.

A Passage to India is his fifth novel, and his first for fourteen years. Those who fear that his peculiar gifts may be wasted in a novel about India can be reassured; they have full scope. He can make even these brown men live; they are as alive as his Cambridge undergraduates, his London ladies, his young Italians, his seaside aunts; they are drawn with an equal and a more amazing insight and vision. And in the Anglo-Indians, male and female, he has material the most suitable ready to his hand.

The Ruling Race

Never was a more convincing, a more pathetic, or a more amusing picture drawn of the Ruling Race in India. A sympathetic picture, too, for Mr. Forster is sympathetic to almost everyone. Here, for instance, is the Club, after a supposed insult offered by an Indian to an Englishwoman:

> They had started speaking of 'women and children'—that phrase that exempts the male from sanity when it has been repeated a few times. Each felt that all he loved best in the world was at stake, demanded revenge, and was filled with a not unpleasing glow. . . . 'But it's the women and children,' they repeated, and the Collector knew he ought to stop them intoxicating themselves, but had not the heart.

Somewhere between the two camps, the Anglo-Indians and the Indians, are the newcomers to India—an old lady and a girl, not yet hardened and harrowed into the Anglo-Indian outlook, but full of honest, interested curiosity. These two women are alive with all the imaginative actuality with which Mr. Forster invests his old and his young females. He is almost alone in this, that he enters into the minds of old ladies, and attributes to them those sensitive reactions to life, those philosophic, muddled speculations as to the universe and personal relationships, which most novelists only find younger persons worthy to contain or to emit. The old lady in this book is the most clear-sighted, sensitive, civilised and intellectually truthful person in her circle. She speculates like a male or female undergraduate. 'She felt increasingly (vision or nightmare?) that, though people are important, the relations between them are not, and that in particular too much fuss has been made over marriage. Centuries of carnal embracement, yet man is no nearer to understanding man. And to-day she felt this with such force that it seemed itself a relationship, itself a person who was trying to take hold of her hand.' What other novelist would attribute such thoughts to a lady of sixty-five who has just been told of the engagement of her son?

A Civilised Girl

It is such patient, imaginative realism as this that distinguishes Mr. Forster from most writers. His young woman, too, is an achievement—a queer, unattractive, civilised, logical, intellectually honest girl, who wanted to understand India and the Indians, and came up against the wall of Anglo-India between herself and them. *A Passage to India* is really a story about this Anglo-Indian wall, and the futile occasional attempts, from either side, to surmount it. I suppose it is a sad story, as most truthful stories of collective human relationships must be; it is an ironic tragedy, but also a brilliant comedy of manners, and a delightful entertainment. Its passages of humour or beauty might, quoted, fill several columns. But they cannot profitably be isolated; Mr. Forster is not, in the main, a detachable epigrammist; his wit and his poetry are both organically contextual. This novel has a wider and a deeper range than any of his others.

He has quite lost the touch of preciousness, of exaggerated care for nature and the relationships of human beings, that may faintly irritate some readers of his earlier books. He used once to write at times too much as a graduate (even occasionally as an undergraduate) of King's College, Cambridge (perhaps the most civilised place in the world), who has had an amour with Italy and another with the god Pan. In *A Passage to India* (as, indeed, in *Howards End*), Pan is only implicit, the mysticism is more diffused, the imagination at once richer, less fantastic, and more restrained. It is a novel that, from most novelists, would be an amazing piece of work. Coming from Mr. Forster, it is not amazing, but it is, I think, the best and most interesting book he has written.

But I should like very much to know what Anglo-Indians will think of it.

94. Unsigned review, *The Times Literary Supplement*

no. 1169, 12 June 1924, 370

Not the least distinctive quality of Mr. Forster is his fairness; his judgements are marked by an unfailing sincerity. The accurate blending of observation and insight is his outstanding virtue. His new novel, *A Passage to India*, is the first he has published for fourteen years—since *Howards End*. Its artistry is of the same finished kind, its vision as original, as that of the foregoing novel: it has the beauty and pathos which belongs to Mr. Forster's best work. But because it is essentially a definite picture rather than a creative imagining, it is a different kind of achievement from *Howards End* or *A Room with a View*; its form is stricter, its appeal more precise.

Adela Quested, who has come out to Chandrapore in order to decide whether she will marry Ronny and spend the rest of her life there, wants to 'see' India. The superficial glamour of its picturesque figures has faded. She sees India always as a frieze, never as a spirit, and she cannot understand the apathy and complacent aloofness of the official Anglo-Indian community. The men are content to occupy themselves with the routine of administration and to eschew all personal interest in local affairs, and for the rest, the women attempt to model the colony on the lines of an English suburb. The Lesleys and the Callendars and the Turtons and the Burtons look in at the club every evening, and shun social intercourse with the natives like the plague. Ronny, the City magistrate, says candidly that it is not part of the job of a servant of the Government to fraternize with insurgent India: 'I'm not a missionary or a Labour member or a vague sympathetic sentimental literary man'. Mr. Forster does not minimize the difficulties; if Ronny's arrogance is to some extent the result of an ignoble tradition, Adela's enthusiasm is due largely to inexperience. She can see India only as a frieze precisely because she cannot understand its spirit. Ronny's mother and Fielding, the Principal of Government College, can overcome the suspicion and compel the friendship of Aziz because they realize his need for emotional intimacy. Aziz, the young doctor who quotes Persian poetry on the decay of Islam and the brevity of love, exuberant, sincere and distrustful, epitomizes the manners and sentiments of the educated Indian. He is naturally resentful of the English authority, but willing to co-operate in the common task. What arouses his fanaticism and prompts his excesses is the contemptuous indifference with which his advances are met. Sooner or later that indifference is bound to culminate in personal disaster. When Adela blindly accuses Aziz of insulting her in the polished gloom of the Marabar caves, East and West take sides. Fielding, believing in Aziz's innocence, champions him against the self-righteous fury of the ruling caste, and is ostracized for his disloyalty. Adela has an intuition of her mistake and, to the horror of her friends, withdraws the charge. Her repentance is worthless to Aziz. Without a violent show of passion, justice and honesty mean little in India.

With its subtle portraiture, its acute studies of the Moslem and the Hindu mind, its irony and its poetry, the story has imaginative breadth and generosity. The contrast between Adela's logical honesty and Mrs. Moore's mystical apprehension is finely conceived. Mr. Forster seldom lacks the power to go beneath the surface of the trivial occurrences of everyday life. He suggests the hidden workings of the soul in all the commonplace incidents of Aziz's experience.

95. A. C. Benson, letter to E. M. Forster

14 June 1924

I was sent to bed yesterday so I have had a real opportunity of reading your book continuously [. . .] Let me say first that I think it beautifully written. You have a technique which makes light of difficulties, and you seem to be able to express the subtlest idea both suggestively and clearly. Henry James, I used to think, latterly had the power of expressing a perfectly simple thought tortuously and intricately.

Then the characterisation is *admirable*.

I once made real friends with a Hindu here, who told me amazing things—and amazing things happened to him. He became unpopular at one time with some of his brethren about a small matter—and bags of offal and organs were left in his room as one might leave a card. He reminds me of Aziz in his flexibility and loving-kindness, and his sudden startled lapses into subconscious nationality.

The figure I feel I don't understand is Mrs. Moore. She is charming up to a point—but I don't grasp the significance of the echo, or her sudden lapse into peevish exhaustion. But the other figures are all *tremendously* alive, and vitally inconsequent.

I'm a little bewildered by the Hinduism of Godbole, though it seems to me marvellously like the mental attitudes of Roman Catholics. But what chance has one of penetrating these things? How much would the wisest Hindu grasp of a Bible Xtian revival in Cornwall? It seems to me that the inner impulse is probably the same, and that it leads to a sort of joyful levity about ceremonies which disconcerts one, because it seems to evoke all that is most irresponsible.

But I must thank you for some hours of very great intellectual, emotional, and artistic pleasure.

96. H. C. Harwood, review, *Outlook*

14 June 1924, 412

H. C. Harwood (1893–1964), journalist, was called to the Bar in 1922. He published short stories and contributed to the *Encyclopaedia Britannica*.

In literature this is an age of irony, for which, as for so many other unpleasant phenomena, the war may be safely blamed. Before the pressure of enormous destruction and crowd emotionalism so many persons found refuge in sour laughter. On certain events the only possible comment was: 'What fools these mortals be.' This ironical attitude, at first adopted by the mind in self-defence, has become a habit, and, because a tedious, an oppressive habit. There is this to be said for it, that it does demand, as simple earnestness and quaint pastorals do not, a modicum of intelligence, and though the majority (for obvious reasons) may prefer the company of fools, they are prepared to tolerate and even, surreptitiously, to favour intelligent books. This, too, may be said, that for those naturally more amused by than interested in life—a class in which it is difficult to avoid reckoning Mr. Lytton Strachey—anything but irony would be excessively ungraceful. Only Mr. E. M. Forster, perhaps because he has been ironical so much longer than the rest, seems to me to add interest to amusement. His is not the facile superiority behind which lurks the great fear of being either bored or conscribed. His irony is not an asylum, but a watch-tower. He has taken some pains before he smiles and shrugs at a problem or a frenzy to discover whether the one be in fact insoluble, the other in practice incurable. In *A Passage to India* he has analysed relations less personal than it is his wont to consider. This is a remarkably good novel, his best, may be, and the characterisation is no less subtle, the descriptions no less forcible than those of *Howard's End*, but even if it were a bad novel it would be necessary for all those desiring to correct the extravagances of Indian partisans, whatever their race, by a clear and convincing summary of modern conditions to study and to keep it. That summary I will not attempt further to summarise, and will abandon politics with an apology for having mentioned them. Enough to note that they give this novel half at least of its value.

The central figure of *A Passage to India* is one Aziz, a young Mahommedan doctor in Chanderapore; a simple-minded, almost childish person, for whom you are made to feel exasperated affection, so pathetic he is in adversity and so presumptuous in success. He is a poet, too. That is, he is thrilled by the mention of roses and bulbuls and of the melancholy fact which so many poets, Persian and others, have remarked that though this man or that man die, roses and bulbuls go on. And he is in a sense religious. Mere aestheticism enters into his spiritual experience, and so does party feeling, but there is something more. With all his defects he is a very decent little fellow, and as it happens his ruin is quite accidental. Aziz's constitutional indolence, the effects of a very trying climate on that bothered spinster, Miss Quested, an unlucky coincidence; how do these things start and how do they end? Nowhere and nohow. Out of nothing emerges a local crisis, with angry civil servants gathering together to talk of women and children, with native pleaders hastily imported to make scenes and excite sedition, with moderate men earning for their moderation general dislike, a small riot, legends. . . . Something has kicked an anthill, and after scurrying hither and thither the insects repair the damage. The novel is hardly more dramatic in its conclusion, for embittered Aziz goes to a native State and there drops his science, in which he never firmly believed, for charms. Between chilly English and flabby Hindus, what is a simple and passionate Mahommedan to effect?

97. Leonard Woolf, 'Arch beyond arch', *Nation & Athenaeum*

14 June 1924, 354

Leonard Woolf (1880–1969) was the husband of Virginia Woolf and co-founder with her of the Hogarth Press. He was also an important political theorist and a member of the Fabian Society. His earlier years were spent in Ceylon as a colonial administrator; his last in writing his five-volume autobiography with its many invaluable descriptions of the 'Bloomsbury Group'.

A little while ago I wrote in these columns that the book of this publishing season to which I looked forward most eagerly was Mr. E. M. Forster's new novel, *A Passage to India*. And now it has appeared and I have read it and—— Well, there are few things more exciting than to look forward to the publication of a new book, by a living writer, to read it, and to find one's hopes realized. That, at least, has happened to me with *A Passage to India*. But it only adds to the difficulty of writing about it. It is very easy to criticize a book which you know to be bad or which you think to be good; your real difficulties begin with a book by a contemporary which seems to you to be very good. There is, for instance, that terrible question: 'How good?' a question which, in the case of Mr. Forster, it is hopeless to try to answer in 1,200 words.

* * *

There are, first, certain obvious things which must be said about *A Passage to India*. It is superbly written. Mr. Forster seems now to have reached the point at which there is nothing too simple or too subtle for his pen; he is able to find words which exactly fit, which perfectly express, every thought which comes to him, and neither the thought nor the words are those which would come to anyone else in the world except Mr. Forster. If that is not one of the essential characteristics of a great writer or of great writing, then I have no knowledge or understanding of either. Let me quote:—

She had come to the state where the horror of the universe and its smallness are both visible at the same time—the twilight of the double vision in which so many elderly people are involved. If this world is not to our taste, well, at all events there is Heaven, Hell, Annihilation—one or other of those large things, that huge scenic background of stars, fires, blue or black air. All heroic endeavour, and all that is known as art, assumes that there is such a background, just as all practical endeavour, when the world is to our taste, assumes that the world is all. But in the twilight of the double vision, a spiritual muddle is set up for which no high-sounding words can be found; we can neither act nor refrain from action; we can neither ignore nor respect Infinity. Mrs. Moore had always inclined to resignation. As soon as she landed in India it seemed to her good, and when she saw the water flowing through the mosque-tank, or the Ganges, or the moon, caught in the shawl of the night with all the other stars, it seemed a beautiful goal and an easy one. To be one with the universe! So dignified and so simple. But there was always some little duty to be performed first, some new card to be turned up from the diminishing pack and placed, and while she was pottering about, the Marabar struck its gong.

* * *

In this book there are all the elements which made Mr. Forster's previous novels of such promise. There is the extraordinarily subtle and individual humour, the lifelikeness of the characters, the command of dialogue, the power of opening windows upon what is both queer and beautiful. The difference between *A Passage to India* and the former novels is that now Mr. Forster knows exactly how to use the elements of his genius. The promise of *Where Angels Fear to Tread* was renewed, but not fulfilled, in *Howards End*. None of these former books 'came off,' and there were in them disconcerting lapses into 'silliness,' if I dare say so—the silliness, not of a stupid, but of a clever man. But there is no silliness, no lapse, no wobbling in *A Passage to India*; it marches firmly, triumphantly, even grimly and sadly—the adverbs can only be explained by reading the book—through the real life and politics of India, the intricacy of personal relations, the story itself, the muddle and the mystery of life.

* * *

I have left my last paragraph for what I shall find most difficult to say. I ought, I know, to have said something about the plot, the story, the novel. They are extraordinarily interesting, but they are the superficies of the book. Even what I have been writing about in the previous paragraphs is on, or only just below, the surface. Nearly all great books, certainly nearly all great novels, have deep beneath their surface a theme or themes which are what give to the whole book its form, real meaning, greatness. Most writers are content with a single informing idea of this sort as the basis of their book, but what makes Mr. Forster's novel so remarkable is that he has a large number of such 'themes,' which, interwoven with great imaginative subtlety, weave a strange and beautiful texture for the book itself. The old lady, Mrs. Moore, a superb character in the book, felt that 'outside the arch there seemed always an arch, beyond the remotest echo a silence.' I feel the same about the book, when I look back on it, if one adds, perhaps, that beyond the remotest silence there is again an echo. There is the story itself with the two ladies who wanted to see India, the Anglo-Indian society of Chandrapore, and Aziz the only living Indian whom I have ever met in a book, and his friendship—which failed to be a friendship—with the Englishman Fielding. Behind that is an arch of politics, the politics of Anglo-India and the nationalist India. And beyond that is another arch, half mystery, half muddle, which permeates India and personal relations and life itself—'and all the time,' as Mrs. Moore says, 'this to do and that to do and this to do in your way and that to do in her way, and everything sympathy and confusion and bearing one another's burdens. Why can't this be done and that be done in my way and they be done and I at peace? Why has anything to be done, I cannot see.' And beyond that the terrible arch of 'personal relations'—do 'we exist not in ourselves, but in terms of each other's minds'?—and 'the friendliness, as of dwarfs shaking hands.' And beyond that the still more terrible arch of disillusionment—'the shadow of the shadow of a dream.' So the book builds itself up, arch beyond arch, into something of great strength, beauty, and also of sadness. The themes are woven and interwoven into a most intricate pattern, against which, or in which, the men and women are shown to us pathetically, rather ridiculously, entangled. That is how the book presents itself to me immediately after having read it, and perhaps my description may be hardly intelligible to anyone who has not read it. If so, all I can do is to advise him to rush out to the nearest bookseller, buy a copy of the book, and read it for himself.

98. H. W. Massingham, 'The price of India's friendship', *New Leader*

27 June 1924, 10

H. W. Massingham (1860–1924), journalist and Editor of the *Daily Chronicle*, died two months after this review appeared.

I read the other day a notice, in *The Nation*, of Mr. E. M. Forster's novel, *A Passage to India*. It was a very laudatory notice, written by a gentleman who expressed, with evident sincerity, his sense of the æsthetic and spiritual qualities of Mr. Forster's book, and gave an alluring picture of the delicacy and complexity of its structure, built up in 'arch beyond arch' of individual and personal and political relationships. At that point the criticism came to an end, with an asseveration of the extreme beauty of this production of Mr. Forster's. But on the actual subject of his work, beyond a general remark that it dealt with India, with the politics of Anglo-India, with Nationalist India, and with the visit of two English ladies to India, the article threw no light whatever. For all that one could tell, Mr. Forster might have written in a sketchy-spiritual way anything about India that had come into his head to write. The one palpable fact which was made clear to the reader was that he had strongly impressed Mr. Leonard Woolf with the beautiful way he had written it.

A Satire of Contrasts

Now, this habit of our latter-day critics of writing on literature as if its form-pattern, or its spiritual rhythm, and not its meaning and content, were the most important thing about it, is very characteristic of them, and it is quite true that Mr. Forster's wonderful style offers itself to this kind of admiration. He has the modern writer's gift of analysis, of spiritual discernment of the concealed or half-concealed sides of human nature. The irony of the contrast between what we say and even think, and the dark current of instinctive life that flows on beneath all this seeming, presses on his mind, just as it presses on the sterile, not to say the malign, genius of Mr. D. H. Lawrence. He has the art of presenting both the thoughts of men and the scenes in which they develop—witness the brilliant descriptions of the trial at Chandrapore and the festival of Krishna in Mau, the Indian State. And his detail is at once rich and curious. None of his contemporaries has a finer power of suggesting the colour and movement of life, and can be at once so disdainful and so sympathetic about it.

Nevertheless, it is just as informing to talk merely of the beautiful manner in which *A Passage to India* is written as it would be to remark of the *Decline and Fall* that 'Mr. Gibbon had composed a wonderful architectural work on the early and late Roman Empire.' Gibbon, of course, had the most definite thing to say about Imperial and Christian Rome, and he took care to say it on nearly every one of his thousands of crowded pages. In the same way, Mr. Forster has something extremely pointed to say about India, and he says it directly and passionately, or ironically and suggestively, just as the current of his thought sweeps him along.

That is by no means to say that he has written a pamphlet. *A Passage to India* is, indeed, a satire of contrasts, much in the same sense that the *Voyage to Lilliput* is a satire of contrasts. As Swift sets against the grossness of Gulliver the pettiness of the race of little men, so Mr. Forster portrays the super-sensitiveness, the impulsiveness, the charm and the weakness, of Mohammedan and Hindu India, in order to emphasise the honesty, the arrogance, the intellectual shallowness, the physical courage and the moral tremors of the governing caste, in all its haughty and unimaginative segregation. In effect, the book is addressed to the Dyers and the O'Dwyers of India, and to those who keep up the political repute of these people in this country. It says: 'Keep your bad manners if you will, but realise that they are losing you India, if they have not already lost it.' Only all this is said or inferred in the manner of the artist, not of the didactic writer. The latter can bring theory, rhetoric, argument, into the case. The artist can only contribute his love or his æsthetic and moral aversions.

Now Mr. Forster's temperament draws him towards native India, as it draws him away from the temper and spirit of Anglo-Indianism. Thus the exquisite picture of Dr. Aziz is touched with sympathy, as the picture of Major Callendar is deeply bitten with disdain. But both sketches are in proportion. Mr. Forster knows well where the weakness of a non-English India, an India from which we had withdrawn in anger or despair, would be—an India in which the affinities and repulsions of Professor Godbole, the Brahman, met the affinities and repulsions of Dr. Aziz, the Mohammedan, without the screen of British indifference thrown between them. And he seems—perhaps he only seems—to suggest that if such Englishmen as Mr. Fielding and such Englishwomen as Mrs. Moore could have their say, the irreconcilable might be reconciled, the all-but-impossible accomplished. But Mr. Forster's serio-comic picture of the India of to-day is not of a thing that can last. It is the image of a phantasm, almost a joke of the Time-spirit. If India is governed from the bridge-tables and tennis-courts of Chandrapore—well, the day is coming when she will be so no longer.

Warring Spiritualities

This, then is the theme of *A Passage to India.* Its illustration is in the main through a single piece of portraiture. Dr. Aziz, the victim of an hysterical woman and an equally hysterical society, is also the hero of the story. He is imagined in such a glow of feeling and drawn with such delicacy of touch that it seems natural to guess an original. But it is clear that Mr. Forster means us to take him for a good deal—not all—of India. In the rich profusion and confusion of her creeds and loyalties he stands out for something tangible, to be apprehended with sympathy and won, as far as India is to be won at all, with a price. Mrs. Moore wins him in a moment, with a single touch of spiritual generosity. The Collector and the 'Bridge Party' lose him again, it seems for ever. Mr. Fielding attempts a recapture, and the effort fails, because both men feel that the time of Anglo-Indian reconciliation is not yet. There is too much between—too little character and clear purpose on the one side, not enough understanding on the other. Perhaps when the problem of Krishna and his worship, the problem of Professor Godbole and his food, and the problem of 'Ronny' and his rawness, have all been solved together, the peace-makers can begin to talk.

Therefore it is not enough to ignore the subject of Mr. Forster's story, and to content oneself with the delicate ornament that so delights Mr. Woolf and the rest of the readers of *A Passage to India.* Yet it is true to say that its charm lies equally in its precision of detail, and in the way in which, when once the vivid impression of reality is attained, the study as a whole recedes into a mystical background, where the half-revealed forces have their play—the dim prophecies and blank misgivings of Mrs. Moore, the ecstasies and (to the European mind) the absurdities of the Brahman, to whom mere happenings are nothing, and 'whose conversations frequently culminated in a cow.' Obviously, the Anglo-Indian scene is a tangle of such obscure and warring spiritualities as these. But it is also a little absurd. Absurd are the Collector and the frightened gathering in the Chandrapore club, scenting a second Mutiny because Miss Quested has had an attack of nerves.

[Quotation follows]

Absurd, too, is Aziz himself, melting in a moment when the governing caste behaves a little decently to him, and blazing up into wrath as it falls back to its habitual mood of cold intolerance. Mr. Forster's conclusion is, perhaps, a little difficult to state. Fear, and the concealment of thought that fear brings, govern, to his mind, the whole Anglo-Indian relationship. The Indian dreads the fury of a second Amritsar. The Englishman knows himself hated, a stranger in an unknown and a complicated land, and feels that the hatred is unjust. Reconciliation might come through love and understanding. But how can India understand our shy, distant race? And what is an Englishman to make of a people that bows down to the strangest kinds of idols, and yet somehow enjoys the easy and scandalous intimacy with Godhood which Mr. Forster describes in his brilliant picture of the celebration of the Birth of Krishna?

[Quotation follows]

Alas! it seems impossible for an Englishman (unless he is a Scotchman) to enjoy God. But it ought to be within his competence to begin to realise what a task the Indian spirit has laid upon him, and to resort to such interpreters of it as the author of *A Passage to India.*

99. Unsigned review, *Observer*

no. 6942, 15 June 1924, 5

Some of us were beginning to fear that *Howard's End*—it must be nearly fourteen years since it was published—was to be Forster's end: but now the novelist has broken his silence with a book which does not repeat the amazingly ingenious, but hopeless, life of his last novel, but the far greater, more spiritual, less insolently bored tone of that much finer book, *A Room with a View*. There are still passages in Mr. Forster's work which proclaim too certainly that he was of King's College, still traces of the narrow anti-Christian bias affected by those who, as a distinguished Cambridge historian once said, 'cannot see the difference between Lowes Dickinson and Plato': but on the whole *A Passage to India* is the work of that wiser, more sensible Mr. Forster, who is incredibly aware of the niceties of human feeling, has a sympathy which is extended gladly (if sometimes with a gay malice) to his enemies, and will call no man or woman a fool unless he boasts himself wise.

[. . . . .]

Two of his Indias Mr. Forster knows exquisitely, and portrays with a searching justice, an imaginative justice: these are Anglo-India and the Mahommedan India. Of his Hindu India he makes a plausible picture, but we feel it is slightly invented, while his Brahman India, expressed in Professor Godbole, seems purely fanciful. Of course, it need not be the less true, but its truth is not of the same kind as Mr. Forster's rendering of the world of the British in India, of Dr. Aziz and his friends, of Fielding, the pro-Indian. The story is simple, but its interest is so great and so vivid that Mr. Forster might well become a popular novelist on the strength of his power as a story-teller. It is long since we have been so moved as by some of the scenes in this book. Aziz's first meeting with Mrs. Moore; the expedition to the caves; the trial of Aziz, an amazing piece of descriptive writing; and, finally, the gorgeous account of the great festival of Krishna, in the native state of Mau. Yet the story is only used as a means of getting us to understand Aziz and Fielding, Mrs. Moore and Agatha. The last is the prime mover of the story: her impersonal, academic interest in India; her inability to make anything out of what she sees and hears; her disastrous mistake about Aziz—all these drop like pebbles into a pond, making ring after ring, all uncontrolled by the precise, plain little woman who has come out to India to see how Ronnie 'behaves to the natives'. The minor characters, from Anthony, the insolent servant, and Mahmoud Ali, the violent barrister, to Turton and Hamidullah, are as vivid and life-like as the chief persons, and they all move against a background which is as vital as they are, a background full of colour, and echoing with the traditional and difficult experiences of an age-long civilisation.

100. 'C. M.', review, *Manchester Guardian*

20 June 1924, 7

The first duty of any reviewer is to welcome Mr. E. M. Forster's reappearance as a novelist and to express the hope that the general public as well as the critics will recognise his merits and their good fortune; the second is to congratulate him upon the tone and temper of his new novel. To speak of its 'fairness' would convey the wrong impression, because that suggests a conscious virtue. This is the involuntary fairness of the man who sees. We have had novels about India from the British point of view and from the native point of view, and in each case with sympathy for the other side; but the sympathy has been intended, and in this novel there is not the slightest suggestion of anything but a personal impression, with the prejudices and limitations of the writer frankly exposed. Mr. Forster, in fact, has reached the stage in his development as an artist when, in his own words about Miss Quested, he is 'no longer examining life, but being examined by it'. He has been examined by India, and this is his confession.

There can be no doubt about the principal faculties which have contributed to its quality: imagination and humour. It is imagination in the strictest sense of the word as the power of seeing and hearing internally, without any obligation to fancy—though Mr. Forster has fancy at his command to heighten the impression, as in his treatment of the echoes in the Marabar Caves. 'Even the striking of a match starts a little worm coiling, which is too small to complete a circle but is eternally watchful'. To speak of his characters as being 'well-drawn' would be crude; they draw themselves, and mainly in their conversation. More remarkable even than his vision is Mr. Forster's power of inner hearing; he seems incapable of allowing a person to speak out of character, and Dr. Aziz strikes one as less invented than overheard. Equally pure is Mr. Forster's humour. His people, British or native, are not satirised or caricatured or made the targets of wit; they are simply enjoyed.

[There follows a sensitive and neat summary of the story, ending with the last few phrases of the book.]

Thus we are left with the feeling that the blending of races is a four-dimensional problem. In his presentation of the problem Mr. Forster leans, if anywhere, towards his own race in his acute sense of their difficulties, but not more than by the weight of blood; and, again, fairness is not the word for his sensitive presentation. It is something much less conscious; not so much a virtue as a fatality of his genius. Whether he presents Englishman or Moslem or Hindu or Eurasian he is 'no longer examining life, but being examined by it' in the deeps of his personality as an artist.

101. Unsigned review, *Birmingham Post*

20 June 1924, 3

Reproduced by courtesy of the *Birmingham Post* (England).

The admirable self-restraint by which Mr. E. M. Forster has limited his output produces an undeniable drawback—that the public are not familiar with his style; yet no modern writer is so distinctive in all his work. The manner, which so closely recalls, without a trace of imitation, the unique methods of Henry James is not quite so obvious in *A Passage to India* as elsewhere; but, in the end, becomes once more revealed as its dominating characteristic. The earlier chapters, extending, indeed, well beyond the middle of the story, are used for that quiet, penetrating, creation of an atmosphere, and for that subtle analysis of character which appear to move on the surface of things, while mysteriously suggesting a hidden profundity of emotion that absolutely eludes precise expression, and cannot therefore be found: the peculiar gift of both writers.

In this story, of course, we remain uncertain (until the crisis) whether the suspected undercurrent will prove to be anything more individual than the eternal mystery of the soul-barrier between East and West. For all their comradely betrothal, there is an obvious antagonism between Adela's 'open mind' and the arrogant 'Anglo-Indianism' of Ronny Heaslop, who was 'not there to behave pleasantly' —outside his 'own class.' Aziz impresses one as the most absolutely 'real' Indian to be found in fiction: a living son of that baffling people for whom 'truth is not truth unless there go with it kindness and more kindness and kindness again,' to whom 'justice and honesty' in themselves make no appeal. But philosophy or atmosphere, however subtle, were never enough for either Henry James or Mr. Forster. And here, once more, without the slightest warning or preparation, we are plunged into the most intense and rapid, personal, plot-thrill that approaches melodrama. East and West alike wake up, as it were, to naked passions of loyalty and hate; and, without for one moment losing his unique control of differentiated race-temperaments, Mr. Forster almost rushes us through a storm of emotion that strips man down to human nature. Then, as suddenly as it flared up, the personal element dies away—but India remains. The passions have broken themselves, and those who felt them: we are left with only East and West—as before; together, and yet apart. It is a remarkable, almost a brilliant, book.

102. Sylvia Lynd, 'A great novel at last', *Time and Tide*

v, no. 25, 20 June 1924, 592–3

Sylvia Lynd (1888–1952), poet and novelist, and wife of the essayist Robert Lynd (1879–1949).

Reader, lo here, at last, a great book. There have been brilliant books in recent years, witty books, original books, books written in limpid and exquisite English; but not until now has there been a book that was all these things, and at the same time a book of large plan and sustained achievement, a book of new knowledge as well as of wisdom and imagination, a book that illumines a social and political problem and leaves it so revealed that the old revelations of it fade into trumpery insignificance. All this and more may be said of *A Passage to India*. When elderly persons, asking less for the sake of information than in order to bring home to the present generation that it is a generation of vipers, ask 'Where are our great books nowadays?' they can henceforth confidently be answered with: *A Passage to India*.

It is to Jane Austen that one must turn for a parallel in English fiction to the work of Mr. Forster. Like her he has the supreme gift of making things happen 'naturally,' he has her ear for the exact turn of speech that contains character and humour perfectly sharpened but without the faintest exaggeration of caricature, he has her gift for making a procession of ordinary events as exciting as such processions are in reality, and like her he sees both young and old with equally interested and detecting eyes. The impartiality, the humour, the irreverence, and the candour, not imprisoned in lady-hood, of Jane Austen—imagine all these applied to an examination of the relationships of east and west in India at the present day, of India seen not only from the English club but also from the native bungalow and the native palace, and you have some idea of the richness, the variety and the astonishingness of *A Passage to India.* To call it a beautiful book, beautiful as is its style and beautiful as is the poise of its author's spirit, would be misleading. Neither Western civilisation nor Eastern civilisation is beautiful nor are they beautiful in impact. *A Passage to India* is a delicious and terrible book. It is at once comical and agonising.

Mr. Forster takes a group of some dozen characters, English, Moslem and Hindu, and measures to each his share of sympathy, understanding and derision. The Indians in this book are not, as in all other Anglo-Indian novels, deplorable but unavoidable pieces of the scenery. They are not cast for the roles of simple villains or clowns. They are men with different conventions from Englishmen—how different has never been revealed before. And they are not of one pattern. Professor Godbole, the Brahman, is as different from Dr. Aziz, the Mohammedan with the English medical degree, as both are from Cyril Fielding the liberal Englishman, eccentric in India, and as he is from Mr. Turton of the Residency, and as Mr. Turton, the fine austere Anglo-Indian is from the brutal Major Callendar.

To visit Ronny Heslop the young magistrate, in Chandrapore, come his mother Mrs. Moore, the best type of intelligent Englishwoman, and Miss Quested, a plain, conscientious English girl to whom he is half-engaged. Miss Quested is anxious to see 'the real India.' This can only be done by becoming personally friendly with Indians, a state of affairs that English rule does not encourage. Attempts to bridge the gulf always end disastrously, declare the English residents of Chandrapore. They prefer to act 'Cousin Kate' and play bridge. Mrs. Moore and Miss Quested are not deterred, however, Mrs. Moore because her naturalness and free mind put her at once into sincere relations with everyone, Miss Quested because she feels that to try to 'understand' India is the right thing to do. By touch after touch of delicate comedy and delicate revealing detail, Mr. Forster conveys the exquisite discomfort of the attempt to bridge the gulf.

Dr. Aziz, out of mixed motives of vanity and friendliness, organises an expedition for Mrs. Moore and Miss Quested to some famous caves in the neighbourhood of Chandrapore. He expends vast sums on the entertainment. He borrows an elephant. He sleeps overnight at the railway station for fear of being late. The whole thing worries him desperately. Mrs. Moore and Miss Quested are not at all anxious to go; but out of politeness they do not like to refuse. And so the party sets off for a disaster as complete as the wildest prophets among the *mem-sahibs* could desire. Mrs. Moore gets a touch of sun and becomes a crabbed, dying woman, instead of a figure of health and wisdom. Miss Quested for some reason less comprehensively explained, flees from the caves believing herself the victim of attempted outrage. It is a horrid picnic. Race prejudice bursts in upon it like an infuriated bull. Mr. Forster now hovers above a world not only filled with absurdities and misconceptions, but churned to frenzy with hatred and the desire of vengeance. Each of his characters shows himself as he is at a crisis as clearly as he did among every-day occurrences. The description of the trial of Dr. Aziz is one of the most overwhelmingly exciting things in English literature. It is like the gliding of the pilgrim ship at the beginning of *Lord Jim*, or the chase between that other Jim and Israel Hands in *Treasure Island*. It is the pinnacle of the miserable comedy. It does not cease to be grotesquely funny because it is also sternly serious.

Mr. Forster seizes his opportunity with the finest precision whether he is twisting the emotions of his characters into the knot of conflict or disentangling them into the innumerable strands of triumph and humiliation and dismay that follow it. Fielding, whose sense of justice is stronger than his racial feeling has taken the side of Dr. Aziz in the struggle. Fielding is garlanded with flowers, but he finds himself irresistibly impelled in the end to call Dr. Aziz 'little rotter,' though he knows it to be less than half the truth. East and West are left by Mr. Forster as completely separate as in the most stirring melodrama of the Mutiny, or in the plainest tale from the hills.

This may not be the moral of Mr. Forster's novel for everyone, however. *A Passage to India* is one of those books so rich in implication as well as in statement, that each reader may draw his own conclusion from it, just as each of us draws a different conclusion from what he experiences of life. One thing is certain, friendship whether between nations or individuals can only be based on knowledge, and it is an enlargement of knowledge, not only of India, but of human motives, that Mr. Forster has made so superb a contribution. I should like to quote passage after passage to illustrate Mr. Forster's beautiful fairness, perceptiveness and sense of the mystery of life, but where the excellence is so consistent every page demands quotation and I must direct my readers straight to the book itself.

103. Gerald Gould, review, *Saturday Review*

cxxxvii, 21 June 1924, 642

Gerald Gould (1885–1936), poet, essayist and reviewer. Associate Editor of the *Daily Herald* from 1919 to 1922. Published *The English Novel of Today* (1924); *Collected Poems* (1929).

To that portion of the novel-reading public which takes the novel as a form of art and not merely as a form of dissipation, the publication of a new book by Mr. Forster is probably the event of the year. He would, indeed, be the best of the younger novelists, if he were a novelist at all. But his medium is really the fairy-story; for in a fairy-story the characters may be as thin and faint and fantastic as you please, or as Mr. Forster pleases, and yet the enchantment will remain.

No doubt *A Passage to India* has been given a deliberately misleading title. There is nothing in it about the passage to India in the ordinary sense of the words: all the action passes *in* India: and the passage is of the spirit. The one weakness is that Mr. Forster cannot lodge his spirits in human bodies. He can give them every finest shade of feeling and perception; he can mercilessly record their language, their thoughts, even the hinterland of their thoughts; but he cannot make them come alive. His wealth of wit and poetry is marked, or at any rate limited, by something between pity and contempt for that witless and unpoetic race, the human. It is clear that he does not like either Indians or Anglo-Indians: not that he dislikes them *as* Indians or

Anglo-Indians, but that he sees them involved in the vast purposeless sufferings and pathetic-comic enjoyments of man. Is his book a contribution to the 'problem' of India? Not specifically. One gathers that for him there is only one problem in the world, and that insoluble.

He does not regard it as possible that the Englishman should understand the Moslem or the Hindu, or the Hindu and the Moslem understand the Englishman or each other: he does not think it possible that one human being should understand another human being. His people of each several race are as much at cross-purposes among themselves as with the people of other races. It is true that occasionally he is tempted into cheap generalizations, but only when he has lost touch with his own theme. 'Like most Orientals, Aziz overrated hospitality, mistaking it for intimacy, and not seeing that it is tainted with the sense of possession.' A moment's thought or five minutes spent in the bar of a public-house would have enabled Mr. Forster to write 'like most Occidentals' there. The human heart, capable of very little intimacy and hungry for more, is always and everywhere parading hospitality in its place. 'What's yours?' and 'Have one with me' are not peculiarly oriental expressions. Again:

> Suspicion in the Oriental is a sort of malignant tumour, a mental malady, that makes him self-conscious and unfriendly suddenly; he trusts and mistrusts at the same time in a way the Westerner cannot comprehend. It is his demon, as the Westerner's is hypocrisy.

If Mr. Forster will re-read his own book (which I confidently recommend to him), he will find the East just as hypocritical as the West, and the West just as suspicious as the East. These be the maladies of flesh-and-blood.

Dr. Aziz, a Mohammedan surgeon and poet, makes the acquaintance of Mrs. Moore in a mosque. She has thoughtfully removed her shoes, which delights him: she talks to him as to an equal, which delights him more: she understands what he is talking about, which delights him most of all. But hence tragedy, or the inept and ungraceful antics of pain which life sometimes offers us in place of the tragic dignity. Mrs. Moore is an old lady, mother of the City Magistrate of Chandrapore: she has come out to visit him, and to chaperone Miss Quested, the plain young woman whom he is vaguely supposed to be going to marry. Aziz plans a picnic at the Marabar Caves, twenty miles out of the city: by a series of accidents, he is left alone with Miss Quested near the caves: he goes into one, she into another:

and she comes out insane, alleging that he followed her in and insulted her. What exactly did happen in the cave we are never told: a heavy veil of mystery hangs over all. But the incident, the subsequent arrest and trial, let loose two conflicting storms of racial passion, and the excitement comes to a climax in court, when Miss Quested recovers sufficient sanity to withdraw her charge. This is the central theme of a long carefully-written story, of which the details are more important than the centre. For neither Miss Quested nor Dr. Aziz has any separate life. Their fortunes, their thoughts, might have been written down about anybody; but by no one except Mr. Forster could they have been written down with such delicacy, such restraint, such an indulgent tone of romance redeemed from horror by humour. It is no hyperbole to say that almost every sentence is a work of art. 'He was pleasant and patient, and evidently understood why she did not understand. He implied that he had once been as she, but not for long.' 'She owed him an explanation, but unfortunately there was nothing to explain.' 'They were softened by their own honesty, and began to feel lonely and unwise.' The story is built up out of thousands of such touches, malicious and delicious. And in the 'big scenes,' the descriptive power, the narrative power, are terrific. To call the book 'good' would be a ludicrous understatement: over and over again, as one reads, one thinks: 'This is great'; and yet the total effect is not of greatness, in the sense in which one predicates greatness of great novels. The real, some philosophers tell us, speaking truth, is the individual: in other words, the answer to that insoluble problem of Mr. Forster's is the problem itself, presented concretely in the shape of men and women: great art, in the narrative or dramatic form, gives us reassurance by its sheer power of creation: and it is through this one lack that all Mr. Forster's dazzling and baffling wisdom leaves us only dazzled and baffled.

104. Ralph Wright, review, *New Statesman*

xxiii, 21 June 1924, 317–18

It is a commonplace exaggeration among reviewers to say that the literary world has been waiting breathlessly for Mr. X's new book. Thirteen years have passed since Mr. Forster's last novel appeared, and even a literary world cannot maintain its breathlessness for so long as that. Yet Mr. Forster has never been forgotten, and there are a good many people who, whenever they have found themselves re-reading his earlier books, have felt a certain grudge against an author they knew to be still young for ceasing to try and produce the novel they were persuaded he alone, as representative of his generation, was likely to give them.

Now this generation, we all know, has many faults, but it has above other more brilliant ages one clear virtue, that of truthfulness. Not Truth with a large T perhaps, but at all events a desire to state the facts of a case as fairly and dispassionately as possible. It may not be so interested as other generations in the meaning of the universe, but it tries harder to find out what is happening and has happened. Why, even its historians view the past no longer as a lesson book.

Mr. Forster has other great merits as a novelist, but if there is one that stands out far ahead of the others, it is this sensitiveness to truth. He does mean to find out about the characters who in life and still more in novels, are usually viewed as backgrounds against which the more heroic and adorable people can display the obvious virtues. It is not so much that he wishes to stand up for the unpopular; that after all is merely the old game reversed; he is not seeing what can be said for them, he is merely trying to see what they are really like. Of course to do this successfully requires an extremely sensitive mind and a very accurate and subtle sense of words. But these in Mr. Forster's case are, one feels, secondary, though all important, things; what comes first is this desire to know how people think and feel and act in relation to one another.

In *A Passage to India* he has chosen a subject of enormous difficulty. Race feeling, or the violent reaction from what seems the intolerable race feeling of our fellows, is strong in every one of us. It is almost impossible to start a conversation on India, at dinner or in a railway carriage, even in this country, without producing a heated quarrel. For in the case of India there is much more than even race feeling, which is strong enough, to disturb us. There is our behaviour to a conquered country. There is a ticklish question of conscience. There is great ignorance. There is a quite genuine hatred of muddling, and a suspicion that whatever we do, go or stay, we shall produce disaster. It is race feeling multiplied by the old Irish situation multiplied by money. There is hardly one man in a million who can keep his head when the subject turns up, or one man in a hundred thousand who will try to. And it is on this almost fratricidal subject that Mr. Forster has chosen to be fair. At least we can be certain of one thing, that patriots on neither side will bless him for it.

The opening of the book is admirably planned. We are shown a group of educated Indians discussing quite calmly whether or not friendship with an Englishman is a possibility. We are used to this discussion the other way on; and the dispassionateness of the shifted angle sets the tone of the book from the outset. The conversation is desultory. It is not, one feels a set piece of propaganda. The characters are not speaking to an audience and there are no points to score. And almost at once one falls into Mr. Forster's mood of refusing to score a point for either side, of realising that there is an interest in people for their own sake and not as representatives of political idealisms or pawns in the hands of political or commercial forces. The English are treated as fairly as the various Indians, they remain even, in spite of their superior attitude, on the whole the most sympathetic to us.

> He spoke sincerely. Every day he worked hard in the court trying to decide which of two untrue accounts was the less untrue, trying to dispense justice fearlessly, to protect the weak against the less weak, the incoherent against the plausible, surrounded by lies and flattery. That morning he had convicted a railway clerk of over-charging pilgrims for their tickets, and a Pathan of attempted rape. He expected no gratitude, no recognition for this, and both clerk and Pathan might appeal, bribe their witnesses more effectually in the interval, and get their sentences reversed. It was his duty. But he did expect sympathy from his own people, and except from new-comers he obtained it.

The new-comers are his mother and the girl to whom he is expecting to become engaged. Both of them are anxious to see India with their own eyes, to judge for themselves, to be fair.

On the Indian side we have among others the Mohammedan Aziz, a doctor, and the almost incomprehensible Hindoo, Godbole. Aziz seems almost as if he were a portrait, so clearly seen is he, in his enthusiasms, his volatile feeling, his vagueness, his quickness to take unreasoning offence, his folly and his limitations. 'He was sensitive rather than responsive. In every remark he found a meaning, but not always the true meaning, and his life though vivid was largely a dream.'

For a time all goes on as usual. The mother and the girl make the acquaintance of Dr. Aziz. There is a ridiculous 'Bridge party,' a party meant to bridge the gulf between the English and the Indians, which naturally only serves to emphasize it. And then a terrible thing happens. Aziz is accused of an assault upon the girl. What actually happened we never really know. We only know that Aziz is innocent, and that one of those ghastly moments of tension in India between the two populations has arisen:

> The collector could not speak at first. His face was white, fanatical, and rather beautiful—the expression that all English faces were to wear at Chandrapore for many days. Always brave and unselfish, he was now fused by some white and generous heat; he would have killed himself, obviously, if he had thought it right to do so.

An Englishman with a fair mind dares to take the Indian's side:

> The collector looked at him sternly, because he was keeping his head. He had not gone mad at the phrase 'an English girl fresh from England,' he had not rallied to the banner of race. He was still after facts, though the herd had decided on emotion. Nothing enrages Anglo-India more than the lantern of reason if it is exhibited for one moment after its extinction is decreed. All over Chandrapore that day the Europeans were putting aside their normal personalities and sinking themselves into their community. Pity, wrath, heroism, filled them, but the power of putting two and two together was annihilated.

This event, which one is inclined to resent as melodramatic at first, is of the utmost importance in the scheme of the book. The evil thing has happened thereby. Individuals have ceased their individual existence for the time being, and become part of one of the herds. Unreason is loose, Indians and English become angry and futile in equal measure though in different ways. Only old Godbole, the learned Hindoo, remains unmoved. And he, though he knows what has happened, asks blandly and politely if the party which has led up to this has been a success? The whole community is momentarily mad, and phrases and catch-words rule the minds of men.

Further than this into the plot it is hardly fair to Mr. Forster's readers to go. It is enough to show the problem he has set himself, and stress the sympathy and fairness of his treatment. And this fairness is no judicial fairness. Nothing is further from his mind than the delivery of a judgment. The whole aim is sight and insight—the distinguishing of the individual problem from the obscuring mass.

M. Gide in an excellent passage on Proust, in his new book, tells us how a lady he knew had suffered from bad sight as a child. It was not until she reached the age of twelve that her parents realised this and gave her spectacles. 'Je me souviens si bien de ma joie,' he reports her conversation. 'Lorsque, pour la première fois je distinguai tous les petits cailloux de la cour.' It is in this power of distinguishing 'tous les petits cailloux' where most people see nothing but masses that Mr. Forster's special talent seems to lie. And it is from this ability that his special kind of fairness takes its birth. Again and again, even in such a tempting ground as that of the relations between Indian and Anglo-Indian, he refuses to generalise. That he leaves to his characters, and it is clear that it is from this habit of thinking in generalisations that most of their troubles spring. And naturally he comes forward with no solution. At the end of the book we are left with a scene of reconciliation between Dr. Aziz and Fielding, the Englishman who had taken his part, and with whom he had subsequently quarrelled:

[Quotes last phrases of book.]

The book seems to me to be a real achievement. There are things in it that I would have otherwise. There is a queer kind of mystery connected with the caves, where the terrible thing occurred, which is never cleared up. This in itself would hardly matter. What does seem to me to matter is a kind of mystical attitude to the caves, a suggestion of nameless horror that it is *impossible* to explain. I do not believe in nameless horrors, and I suspect Mr. Forster of doing so. Again, there is no one in the book that one can really care for. But that, on second thoughts, I would perhaps not have altered. It is, I think, an integral part of the book. Its reason is the same as that which refuses to allow Mr. Forster to give his heroine any physical attractions. It is a fear of loading the dice.

But even a reader who insists that some characters in a novel should engage his sympathy completely cannot miss the peculiar merits of the book. It is written with great care. It is so full of knowledge and so beautifully perceptive. It is most delicately written. We have had a long time to wait since *Howard's End*, and if Mr. Forster continues to write like this the waiting is worth it. *A Passage to India* is a better book than any earlier ones. It is as sensitive as they were, it is far better proportioned, and the mind which made it is more mature.

105. L. P. Hartley, review, *Spectator*

28 June 1924, 1048–50

Leslie Poles Hartley (1895–1972), novelist. His first book appeared in 1925, but he is best known for his *Eustace and Hilda* trilogy and for *The Go-Between* (1953).

Of all the novels that have appeared in England this year, Mr. Forster's is probably the most considerable. If it had merely been up to his standard, its pre-eminence would scarcely have been challenged; and in its scope and its effect it surpasses his previous books. In them, delightful as they were, evidences of partiality, imperfect sympathy, eccentricity of outlook so pronounced as sometimes to seem an obsession, spoiled the exquisite flavour and distinction of his work. Perhaps spoiled is too strong a word; but they gave it a partisan air, almost an air of propaganda; as though it were Mr. Forster's mission to show that all the evil in the world came out of Philistinism, suburbanism and the Public Schools. One trembled for the stupid well-meaning person who blundered into Mr. Forster's pages, disturbed his fawns at their play, and recommended corporal punishment for them. Such a one did not get off lightly.

Some such distinction between types Mr. Forster preserves in his last, and as we think his best, book. The Anglo-Indians stand for much that Mr. Forster dislikes: insensitiveness, officialdom, stupidity, repressiveness, rudeness. The Indians are the children of Nature, affectionate, courteous, eager, irresponsible, wayward. Mr. Forster's heart lies with them, but his sympathy does not blind him to the defects of their qualities; their impracticability, their double-dealing, conscious and unconscious, the crust of shallow intrigue which makes action, when they take it, of none effect. Nor does he fail to do justice to the redeeming qualities of their rulers. They are, of course, the qualities that make themselves felt in a crisis; and a crisis is foreign to the spirit of the East, which does not so much rise as sink to an emergency.

A Passage to India is much more than a study of racial contrasts and disabilities. It is intensely personal and (if the phrase may be pardoned) intensely cosmic. The problem of the English in India lies midway between these two greater considerations, linking them up and illuminating them. To the question, can the English as a foreign ruling caste arrive at a working arrangement with the Indians? Mr. Forster answers perfunctorily, No. And to the question (more interesting to the novelist) can an individual Englishman with the best will in the world reach terms of intimacy with an Indian similarly disposed? Mr. Forster again seems to say, with infinite hesitation and regret, that he cannot:—

'"Why can't we be friends now?" said (Fielding) holding him (Aziz) affectionately. "It's what I want. It's what you want."

But the horses didn't want it—they swerved apart; the earth didn't want it, sending up rocks through which riders must pass single file; the temples, the tank, the jail, the palace, the birds, the carrion, the Guest House that came into view as they issued from the gap and saw Mau beneath: they didn't want it, they said in their hundred voices, "No, not yet," and the sky said "No, not there."'

All the characters except perhaps Fielding, the unconventional Anglo-Indian schoolmaster whom the ladies of the station in their spiteful way called 'not quite pukka,' are at the mercy of their moods and nerves. Most novelists take it as a postulate that personality is capable of little variation, that it is within narrow margins determinable and accountable, and on this assumption work out problems of relationship to a logical conclusion. Mr. Forster sees human beings very differently. They have little sure hold over themselves; they are subject to skiey influences and 'dangers from the East'; they reach out for a prevailing mood and find it gone. They are infinitely receptive and 'suggestible.' Hence their failure to come into touch with each other. They desire the most intimate spiritual contacts, but they have no assurance of success because they do not know, from one moment to another, where the weight of their desires will lie: gravity pulls their personalities this way and that, they cannot count on themselves. The 'incident' of the Marabar Caves would have been a strain on the most tough-minded person; its effect on the two sensitive ladies who had come out, with the best will in the world, to find what India meant, was little short of disintegrating. It is the central fact of the book, this gloomy expedition arranged with so much solicitude and affection by Dr. Aziz to give his guests pleasure. A lesser novelist than Mr. Forster could have shown everything going wrong, could have emphasized the tragic waste of Aziz's hospitality and kind intentions, could have blamed Fate. But no one else could have given the affair its peculiar horror, could have so dissociated it from the common course of experience and imagination, could have left it at once so vague and so clear. Unlike many catastrophes in fiction, it seems unavoidable whichever way we look at it; we cannot belittle it by saying that the characters should have behaved more sensibly, the sun need not have been so hot or the scales weighted against happiness. And not only by the accident of the caves does Mr. Forster illustrate the incalculable disastrous fluctuations of human personality, but he subtly works in the black magic of India, crudely presented to us in a hundred penny-dreadfuls about the stolen eyes of idols and death-bearing charms.

A Passage to India is a disturbing, uncomfortable book. Its surface is so delicately and finely wrought that it pricks us at a thousand points. There is no emotional repose or security about it; it is for ever puncturing our complacence, it is a bed of thorns. The humour, irony and satire that awake the attention and delight the mind on every page all leave their sting. We cannot escape to the past or the future, because Mr. Forster's method does not encourage the growth of those accretions in the mind; he pins us down to the present moment, the discontent and pain of which cannot be allayed by reference to what has been or to what will be. The action of the book is not fused by a continuous impulse; it is a series of intense isolated moments. To overstate the case very much, the characters seem with each fresh sensation to begin their lives again. And that perhaps is why no general aspect or outline of Mr. Forster's book is so satisfactory as its details.

106. J. B. Priestley, review, *London Mercury*

x, no. 57, July 1924, 319–20

John Boynton Priestley (1894–), novelist, dramatist, essayist, critic and social historian. He contributed a volume on Meredith to the *English Men of Letters* series in 1926, and his novel *The Good Companions* (1929) was a best-seller.

Mr. E. M. Forster has had a very different fate from that of any other member of that group of promising, brilliant young novelists, the 'coming men' of, say, nineteen-hundred-and-ten to-twelve. Many of his colleagues, instead of writing themselves 'in,' have by this time succeeded in writing themselves out. Mr. Forster, after the publication of his very successful *Howard's End*, apparently stopped writing fiction, and this new story of Anglo-Indian life is the first novel he has produced for at least twelve years. His return should be regarded by every intelligent reader of fiction as an event. He has brought back his own exquisite sanity into the English novel, and his curious sensitiveness, honesty and, perhaps above all, his civilising quality (for surely he is the most civilised writer we have), make some of our more recent discoveries among novelists look very cheap. Once more we are given a real novel, an honest thing in three dimensions, and not an amusing literary gesture, a bag of coloured tricks, seven shillings worth of careless and dishonest autobiography served up with sixpenny worth of creative effort. Everything is present, ideas, character, action, atmosphere—a genuine civilised narrative. While I enjoyed every moment of this book, however, I cannot help feeling sorry that Mr. Forster did not choose to mirror contemporary English society in that astonishingly just and sensitive mind of his. Anglo-India is caught here, I imagine, as it has never been caught before, and its sharp divisions, its crushing institutionalism and officialism, its racial and herd thought and emotion, provide an excellent background for Mr. Forster's somewhat elusive philosophy of personal relationships. But it is too much of a 'special case,' and unless we too happen to be Anglo-

Indians, Mr. Forster's little thrusts are too apt to give us the pleasant task of applauding the discovery of weaknesses outside ourselves instead of the less pleasant but more salutary and exciting business of acknowledging our own weaknesses. But how cunningly the scene is presented, and with what extraordinary justice. Two ladies arrive from England, one, Mrs. Moore, the old mother of the district magistrate, the other, Miss Quested, his prospective wife and their presence in Chandrapore, their desire to know 'the real India,' and their distrust of the official Anglo-Indian attitude have the same effect as a stone flung into a pool. Mr. Forster has distributed his interest, so that this is nobody's story, or rather it is everybody's. Person after person; Mrs. Moore, old, weary of the needless complications, the fussiness of life, looking for an hour or so of quiet with the huge staring universe; Miss Quested, so curiously barren like all her kind, who laboriously desire to do right without really spending themselves; young Heaslop, the conscientious Indian civilian, only frustrated by the knowledge of his own rectitude; Aziz, the Europeanised Oriental, drifting, emotional, and only contemptible when glimpsed against a background that is not his; and so on and so forth; person after person is brought before us in the shifting and re-shifting of the action, and everyone is treated as real persons should be treated—with a certain detached sympathy that is the very height of human justice. So too, group after group, Anglo-Indians, Mohammedans, Brahmans, are similarly caught. And what a wealth of ideas and impressions the narrative holds, from such flicks of the whip as these:

They (the Anglo-Indians) had started speaking of 'women and children'—that phrase that exempts the male from sanity when it has been repeated a few times. Each felt that all he loved best in the world was at stake, demanded revenge, and was filled with a not unpleasing glow, in which the chilly and half-known features of Miss Quested vanished, and were replaced by all that is sweetest and warmest in the private life, "But it's the women and children," they repeated, and the Collector knew he ought to stop them intoxicating themselves, but he hadn't the heart.

to such characteristic passages of dialogue and subtle impression as this:

'But it has made me remember that we must all die: all these personal relations we try to live by are temporary. I used to feel death selected people, it is a notion one gets from novels, because some of the characters are usually left talking at the end. Now "death spares no one" begins to be real.'

'Don't let it become too real, or you'll die yourself. That is the objection to "meditating upon death". We are subdued to what we work in. I have felt the same temptation, and had to sheer off. I want to go on living a bit.'

'So do I.'

A friendliness, as of dwarfs shaking hands, was in the air. Both man and woman were at the height of their powers—sensible, honest, even subtle. They spoke the same language, and held the same opinions, and the variety of age and sex did not divide them. Yet they were dissatisfied. When they agreed, 'I want to go on living a bit,' or, 'I don't believe in God,' the words were followed by a curious back-wash as though the universe had displaced itself to fill up a tiny void, or as though they had seen their own gestures from an immense height—dwarfs talking, shaking hands and assuring each other that they stood on the same footing of insight. They did not think they were wrong, because as soon as honest people think they are wrong instability sets up. Not for them was an infinite goal behind the stars, and they never sought it. But wistfulness descended on them now, as on other occasions; the shadow of the shadow of a dream fell over their clean-cut interests, and objects never seen again seemed messages from another world.

It is some time since I read *Howard's End*, and it has not been possible for me to read it again for the purpose of comparison, a matter of some interest after such a long silence on the part of an author. Writing, then, after such a long interval, I can only suggest that a certain curious evocative power, a certain unusual and very characteristic pregnancy of style, which was at its height in the earlier work, has not been here entirely recaptured. On the other hand, this is the more rounded, complete and satisfying narrative, if only because it never for a moment ceases to be entirely convincing, whereas in *Howard's End*, the two most important incidents in the narrative, the seduction of one sister and the marriage of the other, never failed to leave me frankly incredulous. No, Mr. Forster has not returned to disappoint us. Unlike his Anglo-Indian males, he is one of those fortunate few who are able to allow nothing to 'exempt them from sanity,' and now that he has come back, as a novelist, to a world that is even more insane and even more in need of his clear-sighted exquisite charity, than the world he stopped writing about so many years ago, now that he has returned we should celebrate the event. In that neurotic's home and that dreary smoking-room which together represent contemporary fiction, a window has been opened and once more we can catch a glimpse of the mountains and the stars.

107. R. Ellis Roberts, review, *Bookman* (London)

lxvi, no. 394, July 1924, 220–1

Richard Ellis Roberts (1879–1953), author and journalist, Literary Editor of the *New Statesman* from 1930 to 1932.

We knew from Mr. Forster's earlier work that he had a surprising grasp of the modern character and the modern temperament; even if he was, as some unkind critics of *Howard's End* asseverated, 'by Cambridge out of Kensington,' he had the sympathy and sense to know that both those homes of culture were inhabited by quite real people. Most novelists of manners and society only mimic the gestures of their puppets; he, with Mr. Charles Marriott, feels the flesh and blood in the most unlikely persons. But few, except those who have read with understanding books of Mr. Forster which are not fiction, could have guessed that he had in his power the making of a novel so rich in colour, so lively in sensation, so varied in aspect as *A Passage to India*. There was depth as well as humour and sympathy in *A Room With a View*; but in that enchanting book the line between fancy and imagination, between whim and wisdom was rather insecurely kept. I would give nothing for a Mr. Forster who had forgotten how to be freakish; but in this book he knows when he is being freakish—or at least almost always knows; and he deals with a world larger and more significant than any he has dealt with, and yet still remembers that it is men and women who matter most.

There are three worlds in *A Passage to India*: the Anglo-Indian world; the world of cultured India; and the world—on which both these depend—the world of the old, primitive, uneducated Indian, a world very wise, very determined and very difficult. Agatha Quested comes to Chandrapore with Mrs. Moore to see Ronny Heaslop, Mrs. Moore's son, an Anglo-Indian official. They are not engaged. Agatha wants first to see Ronny at work, and this is the story of what she saw. Her desire directly she lands is to see India. She is tired of the official life, of the servant life, of the parasitic life; and she pictures all these as a screen behind which, waiting patiently and magnificently, is the real India. The unfortunate girl is entirely sincere, if rather stupid. She has no real capacity for sight at all. Mrs. Moore, who has no theories but much sense, great sympathy and a curious mystic understanding of people, sees India very quickly in a very simple way. She sees one Indian, Dr. Aziz, the Indian assistant of Major Callendar. Aziz is young, forceful, alternately bored and furious at the English professions of superiority; he has no English friends until he makes one of Fielding, a schoolmaster who is old enough and sensible enough to know that men and women are very much alike in their sillinesses and sensitivenesses. The way in which Mr. Forster shows us Aziz and his reactions makes one of the best pieces of psychological fiction I have read for years. Henry James never did anything better than some of the chapters in which Aziz communes with himself; and Mr. Forster is straightforward when James would have been ponderously sly and incredibly involved. Equally masterly is the analysis of the direct Fielding, the simple, not very intelligent but competent Ronny, and of the Mohammedan group in which Aziz finds his friends. With Professor Godbole, the Brahmin, Mr. Forster is not quite so successful: he is anxious that we should grasp Godbole's surprising aloofness, his 'polite and enigmatic' manner, the way in which at a tea-party 'he took his tea at a little distance from the outcasts, from a low table placed slightly behind him, to which he stretched back and as it were encountered food by accident.' He does give us Godbole's externals, but I do not feel he knew him or understood him as he understood the other people in his story.

The story is as vivid and as exciting as the characters. No one need be afraid that Mr. Forster has written a 'highbrow' book. *A Passage to India* not only has plenty of incident and plenty of humour, but it has scenes of description which are as richly portrayed as they could be by more spectacular novelists. A good example of Mr. Forster's narrative style is that in which Mrs. Moore reflects over her adventure in the Marabar cave:

> The more she thought over it, the more disagreeable and frightening it became. She minded it much more now than at the time. The crush and the smells she could forget, but the echo began in some indescribable way to undermine her hold on life. Coming at a moment when she chanced to be fatigued, it had managed to murmur, 'Pathos, piety, courage—they exist, but are identical, and so is filth.' Everything exists, nothing has value. If one had

spoken vileness in that place, or quoted lofty poetry, the comment would have been the same—'ou-boum.' If one had spoken with the tongues of angels and pleaded for all the unhappiness and misunderstanding in the world, past, present and to come, for all the misery men must undergo whatever their opinion and position, and however much they dodge or bluff—it would amount to the same, the serpent would descend and return to the ceiling. Devils are of the North, and poems can be written about them, but no one would romanticise the Marabar because it robbed infinity and eternity of their vastness, the only quality that accommodates them to mankind.

In the caves of Marabar, to which Aziz has taken them on a picnic, Mrs. Moore and Agatha both have strange experiences. Mrs. Moore's only affects herself, unless her thought perhaps dragged in Agatha and made her feign (sincerely but mistakenly) that Aziz had insulted her. After that feigned insult the story gains in power. The feeling at the club, the gossip in the bazaar, the trial and Agatha's confession are all presented with extraordinary feeling and beauty. Mr. Forster has published no novel for fourteen years. I would wait as long for another book as good as this, but I hope he will make the interval a shorter one.

108. Marmaduke Pickthall, letter to E. M. Forster

18 July 1924

Marmaduke William Pickthall (1875–1936) wrote novels, usually on Middle Eastern themes, and edited the *Bombay Chronicle* from 1920 to 1924. He travelled and lived in the Middle East, particularly Egypt and the Lebanon, and entered the Educational Service of the Nizam of Hyderabad in 1925. I regret not having been able to trace the review he planned to write for the *Bombay Chronicle*.

How very kind of you to send me your *Passage to India*. I have read it with a strong desire to understand what it is that so depresses all my fellow countrymen here, except of course the purely animal among them. I cannot say that I have fathomed it exactly, but your book has given me ideas which I shall try to express when I review it in the *Bombay Chronicle*.

. . . .

My compliments on your success in portraiture [of the 'solidarity' of the 'fluttered English']. I do not like your Indians half so well.

109. D. H. Lawrence, letter to Martin Secker

23 July 1924

Cf. No. 123.

Am reading *Passage to India*. It's good, but makes one wish a bomb would fall and end everything. Life is more interesting in its undercurrents than in its obvious, and E. M. does see people, people and nothing but people: *ad nauseam*.

110. John Middleton Murry, 'Bo-oum or Ou-boum?', *Adelphi*

ii, no. 2, July 1924, 150–3

John Middleton Murry (1889–1957), author of *Keats and Shakespeare* (1925), *Son of Woman* (1931), etc., was Editor of the *Adelphi* from 1923 to 1948.

It was only to be expected that Mr. E. M. Forster's novel when it did come, after a silence of fourteen years, would be a remarkable one. What might further have been expected was that it would in itself contain an explanation of that abnormal interlude. *A Passage to India* does this: it tells us that the miracle is not that Mr. Forster should have taken fourteen years to write it, but that he should have written it at all. For evidently the best part of those fourteen years was occupied not in writing this very fine novel, but in wondering whether there was indeed anything on earth, or in the heavens above, or in the waters under the earth, worth writing about. And even then, in that long space of years, Mr. Forster did not *decide* that there was. No, the balance faintly inclined, the pointer dribbled over towards 'To be,' and the silence was interrupted.

I scarcely think it will be interrupted again. The planning of Mr. Forster's next novel should carry him well on to the unfamiliar side of the grave. It will take him, I imagine, a good deal more than fourteen years to find the word which will evoke a different echo from the primeval cave of Marabar: and I fancy (such is my faith in his intellectual honesty) that he will not speak again without the assurance of a different reply.

But what is the echo of the cave of Marabar? This is what it is absolutely:

> The echo in a Marabar cave . . . is entirely devoid of distinction. Whatever is said, the same monotonous voice replies, and quivers up and down the walls till it is absorbed in the roof. *Boum* is the sound as far as the human alphabet can express it, or *bou-oum*, or *ou-boum*,—utterly dull. Hope, politeness, the blowing of a nose, the squeak of a boot, all produce *boum*. Even the striking of a match starts a little worm coiling, which is too small to complete a circle, but is eternally watchful. And if several people talk at once, an overlapping howling noise begins, echoes generate echoes, and the cave is stuffed with a snake composed of small snakes, which writhe independently.

And this is what it was to an elderly woman who was gifted (or cursed), like her creator, with 'the twilight of the double vision':

> The echo began in some indescribable way to undermine her hold on life· Coming at a moment when she chanced to be fatigued, it had managed to murmur, 'Pathos, piety, courage—they exist, but are identical, and so is filth. Everything exists, nothing has value.' If one had spoken vileness in the place, or quoted lofty poetry, the comment would have been the same—*ou-boum*.

A cave of Marabar is the symbol of the universe for Mr. Forster: no wonder then that he should have waited so long before inviting an echo from it. He might almost as well have waited an eternity. 'It is a good book'—*bou-oum*; 'it is a bad book'—*ou-boum*; 'it is a good bad book'—*bou-oum*; 'it is a bad good book'—*ou-boum*.

To be or not to be? was once the question. But now, *Ou-boum* or *bou-oum*? Of these one is as good as the other. And yet, I wonder, is that indeed the only echo which reaches Mr. Forster's metaphysical ear? Is *ou-boum* or *bou-oum* really the rich and rippling recompense for the dropping of this novel into the everlasting void? If it is, then Mr. Forster is a hero: but if it is not. . . .

I am speaking not of the outward fiction, which is brilliant and dramatic and absorbing, but of the inward significance of *A Passage to India*. That is the same (though expressed in how different a dialect!) as the significance of Mr. Joyce's savage and hyperborean *Ulysses*. The outward fiction politely declares: 'I am revealing a strange and unknown continent—India—as it has never been revealed before.' That is true. But the inward significance whispers: 'I am obeying the word: Command that these stones be made bread.' And that not even Mr. Forster can do.

One after the other they go, the talents of our age, dropping into the void. *Ou-boum* or *bou-oum*? The echo of *A Passage to India* is one of the greater ones: so many of the others are no more than 'the little worms coiling, too small to complete a circle.' Mr. Forster's echo completes a circle utterly. And that is a great achievement. But what then? When the subtle, delicate, wistful voice of Mr. Forster evokes the same response as the vulgar braying of *****? Is it enough to have given companions he would despise a symbol they will not understand? Can it be that one so skilful should have lost his way because he has forgotten a simple but difficult truth: that the head cannot really find room for that which the heart rejects, or both will wither and grow old? Can it be that, like his own Mrs. Moore, Mr. Forster

has come to that state where the horror of the universe and its smallness are both visible at the same time—the twilight of the double vision in which so many elderly people are involved. If this world is not to our taste, well, at all events there is Heaven, Hell, Annihilation—one or other of those large things, that huge scenic background of stars, fires, blue or black air. All heroic endeavour, and all that is known as art, assumes that there is such a background, just as all practical endeavour, when the world is to our taste, assumes that the world is all. But in the twilight of the double vision, a spiritual muddledom is set up for which no high-sounding words can be found; we can neither act nor refrain from action, we can neither ignore nor respect Infinity.

Whether or not this is Mr. Forster's condition, in that last half-sentence is contained the genesis and the import of *A Passage to India*.

111. Unsigned notice, *Times of India* (Bombay)

23 July 1924, 13

Reprinted by permission of the *Times of India*.

This book is quite devastatingly clever; and fully representative of Mr. Forster's highly original talent. There is always a risk that when a novelist who has won reputation in other fields begins to turn his attention to India, the end of all things, so far as he is concerned, is near. For this luckless country is at the moment decidedly over-written. But there is room, and more than room, for such works as this. Often and often has the life of Anglo-India been satirised, derided, or eulogised. Here we have it portrayed in a series of vignettes which, for their delicacy of touch and perfection of detail, remind us of the Flemish School. But it is not the studies of Anglo-Indian life which lend to the book its remarkable interest. The central figure of the story is a young Mahomedan doctor; and it is round his relation with Anglo-India that the theme revolves. We have never encountered a more finished study of the psychology of Educated India—deft, incisive, sympathetic, but disillusioned. The mental complexes and inhibitions; the mysticism; the modernism; the racial pride; the intellectual alertness; the supersentiveness, are all there. We are frankly amazed at the skill with which the scalpel is used to lay bare, as it were, each quivering nerve and to expose every morbid growth. And yet with it all, the book is enthralling in its interest; the poor little tragedy round which it centres grips the imagination. No one, we think, can pick it up without feeling compelled to turn its searchlight upon himself. It is a very genuine contribution, at once powerful, original, and thought-provoking, to the central problem in India to-day—that of the relations between the races and creeds whom Fate has brought together in this distracted land. If it is read as widely as it deserves to be, it may exercise a salutary influence. For, like many of those drugs which relieve the ills of mankind, its bitterness in the mouth augments, rather than detracts from, its cathartic properties.

112. Laurence Stallings, review, *World* (New York)

13 August 1924, 9

'When Rudyards cease their Kiplings and Haggards Ride no more'.

Laurence Stallings (1894–1968) was born in Georgia and edited the literary column of the New York *World*. He published a novel, *Plumes*, in 1924, but is better known as the author of a number of plays in collaboration with Maxwell Anderson, and of many film-scripts.

E. M. Forster's new book is so good a novel that even a reviewer faced with groaning tables of new fall fiction cannot hasten through *A Passage to India* to get on with the fall reading. It is Mr. Forster's first novel in some time, perhaps ten years. He has contributed short stories, essays and sketches since he published *Howard's End*, until one no longer thought of him as a novelist. Two slight books he published last year through Knopf were *The Celestial Omnibus* and *Pharos and Pharillon*. The first was a collection of fantastic stories, which this department boomed so raucously it never has been heard of since. The other was a series of essays on the Alexandrian lighthouse and its legends. Since *Howard's End*, however, he has forsaken the novel until now. In the mean time his colleagues, to quote the *London Mercury*, 'instead of writing themselves in, have succeeded in writing themselves out.'

* * *

I doubt that any other book of the fall will supplant *A Passage to India* as the most sensitive piece of fiction in years. Yet it will require a disinterested American reader to follow it through, for it is concerned solely with British India, and not as a romantic quarry for an outlandish story. It is concerned rather with transmissions of ideas (or with the welter of misunderstanding) between one race and another. With a thousand shades and delicacies of writing, he seems to have pulled a page from the life of British India. But you would not read *A Passage to India* for this page; it would not be worth your while, perhaps. But you will read *A Passage to India* for yourself and find that here, if ever, the Western mind and the Eastern one have been imprisoned and photographed with the most sensitive of lenses, upon the plate of E. M. Forster's mind.

About India: He is as thoroughly saturated in his fields as was Mr. Conrad in his when he came to London, to quote Philip Guedalla, 'with a remarkable prose style and a vivid memory of the Dutch East Indies.' But Mr. Forster's style is remarkable for its clarity, its smooth penetration. There is nothing diffuse about him, nothing interminable. Nor has *A Passage to India* the externals of romance, the theme almost inevitable when a novelist is given the rim o' the world, varied races, shaded skins.

* * *

The story is of the slightest. Two Englishwomen, a Mrs. Moore and a Miss Quested, come to a small, boresome hole called Candrapore. The unmarried woman is chaperoned there to visit her fiance, a small cog in the British civil machine. Miss Quested, a courageous and conscionable prig, makes a grave charge as to the conduct of a certain native M.D., a Moslem named Aziz. And reason is thrown to the winds.

Until this charge is made Mr. Forster has been painting his scene, drawing his lines, sketching in his figures, turning out their minds to the reader's inspection. Once the charge is made and he sets the whole community in motion—Moslems, Hindus, English, Pathans—concerning himself, [with] the measureless differences between the two mass minds, European and Indian. He does so without the faintest intimation of prejudice for one side or another. He is at pains to show that he is dealing with second rate figures: that his British are the second rate Government officials exported in large quantities by the tight little isle of the North Sea: that his Indians are only medium grade, and touched too with the crazy quilt of engrafting a smattering of Occidental science upon Oriental metaphysics. The essence of propaganda, of blanket indictment of one race or another, is not in

A Passage to India. Mr. Forster is too good a novelist, has too finely proportioned a reasoning faculty, to be concerned with 'issues' in his fiction. Only as an artist he is busy in aligning the forces within his ken.

I should like to quote from *A Passage to India*. But the prose does not come apart readily, will not easily permit of disintegration. A train of ideas, set sputtering at the outside gives way to a thousand succeeding grains of thought, volatile, powerful, capable of catastrophe, of enormous explosion. It is difficult to segregate one. I might give for one example, however, Fielding's (the best of the Europeans) philosophy.

The world, he believed, is a globe of men who are trying to reach one another, and can best do so by the help of good will plus culture and intelligence—a creed ill-suited to Chandrapore, but he had come out too late to lose it. He had no racial feeling—not because he was superior to his brother civilians, but because he had matured in a different atmosphere, where the herd instinct does not flourish. The remark that did him most harm at the club was a silly aside to the effect that the so-called white races are really a pinko-grey. He had only said this to be cheery, he did not realise that 'white' has no more to do with color than 'God Save the King' has to do with a god, and that it is the height of impropriety to consider what it does connote. The pinko-grey male whom he addressed was subtly scandalized, his sense of insecurity was awoken, and he communicated it to the rest of the herd.

* * *

And what a book this is, what flights of writing, turns of philosophy. A small handbook of thoughts and 'pensees' could be made from its asides. In the feeling for its subject matter, one instantly is provoked to make the inevitable comparison of Kipling's India. What a long way we have all of us come since then, despite the botching at Versailles and massacre at Amritsar. Young men who bow before the castiron effectiveness of Kipling's prose have long since learned to laugh at his absurd and lily-white Jehovah with the reeking tube and iron shard. But here is Forster, an Englishman too, cracking the whip of reason over this philosophy Kipling followed. And how sharp and incisive the flicks of its lash, how stinging, how accurate! *A Passage to India* should be your first purchase from the fall list.

113. Edward Carpenter, letter to E. M. Forster

14 August [? 1924]

Edward Carpenter (1844–1929) described himself in *Who's Who* as a 'democratic author and poet'. He was originally in Holy Orders and a Fellow of Trinity Hall, Cambridge, but relinquished both Orders and Fellowship, leaving Cambridge in 1874. He worked in various Northern towns for the University Extension Movement until 1881, and in 1883 settled on a small farm at Holmesfield near Sheffield, being occupied with, as he described it, 'literary work, market gardening, sandal-making, socialist movement, street corner propaganda'. He visited Walt Whitman in America in 1884. For his connection with Forster's *Maurice* cf. No. 167.

The *Passage to India* has arrived—and it is already a great joy to me! The people move through the book like real people and have character and decision—Ronny and Miss Quested and Mrs. Moore and the Nawab and Aziz and Fielding. I know now that I shall *finish the book!* —though I have read hardly more than a hundred pages. It gives me quite the feeling of India—the Anglo-Indian life—and I think the picture of that life as shown will have a considerable and a very sane and stimulating influence upon public opinion in England. Yet you are perfectly impartial and fair, and do not take sides anywhere that I can discover—always drawing the life (as nearly as can be) *as it is*, and keeping yourself out of sight. I could not write (a novel) like that. (Should tend to be drawn into the fray!) but it is a high class of art, and I congratulate you on it. The only fault I find with the book—and that is chiefly owing to my own slowness of apprehension—is that you put in so few signposts to direct the traveller! Often I have to *turn back* 2 or 3 pages to find out *who* is talking—but that as I say is chargeable to my own obtuseness! There is a quiet current of humour runs through the book ('a fabric bigger than the mosque fell to pieces') and I like the touches about the scenery throughout. I shall finish it as I say and write to you again.

. . . .

114. 'A striking novel', *Statesman* (Calcutta)

15 August 1924, 6

An unsigned review.

Mr. Forster's book has been widely praised as one of the great novels of the year, and even the reader who quarrels with his views will admit it to be a work of outstanding ability. The story is of the simplest; indeed, there is scarcely any. To Chandrapore, an up-country station, come two ladies from England—the mother of the city magistrate and the lady who contemplates marrying him. They wish to 'know India,' a wish which leads to various inconveniences and embarrassments, and ultimately to an accusation by the younger lady against a Mahomedan doctor of having assaulted her. There is a trial, an acquittal, racial friction, fears of a rising, and finally a few chapters on a Native State and gods and idols to help it all to a conclusion which is only a leaving-off. It is in his drawing of his few characters that Mr. Forster bewitches. He stands apart and views them, European officials and their wives, Hindus and Mahomedans, in their human littleness against the mighty background of the clash of creeds, races, sentiments, prejudices, resentments, that is India. The officials strut in their tiny dignity, the others falter in their uncertainties, while the gods play shuttlecock with all. Mr. Forster has taken a malicious pleasure in making most of his characters trivial and unlovable. The bullying civil surgeon, with a wife who held that 'the kindest thing one can do to a native is to let him die,' the policeman's wife who was 'all for chaplains and all against missionaries,' the collector's wife, always saving up her courtesy and kindliness for important visitors, —all are gathered together. If Chandrapore were a type of the Indian station, India would certainly be a lost dominion.

The men's point of view may be exemplified by Ronnie, a civilian of one year's standing. He is self-complacent, censorious, unsubtle; indifferent to the feelings of others; always right, or if wrong, certain that it does not matter; consciously upright and conscientious. He is not in India to behave pleasantly, but to do justice and keep the peace; in short, 'to work, and to hold this wretched country by force.'

When his finance becomes unpleasantly involved in a public case, he releases himself from the engagement because marriage with her now would retard his advancement. It is an unattractive character, but Mr. Forster is not kind to the official in India. Still, he has a word of appreciation for the policeman, the 'most reflective and best educated' of the Chandrapore officials, who, 'owing to an unhappy marriage, had read and thought a great deal, and evolved a complete philosophy of life.' Also for the Lieutenant-Governor, who appears on the scene for a moment. Not an enlightened man, he held enlightened opinions; 'exempted by a long career in the Secretariat from personal contact with the peoples of India, he was able to speak of them urbanely, and to deplore racial prejudice.' The Indian characters are in general dealt with more gently, with some pity for the confused circumstances of their lives, but with the exception of Dr. Aziz, the chief Mahomedan character, with less distinctness of outline.

The account of the Mahomedan doctor's trial on the charge of having insulted an English lady is a serious blemish in the book, and as thousands of readers in England will doubtless take it as gospel, it is calculated to do grave mischief. All the codes appear to have been specially suspended for the occasion. An Indian of good social and official position is arrested summarily. It is a bailable offence, but bail is at first refused, then granted, and then again revoked. The superintendent of police conducts the prosecution before an Indian joint magistrate, and the European officials gather on chairs round the magistrate on the platform, interfering and interrupting. When they are made to leave the platform it is felt as a national humiliation, while all the Indians rejoice. Finally, when the prisoner is discharged without a stain on his character, 'the flimsy framework of the court broke up, the shouts of derision and rage culminated, people screamed and cursed, kissed one another, wept passionately.' The account is so full of technical error—indeed, so preposterous, that it cannot even be called a travesty. It is much to be regretted that a writer with Mr. Forster's evident knowledge of the country should have thought fit to supplement his experience by so reckless a use of his imagination. If he did not himself know how an Indian trial is conducted, why did he not ask for information from someone who did?

But indeed, the whole story produces a curiously ill-balanced effect on the informed reader. In his treatment of some aspects of Indian life, Mr. Forster is almost photographic in his accuracy; in others, he seems to be depending on a blend of hearsay and invention. On the one hand, his account and interpretation of the ceremonies at the Gokul Aohtami will be read with keen delight: on the other, his picture of the life of an Indian mofussil station is a caricature and not even a clever caricature. One is led to speculate as to what Mr. Forster's Indian experience may have been. Was he taken round the country by the gifted lady president of the Theosophical Society?

115. An Anglo-Indian view

August 1924

E. A. Horne, letter to the editor, *New Statesman* xxiii, no. 591, 16 August 1924, 543–4

E. A. Horne was a member of the Indian Education Service; his letter, of 23 July, was sent from Patna.

Sir,—The publication of a new novel by Mr. Forster, after twelve years' silence, is a great event—perhaps, *the* literary event of the year. This, in itself, is sufficient excuse for a good deal of ink being spilt about it; but, apart from its character as a literary event, the book is one which I think will be much discussed. Mr. Ralph Wright has already reviewed it in *The New Statesman*; and what I now feel impelled to write is not another review, but something which will convey to English readers how the book strikes an Anglo-Indian—a task for which I claim to possess qualifications, having spent the last fourteen years of my life in Chandrapore itself. And with all respect to English literary critics, a knowledge of Cambridge and the suburbs of London, while it may equip them to appraise Mr. Forster's earlier novels, is scarcely sufficient for the appraisement (apart from the purely literary merits of the work, to which they have done full justice) of this latest one. For, after all, this is not a case of mere local colour, as in novels one might mention, the scene of which is laid in Egypt or Morocco, but of Mr. Forster's own 'passage to India.' The centre of his universe is shifted, for the time being, from Surbiton to Chandrapore. It is this rare faculty to identify himself with the little world he is describing, to live its life from the inside, which gives to all Mr. Forster's novels their special quality; and, incidentally, as I shall try to show later, it is to this peculiar faculty of his that his latest novel owes not only what is so strangely beautiful and true, but elements which are unreal and strangely distorted.

A Passage to India is a novel, not about India (though the Indian background is wonderfully worked in), nor about Indian 'problems' (though these are plentifully implied), but about Indians—and more particularly, Indian Muhammadans. Fielding, who is the author's mouthpiece, when asked how one is to see the real India, replies: 'Try seeing Indians.' This is the way in which Mr. Forster himself has seen India; and it makes his book different from all other books about India. Mr. Forster has created some wonderful characters. The dear old Nawab Bahadur (whose favourite remark was: 'Give, do not lend; after death who will thank you?'); the polished and charming Hamidullah; Mohammed Latif ('a distant cousin of the house, who lived on Hamidullah's bounty and who occupied the position neither of a servant nor of an equal . . . a gentle, happy and dishonest old man'); Hassan (Aziz's servant)—Aziz himself. And some wonderful scenes! How perfect is Aziz's first appearance in the book; and how it strikes a key-note! 'Abandoning his bicycle, which fell before a servant could catch it, the young man sprang up on the verandah. He was all animation.' The first meeting of Aziz and Fielding, and the incident of the collar-stud. The chapters—among the most beautiful in the book, and to me the most moving—when Fielding calls on Aziz. ('Aziz thought of his bungalow with horror. It was a detestable shanty near a low bazaar.') Aziz is in bed, with slight fever. The room is full of people, many of them sitting on his bed. Of some he is acutely ashamed—'third-rate people.' His spiritual restlessness and discomfort —until he gets rid of the others, and has Fielding to himself, and shows him the photograph of his wife. The gorgeous episode at the railway station in the early morning, when Fielding and Godbole miss the train to the Marabar hills—the elephant, the caves and the picnic—all sustained on the full-spread wings of comedy until the crash into sordid tragedy. Such portraits, such scenes, by the hand of a Westerner, are something never before achieved, and are worthy of the cunning of Mr. Forster's hand at its deftest. And how lovingly are these characters studied—with the affectionate understanding which, while it glosses over none of their faults (some of them very odious), just because it understands, forgives. There is one thing, for me, unsatisfactory about Aziz. We are told too little, we are told practically nothing, about his social and spiritual antecedents. ('Touched by Western feeling' is the most that we are told on the subject.) Hamidullah we can 'place'; but Aziz we cannot, and are left groping.

Many readers will be dissatisfied with the central incident in the book—the thing, unpleasant but nameless (since no one can say what really happened), that befell Adela in the cave on the Marabar hills. Here is rich material for the psychoanalyst. My private theory is as follows. The 'hallucination' was not Adela's, but Aziz's. His the sexual vanity, the physical obsessions (on which Mr. Forster lays somewhat painful stress throughout the book); not Adela's, with her college-bred questionings about love. When she 'innocently asked Aziz what marriage was like,' it was the man who was thrown off his balance; 'and she supposed that her question had roused evil in him.' That it did, we may conclude from the gross image which Aziz conceived of the girl's attitude afterwards, putting these words into her mouth: 'Dear Dr. Aziz, I wish you had come into the cave; I am an old hag, and it is my last chance.' The hallucination was Aziz's; but it communicated itself to Adela, just as old Mrs. Moore's obsession by 'evil spirits' communicated itself to the girl's impressionable mind.

To some readers, the epilogue or pendant to the book (Part III., Temple), of which the scene is laid in a Native State on the other side of India, will savour of an impertinence. But a virtuoso passage of the finest is the description of the Hindu festival, the Gokul Ashtami (the birth of Krishna).

It is when one turns from the Indians, who are the real theme of the book, to the Anglo-Indians, who are its harsh but inevitable accompaniment, that one is confronted by the strangest sense of unreality.

The 'English' people are real enough. Fielding, the author's mouthpiece; Adela, with her frank, questioning, but ever baffled nature; old Mrs. Moore, with her rather shiftless, rather tiresome, mysticism, but her authentic beauty of soul. Indeed, they are types with which the reader of Mr. Forster's earlier novels will feel instantly at home. But the Anglo-Indians? Where have they come from? What planet do they inhabit? One rubs one's eyes. They are not even good caricatures, for an artist must see his original clearly before he can successfully caricature it. They are puppets, simulacra. The only two of them that come alive at all are Ronny, the young and rapidly becoming starched civilian, and the light-hearted Miss Derek.

Many of Mr. Forster's generalisations about Anglo-Indian society are both witty and penetrating. This, for example: 'The orchestra played the National Anthem. Conversation and billiards stopped, faces stiffened. It was the Anthem of the Army of Occupation. It reminded every member of the club that he or she was British and in exile. It produced a little sentiment and a useful accession of will-power.' Or, again: 'Their ignorance of the Arts was notable, and they lost no opportunity of proclaiming it to one another; it was the Public School attitude, flourishing more vigorously than it can yet hope to do in England. The Arts were bad form.' The incident of Aziz's tonga, commandeered without a word of explanation or apology by two ladies wanting to get to the club, rings true. The self-complacency too, of a young man like Ronny, when faced with the apparent impossibility of mixing with Indians on terms of social equality. 'One touch of regret would have made him a different man, and the British Empire a different institution.'

Even about the general background, however, there is a slight air of unreality. This is partly because the picture is out of date. The period is obviously before the War. Not that this matters, provided it is clearly understood. It is not only that Lieutenant-Governors and dog-carts are out of date. All the fuss about the 'bridge' party will strike the Anglo-Indian reader as hopelessly out of date, it being nowadays very much the fashion—not in Delhi and Simla only, but in the humble mofussil station also—to entertain and cultivate Indians of good social standing.

But it is of Mr. Forster's Anglo-Indian men and women that I wish to speak. Of Turton, the Collector, who is addressed individually and in chorus, and at every turn—as by children in school—as 'Burra Sahib'; and about whom all the other Europeans scrape and cringe.

Turton, who is for ever hectoring Fielding, a man not much his junior in years and occupying a sufficiently important official position, telling him (speaking 'officially,' whatever that may mean) to stand up, or 'to leave this room at once,' or to be at the club at six, always addressing him as 'Mr.' Fielding. 'Pray, Mr. Fielding, what induced you to speak to me in such a tone?' This man is not an Indian civilian; he is a college don, and ridiculous enough as that. Of Callendar (of the Indian Medical Service), that incredible cad and bully. Of McBryde, the Superintendent of Police, who, though he does use phrases (speaking of the Collector) like 'Sort of all-white thing the Burra Sahib would do,' is represented as being, morally and intellectually, by far the best of the bunch. And yet we are asked to believe that McBryde commits adultery with Miss Derek while she is staying in his own house, and his wife in the next room! And what is one to make of the women? But I think they are scarcely worth discussing, so inhuman are they without exception. And if these people are preposterous, equally preposterous are the scenes which they enact. The scene at the club, when an 'informal meeting' is held to discuss the situation created by the alleged assault on Adela; the scene in the court-room at the trial, which ends with Callendar ('on a word from Turton') standing up and bawling: 'I stop these proceedings on medical grounds.'

And why is this? Why are these people and these incidents so wildly improbable and unreal? The explanation is a singular but a simple one. Mr. Forster went out to India to see, and to study, and to make friends of Indians. He did not go out to India to see Anglo-Indians; and most of what he knows about them, their ways and their catchwords, and has put into his book, he has picked up from the stale gossip of Indians, just as the average Englishman who goes out to India picks up most of what he knows about Indians from other Englishmen. It is a curious revenge that the Indian enjoys in the pages of Mr. Forster's novel which profess to deal with Anglo-Indian life and manners; and some would say a just one. All the same, it is a thousand pities that Mr. Forster did not see the real Anglo-India, for he would have written an incomparably better and truer book; and we venture to suggest to him, next time he goes to India: 'Try seeing Anglo-Indians.'

But there is yet another reason why Mr. Forster's picture of Anglo-Indian society is distorted; and this may be told by means of a parable. Even when Aziz blasphemes hideously against their friendship, accusing Fielding of having made Adela his mistress (immediately after the trial); even under this provocation, Fielding understands and forgives his friend. But for the offending members of the European club, he has in his heart no understanding, no forgiveness. To Aziz 'he made a clean breast about the club—said he had only gone under compulsion, and should never attend again unless the order was renewed.' I have said that Fielding is Mr. Forster's mouthpiece; and nobody can describe people as they really are unless he has some affection for them.

116. Another Anglo-Indian view

August 1924

S. K. Ratcliffe, letter to the editor, *New Statesman* xxiii, no. 592, 23 August 1924, 567–8

Samuel Kerkham Ratcliffe (1868–1958) was Acting Editor of the *Statesman* (Calcutta) from 1903 to 1906. He was a member of the National Liberal Club, contributed frequent articles to the monthly reviews and, in 1923, published *Sir William Wedderburn and the Indian Reform Movement.*

Sir,—Mr. E. A. Horne of the Indian Education Service is prompt and right on the target. He has got in first with the kind of letter which, it was certain, many critical Anglo-Indians are eager to throw after reading Mr. Forster's book. *A Passage to India* has, of course, been dealt with by the reviewers as a very remarkable novel. Mr. Horne opens the debate upon it as something altogether different—*namely*, an event of imperial significance. I can think of no piece of imaginative writing in our time which possesses that character in an equal degree.

Mr. Horne, I think, is happy on the whole in his selection of typical incidents and characters that seem to him worthy of praise, but I should dissent from him strongly in regard to some of those cited by him. For instance: almost the last thing I should say about Mr. Forster's

Indian characters is that they are 'lovingly studied'; few readers who know anything of India would share Mr. Horne's difficulty about 'placing' Dr. Aziz, and fewer still, I believe, would wish to describe the last part of the book as an impertinence—unless (and there I should sympathise) they resented the author's use of the discredited long arm of coincidence.

It is, however, upon Mr. Horne's criticism of Mr. Forster's Anglo-Indians that I wish particularly to comment. Where, he asks, has Mr. Forster got them from? 'What planet do they inhabit?' Mr. Horne admits that many of Mr. Forster's generalisations about Anglo-India are witty and penetrating and he notes one or two incidents as ringing true. That, however, is the utmost he will allow to the Anglo-Indians in the book. His charge is that Mr. Forster simply has not observed the official English in India.

Here, I submit, Mr. Horne is at fault. He has no difficulty in showing that the Anglo-Indian scenes are out of drawing—the station club, for example; the curious forms of speech and address; the out-of-date details of station life. In regard to such matters, indeed, Mr. Horne might have gone a good deal further. My own especial complaint, in this connection, is the scene in the court-room which Mr. Horne in a sentence dismisses as preposterous. Now, as a piece of narrative this is so brilliantly written that it will probably, by most English readers, be voted triumphant. It seems necessary, therefore, to amplify Mr. Horne's criticism. The trial of Aziz by the Hindu magistrate is the centre scene of the book. The story proper ends with it. And yet it will not do. British officials could not have behaved in court as Mr. Forster makes his behave. The procedure is altogether wrong. The Superintendent of Police does not conduct the case against the accused: that is the job of the Government prosecutor. And if, as in the case of Aziz, an eminent Indian barrister were brought up from Calcutta, he would refuse to appear in so farcical a court and would insist, successfully, upon a transfer to another district.

In other words, I agree with Mr. Horne as to the unreality of the Anglo-Indian background, but I think he is mistaken in his general conclusion. Mr. Forster's externals are continually wrong. His court-room and club are absurd. His Turtons and Burtons (as Aziz calls them, contemptuously and compendiously) are not recognisable in detail. But they are true in the essentials of character and attitude. And the tremendous import of *A Passage to India* for our people is this: for all its mistakes and misreadings, it presents a society, a relation, and a system, which are in the long run impossible. Thirty years ago the station pictures of Rudyard Kipling flashed this truth for the first time over England. Mr. Forster's delicate pen is a far more deadly weapon.

But if this is, as I am convinced it is, the moral for us of *A Passage to India*, I wonder what moral will be discernible by Mr. Forster's Indian friends. Mr. Horne is impressed by, and delighted with, the Indian portraits in the book. They are vividly seen and presented: but of what kind are they? One reason suggested by Mr. Forster for the failure of the official garden party was that the Collector knew something to the discredit of every Indian present. Mr. Forster's Indians are all miserable creatures, feeble, fawning, dishonest, treacherous, or what not. True, they are shown usually, though not entirely, in relation to Anglo-Indians. But the fact is there, and here is the point: we knew enough of Mr. Forster's intellectual character and attitude to know that he must depict the representatives of the ruling race with severity; and we assumed that, of necessity, he would find examples of contrasted nobleness among the Indian people. He has not done so; and I suspect that to-day in the club of Anglo-India the *Sahib-log* are asking derisively what need there can be of a defence for their own position and behaviour, if this is all that their merciless critic has to say for the educated Indians.

117. Rebecca West, 'Interpreters of their age', *Saturday Review of Literature* (New York)

i, no. 3, 16 August 1924, 42

It is always entertaining to speculate as to who of the younger writers are going to step into the places of the acknowledged great men when they go; and there has been a book published recently which hints at one who next will strike this generation as mirroring the changing spirit of the age with this impressiveness, and what that change will be. That book is Mr. E. M. Forster's *A Passage to India*. I am a little frightened lest readers on the American side of the Atlantic fail to appreciate it, for it is primarily a very conscientious study of a certain problem of the British Empire. It is a political document of the first importance; and since it will be filed in our archives and not yours that may seem against it. But note that it is full of passages of universal beauty, of universal interest, that one simply cannot compare with anything save the mystical poetry of Vaughan the Silurist. There is, for instance, the description of the caves of Marabar:

> They are dark caves. Even when they open towards the sun, very little light penetrates down the entrance tunnel into the circular chambers. There is little to see, and no eye to see it, until the visitor arrives for his five minutes, and strikes a match. Immediately another flame rises in the depths of the rock and moves towards the surface like an imprisoned spirit; the walls of the circular chamber have been most marvellously polished. The two flames approach and strive to unite, but cannot, because one of them breathes air, the other stone. A mirror inlaid with lovely colors divides the lovers, delicate stars of pink and grey interpose, exquisite nebulae, shadings fainter than the tail of a comet or the mid-day moon, all the evanescent life of the granite, only here visible. Fists and fingers thrust above the advancing soil—here at last is the skin of its body, finer than any covering acquired by the animals, smoother than windless water, more voluptuous than love. The radiance increases, the flames touch one another, kiss, expire. The cave is dark again, like all the caves. . . .

That is only the first verse of a poem about the caves which in the end creates a symbol of that willingness to imagine an eternity that is not motherly, an infinity which is not kind, an absolute that is not comforting, which makes certain forms of Indian mysticism terrifying to the Western mind.

Beautiful that writing, perfectly beautiful in a strange way that occasionally recalls *Kubla Khan*; and an entirely adequate symbol. Mr. Forster possesses the secret of all poets, which is intensity of perception. Thinking of Eastern mysticism, he sees all aspects of it, and the essence of each. Thinking of the caves, he sees all of them, the faintest scratch on the polished wall of the least visited of them, and he remembers the most tedious whisper of the blind guide concerning them. Being in possession of all the facts he can synthesize them, make them serve the interests of the truth at which he has arrived after this fullest possible consideration of the evidence. Thus does he do with every conceivable aspect of Indian life, culminating in the superb trial scene, where the account of the pitiful contentions of the Anglo-

Indians and the Indians is given its right values by the description of the man who pulled the punkah. He is seen at the beginning . . .

Almost naked, and splendidly formed, he sat on a raised platform near the back, in the middle of the central gangway. . . . He had the strength and beauty that sometimes come to flower in Indians of low birth. When that strange race nears the dust and is condemned as untouchable, then nature remembers the physical perfection that she accomplished elsewhere, and throws out a god—not many, but one here and there, to prove to society how little its categories impress her. . . .

He is seen at the end . . .

Before long no one remained on the scene of the fantasy but the beautiful naked god. Unaware that anything unusual had occurred he continued to pull the cord of his punkah, to gaze at the empty dais and the overturned special chairs, and rhythmically to agitate the clouds of descending dust.

Apt symbol he is for the pointing of the just view of the contending parties, which is also a merciful view. He was beautiful because he was in the dust and nature plays such tricks, and he was in harmony with the dust and with nature. The litigants had lost their beauty, because they were trying to rise above the dust, to bring a higher order into nature. He can use the punkah-wallah so well because he has observed him with this intensity of perception which is the result—like his choice of this complex and disputatious subject—of an enormous, an insatiable will to understand.

It is perhaps in Mr. Forster's possession of that quality that he is mirroring the change in his age. Was there ever, indeed, a period of the world since time began when humanity so simply, so purely, so exclusively, wished to understand? Even the Greeks complicated their desire for comprehension by discussing the connection between knowledge and virtue, and later ages made no bones about wanting it as a basis for the most effective action. But now we wish to understand, apparently for the sake of understanding alone. The books that men read concerning the late war are not celebrations of its valors nor denunciations of its cruelty, but analyses of its causes. To take this novel itself as an example, the average Englishman was used to regard India with the pride of the possessor; it was desirable for his national prosperity that he should; but now he would rather understand it, and he is reading *A Passage to India* with avidity. It may be that this desire for understanding may result in an age of impotence. That has been the belief of the men of action in all ages. Few armies have not held that it was the duty of a good soldier to die mentally in the service of his country. Yet we are safe in assuming that this age also is going to be glorious, for its celebration by its appropriate artist has the authentic sacramental quality.

118. Henry W. Nevinson, 'India's coral strand', *Saturday Review of Literature* (New York)

i, no. 3, 16 August 1924, 43

Henry Nevinson (1856–1941), journalist and author of many books, including *Ladysmith* (1900). He was on the staff of the *Nation* from its inception in 1907 until 1923. He travelled widely, either as a correspondent or privately, usually to places where political or military action was afoot. In 1904/1905 he visited Central Africa and exposed the Portuguese slave trade in Angola. In 1939 he was President of the Council for the Defence of Civil Liberties.

It is unfortunate that the very name of India arouses despair or indifference in British hearts. Our average citizen thinks vaguely of a vast country inhabited by hordes of brown or blackish 'natives,' who worship strange and improper gods, are given to atrocious mutinies and massacres, and would fight horribly among themselves if the controlling power of England were withdrawn. To some of us India is a field for missionary enterprise, to others a field for the lucrative employment of our sons, to others, again, a market for our cotton goods. There have been stages in our knowledge or our ignorance. There was the stage of the 'Nabobs,' when India was a dream of diamonds and gold and pearls; a country which we had acquired by the might of our sword for our own advantage, and to which no one questioned our right. There was the stage of 'India's coral strand'—the stage when India was to us the scene of widows burnt alive, madmen swinging themselves by hooks from poles as an act of sanctity, and worshippers flinging themselves beneath the bloody wheels of Juggernaut; from which abominations only English missionaries could save them. In that stage I was brought up, but about thirty years ago it was succeeded by the Kipling stage, when India was seen revealed as the home of incomprehensible 'natives' and jungley beasts, dominated for their own good by the British sons of 'The Blood,' who spent their time in deeds of amazing courage and the seduction of each other's wives.

At each stage our conception was entirely false—as false as the 'coral strand' of India, where, I believe, not a bead of coral could be found. And so it came about that, as each stage passed, most of our people felt a chill of despair or indifference when the name of India was mentioned. When 'the man in the street' sees a column of news from India in his morning paper, he hastily turns the page to a full-blooded murder in Eastbourne or the suburbs. Till quite lately, a debate on India in the House of Commons was taken as a signal for a members' holiday, like the Derby Day. India has become a subject passing the wit of 'the man in the street.' Surely we must be content to leave it to our experts—our well-paid Viceroy, our Lieutenant Governors, our Collectors and Commissioners, our trustworthy police, or, if the worst comes to the worst, our gallant British troops, which are maintained in the country at India's expense, and for her benefit. Are not our Judges a marvel of Justice? Is not our Indian Civil Service the wonder of the world?

That was the ordinary attitude of this country while I was in India during the period known as 'The Unrest.' But lately I have noticed some small change in opinion. It has been caused partly by the general upheaval of all traditions and ideas since the Great War; partly by the growing insistence of Indians themselves, as seen by the present delegation of Srinivasa Sastri and other leaders who are now in London with Dr. Annie Besant; but chiefly by the widespread horror at the Amritsar massacre about five years ago, the shameful speeches about it in the debate in the House of Lords, and what appears to me the still greater shame of the methods and judgment in the recent libel action upon that very point brought by Sir Michael O'Dwyer against Mr. Sankaran Nair, one of the most eminent and moderate of Indian statesmen. And now, just at what our scientific novelists call 'the

Psychological Moment,' comes this book of Mr. E. M. Forster, long recognized as one of our best and most thoughtful writers, not only of fiction.

Certainly the book is fiction of a kind. It may be called a novel, for it is an imaginary story with a carefully devised and elaborated plot, a certain amount of 'love interest' (not much, thank heaven!), a beginning, a middle, and an end, like all works of imaginative art. At its climax the story even becomes exciting—all the more 'intriguing' (if one must use that tiresome French word) because the heart of the mystery is never precisely explained. Just as a story it is excellent, being written with all the humor and irony of style that one expects from its distinguished author. Humor, irony, and sympathy are, in fact, his distinctions, and I could only question his dubious use of the pronoun 'he,' which often leaves me in doubt what 'he' is referred to. The use is so frequent that I suppose it is intentional, but it puzzles a careful reader like myself, and is repeatedly driving him back to solve a problem that should not exist.

But the story, though fine and full of characters finely suggested, is not the vital or most significant part of the work. It is the picture of Anglo-Indian life and character on the one side, and of Indian life and character of the other that is vital and significant. I have read many volumes written from both sides. At one time I knew both the missionary books and the Kipling books almost by heart. Since then I have travelled far and wide through India, and have consorted with Anglo-Indians of all ranks, and with Indians of all castes and classes. But I have never known so accurate, so penetrating, and so sympathetic an account of these divergent characters and lives as this. It is sympathetic with both sides. On the one hand we are shown the British official in all his real glory—devoted to his routine, inflexible in what he thinks justice, above suspicion of corruption, toiling almost incessantly upon work for which he receives no thanks, no recognition; separated from his wife, who must go to the hills or 'home,' and from his children who must be brought up far away in England; fairly paid but obliged to spend largely, unknown in his own country, and in the end destined, if he survives the fevers and the heat, to spend an old age upon the golf links or in the sanatoria of Cheltenham and Harrowgate. I have known these people well, and, on my word, there is no class of mankind that I admire more. So calm they are in the midst of perpetual dangers, so dignified in behavior, and so silent.

That side of our British workers Mr. Forster shows us, but he also shows us the other—the stiff aloofness, the pride refusing intercourse with 'natives,' the contempt, especially for the 'educated Indian,' the degrading use of spies—an abomination from which even I suffered much when I was in India. We are shown also the occasional outbursts of insensate and unreasoning passion, especially in the case of the Anglo-Indian women, who are our stiffest obstacle in attempting any friendly intercourse with the Indian peoples. As an Indian says in the book, an Englishman comes out intending to be a gentleman, but is told it will not do. It is the women who tell him so. It may take two years to make him like every one else, but it takes only six months for a woman. And so with time—and not a long time—the state of mind is reached depicted in the two following paragraphs:

> Nothing enrages Anglo-India more than the lantern of reason if it is exhibited for one moment after its extinction is decreed. All over Chandrapore that day the Europeans were putting aside their normal personalities and sinking themselves in their community. Pity, wrath, heroism filled them, but the power of putting two and two together was annihilated.

Or again, when women are discussing the same incident—the wrongfully imagined assault upon an English girl by a 'native'—

> 'I say there's not such a thing as cruelty after a thing like this.'
>
> 'Exactly, and remember it afterwards, you men. You're weak, weak, weak. Why they ought to crawl from here to the caves on their hands and knees whenever an Englishwoman's in sight, they oughtn't to be spoken to, they ought to be spat at, they ought to be ground into the dust; we've been far too kind.'

That is the spirit which makes Amritsar massacres, and afterwards glories in them, and gets up subscriptions for the agent. It is an illustration of what I myself wrote from India some years ago:

> The deterioration of a new-comer who has been sent out with the usual instincts of our educated classes in favor of politeness and decency, is often as unconscious as it is rapid. The pressure of his social surroundings is almost irresistible. If he does not wish to cut himself off altogether from the society and amusements of his own people, he will be driven to conform to the code of insolence established among them.

Set such a man to govern the Indian peoples, among whom reverential manners and deferential politeness are ingrained by birth—imaginative peoples, sensitive to slights, but always tempted to cringe and to flatter and bribe the man in power, and then what a degeneration of two great races, British and Indian, is likely to ensue! That is the root problem of India now, and I have never seen it so plainly stated as in this discerning story of manners and characters opposed.

For Mr. Forster does not deal only with the weakness of our British nature when placed in so unnatural a position as in India. He shows us the weakness of the Indian too—his tendency to break down and sob, his habit of wandering off into futile discussions when the moment calls for action, his want of persistence, his readiness to submit to orders, his fanatical unreason, and above all his suspicion of every Anglo-Indian action whether good or bad. As to the 'efficiency' that Lord Curzon preached for India, one of the Indians in the story admits they have not got it:

> We can't coördinate, we can't coördinate, it only comes to that. We can't keep engagements, we can't catch trains. What more than this is the so-called spirituality of India?

Moslems and Hindus are mingled in the story, and we are shown the marked difference in character, though there is no hostility, and little boasted superiority of the one form of religion over the other. That is one of the author's triumphs, and for the descriptive style of a quiet and discerning eye, I may quote the following picture of an Indian eventide as all who have lived in India know it:

> The promontory was covered with lofty trees, and the fruit-bats were unhooking from the boughs and making kissing sounds as thay grazed the surface of the tank; hanging upside down all day, thay had grown thirsty. The signs of the contented Indian evening multiplied; frogs on all sides, cow-dung burning eternally; a flock of belated hornbills overhead, looking like winged skeletons as they flapped across the gloaming. There was death in the air, but not sadness; a compromise had been made between destiny and desire, and even the heart of man acquiesced.

119. 'D. L. M.', review, *Boston Evening Transcript*

3 September 1924, 6

There are few writers of the present day from whom we have the right to expect more than we do from Mr. Forster. He has given us fine work before, and always within his work there has existed the clearly defined promise of better things to come. He possesses a keen and sympathetic sense of words, a possession which makes it possible for him to express much more within the compass of a sentence than can be accomplished by the majority of writers. So in *A Passage to India* we may almost escape recognition of his skill, so completely has his language become the medium of his ideas and impressions. In a period when many people write carelessly it is worthy of notice that he never has to strain for his effects, that he always is master of his medium.

A Passage to India seems to be the most significant of the many Anglo-Indian novels which have come to us in recent years. It goes deeper into the problems of Anglo-India, while at the same time it offers us as clear and as accurate a picture of the conditions under which English and Indians live as any we have read. It has to be confessed that a great number of books of Anglo-India mirror only the least significant of the problems of English life there. For all those writers are concerned, there might exist nothing except the handful of English men and women who represent England there, administer her government, and execute her commands. For the Indian in his home country we have had to look to a different type of books entirely. A certain few writers have pointed out that Englishmen, and to a much greater extent Englishwomen, have no desire at all to know anything of the native population of the country. There has been an occasional voice to point out that while under any conditions such blindness is disastrous, in India it is especially so, because the Indian is neither primitive nor uneducated, and because there is nothing in his history which marks him as a person to be ignored.

Mr. Forster is not weakly partisan. He does not argue for either side in this very difficult question. He is, on the other hand, quite ruthless in his portrayal of the weaknesses of both. We cannot admire the English who after the first few months in the country invariably lose even the vestiges of common courtesy in dealing with Indians of all ranks. The most striking and memorable instance of this attitude is in the fact that one of the women had never learned anything but the imperative form of the verb in speaking the dialect. Consequently when her husband was entertaining well-born Indians and purdah women she still spoke to them in the imperative. Only an outsider—or one of the subject race—could appreciate the extent to which this lack of courtesy reaches. Ronny Healsop is a nice boy. We imagine that back in England he must have been quite likeable. Yet here we find him coming into a room where are being entertained his mother and the girl he expects to marry, and completely ignoring the Indians who are also being entertained there.

Not even Adela's surprise rouses him to the enormity of his impolite action. Coming out to Chandrapore a nice English boy, his whole effort apparently has been to absorb the English ideas and the English attitude. Watching Ronny, we see why it is that English authors can write novels of Anglo-India where the only reference to Indians is an occasional mention of a servant. Yet Ronny is not bad. He is merely excessively afraid of being thought queer, of not being on the right side. There are hints—though Mr. Forster is fairly chivalrous in what he actually says—that a great part of the actual enmity is stirred up by the women. The women of Anglo-India invariably show up in a much worse light than the men. Mr. Forster explains quite carefully that these women are largely the result of their environment. The men never read anything, and the women never do anything which they cannot do with the men. This narrows their lives to a much greater extent, because they have not the men's interest in their work. The women of Chandrapore show very badly indeed in this novel.

On the other hand, though Mr. Forster shows us quite clearly the weakness of the English position, he also shows us the weakness of the Indian in his relation with the English, his unreliability, the vivid use of his imagination and the difficulty inherent in a position where one race stresses the speaking of the truth and the other fits his facts to the occasion. We realise how irritating this faculty of the Indian must be in direct contact, though it has its element of amusement for us, when we find Dr. Aziz for artistic reasons stating that his dead wife is merely out of the city at present, or when we hear him describing the hospitality which will be extended to the English ladies when they visit his home, though in his mind's eye he has the picture of that wretched little bungalow where he lives and the hordes of black flies which infest it.

On both sides we find the same sense of fatalism. The English express no desire or intention of coming to a better understanding with the Indians. The common expression is that Indians are not worth the effort. On their part we find these better-class Indians expressing the opinion that it is useless to try to be friends with the English, that even those who come to India well inclined are soon corrupted by their companions. Nothing can express more clearly the attitude of the two races to each other than the drama enacted upon the mere announcement by Adela Quested that she had been attacked by Dr. Aziz! No one among the English stops to consider the truth of the question, the condition of Adela or the possibility of her being wrong. Mrs. Moore—the visiting Englishwoman—and Fielding—who is never very popular with his own kind,—are the sole two who suggest that the girl might have been mistaken. We see how quickly the smoldering enmity can flame into open strife.

No matter whether or not Adela Quested had been popular before the incident, the Englishwomen rush to her defense under these conditions. The men form a hostile camp giving orders which presume a virtual state of warfare between the English and the Indians. No reader should miss the significance and the skill with which Mr. Forster builds up this case and smashes it suddenly because this English girl is honest enough to withdraw her charge when she realizes that she may have been mistaken. We suspect that she is the only one of the Englishwomen there who would have been brave enough to withdraw it—no matter what the consequences to themselves. Adela finds herself suddenly an outcast among her own people. She realizes that Heaslop no longer desires to marry her and before she leaves the country she learns that her name has been linked disastrously with that of Fielding, the sole man left to befriend her.

The story would have been more effective if it had closed with the departure of Adela Quested from the country after her most disastrous sojourn there. There is irony in the after glimpses which we have of Aziz and Fielding, of Mrs. Moore's other children, and of the remnants of that one splendid friendship which was to have existed between an Indian and an Englishman, but it injures the dramatic perfection of the story. It is a book abundantly worth reading as a story, but it is even more potent in significance as we realize the subtlety and power with which Mr. Forster has revealed to us the Moslem and the Hindu mind and that strange anomaly, the mind of the Anglo-Indian.

120. 'Indians and Anglo-Indians: as portrayed to Britons'

September 1924

St Nihal Singh, review in *Modern Review* (Calcutta), xxxvi, September 1924, 253–6.

St Nihal Singh (1884–), prolific Indian factual writer and widely-travelled journalist, educated at Punjab University. He was special correspondent for the *Observer* during the Prince of Wales's visit to India in 1921–2.

A Passage to India is of an entirely different character. Not that it refrains from showing up the weak traits in the Indian character. On the contrary, it gives the impression that there is no such thing as an Indian, for the Muslim disdains the Hindu and is in turn hated by the Hindu and Hindus and Muslims alike are slack, prevaricating, not quite honest, unreliable, sexually loose—in a word, inefficient from every point of view. The author is, however, not content with such an expose but mercilessly tears away the gaudy vestments and gew-gaws which Anglo-Indians, or 'Europeans' as they prefer to call themselves, have draped about themselves and displays a sight which will revolt some persons, shame others and enrage still others.

The scene is laid in a small civil station probably in Behar and Orissa, where the universe revolves round the Collector. His assistant, who is also the City Magistrate, the District Superintendent of Police, and the Civil Surgeon, a Major in the Indian Medical Service, constitute his satellites. The only Briton who does not kow-tow to him, or care to associate much with the others, is the Principal of the Government College.

Into this 'little England' enter the City Magistrate's mother and the girl who has come out from 'Home' to look him over and decide whether or not she wishes to marry him. They insist upon knowing the 'real India', and since the people among whom their lot is cast loathe and despise India and Indians, they have to seek the good offices of the teacher-man, who is the only 'European' who associates with the 'natives.'

The one Indian—the Assistant-Surgeon (Dr. Aziz)—with whom these two ladies become really acquainted, is a little later accused by the younger woman of attempted assault. He is promptly locked up by the Collector; the District Superintendent of Police works up a case against him, and denies the Principal of the College, who believes in his innocence, the opportunity to see him; the elder Englishwoman, who also believes him innocent, is packed off lest she may complicate matters for the prosecution. The City Magistrate's fiancee however realises in the middle of the trial, that hysteria had led her to make the charge and withdraws it.

Dr. Aziz has become so embittered by the treatment which he has received at the hands of the British Colony that he resigns his position and takes service under a Hindu Raja. The Englishman in the Educational Service, who had stuck to him during his days of trial even at the expense of ostracism from the Anglo-Indians, pays a visit to that State, accompanied by his wife (who happens to be a step-sister of the City Magistrate) and her brother. Aziz avoids him because he is an Englishman, and he has had enough of them.

Chance brings them together, however, and an attempt at reconciliation is made but proves useless, because the iron has sunk too deep into the Muslim doctor's soul, while the Englishman, now an Inspector, has himself become an Anglo-Indian.

The plot, though quite thin, has enabled the author to accomplish two purposes. It has first of all given him the opportunity to show how the British in India despise and ostracise Indians, while on their part the Indians mistrust and misjudge the British and how the gulf between the two is widening and becoming unbridgeable. It has further given him a chance to demonstrate the utter hopelessness of expecting any improvement from the efforts of Englishmen of superior education who arrive in India at a mature age, because they can resist the bacillus of Anglo-Indianitis only for a time, and even then not completely, and in the end fall victim to it.

The author's pictures are faithful and vivid. That is particularly the case in regard to the Anglo-Indian characters he has created.

In making that remark, I do not mean to suggest that the Hindus and Muslims depicted by Mr. Forster are not faithfully sketched. On the contrary, there are unquestionably young Muslims in India like Dr. Aziz who, despite the advantages of education they have enjoyed, look down upon Hindus and belittle their culture, and fall below even a reasonable standard of truthfulness and efficiency. There also are Hindus like Professor Godbole and Dr. Panna Lal, who return the compliment to men like Aziz and are not his superior either in respect of truthfulness or efficiency.

There are, however, Indians who are neither full of religious prejudices nor the footling muddlers that Mr. Forster has painted. Perhaps his limited opportunities did not permit him to come in contact with them, or possibly the plan of his book did not permit him to introduce them into it. Unfortunately, however, the British reader, as a rule, is so ignorant of India of our day that he is likely to take Aziz and the others as typical of all modern Indians, and, therefore, become confirmed in his prejudices. Such as the notion that India is a congeries of clashing races and creeds, that the Indian standard of morality is low, that Indians cannot dispense with the British crutches, and the like.

Any harm, which the book may do to the Indian cause by laying such emphasis upon our shortcomings will, however, be more than counterbalanced by the good that may result through the exposé of Anglo-India by an Englishman who has evidently taken the trouble to study it and who possesses the moral courage to tear from it all the sham trappings which a spirit of self-adulation had wrapped round a hideous skeleton.

The head of the district is described as a man who 'knew something to the discredit of nearly every one of his (Indian) guests at the bridge party' (not the game 'but a party to bridge the gulf between the East and the West'), and was consequently perfunctory. 'When they had not cheated, it was *bhang*, women, or worse, and even the desirables wanted to get something out of him'. He had had twenty-five years' experience in India and had 'never known anything but disaster result when English people and Indians attempt to be intimate socially. Intercourse, yes. Courtesy, by all means. Intimacy—never, never.' The whole weight of his authority was against it. 'When he saw the coolie asleep in the ditches or the shopkeepers rising to salute him on their little platforms, he said to himself, "You shall pay for this, you shall squeal" '. 'He longed for the good old days when an Englishman could satisfy his own honour and no questions asked afterwards.' As it is, not only the Indians, but 'the Government of India itself also watches—and behind it is that caucus of cranks and cravens, the British Parliament.' In India 'the Turtons (the Collector and his wife) were little gods; soon they would retire to some suburban villa and die exiled from glory.'

The City Magistrate is made out to be a man who lives up to the principle that the British are not in India for the purpose of behaving pleasantly. They are there 'to do justice and keep the peace.' 'Here we are, and we're going to stop, and the country's got to put up with us,' he declared. He was out in India 'to work, mind, to hold this wretched country by force.' He was 'not a missionary or a Labour Member or a vague sentimental sympathetic literary man. . . . Just a servant of the Government.' The British, he said, were 'not pleasant in India' and do not 'intend to be pleasant.' His task was a difficult one. 'Every day he worked hard in the court trying to decide which of two secretive accounts was the less untrue, trying to dispense justice fearlessly, to protect the weak against the less weak, the incoherent against the plausible, surrounded by lies and flattery. That morning he had convicted a railway clerk of over-charging pilgrims for their tickets, and a Pathan of attempted rape. He expected no gratitude, no recognition for this, and both the clerk and Pathan might appeal, bribe their witnesses more effectually in the interval, and get their sentences reversed.' When the day's work was over, he wanted to play tennis with his own kind or rest his legs upon a long chair. He frankly did not like the 'natives'. Soon after he came out, he had asked one of the Pleaders to have a cigarette with him. He found afterwards that he had sent touts all over the bazaar to announce the fact—had told all the litigants that Vakil Mahmoud Ali was 'in with the City Magistrate'. And he believed that 'whether the native swaggers or cringes, there's always something behind every remark he makes—if nothing else, he's trying to . . . . . . score.' He did not consider it worth while to conciliate the educated Indians. They would be no good to the British in case of a row, and so did not matter.'

The District Superintendent of Police was the most reflective and best educated of the officials in the place. Himself born at Karachi, his theory was that 'all natives are criminals at heart, for the simple reason that they live south of latitude 30,' and that 'when an Indian goes bad, he not only goes very bad, but very queer.' His attitude was, 'Everyone knows the man's guilty, and I am obliged to say so in public before he goes to the Andamans.' And in the end he, a married man, was caught in a lady's bedroom and divorced by his wife—and probably 'blamed it to the Indian climate.' According to him, there was nothing in India but the weather—it was the Alpha and Omega of everything.

The Civil Surgeon, a Major in the Indian Medical Service, was full of the 'details of operations which he poured into the shrinking ears of his friends. The boredom of regime and hygiene repelled him.' He was not well disposed towards his Indian Assistant, considering that he had 'no grit, no guts,' and was not any better disposed towards him when by operating he saved an English lady's life. It never occurred to him that 'the educated Indians visited one another occasionally. He only knew that no one ever told him the truth, although he had been in the country for twenty years.' He 'put the fear of God into them at the hospital.' As he described to his fellow 'Europeans' at the club the appearance of the grandson of the leading Indian loyalist:

> His beauty's gone, five upper teeth, two lower and a nostril. . . . Old Panna Lal brought him the looking glass yesterday and he blubbered. I laughed; I laughed, I tell you, and so would you; that used to be one of these niggers, I thought, now he's all septic; damn him, blast his soul—er—I believe he was unspeakably immoral—er—. He subsided, nudged in the ribs, but added, 'I wish I'd had the cutting up of my late assistant too; Nothing's too bad for these people.'

The womenfolk of these persons, as described by Mr. Forster, are a vulgar lot. They were amazed when the heroine and the lady who expected to be her mother-in-law expressed a desire to see Indians. 'Wanting to see Indians!' they exclaimed, 'Natives! why fancy!' and they explained that 'Natives don't respect one any the more after meeting one.' The kindest thing one could do to a native was to let him die.

When the Collector gave a 'bridge party,' his wife refused to 'shake hands with any of the men unless it has to be the Nawab Bahadur.' She reminded the strangers that they 'were superior to every one in India except one or two of the Ranis, and they're on an equality.' She 'had learnt the lingo, but only to speak to her servants, so she knew none of the politer forms and of the verbs only the imperative mood.' She was more distant with Indian ladies who had travelled in Europe and 'might apply her own standards to her.' She told the men that they were 'weak, weak, weak.' The Indians ought to be made 'to crawl from here to the caves on their hands and knees whenever an Englishwoman's in sight, they ought not be spoken to, they ought to be spat at, they ought to be ground into the dust, we've been far too kind with our Bridge Parties and the rest.' No wonder her husband thought that 'After all, it's our women who make everything more difficult out here.'

Then there was the wife of the District Superintendent of Police, who, at her husband's bidding, gave purdah parties until she struck; and the lady who was visiting her, who was companion to a Maharani in a remote Native State, who had taken leave 'because she felt she deserved it, not because the Maharani said she might go.' She burgled the Maharaja's motor car at the junction, as it came back in the train from a Chiefs' Conference at Delhi. 'Her Maharaja would be awfully sick, but she didn't mind, he could sack her if he liked.' 'I don't believe in these people letting you down,' she said. 'If I didn't snatch like the Devil, I should be nowhere. He doesn't want the car, silly fool! Surely it is to the credit of his State I should be seen about in it at Chandrapore during my leave. He ought to look at it that way. Anyhow he's got to look at it that way. My Maharani's different . . . my Maharani's a dear. That's her fox-terrier, poor little devil. . . . Imagine taking dogs to a Chiefs' Conference! As sensible as taking Chiefs, perhaps, she shrieked with laughter.' She it was in whose bedroom the District Superintendent of Police was later caught.

The Anglo-Indians are not used to being talked about in this manner. They will hate Mr. Forster for giving them away.

I wonder if the book will open the eyes of the British people. I see that it is being widely reviewed in the London and the provincial press, and the critics are writing of it in glowing terms. I have not seen it pointed out anywhere, however, that the author has come to realise that the Anglo-Indians are acting in the manner in which he has described them as acting because they are determined to hang on to India and because they feel that that is the only way they can hang on. The problem, in other words, is not social, but political, and therefore, no end of homilies can have any effect upon improving the manners of the British in India. The political elevation of Indians is the only remedy which can cure them of their habit of looking down upon us—of belittling our past and our capacity—of desiring to keep us at a distance.

121. 'C. W. G.', review, *Englishman* (Calcutta)

25 September 1924, 11

There are three types of fiction written about India by English novelists. The most attractive to those who know the country is the historical romance placed for the most part in the time of the Moguls. The novels of Flora Annie Steele give more life and interest to the Northern provinces than pages of their tangled history. The type of novel most widely read however, both at home and in India, is that written around the life of the European station for its own sake. It is the fortunes and love affairs of their own people that interest the generality of British readers in fiction about India. It is this news that desperately fills the pages of struggling letters to friends at home when the strangeness of Indian sights and sounds no longer affords the effusive resources of the first months. And when readers at home tire of our correspondence, as we no less of writing, it is for the same interests that they look to 'a really good novel about India'. The romances and adventures of the British in this least romantic and most unadventurous environment, of Indian station life, are the mainstay of popular fiction relating to this country.

There is however a third class of fiction coming into evidence concerned not with station life in an ethnological void, but with the contact of the British and Indian peoples. It is an offshoot of the penchant for psychological elaboration which characterizes the present-day novelist. Races not individuals become the characters, and it is the feelings of communities rather than of hero, heroine and villain that are spun fine in psychological analysis.

To fiction of this kind special responsibilities attach. It is almost impossible for a novel of this type to avoid some shade of political implication. And provided that the story is well-planned and vigorously written, it will carry a far more powerful message to the British public than a vast amount of more deliberatively informative writing. Nine-tenths of the voting force in Britain, or rather of that section of it which forms any conception of Indian questions, derives its ideas as much from readable fiction as from authoritative books and articles. Even within the boundaries of India the resident population of the large towns probably derives its acquaintance with the daily life of the interior from this source to a greater extent than would be readily admitted. The novel which sets out to deal with the social psychology of station life in relation to its Indian environment exercises, therefore, a half-unconscious influence, which will be the more pronounced in proportion, not to the accuracy of the picture, but to the interest and vivacity of the narrative. And this responsibility implies a corresponding claim that the picture should be drawn from intimate and expert knowledge, without prejudice, in delicate and careful delineation of a most difficult subject. Failing these qualities, avaunt the novelist from the tempting opportunity.

Unfair fiction

But unfortunately intensive study and cautious impartiality are commodities of poor value on the counter of Fiction. It is bias and exaggeration that pay. They make the better story and the easier hit. And the traditional aloofness of the British Community offers only too ready a material for the jerry-built fabric of fiction soonest put together and quickest told.

An illustration of this will be found in one of this year's recent novels which has met with considerable success. *A Passage to India* is a study of station life in India based on the peculiarly far-fetched theme, of an English girl involved through genuine mistake or hallucination in a false charge against an Indian doctor. It is round the latter character that interest is centred, and its portrayal would obviously be a task of infinite difficulty for a writer in close touch with the Indian mind. The representation is probably meant to be flattering, and, however, crude and theatrical it may be, it does no one any harm. One may assure the writer that the most impulsive young Indian Doctor, and the most friendly European in the local College would not really be found, on their second meeting, at the former's house discussing the photograph of the Doctor's deceased wife, and the local young civilian's fiancee, with special attention to the flatness of her bust. But this after all is no more than a mistake, a flaw in the picture, a touch of inoffensive exaggeration. There is much else of the same kind, but herein lies no touch of prejudiced representation or slanderous savour. It is in depicting the attitude of the European station as a whole, and of the officials individually that one feels that the element of unfairness does obtrude. Nor can a stronger term b withheld when the writer describes the Civil Surgeon as ill dispose to his Indian subordinate because of the latter's higher professiona skill, or as venting his spleen against the Indian community ove surgical treatment of patient. Such passages are of the wickedness o fiction. 'Quosque tanden abutere patientia nostra.'

Ladies in the Club

The superficiality of this novel as a study of life at District Head quarters, will be apparent in the absurdities of its situations. Let u glance at one, and that fairly familiar to all who have lived in th interior during the past three or four years. Communal feelings hav been aroused and reciprocated. There is a certain nervousness in th Club, tom-toms too near, shouting too loud, and an unpleasan bazaar to drive through. And in real life there may have been a fev unnoticed precautions and a quiet word spoken aside to reassure nervous woman.

Not so in Chandrapur of the novelist. The Collector 'clapped hi hands for silence' and makes a brief speech to the ladies. The Civi Surgeon's wife indiscreetly discloses that the Superintendent of Polic is 'in the city disguised as a holy man'. The Collector closes his remark 'It is all I ask. Can I rely on you?' Yes indeed, Burra Saheb they chorused out of peaked anxious faces.' Faded curtains of the ladies rooms in all the Clubs in India, that have witnessed strange scenes an heard stranger scandals, did you ever yet hear the wives of the Distric Officials 'chorus out Burra Saheb' to the Collector? After this, one i not surprised to find a similar reception in the smoking room wher the Collector proceeds to speechify to the men, or to read of th Principal of the local College, in the educational service, 'rising wit deference' and addressing as 'Sir' the Assistant Magistrate in his firs year out. Nor need we thrust ourselves into the crowded court room where our friends now all witnesses are assembled from the beginning of the proceedings, and the Superintendent of Police conducts th prosecution in person, with the help of leading questions that evok no protest from the brilliant young Calcutta barrister named Amrita Rao. Enough has been said to show how spurious an acquaintance wit the facts of the inter District life the novelist presumes to draw on and the exposure of the ludicrous may do something to counterac the injurious tendencies of this type of fiction.

122. I. P. Fassett, review, *Criterion*

iii, no. 9, October 1924, 137–9

Fassett was a regular contributor of reviews to the *Criterion* at this time.

Mr. Forster has asked himself the questions: What *is* essential India? Why is she esteemed so great? What can be done to help her to express herself? What, indeed, is her message? And in his honesty he has not been able to find a really satisfying answer to any of his queries; nor does he believe they can be answered in our time. He points to the Marabar Caves that lie under the Marabar Hills (described as a group of fists and fingers), and we take them for a symbol representing present-day India.

The caves consist of a number of small tunnels leading each one into a small circular chamber. They have no sculpture, no ornament, no stalactites even. When you scratch the walls there is an echo, and that is all. And the caves are held in unquestioned and unexplained reverence by all white men and all Indians.

Why do we have to remind ourselves so incessantly that Mr. Forster's work is admirable? In this book he responds to a call to write about India. He has worked in the power of a clear-thinking, well-informed mind; therefore he has produced a logical book. The individual points of view of the various characters could only have been determined by a man of great sensibility. The subject matter is handled so competently that nothing is superfluous or out of place. Mr. Forster is so very clever—what is it that his work lacks? What is it that we miss in *A Passage to India*? Something that could lift it above the level of Sound Contemporary Fiction where it must inevitably lie.

Is it possible that Mr. Forster has tried to supply this something in Mrs. Moore, that sinister, obscure, horrible woman whom he persists in twining so tightly into the thread of his story? I have said that there is nothing superfluous in *A Passage to India*, but I confess that it *would* be nice not to have to bother with Mrs. Moore. In her Mr. Forster has not given us one of his clear, cleancut figures. He has been very subtle. He throws out suggestions here and there as to the key to her nature. He surrounds her in mystery. Psychic influences play about her. It is all very vague.

The development of the book hangs on the visit to India of Miss Questead, an intelligent young woman, who, although she becomes engaged to an English civil servant of some importance, wishes to investigate the life and point of view of the Indian: an impossible combination of purposes. She manages to become acquainted with Doctor Aziz, assistant to the English doctor at Chandrapore, a Moslem of high type with an English education. In spite of a strong English opposition, she accepts the invitation of Aziz to be the guest of honour at a picnic in the Marabar Caves. A scandal ensues. Miss Questead returns from the picnic ahead of the others in a state of collapse, and the news spreads rapidly that Aziz has insulted her in one of the Marabar Caves. So Miss Questead and Doctor Aziz, two earnest workers for a mutual understanding between English and Indians, find themselves the chief figures in a more than usually violent white men-*versus*-Indian disturbance. A temporary illusion of imminent co-operation and good feeling is of course dispelled. There is a fantastic trial, at the crisis of which Miss Questead states that she can make no accusation against Aziz: the man who insulted her may have been someone else, or the whole episode may have been an hallucination. After the excitement caused by the trial has died down, the Public School Englishmen sink back into complacency and condemn the Indians as—well—niggers, and the educated Indians see the English more clearly than ever as double-faced tyrants, the instigators of vile and complicated plots. Doctor Aziz and a certain Mr. Fielding, the best of the Englishmen, find that their personal friendship which they had prized so highly, and for which they had worked so hard, is irrevocably destroyed. Aziz retreats into unanglised India, where Brahmanism flourishes and the schools are used as storehouses for grain. India is his country, and India shall one day be united as one nation and throw off the English yoke. 'We may hate one another', he tells Fielding, 'but we hate you most . . . we shall drive every blasted Englishman into the sea . . . and then you and I shall be friends'.

Mr. Forster's main argument is so sound, and he brings so much relevant matter to bear upon his point, that he does succeed in convincing us that he is right—an unusual achievement. It is chiefly by his clear exposure of conflicting points of view that he proves to us why, in Miss Questead's words, 'India is not a promise, only an appeal'.

123. D. H. Lawrence, letter to John Middleton Murry

3 October 1924

From *The Letters of D. H. Lawrence*, ed. Aldous Huxley (Heinemann, 1932), 615. Copyright 1932 by the Estate of D. H. Lawrence, 1962 by Angelo Ravagli and C. M. Weekley, Executors of the Estate of Frieda Lawrence Ravagli.

This letter was written from the Del Monte Ranch, Questa, New Mexico.

All races have one root, once one gets there. Many stems from one root: the stems never to commingle or 'understand' one another. I agree Forster doesn't 'understand' his Hindu. And India is to him just negative: because he doesn't go down to the root to meet it. But the *Passage to India* interested me very much. At least the repudiation of our white bunk is genuine, sincere, and pretty thorough, it seems to me. Negative, yes. But King Charles *must* have his head off. Homage to the headsman.

124. Elinor Wylie, 'Passage to more than India', *New York Herald Tribune*

5 October 1924 (Review of Contemporary Literature, i)

Elinor Wylie (1885–1928), American poet and writer of historical novels.

One excellent effect, among his many excellencies, may possibly be Mr. E. M. Forster's supreme contribution to contemporary literature; he has carried the art of writing prose to such perfection that he may very well succeed in discouraging a vast number of us from attempting, lamentably to fail, like miracles of subtlety and ease. For if I had a modern story to tell—and, of course, I have just that, in common with the rest of even faintly literate mankind—I should never begin to tell it until I had exhausted every hope of persuading Mr. Forster to tell it for me, in the absolute conviction that he alone of living writers can understand without effort and relate without obscurity the smallest and the greatest revolution of the human mind.

When I read *Howard's End*—and that was in 1910—I was rather young, and I am forced to believe that the whole world was rather young in my company, which is to say rather ignorant. Because a re-reading of that distinguished work reveals it as far less surprising, if even more satisfactory, than my opinion pronounced and an intelligent public proclaimed it. The conclusions and—if I may be permitted so despicable a word—the wisdom of the book are now admittedly foregone and bitterly acquired by myself and the world, and *Howard's End* is no more amazing than life; it is simply true.

I have long been one of Mr. Forster's most slavish admirers, and I did not truly credit a prophecy that he would ever excel his own performance in *Howard's End* or the adorable *Room With a View*; I came to *A Passage to India* with a slightly jaundiced eye and a liverish aftertaste of Kipling. Not that I thought Mr. Forster would fail me; I knew his ideas were the exact opposite of such curried abominations, but I didn't want to read about India at all, and I wished Mr. Forster would stick to England and Italy. I had not read one paragraph before I was completely won, and now I am prepared to follow him into any portion of the earth to which he will chart a passage.

This particular passage, the passage to India, is rather a tunnel driven through the dreadful solid obduracy of mortal confusion and ignorance than any fair blue voyage of discovery. It arrives at a blank wall, but its very frustration is more illuminating than the dazzling successes of stupidity, which batters its head against this same blank wall and sees the stars of empire. The portraits of individuals—and these are brilliantly executed, beautiful in their precision and contrasted essences—are, I think, less important than the informing spirit of the book, a humanity, an insight, a curious disturbing justice which is beyond praise and certainly beyond my power to define.

Mr. Forster sees so very clearly and writes with so magical a fluid, compounded of beauty and ironic salt and limpid clarity, that he is as great a despair to my muddled creative mind as he is an enchantment to my taste and critical faculties. Therefore I find it difficult to say with becoming authority the many things I wish to say. I must content myself with telling every one to read this book, this *Passage to India*, because it is beautiful and ironic and clear as divining crystal. Therefore, also, I do not speak of the story, which is subtle and casual and surprisingly exciting, nor of the characters, who are extraordinary and commonplace and touching even when they are detestable. I tell you to read the book. It contains a magic which transmutes a gold-plated collar button into something more significant than the hero of another novel. It contains delicate humor and a durable fabric of understanding. It is exquisite and profound. As for Mr. Forster's style I will steal his own words, which he has used to describe the surface of a granite cave. I will use them to describe the language wherein he clothes his mysterious and piercing thoughts . . . 'here at last is their skin, finer than any covering acquired by the animals, smoother than windless water.' . . . That is poetry, of course, but 'A Passage to India' is poetry, as it is also melodrama, and philosophy and 'realism,' if that word by any chance means life.

125. Edwin Muir, review, *Nation* (New York)

cxix, 8 October 1924, 379–80

Edwin Muir (1887–1959), Orkney-born poet and, with his wife Willa Muir, translator of Kafka. During the 'twenties he lived in London by translating and reviewing; later he worked for The British Council in Edinburgh, Prague and Rome. He published his first poems in 1925 and *The Structure of the Novel* in 1928.

Reprinted by permission of the *Nation* (New York).

Mr. E. M. Forster stands apart from the main movements of present-day English literature. He has a striking lack of eagerness for doing the things which other writers do, a striking freedom from the mob instinct in a region where it is today strongest, among writers and artists. He is inclined toward the ironical school of which Mr. Lytton Strachey is the instructor, but he differs from Mr. Strachey's pupils in an important respect: they underline their inclination until they succeed in making it resemble Mr. Strachey's as closely as possible, but Mr. Forster lets his remain where it is, supported on itself. His work is a work of inclinations, adroitly balanced, and rarely slipping into the faux pas of a decision. With great tact he knows how to go half-way in any given direction, and his talent consists in knowing exactly where the half-way point is. This knowledge implies a great deal of experience in reserve behind it, and there is no doubt that that experience is real. Mr. Forster gives his reservations the weight of categories which everybody would be more intelligent by accepting; and no doubt they would, though Mr. Forster attaches too much importance to intelligence. He writes always as a man who knows better than any one else while not insisting on the fact. And he writes thus because he is, first, a capable man, and, secondly, a man of taste. He knows where he stands; he has found his place, and there is a note of assurance, accordingly, in all he says. But although his utterance is genuine as that of few of his contemporaries is, one doubts whether it is profound. The intellect is not exercised to its utmost in going half-way in all directions. Practical expedience, intelligence of a rare kind, may be shown in doing that; but hardly wisdom, not the passion for truth which animates great art. Mr. Forster does not possess these qualities; on the other hand, he has an intelligence of greater force and purity than that of any other imaginative writer today. That intelligence is a scrupulously truthful one; but its distinguishing character is its refusal to pursue truth beyond a certain point. This is why his books, in spite of their skill, produce a total effect which is not decisive.

A Passage to India is a very accomplished novel. It is the kind of novel which could be written only by a very cultivated man, but it shows Mr. Forster's cultivation more clearly than it does his intuition. He does not convince one that he understands his characters; he convinces one only that he understands their misunderstandings, that he knows where they are wrong. His theme is the antagonism, founded largely upon misapprehension, between a colony of Anglo-Indians in a little Indian town and the natives; but although he never shirks the subject he never gets to close grips with it. His picture of mutual misunderstanding is consummate. He presents English people and Indians speaking together, the Indians at a word flying off at an incomprehensible tangent, the English blankly amazed. Nothing could be better than his account of the party at Fielding's, where some English people and two Indians, chatting amiably, find themselves, without knowing why, moving poles asunder. There is the most exquisite artifice in this economically managed scene. The trial, too, is beautifully rendered, and the riot after it is wonderfully neat, a little too neat. Mr. Forster always says the right word, selects the significant detail; yet his art is essentially a kind of impressionism. Miss Quested, the open-minded young Englishwoman who comes to India resolved to know it and refusing to be put off with 'a frieze of Indians,' gets little more than that in the end, nor do we; for Mr. Forster's Indians have the coldness of a procession, and, if more delicately exact than Mr. Kipling's, they have less personality. The author gives us glimpses of their psychology, but he does not understand that psychology, and cannot explain it to us. It is here that a reader who wants to pursue one path until he comes to the end will rebel against Mr. Forster's intelligent resolve to go only half the way. There is no end, Mr. Forster would no doubt reply. Here is a picture of the muddle; if you try to probe it farther it will only become more baffling. At any rate, his picture is wonderfully drawn. He holds the balance evenly between the Anglo-Indians and the natives, without a hint of prejudice, idealistic or imperialist, and with no fear of the opinions of the English public. He is above the quarrel, and without much hope for its issue. It required courage of a rare kind to write the book.

The story is simple. Mrs. Moore and Miss Quested, the prospective fiancée of Mrs. Moore's son, come to India, and are at first repelled by the English official attitude to the Indians. When they suggest a more sympathetic attitude they are always told from the height of a ten or twenty years' experience, 'That is not the point'; and baffled by the English, they turn to the Indians. But by these they are baffled in a different way: they find good-will, even gratitude, but they are misunderstood at every turn. Their sympathy eventually involves them in an adventure in which the younger woman is sexually assaulted, or thinks she is (the point is not clear), in a cave to which a young Moslem doctor has conducted her. The doctor, who is innocent, is arrested and tried; there is a prodigious racial fuss raised by the English, and hysterical indignation among the natives. In the end the doctor is acquitted by the testimony of the woman who accused him, who comes to the conclusion that she was suffering from hallucination. For letting them down she is forthwith ostracized by the Anglo-Indians. A tumult follows the legal decision, and the English fear violence, but the riot passes into a farce. The novel, one feels, should have ended here; but Mr. Forster adds a final section portraying, with an unconvincing irony, an aspect of Indian religious life. It is the only feeble part of the novel, and, seeing that it is the end, the part which could least suffer to be feeble. But, apart from it, the book is executed with rare scrupulousness. The writing, when it does not slip into fine writing, as it does once or twice, is a continuous delight. The novel is a triumph of the humanistic spirit over material difficult to humanize. It is this first of all; it is also a work of art exquisite rather than profound. Last of all, it is a peculiarly valuable picture of the state of India seen through a very unembarrassed and courageous intelligence.

126. 'S. A.', review, *Springfield Sunday Republican*

(Springfield, Massachusetts) 19 October 1924, 5a

It is impossible to give anyone who has not read E. M. Forster's newest novel, *A Passage to India*, the faintest notion, even, of its total effect, because in this case one cannot compare the unknown with the known. Mr. Forster surpasses his former achievements. Goethe has said somewhere that 'There are many echoes in the world, but few voices.' In the world of novel-writing, Mr Forster's is one of those voices. He writes like no one else; few know India as he apparently does or attempt to present so intricate and so extensive a scene as his present one; and very few indeed wish to produce his effect of absolute objectivity.

All of this being true, and since one despairs of being able to give an adequate notion of what this novel is like, it is proper to advise anyone wishing to feel pleasure of the keenest and most unexpected sort, to have vicarious experiences entirely out of the ordinary, and to give in return for these the kind of rapt attention that only moving drama of a superior kind can compel, to possess himself of this delightful book and prepare for hours on end of mental exhilaration. The novel is worth reading slowly in order to appreciate its true savor.

The lucidity and graceful ease with which Mr Forster writes are incomparable. 'Here,' one exclaims, 'is style so perfectly suited to its matter as to leave nothing to be desired and, because it is so natural, little to be remarked.' The drifting currents of the Orient move through the book, languidly at times; swiftly and surcharged with meaning at others. The evasive, baffling charm of Indian life is suggested, its regard for formulas, symbols, the underlying spiritual significance of commonplace happening that so eludes even the most eager visitor.

Good as his descriptions are, and Mr Forster is not afraid to describe things in the leisurely fashion of the older novelists, they are no better than his dialog. When his Indians speak, there is always the suggestion that he is translating their language, for about the idiom there hovers a tang of the unfamiliar, and they are betrayed into an occasional formal turn of speech that no native-born Englishman would employ. Says the engaging, humorous, incapable, emotional Dr Aziz, wishing to put himself en rapport with his new friend, Fielding: 'Excuse the following question: have you any illegitimate children?' and there you have not only the alien turn of phrase, but also the utterly alien way of looking at friendly relationship.

Never does the author permit himself the indolent method of reporting speech as it is uttered, with all of its otiose insignificance; rather he gives us speech selected with the utmost skill in order that we may savor from the small sample the delicate quality of the special intercourse of which it is the expression. While his detail seems casual enough, upon examination it all proves to be important.

This novel gives us opportunity to make excursions into characteristic Indian scenes, accompanied by a skilful guide who refrains from making obvious comments. Without friction and with no apparent effort we are conducted from one place to another, from one group of Indians to another, each peculiar to itself, making no attempt to become like anything else. Here, one feels, is a land in which there is no change, where no persons apes another, no class tries to merge with another. 'Let us have leisure that we may taste life and enjoy all of its quality, undisturbed' everyone seems to urge.

Of Kipling's India, with its army and civil social intrigue there is but little, for herein we are on intimate terms not so much with Anglo-Indians as with natives. To be sure, most of these have been in England, some of them have British tradition and training, but when they have come home to live, they have, as a matter of course resumed their Indian ways.

Thus the complexity, the variety of infinitesimal gradations, the subtle beauty and power of Indian manner and mood suffuse the book. Throughout the story, moreover, one is impressed with Mr Forster's willingness to permit his persons and places to speak for themselves; he merely brings us into position where we may hear without effort, and without eavesdropping. We become a part of the company.

Though the tale presents a fair notion of the many problems England faces in trying to govern this alien people, it holds no brief either for England or for India. It is not a problem novel. If one were to guess the author's views, however, one would conjecture that he sympathizes more with governed than governors. In fact, it would be possible to make out a case for his unfairness to a certain group of English shown at the club, though the 'documentation' is so complete that one is inclined to accept the conclusions (if such they may be called) as correct.

Casual readers might accuse him of occasional caricature, but upon fuller consideration it would be discovered that if he sometimes shows mankind at its inconsistent and illogical worst, he does not fail to present its other, better aspects as well. Here is realism not photographic but representative.

There is plot enough to carry the characters along, though toward the end of the book this becomes negligible. As should be the case in novel-writing, character and incident are the life-giving elements, and these are so unusual yet so plausible that they will stamp themselves upon the imagination as few scenes in life can do. Of course, Mr Forster's delicate irony informs the book: an irony which Gilbert Canaan regards as the special note of the novelist as distinguished from other writers.

127. Robert Bridges, letter to E. M. Forster

11 November [1924]

Robert Bridges (1844–1930), a doctor until 1882, became Poet Laureate in 1913 and published *The Testament of Beauty* in 1930. The clavichord referred to in his letter was made by Arnold Dolmetsch and presented to Bridges by his friends on his eightieth birthday.

Published by permission of the Clarendon Press on behalf of the Bridges Estate.

I read your book about India a fortnight ago and ever since have been refraining from writing to tell you how much I admire it. I did not like to take that liberty with a stranger. But the other day Siegfried Sassoon was here, and I was surprised and delighted to see your name among the subscribers to the clavichord that has been presented to me—so I feel that I may put my scruple aside.

Since I cannot tell you anything that you do not know about your book, I have only to say that it seemed to me a masterpiece: it has filled me with admiration for your genius. I have known some Indians pretty well, and among them had one very good friend—I say *had*, for I cannot tell what he may be doing or thinking now—and I can therefore appreciate the truth of your psychological picture. I should not have thought that the thing could have been done so well.

I very seldom read English novels, and therefore it is not strange that I do not know any of your earlier work, though I have heard it praised. But I look forward to the pleasure that I must have missed, though I do not suppose that you can have found any other field with such opportunities for your skill.

128. Clarence H. Gaines, review, *North American Review*

ccxx, December 1924, 375–8

It is a curious fact that Mr. Forster could scarcely have written so effectively (and so impartially) about the futility of attempts at social *rapprochement* between English people and natives of India, if he had not had as the background of his thought the possible futility of all life. Perhaps no other writer since Montaigne has so acutely realized the 'imbecility' of human intellect. But for this he must have written some sort of propaganda. But he has avoided the too sharp issues of the controversialist because he realizes that we all live after all in a kind of stupor: we pretend that we are wide awake all the time, acutely aware, though really we have been half asleep. So all but the most fortunate blunder through life.

In India these things are emphasized. 'Mrs. Moore . . . had come to that state where the horror of the universe and its smallness are both visible at the same time—the twilight of the double vision in which so many elderly people are involved . . . a spiritual muddledom for which no high-sounding words can be found: we can neither act nor refrain from acting, we can neither ignore nor respect Infinity.' As for our ennobling dreams, our mystic insights: 'Visions are supposed to entail profundity, but—wait till you get one, dear reader!'

One thing is perfectly clear: a man who writes in this strain cannot write as a partizan.

Yet Mr. Forster is anything but depressing. He is the tonic satirist, the philosopher possessed with the comic spirit. Though he sometimes makes the ground gape under our feet or cleaves right to the centre of our consciousness with a phrase, his is not the manner of the tragedian. He does not really seek to terrify. Instead of making his satire unendurable, his philosophy makes it kindly—for are not all of us too human? So we are amused—amused by the ineptitudes of the well-intentioned Abdul Aziz, amused by the frustration of the honest-minded, flat-breasted Miss Quested, amused by the officialdom of the 'Burtons and Turtons'—amused and made sympathetic. We enjoy it all like gods, and yet we are not required to strain our minds above the common pitch of nobility.

Unsparing but never cruel, and admirably free from the vice of preaching the 'spirit' of a land as if it were a kind of black gospel (as if one must be a materialist because life is gross in mid-Africa, or a mystic because the desert appears to the observer to be limitless!), Mr. Forster is at once a philosopher, a humanist, and a wit—and hence that complex creature, a novelist!

His wit is unconscionable, but never unkind or atrocious. What other English writer would have dared to make one of his characters think, as Mr. Forster does,—it was the thought of Miss Quested on the eve of the trial in which she was to testify against Aziz,—'God, who saves the King, will surely support the police'? What militant skeptic has said a more shocking thing than Mr. Forster's (quite accidental) remark about 'poor talkative Christianity'? Yet this does not offend; it is all in the picture—a picture irresistibly true. None would wish it incomplete in the least touch.

From his skeptical point of view—with kindness, with impartiality, without solemnity or derision—Mr. Forster gives us a lively, critical view of one portion of British India. The romantic view, as well as the critical view, has its place no doubt, and surely it is a waste of breath at this time to inveigh against romance. But if Kipling has shown us India as a pageant, full of picturesque figures, human enough, yet incomplete, after the fashion of romance, Forster has convinced us, and has proved that the destruction of illusions may be neither a base nor an uninteresting business. Like Chekov, best of realists, he sees not only people's motives, but the very wrinkles in their consciousness. Yet, unlike Chekov, he is always the artist, never the diagnostician. He scarcely approaches the borders of pathology, physical or spiritual. Always he keeps within our range—well within the range of conceivable human interests and passions. And when he is subtlest, he is clearest.

The baffling misunderstandings that enter into all human relations, and especially those between numbers of alien races! No sermon can be preached about them. No clear lesson can be drawn from them. They are too complex, too subtle, and too true! Before the pluralism of life, we are very likely to stand amazed. Aziz says that the only cure is 'kindness, kindness, and then more kindness'—or well, let us say, the millenium! Does Mr. Forster agree with Aziz? One does not know, but one cannot doubt that he has written an exceptional novel—a novel in which all is clear as daylight, and nothing, absolutely nothing, is said as any one else would say it or from the point of view of any common observer. This novel is one of the great literary victories over the inherent commonplaceness of words—a triumphant escape from the stereotyped.

Mr. Forster (besides knowing India) is certainly a master of our astringent modern comedy—a comedy that excludes alike the savagery of the satirist and the wistfulness of the half-repentant skeptic. To be so terrible a philosopher, yet never to boast of it or parade it, or half withdraw it, but to use one's comic spirit zestfully in the criticism of life, is no small thing.

129. Arnold Bennett's Journals

27 January 1925

Reprinted from *The Journals of Arnold Bennett* (Cassell, 1933), 69–70, by permission of A. P. Watt & Son on behalf of the Arnold Bennett Estate.

I finished Forster's *A Passage to India* this morning at about 5 a.m. The central part of this book (the trial etc. of innocent Aziz for an attempt on Adela Quested in a cave) is a magnificent piece of work. I should call it strictly first-class. The herd instinct among the British section of Chandrapore is perfectly done. There are also many other very fine, and even first-class things in the book. It is all very good indeed. The writing here and there slips up over phrasing—is a bit too clever, or a bit too pert or colloquial; but on the whole the style is excellent.

Yet the book left me with a sense of disappointment. I think the reason is that I don't know quite what it is about. Aziz, the Moslem doctor, is the chief character, and he is lifelike. So are all the Indian characters. So are most of the British characters. He gets into a mess with the British Raj through the hysteria of Adela Quested, and gets out of it again through Adela's honesty. You are made to see that there are two sides to the Indian question, with considerable impartiality. But as soon as Aziz is acquitted, the story seems to curve away towards Aziz as himself, scarcely related to the British Raj problem.

Some chapters, then, are a bit feeble because his psychology, and that of others, is merely described, instead of being exemplified in incident. Then the story pulls itself together, and Aziz goes to an Indian native State as doctor. All the life there, especially the religious, is beautifully done; but it doesn't seem to relate itself directly to the problem of the previous part of the book. Also there is a stupid and rather improbable misunderstanding as to the marriage of Fielding, the chief pro-Indian character. Aziz thinks F. has married Adela and he hasn't. Fielding and Aziz meet. All details are good: but the ensemble is fuzzy, or wuzzy. Although I only finished the book three hours ago, I don't recall now what the purport of the end of the book is.

130. 'Hommage à M. Forster' by 'An Indian'

4 August 1928

Article (signed 'A. S. B.'), *Nation & Athenaeum*, 589–91.

I have met the 'sympathetic' Englishman before, and I have always sympathized with him. For who would not sympathize with the Westerner who wears wooden sandals and yellow robes, takes to Gandhi's spinning-wheel and Tagore's hymn-singing and is given a seat of honour in the Indian National Congress as the only God-fearing Englishman alive? Or the ardent missionary who works for the uplift of the Indian peoples and after years of hard work (periodically described in an Evangelical paper) comes home to address Revivalist meetings, taking for his text: 'He maketh the sun to rise on the evil and on the good'? Or the eager Civil Servant who earnestly prays to the Almighty for strength and endurance to 'hold dominion over palm and pine' for the good of the palm and the pine? Or the fervent educationist who is busy devising pedagogic methods in order to inculcate a taste for Milton and Shelley amongst a people who he is certain would be immensely the better for it? Or the robust-minded Englishman who is virtuously hurt at the incapacity of Eastern crowds to form a queue outside a theatre door?

One sympathizes with them, for it is impossible either to censure them or applaud them. Their diversity is evidence of the complexity and a tribute to the immensity of India. Their impatience and fanaticism is a tribute to their simplemindedness and evidence of their narrow vision.

And it is because India is used to this sympathy of the well-meaning propagandist kind, that there is a danger of *A Passage to India* being misunderstood by the majority of Indians. It is nothing to boast of that Mr. Forster has seen India 'from within,' for every retired Anglo-Indian in the Isle of Wight who names his house 'The Shalimar' and arrays Khyber daggers and Benares brass-work on his mantelpiece has done the same. His great achievement is to have held India at arm's length, as it were, to have turned it round this way and that, and to have taken the lid off and looked within. He is a sympathizer who has retained his detachment. In a word, his is the sympathy of the artist. And if we in our turn sympathize with him, we do so in the sense of adequately responding to him and not in the sense of behaving kindly towards him. We do not see his point of view, we submit ourselves to a new orientation.

When I read *A Passage to India*, I was filled with a sense of great relief and of an almost personal gratitude to Mr. Forster. This was not because as an Indian I felt myself vindicated or flattered by the book. Indeed to know oneself is not to feel flattered, as many an Anglo-Indian reader of the book has discovered before me. It was because for the first time I saw myself reflected in the mind of an English author, without losing all semblance of a human face. Had I been a Jew living in the reign of Queen Elizabeth, I would have had a similar satisfaction at witnessing the first performance of *The Merchant of Venice*. Shylock is not exactly a deified Jew, but he is certainly a humanized Jew, which is far better. Mr. Forster in *A Passage to India* has created the Easterner in English literature, for he is the first to raise grotesque legendary creatures and terracotta figures to the dignity of human beings.

My first English book about India was given to me as a prize for reciting Kipling's 'East is East and West is West' at an annual function in my school. It was called *Picturesque India*. On the cover was the picture of an elephant carrying a golden howdah and decked in all the gorgeous trappings that are the privilege of an elephant. It was an account of an extensive tour through India, describing its palaces, monuments, gold work, shawls, Persian wheels, burning-ghats, and all the sights and curios that delight the heart of a cold-weather tourist. The book amused me. It was my first glimpse of the country through a foreigner's eye, and it tickled me to find him stupidly gazing about India and stumbling amongst its mosques and temples. I admit that the author was probably one of those much-travelled men who gradually amass a vast collection of guide books, and who at the end of their lives have the satisfaction of knowing the height (in feet) of every tower in the world. But as I read more and more books about India, I despaired of meeting any other kind of author at all. Each wrote in a slightly different vein, but they all rode through the streets of the East in a hackney carriage and carried luncheon baskets with them. There were the Colonel's 'Letters from India,' where the sole human touch is the highly amusing way in which the worthy Colonel set a trap to catch his dishonest native servant red-handed. There was the Big Game Hunter's journal with photographs of all the man-eaters and cheetahs that he had shot (the frontispiece showing the author himself wearing a pith helmet and a scout's shirt). There was the ecclesiastical gentleman with his statistics of mission schools and true stories of some of the untouchables who had found consolation in the new religion. There was milady, who writes the Society column, romancing about the witchery of the Indian skies (the open-air ball they had at the Club in Delhi on a moonlight night). Even Kipling, with his long experience of India, failed to reach the soul within. 'Kim' is like a curio shop, plus all the entertaining, enchanting, and persuading falsehoods of the curio-dealer himself. He showed his readers the 'Wheel of Life' going round and round, and sought to mesmerize him by its mystic revolutions. The throb of real life escaped his touch. Edmund Candler began as a romance-hunting sightseer—*The Mantle of the East* is a suggestive title—and ended by adopting the tone of a war-correspondent. For some years he rhapsodized about the picturesqueness of the East, and then by degrees found himself engaged in propaganda work. Intelligent and observant though he was, he never rose above the level of a talented journalist. His 'Sri Ram' and 'Abdication' were meant to justify the ways of England to men, and on second thought were cast in the form of novels. So that you have a story but no characters. There is movement, in fact there is a revolution, but there is no life.

I have left out of account as unworthy of my reader's consideration all books that deal with the mythical East of the pseudo-romance-writer's convention. Most of these books are evidently catering for a public whose East is a patchwork quilt of a few odd quatrains from Omar Khayyam, some stories from the *Arabian Nights*, a statue of Buddha seen in a museum or an Indian conjurer seen in a music-hall, a few characters of the musical-comedy stage, and a few anecdotes about jealous polygamous husbands handed down from the days of the Crusades or from the days of the letters of Lady Mary Wortley Montagu. Some of them give an occasional touch of moonlight and palm trees, spread a few carpets, scatter a few jewels or brandish a few scimitars to make things more oriental. They are concerned with lands and peoples that are outside the ken of geography or anthropology, and we had best leave them to their own marvellous travels.

To come back to earth and so to *A Passage to India*. It is dangerous to try and divine the method by which an artist selects his material, but one is tempted to contrast Mr. Forster with Mr. Aldous Huxley. In *Jesting Pilate* Mr. Huxley sought to interpret the domes and minarets of India in terms of the human mind. He went about India in the same way as he would go about Italy or Greece, listening to the voices in the ruins and the echoes in the colonnades. If he misinterpreted a dome, there was little danger of his stumbling over it and finding his mistake. Mr. Forster started at the other end. He talked to the living before he conversed with the dead.

I have said that one felt one owed Mr. Forster a debt of gratitude which was almost personal. Let me be bold and claim that his book has made the life of the Indian visitor to this land more comfortable. I do not mean that people are more hospitable to him because they have read the book. In fact, I would not be surprised if some of the indulgence with which he is often treated were to be felt as superfluous and consequently withdrawn, or some of the glamour that clung to him dissolved into the light of common day. What I mean is that if all the people he met were Forsterized, he would not nearly so often find himself forced into false positions which he has not the least desire to take up and from which he finds it difficult to extricate himself without causing minor disasters. He is conceived long before he is accosted, and finds himself constrained to live up to somebody else's false notion or perhaps a thousand false notions. For the only alternative is to acquire a habit of perpetual self-exposition. And an Ancient Mariner in real life would hardly be tolerated.

I, who never had the courage to protest when people would insist on behaving as if I was a dissolute prince, or an unsaved heathen soul, or a slothful Oriental or a profound occultist or a savage aborigine, when I came to the last page of the book and read:—

> 'Why can't we be friends now?' said the other, holding him affectionately. 'It's what I want. It's what you want.'
>
> 'But the horses didn't want it—they swerved apart; the earth didn't want it, sending up rocks through which riders must pass single file; the temples, the tank, the jail, the palace, the birds, the carrion, the Guest House, that came into view as they issued from the gap and saw Man beneath: they didn't want it, they said in their hundred voices, "No, not yet," and the sky said, "No, not there." '

—when I read this, for a moment I ignored the awful truth of the passage, so elated was I at the discovery that somebody had found ordinary human beings in the East.

131. Forster's picture of India

From Bhupal Singh, *A Survey of Anglo-Indian Fiction* (Oxford University Press, 1934), chapter 9, 221–32.

Mr. Forster's *A Passage to India* is an oasis in the desert of Anglo-Indian fiction. It is a refreshing book, refreshing in its candour, sincerity, fairness, and art, and is worth more than the whole of the trash that passes by the name of Anglo-Indian fiction, a few writers excepted. It is a clever picture of Englishmen in India, a subtle portraiture of the Indian, especially the Moslem mind, and a fascinating study of the problems arising out of the contact of India with the West. It aims at no solution, and offers no explanation; it merely records with sincerity and insight the impressions of an English man of letters of his passage through post-War India, an Englishman who is a master of his craft, and who combines an original vision with a finished artistry. Like all original books it is intensely provoking. It does not flatter the Englishman and it does not aim at pleasing the Indian; it is likely to irritate both. It is not an imaginary picture, though it is imaginatively conceived. Most Anglo-Indian writers, as we have seen, write of India and of Indians with contempt; a very few (mostly historians) go to the other extreme. Mr. Forster's object is merely to discover how people behave in relation to one another under the conditions obtaining in India at present. That he does not win applause either from India or Anglo-India is a tribute to his impartiality.

Mr. Forster's theme bristles with difficulties. He takes for his subject the conflict of races. Race feeling is strong in the English; it is stronger in Anglo-Indians for reasons which can be easily understood. Indians, on the other hand, are very sensitive to insults, real or imagined. Though a conquered people, they have not forgotten their past, nor their ancient culture or civilization. It is what Mr. Ralph Wright has called 'this almost fratricidal subject' that Mr. Forster has chosen as the theme of his novel.

[Two sections follow, summing up the plot and giving examples of Forster's presentation of Anglo-India.]

Mr. Forster's portraiture of Anglo-Indian life has called forth bitter protests from Anglo-India, and he has been accused of ignorance, if not of unfairness, in his delineation of the English colony at Chandrapore. It has to be admitted that most of the Anglo-Indians, from the Collector downwards, do not appear in a favourable light. Turton is a 'burra sahib', much too conscious of his position, before whom other Europeans cringe. His hectoring manner to Fielding is specially offensive and typical of the attitude of a 'Heaven-born' towards a by-no-means unimportant officer of the Indian Educational Department. But Turton's behaviour is the result of Fielding's pro-Indian proclivities. Fielding is not 'pukka'. That is his main fault. His profession inspires distrust, his ideas are fatal to caste. Though the sahibs tolerated him for the sake of his good heart and strong body, it is their wives who decided that he was not a sahib, and for that reason disliked him. He had to pay a heavy price for associating with Indians, and for his unconventionality and independence. Those critics who see in Turton's behaviour to Fielding something unreal, forget that it is not as types that Fielding and Turton have been delineated by Mr. Forster. They are individuals. All Collectors are not Turtons, as all college Principals are not Fieldings. Major Callender, similarly, is not representative of Civil Surgeons. His treatment of Aziz is not typical of the treatment by Englishmen of their Indian subordinates. But Callender's natural contempt and insolence are heightened by the knowledge that his subordinate is more efficient as a surgeon than himself. Mr. Forster is always careful to individualize his characters, even when he is painting them as representatives of a class. The traces of exaggeration, unreality or unnaturalness that Anglo-Indians find in these characters are perhaps due to their habit of confounding the character with the type. The individual and class characteristics have been so cleverly combined in almost all the characters of Mr. Forster's novel, that even his minor characters have an exquisite sense of completeness. Mr. Forster is not so much a portrait painter as a psychologist. He observes human beings under certain conditions. Environment as affecting character is specially marked in his novels. He knows, as 'Affable Hawk' is careful to explain in the *New Statesman*, that often the atmosphere 'distorts human relations, making people behave wildly and foolishly who, under other circumstances, would be neither wild nor foolish'. Just as in the novels of Mr. Wells, clashes of class consciousness and the confusions of the social order make it impossible for people to behave properly towards each other, similarly in *A Passage to India* racial consciousness and the contradictions of a system once established firmly on the distinction between a conquering race and a subject people, but now in the process of rapid decay, make the Turtons and Burtons and Callenders of Chandrapore behave so foolishly that they appear to be 'wildly improbable and unreal'. Turton and Callender, however, are minor characters.

[A section follows on the character of Ronny Heaslop.]

In spite of differences of opinion as regards the reality of Anglo-Indian portraits, and in spite of a few mistakes, Mr. Forster's knowledge of Anglo-India shows insight and penetration.

[An approving summary follows of Forster's presentation of Moslem India.]

It is doubtful whether Mr. Forster knew Hindus intimately. Professor Godbole's conservatism and his religious ecstasy, his good nature and his small lies, his tranquillity and his 'polite enigmatic' manner, are all caught by the deft pen of Mr. Forster. But he is not interesting, any more than Dr. Panna Lal, Mr. Dass the Magistrate, the Battacharyas or Ram Chand. Mr. Forster's description of the Gokul Ashtami in an Indian State is a beautiful picture of Hindu superstitions, faith and fervour, vulgarity and mysticism.

Mr. Forster is not a propagandist. He is scrupulously fair. He has no didactic aim either. But it is possible that in one of the self-communings of Aziz, he is communicating his own vision of India of the future.

This evening he longed to compose a new song which should be acclaimed by multitudes and even sung in the fields. In what language shall it be written? And what shall it announce? He vowed to see more of Indians who were not Mohammedans, and never to look backward. It is the only healthy course. Of what help, in this latitude and hour, are the glories of Cordova and Samarcand? They have gone, and while we lament them the English occupy Delhi and exclude us from East Africa. Islam itself, though true, throws cross-lights over the path to freedom. The song of the future must transcend creed.

132. Roger Fry on *A Passage to India*

1940

Roger Fry (1866–1934), educated at King's College, Cambridge, was an important member of the 'Bloomsbury Group', and painted in 1911 the portrait of Forster in the Evert Barger collection. He was Slade Professor of Fine Art at Cambridge in 1933.

From Virginia Woolf, *Roger Fry: A Biography* (The Hogarth Press, 1940), 240–1, reprinted by permission of the Literary Estate of Virginia Woolf, The Hogarth Press, and Harcourt Brace Jovanovich, Inc.

He greatly admired E. M. Forster's *Passage to India*. 'I think it's a marvellous texture—really beautiful writing. But Oh lord I wish he weren't a mystic, or that he would keep his mysticism out of his books . . . I'm certain that the only meanings that are worth anything in a work of art are those that the artist himself knows nothing about. The moment he tries to explain *his* ideas and *his* emotions he misses the great thing.'

FOUR VIEWS OF FORSTER

1927

133. 'The novels of E. M. Forster'

Translated from Jacques Heurgon, 'Les Romans de E. M. Forster', *Revue de Paris* cxcix, April 1927, 701–9.

Jacques Heurgon (1903–), classical scholar, studied at the École Normale Supérieure in Paris and at the French Institute in Rome. He was a Professor at the University of Lille, then at the University of Paris.

With the translation of *A Passage to India* (which the *Revue de Paris* begins serialising today) the French reader will come to know the most humane and intelligent depiction (and also the most moderate in tone as well as the boldest in its judgements) that has been made for a long time of the relationship between natives and colonials in British India. One sees here, entrenched on a hill outside the town, between their church, their grocer's shop and their club, some dozens of European officials, trying to forget that they are at Chandrapore on the Ganges. They do their duty: administer justice, nurse the sick at the hospital, collect taxes, bring up their children in a school. Around them swirls a pleasant and civilised crowd, eager for sympathy and consideration, and forever disappointed. With a succession of small strokes, Forster leads this breakdown in communication to the most dangerous consequences.

A Passage to India naturally created a scandal in England. In France, where on the one hand India and on the other the problem of colonisation in general excite so much curiosity and concern, it will answer to preoccupations no less urgent. It is a particularly topical book. But above all it is an admirable novel, packed with the experience of a whole life. Even more than the evidence itself, we feel that the man presenting it should be better known to us. The final pages leave us on the track of something important which the reader who has been won over will perhaps go on to seek in earlier works. If he afterwards comes back to *A Passage to India*, this detour will in the end make him discover in this *document* a deeper significance, a more subtle topicality.

The career of E. M. Forster has not been uninterrupted. He first brought himself to our notice, between 1906 and 1910, with a series of novels published one after the other: *Where Angels Fear to Tread* (1906) [*sic*], *The Longest Journey* (1907), *A Room with a View* (1909) [*sic*], *Howards End* (1910), after which (apart from a collection of short stories, *The Celestial Omnibus* (1912) [*sic*]) he was silent for thirteen years. Having been placed, by the vagaries of war, in Alexandria, he brought back from his stay an exquisite little book of impressions, *Pharos and Pharillon*, and a *Guide to Alexandria*. But two visits to India, before and after the war, furnished him with the material for *A Passage to India*, which appeared in 1924.

These novels present themselves first as a dense mass of characters and events. *Packed with so many good things*—so begin nearly all the newspaper articles dealing with him. His prime gift is obviously an inexhaustible ability to invent realistic details. The whole shape of an existence is drawn by a succession of minor but significant facts. Each shade of feeling is presented with a precise and detailed vividness. But despite this care for detail, one must beware of thinking that Forster is some kind of impressionist. The danger that menaces a writer like Virginia Woolf (but the miracle is that she knows how to triumph over it) is that of not being able to separate an individualised human being from the sensations which, so to speak, stifle it. The most dense or the most generous sensation has always something anonymous about it: it is on the inside, at the point where time comes into play, that character becomes identifiable. Forster concerns himself above all with differences. And this is why he tends to neglect everything that does not *denote* an individual reality. When Proust describes a musical evening, he studies the different expressions of the same feeling, affectation, in the audience: his pleasure and ours are produced by the luxuriant variety of faces by which an identical and collective snobbery reveals itself: the exterior exceeds the interior in interest. But here is the beginning of a chapter in *Howards End*. One sees here all that can produce, with a comic sense, a very marked instinct for *discrimination*:

[Quotes paragraph one of Chapter Five—the performance of Beethoven's Fifth Symphony in the Queen's Hall.]

The danger of this exclusive search for the significant might perhaps be a certain airlessness and a lack of that physical density which surrounds and infuses our thoughts and feelings. Forster has not often fallen into this trap; his characters, however unimportant, are filled with a consistent life. His special gift is the play of an incomparably acute subtlety of mind. To follow, in the swarm of individuals, certain lines which criss-cross, without ever getting entangled, is the chief pleasure given by his books: our minds are dazzled. There is nothing more difficult than to show the difference between two sisters who are to all intents and purposes the same age, and have the same character and tastes. We have seen above what the two sisters experienced at the concert: Helen saw heroes and shipwrecks in the flood of the music, Margaret saw nothing but the music. This, taken with a few lines of an earlier chapter, marks the beginning of differentiation:

[Quotes part of penultimate paragraph of Chapter Four, showing certain differences between Helen and Margaret.]

These two intellectuals are attracted by men of action. But Helen, after having once been disappointed, goes to the other extreme—to an intransigent idealism. The other—the one who sees neither shipwrecks nor heroes in the music, but only the music—is more precise, more patient, more reasonable. She will end by marrying, with love but without illusions, a businessman.

Now, in what direction are all these individual destinies pointed? What picture of life does Forster offer us in his novels?

It may be said with fair accuracy that Forster takes his place at the end of that line of English novelists who, from Fielding to Wells, Galsworthy and Arnold Bennett, have insisted on the rights of the individual in the face of a tyrannical society, opposing nature to conventionality, and sincerity to puritan hypocrisy. In this sense *Howards End* could even be called a feminist novel. But such formulae are rather crude and heavy, suited perhaps to the subject-matter of some of these novels if we tell their story in a certain way, but not at all to their quality, their texture, and that sense of hesitant intimacy which is essential to them. It is better to put aside moral notions for a moment. Forster gets to the root of his characters, into an area where the matter at issue is not being this or being that but simply being.

The question that is asked of them is not—is he good? is he bad?—nor, is he strong? is he weak?—nor even, is he natural or unconventional?—but rather—is he real or unreal? And that is the question which their own consciences ask also. Furnished with more sensitivity than vitality, they manœuvre in a world where declarations of belief, irresistible remorse, or the bursting desire for freedom are rare accidents, and where the landscape is, instead, made up of narrow bands of light and shade between which one passes without realising it; except that in one place there is the feeling of living, of being someone real, and in another place, close by, the world suddenly loses all meaning: the feeling, by turns anxious, resigned or limp, of being solid or of being empty. What is it, then, that at certain moments makes us sure that we exist? What is reality? This is the basic theme of E. M. Forster's novels, and the successive answers he has given to this question, or rather the different ways in which he has looked at it, explain the development of his work.

As a young writer, Forster began his career normally by protesting against his social environment. Reality is the complete fulfilment of one's self, in sincerity and joy. It follows from this that there is in the world more unreality than reality: how many people have the courage to fulfil themselves completely? This is the situation found in Forster's earliest novels. Take for example the subject—a standard one—of *A Room with a View*: a young woman, originally engaged in a manner befitting her position, prefers marrying beneath herself for love to a conventional marriage. In such a situation, a Meredith conveys to us above all the feeling of an instinctive force which resists pressure, gives way for a moment, and then bursts out. Here, the general effect is quite otherwise: a crowd of set, unreal masks, amongst which the spirit of life ironically winds; for someone may be imagined behind the scenes—if you like, a vaudeville version of the god Pan. Thus long pages follow each other under a ghostly light: all the efforts these people make to keep themselves to themselves. Suddenly the book lights up with an inner radiance—a sincere word has been spoken. The light spreads more and more widely, and the end of the book is wholly swallowed up in the fire of the young woman's decision to be herself. This contrast between reality and unreality appears again in this book in a striking way, in connection with a subordinate character, the rejected fiancé. From the beginning one senses that basically he is intelligent, that there is something in him, that he exists. But he is none the less detestable. Mechanical gestures and remarks; he carps unceasingly, spoils the pleasure of others, is bored: is he a phantom like the others? The evening when the girl gives him his freedom is more difficult than she has foreseen; she almost regrets having to break off the engagement; suddenly he no longer disappoints her; he lives up to the moment and is profound, sensitive and modest. One suddenly feels the same interior warmth described just before—reality suddenly overcomes him just as a blush suffuses the face, the cut-out figure comes alive, detaches himself from the frozen background and becomes moving, because this ascetic who did not know how to be himself when happy, lives quite naturally at the moment of renunciation.

The Longest Journey, published two years earlier (1907), described a similar but deeper experience. After difficult enough beginnings, Rickie Elliott approaches happiness. His childhood had been unhappy and full of regret at being an only child. At Cambridge he is received affectionately; he has friends; he is going to marry. It is at this moment that chance leads him to suspect the existence of a half-brother who lives in the country, uncultivated, disgraced and disinherited. His fiancée helps him not to linger too much thinking about this, and he almost forgets. But his marriage turns out badly. Everything around him loses its lustre and falls into a kind of languor. Towards the end he tries to become reconciled with his brother, who has taken to drink. He has several clumsy and touching conversations with the drunkard. Then Rickie kills himself in order to save his brother's life. Dying, he refers to his neglected responsibility: 'Ever since', he said, 'I have taken the world at second hand. I was less and less concerned to look it in the face, until not only you but everyone became unreal'. The theme is magnificent. It is a graver version of what *A Room with a View* taught us earlier on: the same thing at stake, the reality or unreality of our being, and the same sole way of attaining it, the fulfilment of what is most sincere within us. Only here that sincerity becomes very demanding: one must seek to the uttermost that fragile opportunity for reality, which shows only transiently and must be caught in passing. One thinks of Rossetti's beautiful sonnet 'The Landmark'.

Howards End, which Forster began in 1908, has the same starting-point: an equally uneasy sense of fate, which makes one think at times of some of the histories of Herodotus. Howards End is the name of a country house: here live Mrs. Wilcox, a woman of strange gentleness, and her family. Suddenly she dies. Everyone is griefstricken.

She had been a model wife and mother, with a consistency of spirit and an unvarying innocence. But her last wishes, conveyed in a letter which arrives a little after her death, contradict all the regularity of an uneventful life. She demands that all her goods, that is, Howards End, be left to an almost unknown friend who herself is far from expecting such a gift. The family, on reflection, decide to disregard this sick woman's fantasy. By what ingenious chain of circumstances Mrs. Wilcox's will, at first neglected, is finally put into effect, is one of the subjects of *Howards End*. It is another *longest journey*. Things go well and easily, then one reaches a turning-point, and makes a mistake, and from then on there is something out of joint in the course of events, and matters are not put right until fate has corrected the false beginning.

Thus, then, at the root of Forster's work there is a spiritual preoccupation which dictates its framework and general outline. And without doubt this spiritual concern is fully registered in the psychological consistency of his characters. (In *The Longest Journey*, it is Rickie Elliott himself, and no one else, who creates his unhappiness by denying his true self.) One often has, however, the impression that the real action is not played before our eyes, that we perceive only coloured reflections of it. Reality is not of this world. We have said that it was to be found in complete self-fulfilment: but can this fulfilment be achieved on a purely human level? One good action done, there remains something unknown still to do. There is no reality other than a mystical one. All that seems real in life is only a symbol . . .: such is at least the deeper meaning of some passages.

But, in proportion as Forster's talent developed, an abundance of human material began to pour into the established mould; and although he always continued to touch on something mysterious, more and more the transparent became dense with life, more and more what was reflection became a source of light, so that at last the balance shifted and reality was brought back to our world.

And in fact, during the time that he was writing *Howards End*, Forster had the opportunity to examine fully its sympathetic character. One may suppose that, after he had at first conceived the novel as the *longest journey* which we summed up above, his heroine, turning away from the abstract subject, led him towards another, or, more exactly, became herself the subject: 'To whom does England belong', she asked herself, 'to those who understand her, or to those who make and re-make her each day?' In *A Passage to India*, an Indian will say: 'At bottom, our spirituality is merely our inability to put two facts together'. She [Margaret] would almost go as far as saying: My spirituality is the inability to organise a ceremony or change my apartment.

Margaret Schlegel, at twenty-nine, slowly and honestly seeks her truth. With her sister Helen and her young brother, she lives in a secluded house where she enjoys her books and the visits of artistic friends. She loves music and the countryside, she gently indulges her sensations, which she analyses with a refined imagination; she looks at landscapes and seeks for their significance. But above all she loves human beings. She is not taken in, either by her culture or her intelligence. She has above all the perfect gift of being able to put herself in another person's place, and of never losing sight of the extent to which we make him what he is. Her sister says to her one day: 'You always wish to keep the golden mean. It is heroic. But I need to be all of a piece. I wish, if it pleases me, to detest someone and tell him so'. So that, when she finds herself in the presence of the Man of Action, a man who quickly makes up his mind and cuts through his scruples—very different from herself and her perhaps sterile understanding of everything—she refuses to despise him, and even admires him.

A delicate sentiment, which affords us the most beautiful and exquisite moments in this book. One is reminded often of *Tonio Kröger*, and of that tender and envious fascination of the artist with the person who pursues a direct course. Margaret Schlegel even begins to question the validity of her solitude. She feels herself to be on the sidelines of life, and wishes to have her share of it. She is weary of taking no action—and she is tired of acting simply because one must, after all, do something. Thus a whole section of *Howards End* gives the reader the almost physical sensation of fatigue, and of a desire to lean on something. The prop will be the Positive Man. He offends her sensitivity in many ways; she is quite sure that to marry him will mean consenting to see the world in a mutilated fashion, and that it will perhaps mean renouncing what she most values in herself. She hesitates, gives herself a breathing space before striking her colours. She comes to terms with her sister on one last romantic evening, in the country, under a beautiful moon. Then there are scenes, tears. Yet she accepts, and at the moment of acceptance she says: 'If only you knew what it is to be loved by a *real* man'. Real: is not there here a complete reversal of the idea? Reality goes in the direction of the Conventional Man; it is no longer a mystical perspective which *the room with a view* opens on; it is not imagined perfection; it is something solid and, without doubt, of necessity incomplete.

Let us not press Forster's ideas too far: it does not follow, because the Wilcoxes are admitted to reality, that the Schlegels are henceforth excluded from it. It is a matter only of putting the helm over towards the world as it is: his two protagonists are now placed at an equal distance in front of him, and he considers them impartially. Each has his real and unreal part; each lives. The beauty of *Howards End* is that when Forster hands over part of himself to the objective novelist, all that remains is enriched. The figure of the Practical Man is no less scrutinised than that of Margaret: to her effort to attain positive life corresponds Mr. Wilcox's clumsy gesture of trying to meet her. The world's Animus and Anima attract each other and seek each other out: it is the amorous rivalry of Thought and Action. Around them, numerous satellite characters embody different solutions to the same problem: we have already spoken of Helen, the idealist extremist. Charles Wilcox, the Businessman's eldest son, is at the opposite pole; not having his father's wealth, he cannot permit himself his father's sentimental weaknesses; he is of an impregnable hardness. There is also the poor devil of a clerk hungry for culture but paralysed by poverty, lack of leisure, a bad marriage, and even his suspiciousness of sympathy: the Miss Schlegels take him to their hearts, and try to civilise and help him. In his eyes they represent the true life. One day they invite him to tea: what a let-down! Having learned that the insurance company he works for is on the brink of ruin, they wish to put him on his guard. He has come to talk about books.

> 'So you like Carlyle?'
>
> He was itching to talk about books and make the most of his romantic hour. Minute after minute slipped away, while the ladies, with imperfect skill, discussed the subject of reinsurance. [Ch. XVI]

It all ends very painfully.—Through the experience of this crowd of characters, so subtly varied, dawns a wisdom it would be vain to express in a formula, except by saying that it is conveyed fleetingly by the personal experience of all those encountered.

After fourteen years which left people thinking that the novelist had dried up, Forster published his masterpiece. The foregoing analyses show that he has not changed his subject. At the source of this impersonal novel the same dialogue is still found: the Indians are in the same relationship to the English as the Schlegels to the Wilcoxes. The conflict which he had tried to express, as far outside himself as possible, but which he had still felt obliged to place in his own country, to dress in the London fashion, blending much imagination in with experience, much unreality with reality—it seems that fate has given him it, one fine day, at last detached from himself, completely spread out before his eyes, localised, fully embodied in other people in new costumes, bogged down—so to speak—in life, to the point of overflowing each instant its abstract significance. All that is left is individuals separated by an unbridgeable gap. Sometimes in *Howards End*, as if it were a matter of revealing 'the influence of the invisible world on the visible', the characters are no more than centres of spiritual exchange. Everywhere exhalations and scents come over stronger than they. In *The Passage to India* the atmosphere is as if purified: all these trails of vapour are dissipated, or rather each character has recalled and reabsorbed them into himself. It acquires a sort of roundness, a gentle fullness. There are also admirable landscapes, most often in a few lines. Instead of being made up of details which arc discordant, contrasted, broken up, so that a supernatural gleam may appear in the intervening gulf, they now resign themselves to spreading out like an unbroken coat of lacquer. The surface of everything becomes smooth. And if the mystery remains all-powerful, it has also taken a visible form: the Marabar caves, clenched like fingers on the horizon. But this concrete richness, which seems taken up with itself, still remains enclosed as with a net of imperceptible cords; so that the phrase which would best sum up the invariable impression would perhaps be this: a delicate balance between form and matter—harmony.

The reader will perhaps now understand what we meant in attributing to the book another kind of topicality than that given to it by setting and subject. This return to reality, an imperceptible transition—fever, frenzy, lassitude, resignation, happiness—is the life story of our greatest writers in the tradition of symbolism. But Forster is perhaps the only one who, without repudiating anything, has pushed the reconciliation so far—as far as a novel perfectly expressed and set there, in front of us, with all the indifference of a lovely and useful object. The life story is also that of many readers who, from *Howards End* and *A Passage to India*, relearn, without illusions or false shame, the exact and definite cost of the inner life.

134. Edward Shanks, 'E. M. Forster', *London Mercury*

xvi, no. 93, July 1927, 265–74

Edward Shanks (1892–1953), poet. Assistant Editor of the *London Mercury* (1919–22); Lecturer in Poetry, Liverpool University, 1926; chief leader writer, *Evening Standard* (1928–35).

Mr. Forster published his first novel in 1905, his second in 1907, his third in 1908, and his fourth in 1910. The first three received much attention, the fourth was a positive success. Mr. Arnold Bennett testified, though without much enthusiasm, to having heard it spoken of in fashionable restaurants, and I myself witnessed a hot dispute on the probability of its incidents, conducted, in the drawing-room of a seaside boarding-house, by a group of indubitable Forster characters. But he was not, it seemed, seduced by any desire to become a perpetual topic of conversation in either fashionable restaurants or unfashionable boarding-houses. At that time there was an increasingly urgent demand for younger novelists, and Mr. Forster was freely nominated for a place. But, so far from responding to this encouragement, he passed from *Howard's End* into a silence which lasted for no fewer than fourteen years, broken only, and that towards its end, by a short story published as a pamphlet and by a book which is best, if inadequately, described as historical topography. The fact that the war took place during these years may have prolonged his silence but can hardly have been its fundamental cause.

We shall probably find a better reason, if we are to look for one, in the character of his four pre-war novels. They had all, at bottom, the same setting and the same theme. The second was not, in certain respects which are to be discussed later, quite as good as the first. The third made an advance on both of these, in breadth and variety as well as in skill of handling. The fourth began the old argument all over again, but with new material for it and in terms less limited. The presentation was more vivid, life-like and complex and conveyed to the reader a greater sense of satisfaction. This book was, as it were, the final statement for which the others were only trial drafts, and with it, not unnaturally, Mr. Forster came to a full stop.

But, even with this, it is probable that one has not found a complete explanation. It may well have been that he paused in some doubt whether the equipment which had enabled him to do so much would enable him to do any more. His own special qualities evidently were, from the first, things that sometimes perplexed and distressed him. Regarded from one point of view, these novels are as subjective as any ever written. Their own considerate impartiality, verging at times on vacillation, as it must ever do in a partial and moving world, is precisely what their author most loves, with a tremulous anxiety, to examine in his principal characters. *The Longest Journey* is perhaps the least satisfactory of his novels, but Rickie Elliott makes the best introduction to Mr. Forster's world. Rickie feared that he had come to a knowledge, not of good and evil, but of good-and-evil, was paralysed by a suspicion that these were necessary and complementary sides in an eternal argument which was never to come to any conclusion. Mr. Forster's first four novels represent an attempt, four times repeated, to deliver his own soul from this disabling situation.

When, however, his moral difficulty is translated into terms of the art of fiction, it becomes his main characteristic, the active principle of his genius. The peculiarly tender, evocative, unemphatic but precise nature of his work depends on his balance, his fairness and his almost wistful appreciation of what is vital in both sides of the argument. And the theme is one that imposes a balance. On the one side, life, active, violent, sprouting in every direction, with no better justification than that it is life and thus must do: on the other, all those bounds of respectability, of culture, of refinement, which life has at one time and another, hardening from its first free impulse, marked out for itself. There is so much to be said for life which follows its own free path, disregarding consequences: there is, alas! so much, too, to be said for the safe and neat walls between which most of us seek to canalise life. For which side are we to declare ourselves? Mr. Forster leaves us in no serious doubt as to the side on which he, at any rate, has declared himself. But the colour of his declaration is the colour given to it by a man who, living on one bank of a river, gets a pretty good, but a distant, view of the other and, not without pangs and not without scrupulously owning a liability to prejudice, proclaims it to be the better.

The terms in which, in these four novels, the opposition is presented have their own particular personal and temporal interest. The pre-war novels are peculiarly pre-war. They reflect in a special way that quarter of a century which preceded 1914, and an aspect of it which can be found mirrored elsewhere, mirrored by very different minds but recognisably the same. The life of the upper middle classes in those unvexed years, Cambridge, residential suburbs, good houses in the country, symphony concerts, visits to Italy, organised discussions on how a millionaire can best leave his fortune by will—it is a whole side of a whole period, and one now so far removed from us that we can see it as a whole, if not with so much impartiality as Mr. Forster even then found for it. This is, seen by other eyes and from another angle, the world of culture into which Mr. Coote and Helen Walsingham sought to lead the simple-minded Kipps. Indeed, if Mr. Wells's Helen Walsingham and Mr. Forster's Helen Schlegel had met at the Pension Bertolini, a resort in Florence known to Mr. Forster's characters, neither would have had any ground for surprise, though they might not have liked one another very much. But to Mr. Wells all this was an episode in passing from the realities of struggling as a draper's assistant to the realities of a wider world: Mr. Forster seems to have stayed longer in that atmosphere, to have been domiciled there, to have found in it and in contrasts to it the core of his material.

He does not, therefore, take it in so robustly light-hearted a spirit. He does, to be sure, find there the elements of comedy, and he seems at times to have a comic spirit that resembles a woman's. Unlike most modern novelists, he is not afraid of criticising his characters in his own person as author and more than once the demure acidity of his comments suggests a twentieth-century Miss Austen, ruffled, perhaps, but not dismayed by the turn of events. He knows the society of residential suburbs and pensions in Florence with an unkind closeness. And yet it is not wholly unkind. The Miss Alans, in *A Room With a View*, write to a clergyman, an old travelling acquaintance, saying that this winter they are going to Greece and 'if you knew of a really comfortable pension at Constantinople, we should be so grateful.' A really comfortable pension at Constantinople! The English travelling spinster stands out for a moment in a light of sublimity: by mere force of taking herself and everyone else for granted she subjugates the results of history.

Not wholly unkind: Mr. Forster cannot be wholly unkind, nor yet can he unreservedly hate even the persons who in his stories stand as the enemies of light. He balances judgment and takes note of the elements of truth and sincerity in all of them. This naturally produces an action of low tones, of suppressed crises. The reader of Mr. Forster's novels must have his wits very actively awake, his sensibilities very ready to be moved, if he is to follow the author's meaning. But here we come upon one of the peculiarities engendered by Mr. Forster's dissatisfaction with his own qualities, a peculiarity that must be considered, because, superficial though it is, it leaps at the reader when he attempts these novels for the first time and may easily mislead him as to their true character. Mr. Forster's stories depend on crises of the mind, subtly conveyed and subtly to be perceived, crises which, being missed, make the whole narrative meaningless. But, contrary to what one might expect, they are by no means without violent events: they are, in fact, full of them. Sudden death is worse than a commonplace with Mr. Forster, it is a vicious habit, and he who reads here for the first time can hardly feel sure of any character that he will survive into the next chapter. Our author does not, indeed, insist unduly on these unheralded shocks. His sudden deaths, sudden as they are, are announced with all possible calm. The death of Rickie's mother, in *The Longest Journey*, is typical of them all.

> It was raw weather, and Mrs. Elliott watched over him with ceaseless tenderness. It seemed as if she could not do too much to shield him and to draw him nearer to her.
>
> 'Put on your greatcoat, dearest,' she said to him.
>
> 'I don't think I want it,' answered Rickie, remembering that he was now fifteen.
>
> 'The wind is bitter. You ought to put it on.'
>
> 'But it's so heavy.'
>
> 'Do put it on, dear.'
>
> He was not very often irritable or rude, but he answered, 'Oh, I shan't catch cold. I do wish you wouldn't keep on bothering.'
>
> He did not catch cold, but while he was out his mother died. She only survived her husband eleven days, a coincidence which was recorded on their tombstone.

The same book is fatal to Gerald, first lover of the girl whom Rickie afterwards marries—'Gerald died that afternoon. He was broken up in the football match.' We learn too, in a retrospective narrative, that Rickie's mother eloped with a lover who was drowned at Stockholm on their unlawful honeymoon—'I heard him call,' she continued, 'but I thought he was laughing. When I turned, it was too late. He put his hands behind his back and sank.' Rickie's child, born lame like himself, dies in infancy—'A window was opened too wide on a draughty day.' And Rickie receives fatal injuries from a train at a level-crossing.

All this is something of a massacre, but it is not exceptional among Mr. Forster's novels. The climax of *Where Angels Fear to Tread* occurs when the abducted baby, poor plot-making parcel, is thrown out of a carriage to die in the darkness and mud of the roadside, and its father just stops short of murdering the abductor, already crippled in the accident, with his hands. In *Howard's End*, Mrs. Wilcox dies briefly as time goes and almost cursorily as the book goes and, later in the same story, Len Bast's vulnerable heart takes him abruptly out of Mr. Forster's world under the stress of Charles Wilcox's violence. Charles gets, in return, a sentence of imprisonment for manslaughter. In *A Room With a View*, Lucy is exposed to the sight of a murder in one of the public squares of Florence. Clearly, Mr. Forster's world is by no means the world of Miss Austen. Stevenson asked, 'Shall we never shed blood?' and Mr. Forster, representing the modern novelist, has done his best.

This taste for violence, unfortunate as it is, is not an accidental eccentricity. It is unfortunate because a sudden death in a story carries its own emphasis, which is outside the author's control. Mr. Forster generally schemes to put his emphasis on much subtler points and then defeats his own purpose. The real crises in *A Room With a View* are two snatched kisses and a young man's refusal to make up a four at tennis—not the Florentine murder. The first of these crises is perfectly described:

From her feet the ground sloped sharply into the view, and violets ran down in rivulets and streams and cataracts, irrigating the hill-side with blue, eddying round the tree stems, collecting into pools in the hollows, covering the grass with spots of azure foam. But never again were they in such profusion: this terrace was the well-head, the primal source whence beauty gushed out to water the earth.

Standing at its brink, like a swimmer who prepares, was the good man. But he was not the good man she had expected, and he was alone.

George had turned at the sound of her arrival. For a moment he contemplated her, as one who had fallen out of heaven. He saw radiant joy in her face, he saw the flowers beat against her dress in blue waves. The bushes above them closed. He stepped quickly forward and kissed her.

Before she could speak, almost before she could feel, a voice called 'Lucy!

Lucy! Lucy!' The silence of life had been broken by Miss Bartlett, who stood brown against the view.

This, in Mr. Forster's intention, is the contrast of the life of reality with the life of sham, Lucy being kissed by a strange young man, with Lucy buying pictures:

She bought a photograph of Botticelli's 'Birth of Venus.' Venus, being a pity, spoilt the picture, otherwise so charming, and Miss Bartlett had persuaded her to do without it. (A pity in art of course signified the nude.) Giorgione's 'Tempesta,' the Idolino, some of the Sistine frescoes and the Apoxyomenos, were added to it. She felt a little calmer then, and bought Fra Angelico's 'Coronation,' Giotto's 'Ascension of St. John,' some Della Robbia babies and some Guido Reni Madonnas.

But Mr. Forster will never quite trust to such a juxtaposition of subtleties to bring out his point. He cannot help invoking as a contrast to the thin-blooded life of substitutes and shams the obvious reality of death. Here, he seems to say, is something you cannot mistake: look at these people playing with their culture and their conventions—and now, see! suddenly one of them is dead. But this makes an unfortunate contrast with the general texture of his work, as alarming and incongruous as a splash of garish colour in a picture by Corot. His fondness for it is not, indeed, hard to understand. It arises from a suspicion that he himself lives in the shadow-world, that he can see only at a distance the spontaneous and natural life he desires: perhaps, he sometimes feels, that distance might be bridged by a sudden violence.

No matter what the reason for it, it remains out of keeping with Mr. Forster's art which, when it is not dispassionately evocative, is compassionately ironical. He does live in 'a room with a view.' Inside all is in delicately distinguished tones of grey. This is an art of domestic interiors, made alive by Mr. Forster's compassion, lit up by his irony. Through the window can be seen a landscape of the outdoor, sometimes of an exotic, world. The contrast of outdoors with indoors is precisely what Mr. Forster is always trying to express. With the one term of the contrast, with the indoors scene, he never fails: his compassion and his irony go hand in hand to make an incomparable picture of those moderately well-to-do people whose lives go evenly enough so long as they remain within the walls of their culture and their conventions and do not look at the view outside except through a closed window so glazed as to take the inconvenient life out of it.

When he tries to describe that significant world beyond the window, his success is more variable. Perhaps he never did it better than in his first novel, *Where Angels Fear to Tread*, which is not, however, in other respects his best. Here Lilia Herriton, a widow, looked at askance by her husband's family on account of her vulgarity, takes an Italian holiday. They regard this as a sign, though a meagre one, of grace in her, but she falls in love with a handsome young Italian, the son of a dentist. He falls in love with her money, she marries him, bears him a son, lingers a little in misery, and dies. Her first husband's brother, goaded by his mother and accompanied by a narrow and righteous spinster sister, makes an expedition to Italy to rescue the child from conditions of supposedly intolerable vulgarity and squalor. The young man finds vulgarity, indeed, and squalor enough, but also, in the child's father and in his town, an outburst of joyous and impenitent life which he dimly understands and deeply envies. Gino is idle and dissolute, vulgar and caddish, but the Englishman discerns in him something very important which is lacking in the cultured residential district of Sawston. He begins to perceive what this is, when, in the company of his sister, he visits the theatre of Monteriano for a performance of *Lucia di Lammermoor*. Harriet, 'though she did not care for music, knew how to listen to it.' She is annoyed because there is talking, and her protest hushes the offenders 'not because it is wrong to talk during a chorus, but because it is natural to be civil to a visitor.'

For a little time she kept the whole house in order, and could smile at her brother complacently. Her success annoyed him. He had grasped the principle of opera in Italy—it aims not at illusion but at entertainment—and he did not want this great evening party to turn into a prayer-meeting. But soon the boxes began to fill, and Harriet's power was over. Families greeted each other across the auditorium. People in the pit hailed their brothers and sons in the chorus, and told them how well they were singing. When Lucia appeared by the fountain there was loud applause, and cries of 'Welcome to Monteriano!'

. . . Lucia began to sing, and there was a moment's silence. She was stout and ugly; but her voice was still beautiful, and as she sang the theatre murmured like a hive of happy bees. All through the coloratura she was accompanied by sighs, and its top note was drowned in a shout of universal joy.

In his search for deeper and fuller expression, Mr. Forster lost something of the happy freshness which is here displayed. Stephen Wonham, in *The Longest Journey*, is a rather extravagant and very unsuccessful attempt to imagine an English Gino. Except in an isolated touch here and there, he has hardly any real existence, and Rickie, his half-brother, the dweller in the indoors world, who looks for a life outside it, is too weak, too much dispersed, and even in his secret thoughts, too inarticulate to arouse much interest. This book depends mostly on veracious studies of some minor characters. *A Room With a View* is a more even performance, the Emersons, direct descendants of Gino and Stephen, being rather sketchy but not at any point unreal, while Lucy is as charming a picture of the perfectly normal human being as any novelist of our time has achieved.

Howard's End is altogether a richer and subtler book than any of the three which went before it. The opposition between the two ways of living is not stated in the same terms nor yet in terms so simple. The author, who before always produced an effect of being anxious to be fair, seems here to be fair out of a transcending artistic necessity: the characters are alive, and he feels he has given them their life, regards them therefore with a loving, not a reasoned, impartiality. It is noticeable that in this novel the writer intervenes with comment and explanation, perhaps not more often than before, but obviously more of intention and with greater assurance. It is noticeable, also, that, in spite of this, he leaves it much more to the reader to draw such conclusions as he pleases from this contemplation of a piece of life. There are the Schlegels, with their cosmopolitan culture and sincere but vague aspirations—'to be humble and kind, to go straight ahead, to love people rather than pity them, to remember the submerged'—and their self-questionings—'Well, one can't do all these things at once, worse luck, because they're so contradictory. It's then that proportion comes in—to live by proportion. Don't *begin* by proportion. Only prigs do that.' There are the Wilcoxes with their serenely unscrupulous material prosperity and their perilous dependence on it, diagnosed by Helen Schlegel as concealing only 'panic and emptiness.' And there are the house, Howard's End, and its mistress, Mrs. Wilcox, vague, inarticulate, but, both of them, instinctively making something secure in an uncomprehended world. This, briefly put, is a conclusion to be drawn from the book. But, when he wrote *Howard's End*, Mr. Forster had attained sufficient certainty in his vision of life not to formulate any conclusions: they are yours, if you like to draw them, not his. I have tried to show that in these books there is what is called 'a reading of life,' but truly what that reading is does not so much matter except in so far as it helps us to appreciate their author's rather unexpected but persuasive *picture* of life—the prisoners in the room, the view outside. It may or may not be true: Samuel Butler (and Mr. Shaw, in *Heartbreak House*) have put it more energetically. But in these four books Mr. Forster does bring a little world of imaginative observation into existence. And, with the fourth book, he came, for a very long time, to a full stop.

Then, in 1920, he published *The Story of the Siren*, a booklet of a dozen or so pages which contains one of the queerest and one of the best short stories of recent years. It begins typically with the young man travelling with (of course) his aunt in Italy, who drops his 'note book on the Deist controversy' out of a row-boat into the Mediterranean:

'Nothing of it but will change into something rich and strange,' warbled the chaplain, while his sister said, 'Why, it's gone into the water.' As for the boatmen, one of them laughed, while the other, without a word of warning, stood up and began to take his clothes off.

'Holy Moses!' cried the Colonel. 'Is the fellow mad?'

'Yes, thank him, dear,' said my aunt: 'that is to say, tell him he is very kind, but perhaps another time.'

And the young man is left behind on a shelf of rock, with the man who is to dive for his note-book, while the boat goes on. The legend that he hears, of the boatman's brother, who dived into these waters without crossing himself, and saw the Siren, and came out changed from the sea, is beyond my explanation. In a phrase or two, Mr. Forster shows that he might have been, if he had chosen, a master of the story of indefinite but powerful horror:

'We pulled him into the boat, and he was so large that he seemed to fill it, and so wet that we could not dress him. I have never seen a man so wet. I and the gentleman rowed back, and we covered Giuseppe with sacking and propped him up in the stern.'

'He was drowned then?' I murmured, supposing that to be the point.

'He was not,' he cried angrily, 'He saw the Siren. I told you.'

I was silenced again.

'We put him to bed, though he was not ill. The doctor came, and took money, and the priest came and took more and smothered him with incense and spattered him with holy water. But it was no good. He was too big—like a piece of the sea. He kissed the thumb-bones of San Biagio and they never dried till evening.'

But it is more than that, it is the recital of a wonder, as meaningless, or as full of unattainable meanings, as *Kubla Khan* or a picture by Blake.

Three years later, Mr. Forster collected, in *Pharos and Pharillon*, some sketches of Alexandria and its history. There is much in these that is delightful. But the religious record of Alexandria has tempted him into displaying, over bishop and theologian and heresiarch, that demurely bloodless gaiety of the intellectual which so disconcertingly makes one think of an atheist counterpart of Gilbert's curates.

This book was an inadequate warning for his masterpiece, *A Passage to India*, which appeared in 1924. The story, as the ordinary reader is at first likely to take it, reaches him under a definite disadvantage. It is about the British in India and the Indians who come into contact with them, and it cannot avoid the air of a political argument, however far removed from immediate politics. I am told by persons who are likely to know that Mr. Forster does exaggerate what he seems to find wrong in the attitude of the British. The plot does seem to me, ignorant as I am of Indian conditions, to show traces of those exaggerations which are natural but not permissible to the novelist—I mean, events, which might have happened, presented as though they must have happened. The English community in Chandrapore might have been as consistently hostile to the natives as it is here shown to be: probably it was not. It almost certainly would have behaved as Mr. Forster says it did, when Dr. Aziz was accused of an attempt to rape Miss Quested. But Mr. Forster has between his English and his Indians a sort of *raisonneur*, one Fielding, principal of the college at Chandrapore, who takes his middle place between the two races with a more conspicuous want of tact than suits the scheme of the book—unless the author had wished, as apparently he does not, to satirise the discomforts of the mediator. At one point he does make a little obvious but effective satire, when Fielding, after the acquittal of Aziz, is crowned with flowers by the triumphant Indians, who have taken the case just as unreasonably as his own fellow-countrymen.

Fielding does nearly spoil the book because his running commentary on the racial problems raised (and, save in isolated moments, he is rather a running commentary than a person) gives it more of the air of a political argument than it should have had. For such a dispute Mr. Forster is not fitted: if he attempted it his impartiality would doom it from the beginning to inconclusiveness. This book is, in essence, but on a higher level, both of conception and accomplishment, the same as his earlier books: it is an agonised and delighted contemplation of the contrasts of different kinds of life. In spite of the one defect of planning, it makes a single, though not an easily describable, impression, and it is written throughout with an exact proportion of effort to purpose which is not to be found elsewhere in Mr. Forster's novels.

It opens, in the description of Chandrapore, with a calm certitude which one does not often feel even in *Howard's End*. Even there Mr. Forster was trying to work out some kind of formula, some table of values, for the conflict he perceived and the effort betrayed itself in a sort of nervousness. But here the diversity of life (so much greater than any to be noted in, or within sight of, the 'room with a view') takes hold of him and he is content merely to suggest its enchantment. The style rises to the new level of the theme. The comedy of Aziz and his friends, particularly of Aziz in his illness, is done with remarkable sureness of touch, and the tragedy of Mrs. Moore is wonderfully suggested. The reader loses her for a little, then finds her subtly changed, feels as he watches, main interest elsewhere, on the focus of the story, mortality creeping over her. He learns of her death on the voyage home as one learns of the death of a friend whose ailing one has unconsciously noted. The book ends with one of the most extraordinary feats of impressionism in modern literature, the festival of the birth of Brahma, as celebrated in a small native state.

[Long quotation follows, beginning 'The corridor in the palace at Mau . . .']

This is but one fragment of a long final episode in which Mr. Forster reaches the climax, not merely of this particular novel, but also of his career as a novelist. He is no longer deliberately impartial, no longer anxious to be fair and to understand what can be said for both sides, he is carried away into an understanding beyond explanation, into the poetic state of mere wonder, and he carries his reader with him. And this book was published three years ago, since when he has again been silent. So erratically and spasmodically has he worked that one cannot think of his genius as in course of development: it comes and goes, apparently, as it wills. But it has given us much, and one masterpiece, and we can only hope that sooner or later it will give us more.

135. T. E. Lawrence on Forster and D. H. Lawrence

6 August 1927

A review of *Women in Love*, *The Lost Girl* and *The Plumed Serpent* in the *Spectator*, reprinted in *Men in Print: Essays in Literary Criticism by T. E. Lawrence*, ed. A. W. Lawrence, the Golden Cockerel Press [1940].

T. E. Lawrence (1888–1935), famous for his First World War exploits in Arabia and for *Seven Pillars of Wisdom* (1926). Lawrence changed his name legally to Shaw in 1927 and was in the Air Force (in India, from 1926 to 1928) at the time of this review. A small edition (of fifty copies) of his book about Air Force life, *The Mint*, had appeared in America in 1926.

In those early days, before the War, readers' hopes lay in Lawrence and Forster. These two heirs, through the Victorians, of the great tradition of the English novel were fortunate to have made good their footing before war came. Its bursting jarred them off their stride, indeed . . . Each man had tired of politics and action, and plunged into the dim forest of character in time to save himself from chaos. In imagination we used to make Forster and Lawrence joust with one another, on behalf of their different practices of novel-writing, as our fathers set Thackeray and Dickens at odds. Forster's world seemed a comedy, neatly layered and staged in a garden whose trim privet hedges were delicate with gossamer conventions. About its lawns he rolled thunderstorms in teacups, most lightly, beautifully. Lawrence painted hussies and bounders, unconscious of class, with the unabashed surety of genius, whether they were in their slippered kitchens or others' drawing-rooms. Forster's characters were typical. Lawrence's were individual. . . .

Forster may love a character, in a gentle, aloof irony of love, like a collector uncovering his pieces of price for a moment to a doubtful audience, as if he feared that an untaught eye might soil, by not comprehending, their fineness. Lawrence is a showman, trumpeting his stock, eager for us to make them ours—at a price. There is no comedy in him. He prods their ribs, prises open their jaws to show the false teeth. It is not very comfortable, on first reading. To be impassive spectators of the slave-market takes a training.

Forster is clever and subtle, Lawrence is not subtle, though he tries, sometimes, to convey emotional subtlety. In the big things his simplicity is shattering. His women browbeat us, as Juno browbeat the Gods at Jupiter's at-homes: but in the privacy of their dressing-rooms they jabber helplessly. Pages and pages are wasted in the effort to make the solar plexus talk English prose.

Both Lawrence and Forster give their main parts to women whenever possible. This is their deliberate choice, for each can draw an admirable man. Look at the youths in the *Longest Journey*: or read what Lawrence has written about Maurice Magnus, or Cipriano, or that splendid Canadian soldier in *The Fox* . . . But Lawrence never draws an average man or an average woman. He gets excited always over our strangenesses, and is the first thrall of his own puppets.

136. Virginia Woolf, 'The novels of E. M. Forster'

November 1927

An article in the *Atlantic Monthly* (Boston) cxv, no. 5, 642–8, reprinted from *The Death of the Moth and Other Essays* (1942) by permission of the Literary Estate of Virginia Woolf, the Hogarth Press, and Harcourt Brace Jovanovich Inc. (copyright, 1942). Copyright, 1970, by Marjorie T. Parsons, Executrix.

Virginia Woolf (1882–1941) was in the middle of her most significant period as a novelist when this essay was written, having published *Mrs Dalloway* in 1925 and *To the Lighthouse* in 1927 itself. Her concern for the formal perfection of her own work perhaps sharpens her criticism of Forster's to too fine a point; nevertheless this remains one of the most perceptive early essays on his novels. Forster returned the compliment in kind, after Virginia Woolf's death, in his Rede Lecture of 1941.

Mrs Woolf's argument is taken up by Howard N. Doughty Jr in No. 151.

I

There are many reasons which should prevent one from criticizing the work of contemporaries. Besides the obvious uneasiness—the fear of hurting feelings—there is too the difficulty of being just. Coming out one by one, their books seem like parts of a design which is slowly uncovered. Our appreciation may be intense, but our curiosity is even greater. Does the new fragment add anything to what went before? Does it carry out our theory of the author's talent, or must we alter our forecast? Such questions ruffle what should be the smooth surface of our criticism and make it full of argument and interrogation. With a novelist like Mr. Forster this is specially true, for he is in any case an author about whom there is considerable disagreement. There is something baffling and evasive in the very nature of his gifts. So, remembering that we are at best only building up a theory which may be knocked down in a year or two by Mr. Forster himself, let us take Mr. Forster's novels in the order in which they were written, and tentatively and cautiously try to make them yield us an answer.

The order in which they were written is indeed of some importance, for at the outset we see that Mr. Forster is extremely susceptible to the influence of time. He sees his people much at the mercy of those conditions which change with the years. He is acutely conscious of the bicycle and of the motor car; of the public school and of the university; of the suburb and of the city. The social historian will find his books full of illuminating information. In 1905 Lilia learned to bicycle, coasted down the High Street on Sunday evening, and fell off at the turn by the church. For this she was given a talking to by her brother-in-law which she remembered to her dying day. It is on Tuesday that the housemaid cleans out the drawing-room at Sawston. Old maids blow into their gloves when they take them off. Mr. Forster is a novelist, that is to say, who sees his people in close contact with their surroundings. And therefore the colour and constitution of the year 1905 affect him far more than any year in the calendar could affect the romantic Meredith or the poetic Hardy. But we discover as we turn the page that observation is not an end in itself; it is rather the goad, the gadfly driving Mr. Forster to provide a refuge from this misery, an escape from this meanness. Hence we arrive at that balance of forces which plays so large a part in the structure of Mr. Forster's novels. Sawston implies Italy; timidity, wildness; convention, freedom; unreality, reality. These are the villains and heroes of much of his writing. In *Where Angels Fear to Tread* the disease, convention, and the remedy, nature, are provided if anything with too eager a simplicity, too simple an assurance, but with what a freshness, what a charm! Indeed it would not be excessive if we discovered in this slight first novel evidence of powers which only needed, one might hazard, a more generous diet to ripen into wealth and beauty. Twenty-two years might well have taken the sting from the satire and shifted the proportions of the whole. But, if that is to some extent true, the years have had no power to obliterate the fact that, though Mr. Forster may be sensitive to the bicycle and the duster, he is also the most persistent devotee of the soul. Beneath bicycles and dusters, Sawston and Italy, Philip, Harriet, and Miss Abbott, there always lies for him—it is this which makes him so tolerant a satirist—a burning core. It is the soul; it is reality; it is truth; it is poetry; it is love; it decks itself in many shapes, dresses itself in many disguises. But get at it he must; keep from it he cannot. Over brakes and byres, over drawing-room carpets and mahogany sideboards, he flies in pursuit. Naturally the spectacle is sometimes comic, often fatiguing; but there are moments—and his first novel provides several instances—when he lays his hands on the prize.

Yet, if we ask ourselves upon which occasions this happens and how, it will seem that those passages which are least didactic, least conscious of the pursuit of beauty, succeed best in achieving it. When he allows himself a holiday—some phrase like that comes to our lips; when he forgets the vision and frolics and sports with the fact; when, having planted the apostles of culture in their hotel, he creates airily, joyfully, spontaneously, Gino the dentist's son sitting in the café with his friends, or describes—it is a masterpiece of comedy—the performance of *Lucia di Lammermoor*, it is then that we feel that his aim is achieved. Judging, therefore, on the evidence of this first book, with its fantasy, its penetration, its remarkable sense of design, we should have said that once Mr. Forster had acquired freedom, had passed beyond the boundaries of Sawston, he would stand firmly on his feet among the descendants of Jane Austen and Peacock. But the second novel, *The Longest Journey*, leaves us baffled and puzzled. The opposition is still the same: truth and untruth; Cambridge and Sawston; sincerity and sophistication. But everything is accentuated. He builds his Sawston of thicker bricks and destroys it with stronger blasts. The contrast between poetry and realism is much more precipitous. And now we see much more clearly to what a task his gifts commit him. We see that what might have been a passing mood is in truth a conviction. He believes that a novel must take sides in the human conflict. He sees beauty—none more keenly; but beauty imprisoned in a fortress of brick and mortar whence he must extricate her. Hence he is always constrained to build the cage—society in all its intricacy and triviality—before he can free the prisoner. The omnibus, the villa, the suburban residence, are an essential part of his design. They are required to imprison and impede the flying flame which is so remorselessly caged behind them. At the same time, as we read *The Longest Journey* we are aware of a mocking spirit of fantasy which flouts his seriousness. No one seizes more deftly the shades and shadows of the social comedy; no one more amusingly hits off the comedy of luncheon and tea party and a game of tennis at the rectory. His old maids, his clergy, are the most lifelike we have had since Jane Austen laid down the pen. But he has into the bargain what Jane Austen had not—the impulses of a poet. The neat surface is always being thrown into disarray by an outburst of lyric poetry. Again and again in *The Longest Journey* we are delighted by some exquisite description of the country; or some lovely sight—like that when Rickie and Stephen send the paper boats burning through the arch—is made visible to us forever. Here, then, is a difficult family of gifts to persuade to live in harmony together: satire and sympathy; fantasy and fact; poetry and a prim moral sense. No wonder that we are often aware of contrary currents that run counter to each other and prevent the book from bearing down upon us and overwhelming us with the authority of a masterpiece. Yet if there is one gift more essential to a novelist than another it is the power of combination—the single vision. The success of the masterpieces seems to lie not so much in their freedom from faults—indeed we tolerate the grossest errors in them all—but in the immense persuasiveness of a mind which has completely mastered its perspective.

II

We look then, as time goes on, for signs that Mr. Forster is committing himself; that he is allying himself to one of the two great camps to which most novelists belong. Speaking roughly, we may divide them into the preachers and the teachers, headed by Tolstoy and Dickens, on the one hand, and the pure artists, headed by Jane Austen and Turgenev, on the other. Mr. Forster, it seems, has a strong impulse to belong to both camps at once. He has many of the instincts and aptitudes of the pure artist (to adopt the old classification)—an exquisite prose style, an acute sense of comedy, a power of creating characters in a few strokes which live in an atmosphere of their own; but he is at the same time highly conscious of a message. Behind the rainbow of wit and sensibility there is a vision which he is determined that we shall see. But his vision is of a peculiar kind and his message of an elusive nature. He has not great interest in institutions. He has none of that wide social curiosity which marks the work of Mr. Wells. The divorce law and the poor law come in for little of his attention. His concern is with the private life; his message is addressed to the soul. 'It is the private life that holds out the mirror to infinity; personal intercourse, and that alone, that ever hints at a personality beyond our daily vision.' Our business is not to build in brick and mortar, but to draw together the seen and the unseen. We must learn to build the 'rainbow bridge that should connect the prose in us with the passion. Without it we are meaningless fragments, half monks, half beasts.' This belief that it is the private life that matters, that it is the soul that is eternal, runs through all his writing. It is the conflict between Sawston and Italy in *Where Angels Fear to Tread*; between Rickie and Agnes in *The Longest Journey*; between Lucy and Cecil in *A Room with a View*. It deepens, it becomes more insistent as time passes. It forces him on from the lighter and more whimsical short novels past that curious interlude, *The Celestial Omnibus*, to the two large books, *Howards End* and *A Passage to India*, which mark his prime.

But before we consider those two books let us look for a moment at the nature of the problem he sets himself. It is the soul that matters; and the soul, as we have seen, is caged in a solid villa of red brick somewhere in the suburbs of London. It seems, then, that if his books are to succeed in their mission his reality must at certain points become irradiated; his brick must be lit up; we must see the whole building saturated with light. We have at once to believe in the complete reality of the suburb and in the complete reality of the soul. In this combination of realism and mysticism his closest affinity is, perhaps, with Ibsen. Ibsen has the same realistic power. A room is to him a room, a writing table a writing table, and a waste-paper basket a waste-paper basket. At the same time, the paraphernalia of reality have at certain moments to become the veil through which we see infinity. When Ibsen achieves this, as he certainly does, it is not by performing some miraculous conjuring trick at the critical moment. He achieves it by putting us into the right mood from the very start and by giving us the right materials for his purpose. He gives us the effect of ordinary life, as Mr. Forster does, but he gives it us by choosing a very few facts and those of a highly relevant kind. Thus when the moment of illumination comes we accept it implicitly. We are neither roused nor puzzled; we do not have to ask ourselves, What does this mean? We feel simply that the thing we are looking at is lit up, and its depths revealed. It has not ceased to be itself by becoming something else.

Something of the same problem lies before Mr. Forster—how to connect the actual thing with the meaning of the thing and to carry the reader's mind across the chasm which divides the two without spilling a single drop of its belief. At certain moments on the Arno, in Hertfordshire, in Surrey, beauty leaps from the scabbard, the fire of truth flames through the crusted earth; we must see the red brick villa in the suburbs of London lit up. But it is in these great scenes which are the justification of the huge elaboration of the realistic novel that we are most aware of failure. For it is here that Mr. Forster makes the change from realism to symbolism; here that the object which has been so uncompromisingly solid becomes, or should become, luminously transparent. He fails, one is tempted to think, chiefly because that admirable gift of his for observation has served him too well. He has recorded too much and too literally. He has given us an almost photographic picture on one side of the page; on the other he asks us to see the same view transformed and radiant with eternal fires. The bookcase which falls upon Leonard Bast in *Howards End* should perhaps come down upon him with all the dead weight of smoke-dried culture; the Marabar caves should appear to us not real caves but, it may be, the soul of India. Miss Quested should be transformed from an English girl on a picnic to arrogant Europe straying into the heart of the East and getting lost there. We qualify these statements, for indeed we are not quite sure whether we have guessed aright. Instead of getting that sense of instant certainty which we get in *The Wild Duck* or in *The Master Builder*, we are puzzled, worried. What does this mean? we ask ourselves. What ought we to understand by this? And the hesitation is fatal. For we doubt both things—the real and the symbolical: Mrs. Moore, the nice old lady, and Mrs. Moore, the sibyl. The conjunction of these two different realities seems to cast doubt upon them both. Hence it is that there is so often an ambiguity at the heart of Mr. Forster's novels. We feel that something has failed us at the critical moment; and instead of seeing, as we do in *The Master Builder*, one single whole we see two separate parts.

The stories collected under the title of *The Celestial Omnibus* represent, it may be, an attempt on Mr. Forster's part to simplify the problem which so often troubles him of connecting the prose and poetry of life. Here he admits definitely if discreetly the possibility of magic. Omnibuses drive to Heaven; Pan is heard in the brushwood; girls turn into trees. The stories are extremely charming. They release the fantasticality which is laid under such heavy burdens in the novels. But the vein of fantasy is not deep enough or strong enough to fight single-handed against those other impulses which are part of his endowment. We feel that he is an uneasy truant in fairyland. Behind the hedge he always hears the motor horn and the shuffling feet of tired wayfarers, and soon he must return. One slim volume indeed contains all that he has allowed himself of pure fantasy. We pass from the freakish land where boys leap into the arms of Pan and girls become trees to the two Miss Schlegels, who have an income of six hundred pounds apiece and live in Wickham Place.

III

Much though we may regret the change, we cannot doubt that it was right. For none of the books before *Howards End* and *A Passage to India* altogether drew upon the full range of Mr. Forster's powers. With his queer and in some ways contradictory assortment of gifts, he needed, it seemed, some subject which would stimulate his highly sensitive and active intelligence, but would not demand the extremes of romance or passion; a subject which gave him material for criticism, and invited investigation; a subject which asked to be built up of an enormous number of slight yet precise observations, capable of being tested by an extremely honest yet sympathetic mind; yet, with all this, a subject which when finally constructed would show up against the torrents of the sunset and the eternities of night with a symbolical significance. In *Howards End* the lower middle, the middle, the upper middle classes of English society are so built up into a complete fabric. It is an attempt on a larger scale than hitherto, and, if it fails, the size of the attempt is largely responsible. Indeed, as we think back over the many pages of this elaborate and highly skilful book, with its immense technical accomplishment, and also its penetration, its wisdom and its beauty, we may wonder in what mood of the moment we can have been prompted to call it a failure. By all the rules, still more by the keen interest with which we have read it from start to finish, we should have said success. The reason is suggested perhaps by the manner of one's praise. Elaboration, skill, wisdom, penetration, beauty—they are all there, but they lack fusion; they lack cohesion; the book as a whole lacks force. Schlegels, Wilcoxes, and Basts, with all that they stand for of class and environment, emerge with extraordinary verisimilitude, but the whole effect is less satisfying than that of the much slighter but beautifully harmonious *Where Angels Fear to Tread*. Again we have the sense that there is some perversity in Mr. Forster's endowment so that his gifts in their variety and number tend to trip each other up. If he were less scrupulous, less just, less sensitively aware of the different aspects of every case, he could, we feel, come down with greater force on one precise point. As it is, the strength of his blow is dissipated. He is like a light sleeper who is always being woken by something in the room. The poet is twitched away by the satirist; the comedian is tapped on the shoulder by the moralist; he never loses himself or forgets himself for long in sheer delight in the beauty or the interest of things as they are. For this reason the lyrical passages in his books, often of great beauty in themselves, fail of their due effect in the context. Instead of flowering naturally—as in Proust, for instance—from an overflow of interest and beauty in the object itself, we feel that they have been called into existence by some irritation, are the effort of a mind outraged by ugliness to supplement it with a beauty which, because it originates in protest, has something a little febrile about it.

Yet in *Howards End* there are, one feels, in solution all the qualities that are needed to make a masterpiece. The characters are extremely real to us. The ordering of the story is masterly. That indefinable but highly important thing, the atmosphere of the book, is alight with intelligence; not a speck of humbug, not an atom of falsity is allowed to settle. And again, but on a larger battlefield, the struggle goes forward which takes place in all Mr. Forster's novels—the struggle between the things that matter and the things that do not matter, between reality and sham, between the truth and the lie. Again the comedy is exquisite and the observation faultless. But again, just as we are yielding ourselves to the pleasures of the imagination, a little jerk rouses us. We are tapped on the shoulder. We are to notice this, to take heed of that. Margaret or Helen, we are made to understand, is not speaking simply as herself; her words have another and a larger intention. So, exerting ourselves to find out the meaning, we step from the enchanted world of imagination, where our faculties work freely, to the twilight world of theory, where only our intellect functions dutifully. Such moments of disillusionment have the habit of coming when Mr. Forster is most in earnest, at the crisis of the book, where the sword falls or the bookcase drops. They bring, as we have noted already, a curious insubstantiality into the 'great scenes' and the important figures. But they absent themselves entirely from the comedy. They make us wish, foolishly enough, to dispose Mr. Forster's gifts differently and to restrict him to write comedy only. For directly he ceases to feel responsible for his characters' behaviour, and forgets that he should solve the problem of the universe, he is the most diverting of novelists. The admirable Tibby and the exquisite Mrs. Munt in *Howards End*, though thrown in largely to amuse us, bring a breath of fresh air in with them. They inspire us with the intoxicating belief that they are free to wander as far from their creator as they choose. Margaret, Helen, Leonard Bast, are closely tethered and vigilantly overlooked lest they may take matters into their own hands and upset the theory. But Tibby and Mrs. Munt go where they like, say what they like, do what they like. The lesser characters and the unimportant scenes in Mr. Forster's novels thus often remain more vivid than those with which, apparently, most pain has been taken. But it would be unjust to part from this big, serious, and highly interesting book without recognizing that it is an important if unsatisfactory piece of work which may well be the prelude to something as large but less anxious.

IV

Many years passed before *A Passage to India* appeared. Those who hoped that in the interval Mr. Forster might have developed his technique so that it yielded rather more easily to the impress of his whimsical mind and gave freer outlet to the poetry and fantasy which play about in him were disappointed. The attitude is precisely the same four-square attitude which walks up to life as if it were a house with a front door, puts its hat on the table in the hall, and proceeds to visit all the rooms in an orderly manner. The house is still the house of the British middle classes. But there is a change from *Howards End*. Hitherto Mr. Forster has been apt to pervade his books like a careful hostess who is anxious to introduce, to explain, to warn her guests of a step here, of a draught there. But here, perhaps in some disillusionment both with his guests and with his house, he seems to have relaxed these cares. We are allowed to ramble over this extraordinary continent almost alone. We notice things, about the country especially, spontaneously, accidentally almost, as if we were actually there; and now it was the sparrows flying about the pictures that caught our eyes, now the elephant with the painted forehead, now the enormous but badly designed ranges of hills. The people too, particularly the Indians, have something of the same casual, inevitable quality. They are not perhaps quite so important as the land, but they are alive; they are sensitive. No longer do we feel, as we used to feel in England, that they will be allowed to go only so far and no further lest they may upset some theory of the author's. Aziz is a free agent. He is the most imaginative character that Mr. Forster has yet created, and recalls Gino the dentist in his first book, *Where Angels Fear to Tread*. We may guess indeed that it has helped Mr. Forster to have put the ocean between him and Sawston. It is a relief, for a time, to be beyond the influence of Cambridge. Though it is still a necessity for him to build a model world which he can submit to delicate and precise criticism, the model is on a larger scale. The English society, with all its pettiness and its vulgarity and its streak of heroism, is set against a bigger and a more sinister background. And though it is still true that there are ambiguities in important places, moments of imperfect symbolism, a greater accumulation of facts than the imagination is able to deal with, it seems as if the double vision which troubled us in the earlier books was in process of becoming single. The saturation is much more thorough. Mr. Forster has almost achieved the great feat of animating this dense, compact body of observation with a spiritual light. The book shows signs of fatigue and disillusionment; but it has chapters of clear and triumphant beauty, and above all it makes us wonder, What will he write next?

ASPECTS OF THE NOVEL

1927

137. E. F. Benson, 'A literary mystification', *Spectator*

cxxxix, 29 October 1927, 732

E. F. Benson (1867–1940), novelist, brother of A. C. Benson. Author of *Miss Mapp* (1922), *Mapp and Lucia* (1932), etc.

Readers of *The Mill on the Floss* will remember that the effect of a clarifying discussion on Mr. Tulliver's mind was to convince him that talking was 'puzzling work,' and this book of Mr. E. M. Forster's, which was delivered as a series of lectures at Cambridge, impels the reader to a gesture of sympathy with Mr. Tulliver. It is full of ideas, but these are only just hinted at, given a moment's dubious illumination, and swiftly abandoned, and the critic hungry for firm guidance figures Mr. Forster as a will-o'-the-wisp light-heartedly hovering over the marshland to which he himself compares the field of his inquiry. He shows a spark here, a glimmer there, but before we can hurry to the source of enlightenment, the phantasmal beacon has guttered out, and we find ourselves more deeply bogged than ever. Towards the end of the book a natural exasperation tempts us to wonder whether our guide is not bogged too.

The process of mystification begins at once. We are bidden to accept Mr. Abel Chevalley's little dictum that the novel is a 'fiction in prose of a certain length' (and, of course, this will guard us from the error of supposing that a sonnet or a short story is a novel), but we are then told to consider that the *Pilgrim's Progress* is a novel, and by inference are forced to conclude that if a writer describes his adventures among cannibal-tribes without ever leaving the four-mile radius, he also is a novelist and his book of travels becomes a novel. But reason revolts and we shall probably continue to call such an author not a novelist but a liar, and his book not a novel but a hoax. Our bewilderment is not diminished by finding that, though Mr. Forster admits that a novel must have a story, he wishes that it needn't, and then he puts out his light, and refrains from telling us what he would substitute for it. Again with a sense of brief enlightenment we are pleased to learn that chronology is a sorry guide to the classification of novelists, but are at once plunged in darkness when we hear that, on the strength of a certain similarity between two short extracts, we should be right to class Samuel Richardson with Henry James. In any student of Henry James's methods so amazing a statement rouses the keenest curiosity, and he longs for an extensive illumination of so appetising a paradox. But Mr. Forster only skips away and glimmers elsewhere.

But we cling to what we have got, and remember that Mr. Forster has agreed (though regretfully) that novels tell stories, and he now concedes that they are about people and the processes they go through during life. Of these he tells us that there are five, birth, food, sleep, love, and death. About birth and death we know nothing first-hand, since we cannot remember the first nor can we get any internal evidence about the other: love he limits to the sex-relation, and thus he leaves out altogether, as fodder or subject-matter for the novel, the processes that happen to the mind. This seems rather a serious omission, but we search in vain for any reasoned consideration of the mental or psychical development (apart from love) which are the whole ground-work of psychological fiction, and must conclude that Mr. Forster prefers a static quality in the characters through whom such a novel functions. He goes on to an examination of these as presented by the novelist, and amusingly divides them into 'flat' and 'round,' according as we are shown only one aspect of them or are made to know them in their entirety. But we must respectfully object to Mrs. Micawber being classed as 'flat,' and as only existing as the lady who will never desert Mr. Micawber. Mrs. Micawber is a rich, round character: Mr. Forster must have forgotten about her Papa, and her grasp of a subject which was inferior to none, and her views as to the branch of the family which was settled at Plymouth. Similarly we resent Lady Bertram being classed as a 'round' merely because she saw the elopement of Julia and the infidelity of Maria 'in all its enormity.' That does not make her round: it is indeed a noble manifestation of her adorable flatness which rivals that of Mr. Woodhouse.

Mr. Forster is a strong and skilful champion of certain modes and masters, but he perhaps allows his personal taste to invade the cool detachment with which every critic should gird himself. His just love for Hardy causes him to be impatient of Meredith, and he doffs his detachment when he calls the latter a suburban roarer, and his visions of Nature 'fluffy and lush.' No doubt Meredith could not have written the opening chapter of *The Return of the Native*, but Hardy is quite as incapable of having written the meeting of Lucy and Richard Feverel on the river. In the same way, though we applaud his admiration of the construction of Henry James's *Ambassadors*, it is curious to find him blind to the constructional neatness of *The Antiquary* and still more curious to see that he fails to put his finger on the real reason which renders *The Ambassadors* such a miracle of dexterity, namely, that the whole of it is seen through the eyes of Strether, and that, in consequence, the point of view is never shifted. We may or may not agree with him as to the advisability of this shifting of the point of view, so that now the author, now one or other of the characters is the showman, but this almost unique unity in *The Ambassadors* is surely worthy of a stressed notice. Possibly the cryptic utterance that this book, like *Thais*, is 'in the shape of an hour-glass,' may convey this, but we want more illumination. Indeed, the final chapter on 'Pattern and Rhythm,' though full of stimulating suggestions, is hardly more than a series of notes, out of which, no doubt, the charming author of *A Passage to India* might build us a palace of shining criticism. We sincerely hope he will, and light it with many of the glimmering mystifications with which he has rather tantalizingly beckoned to us.

138. Virginia Woolf, review, *Nation*

xlii, 12 November 1927
(Nation & Athenaeum Literary Supplement, 247–8)

That fiction is a lady and a lady who has somehow got herself into trouble is a thought that must often have struck her admirers. Many gallant gentlemen have ridden to her rescue, chief among them Sir Walter Raleigh and Mr. Percy Lubbock. But both were a little ceremonious in their approach; both, one felt, had a great deal of knowledge of her, but not much intimacy with her. Now comes Mr. Forster, who disclaims knowledge but cannot deny that he knows the lady well. If he lacks something of the others' authority, he enjoys the privileges which are allowed the lover. He knocks at the bedroom door and is admitted when the lady is in slippers and dressing gown. Drawing up their chairs to the fire they talk easily, wittily, subtly, like old friends who have no illusions, although in fact the bedroom is a lecture-room, and the place the highly austere city of Cambridge.

This informal attitude on Mr. Forster's part is, of course, deliberate. He is not a scholar; he refuses to be a pseudo-scholar. There remains a point of view which the lecturer can adopt usefully if modestly. He can, as Mr. Forster puts it, 'visualize the English novelists, not as floating down that stream which bears all its sons away unless they are careful, but as seated together in a room, a circular room—a sort of British Museum reading-room—all writing their novels simultaneously.' So simultaneous are they, indeed, that they persist in writing out of their turn. Richardson insists that he is contemporary with Henry James. Wells will write a passage which might be written by Dickens. Being a novelist himself, Mr. Forster is not annoyed at this discovery. He knows from experience what a muddled and illogical machine the brain of a writer is. He knows how little they think about methods; how completely they forget their grandfathers; how absorbed they tend to become in some vision of their own. Thus though the scholars have all his respect, his sympathies are with the untidy and harassed people who are scribbling away at their books. And looking down on them not from any great height, but, as he says, over their shoulders, he makes out, as he passes, that certain shapes and ideas tend to recur in their minds whatever their period. Since story-telling began, stories have always been made out of much the same elements; and these, which he calls The Story, People, Plot, Fantasy, Prophecy, Pattern, and Rhythm, he now proceeds to examine.

Many are the judgments that we would willingly argue, many are the points over which we would willingly linger, as Mr. Forster passes lightly on his way. That Scott is a story-teller and nothing more; that a story is the lowest of literary organisms; that the novelist's unnatural preoccupation with love is largely a reflection of his own state of mind while he composes—every page has a hint or a suggestion which makes us stop to think or wish to contradict. Never raising his voice above the speaking level, Mr. Forster has the art of saying things which sink airily enough into the mind to stay there and unfurl like those Japanese flowers which open up in the depths of the water. But greatly though these sayings intrigue us we want to call a halt at some definite stopping place; we want to make Mr. Forster stand and deliver. For possibly, if fiction is, as we suggest, in difficulties, it may be because nobody grasps her firmly and defines her severely. She has had no rules drawn up for her, very little thinking done on her behalf. And though rules may be wrong, and must be broken, they have this advantage—they confer dignity and order upon their subject; they admit her to a place in civilized society; they prove that she is worthy of consideration. But this part of his duty, if it is his duty, Mr. Forster expressly disowns. He is not going to theorize about fiction except incidentally; he doubts even whether she is to be approached by a critic, and if so, with what critical equipment. All we can do is to edge him into a position which is definite enough for us to see where he stands. And perhaps the best way to do this is to quote, much summarized, his estimates of three great figures—Meredith, Hardy, and Henry James. Meredith is an exploded philosopher. His vision of nature is 'fluffy and lush.' When he gets serious and noble, he becomes a bully. 'And his novels; most of the social values are faked. The tailors are not tailors, the cricket matches are not cricket.' Hardy is a far greater writer. But he is not so successful as a novelist because his characters are 'required to contribute too much to the plot; except in their rustic humours, their vitality has been impoverished, they have gone thin and dry—he has emphasized causality more strongly than his medium permits.' Henry James pursued the narrow path of æsthetic duty and was successful. But at what a sacrifice? 'Most of human life has to disappear before he can do us a novel. Maimed creatures can alone breathe in his novels. His characters are few in number and constructed on stingy lines.'

Now if we look at these judgments and place beside them certain admissions and omissions, we shall see that, if we cannot pin Mr. Forster to a creed, we can commit him to a point of view. There is something—we hesitate to be more precise—which he calls 'life.' It is to this that he brings the books of Meredith, Hardy, or James for comparison. Always their failure is some failure in relation to life. It is the humane as opposed to the æsthetic view of fiction. It maintains that the novel is 'sogged with humanity'; that 'human beings have their great chance in the novel'; a triumph won at the expense of life is, in fact, a defeat. Thus we arrive at the notably harsh judgment of Henry James. For Henry James brought into the novel something besides human beings. He created patterns which, though beautiful in themselves, are hostile to humanity. And for his neglect of life, says Mr. Forster, he will perish.

But at this point the pertinacious pupil may demand, 'What is this "Life" that keeps on cropping up so mysteriously and so complacently in books about fiction? Why is it absent in a pattern and present in a tea party? Why is the pleasure that we get from the pattern in the Golden Bowl less valuable than the emotion which Trollope gives us when he describes a lady drinking tea in a parsonage? Surely the definition of life is too arbitrary and requires to be expanded.' To all of this Mr. Forster would reply, presumably, that he lays down no laws; the novel somehow seems to him too soft a substance to be carved like the other arts; he is merely telling us what moves him and what leaves him cold. Indeed, there is no other criterion. So then we are back in the old bog; nobody knows anything about the laws of fiction; or what its relation is to life; or to what effects it can lend itself. We can only trust our instincts. If instinct leads one reader to call Scott a story-teller, another to call him a master of romance; if one reader is moved by art, another by life, each is right, and each can pile a card-house of theory on top of his opinion as high as he can go. But the assumption that fiction is more intimately and humbly attached to the service of human beings than the other arts leads to a further position which Mr. Forster's book again illustrates. It is unnecessary to dwell upon her æsthetic functions because they are so feeble that they can safely be ignored. Thus, though it is impossible to imagine a book on painting in which not a word should be said about the medium in which a painter works, a wise and brilliant book, like Mr. Forster's, can be written about fiction without saying more than a sentence or two about the medium in which a novelist works. Almost nothing is said about words. One might suppose, unless one had read them, that a sentence means the same thing and is used for the same purposes by Sterne and by Wells. One might conclude that 'Tristram Shandy' gains nothing from the language in which it is written. So with the other æsthetic qualities. Pattern, as we have seen, is recognized, but severely censured for her tendency to obscure the human features. Beauty occurs, but she is suspect. She makes one furtive appearance 'beauty at which a novelist should never aim, though he fails if he does not achieve it'—and the possibility that she may emerge again as rhythm is briefly discussed in a few interesting pages at the end. But for the rest, fiction is treated as a parasite which draws its sustenance from life, and must, in gratitude, resemble life or perish. In poetry, in drama, words may excite and stimulate and deepen without this allegiance; but in fiction they must, first and foremost, hold themselves at the service of the teapot and the pug dog, and to be found wanting is to be found lacking.

Strange though this unæsthetic attitude would be in the critic of any other art, it does not surprise us in the critic of fiction. For one thing, the problem is extremely difficult. A book fades like a mist, like a dream. How are we to take a stick and point to that tone, that relation, in the vanishing pages, as Mr. Roger Fry points with a wand at a line or a colour in the picture displayed before him? Moreover, a novel in particular has roused a thousand ordinary human feelings in its progress. To drag in art in such a connection seems priggish and cold-hearted. It may well compromise the critic as a man of feeling and domestic ties. And so, while the painter, the musician, and the poet come in for their share of criticism, the novelist goes unscathed. His character will be discussed; his morality, it may be his genealogy, will be examined; but his writing will go scot free. There is not a critic alive now who will say that a novel is a work of art and that as such he will judge it.

And perhaps, as Mr. Forster insinuates, the critics are right. In England, at any rate, the novel is not a work of art. There are none to be stood beside *War and Peace*, *The Brothers Karamazov*, or *A la Recherche du Temps Perdu*. But while we accept the fact, we cannot suppress one last conjecture. In France and Russia they take fiction seriously. Flaubert spends a month seeking a phrase to describe a cabbage. Tolstoy writes *War and Peace* seven times over. Something of their pre-eminence may be due to the pains they take, something to the severity with which they are judged. If the English critic were less domestic, less assiduous to protect the rights of what it pleases him to call life, the novelist might be bolder too. He might cut adrift from the eternal tea table and the plausible and preposterous formulas which are supposed to represent the whole of our human adventure. But then the story might wobble; the plot might crumble; ruin might seize upon the characters. The novel in short might become a work of art.

Such are the dreams that Mr. Forster leads us to cherish. For his is a book to encourage dreaming. None more suggestive has been written about the poor lady whom, with perhaps mistaken chivalry, we still persist in calling the art of fiction.

139. L. P. Hartley, review, *Saturday Review*

cxliv, 17 December 1927, 858–9

No one is better qualified to write about the novel than Mr. E. M. Forster, for in the opinion of many he is our finest living exponent of the novelist's art. It would be unnecessary to speak of the charm of his style, of his beautiful controversial manners, were it not that they have a part to play in these lectures—the rôle of predisposing us always to assent. Is it possible that these eight exquisite chapters, the very words of which arrange themselves in patterns agreeable to the eye, were originally delivered as lectures? Mr. Forster says so; he even apologizes for their 'informal, talkative tone.' So might the Bird of Paradise apologize for the beauty of its plumes. But though his readers will not readily tire of expressing their gratitude and indebtedness to Mr. Forster, it is possible that he himself may be a little weary of the stream of incense. Though when he pays a tribute himself, how beautifully he does it:

Scheherazade avoided her fate because she knew how to wield the weapon of suspense—the only literary tool that has any effect upon tyrants and savages. Great novelist though she was—exquisite in her descriptions, tolerant in her judgments, ingenious in her incidents, advanced in her morality, vivid in her delineation of character, expert in her knowledge of three Oriental capitals—it was yet on none of these gifts that she relied when trying to save her life from her intolerable husband. They were but incidental. She only survived because she managed to keep the King wondering what would happen next. Each time she saw the sun rising she stopped in the middle of a sentence, and left him gaping. 'At this moment Scheherazade saw the morning appearing and, discreet, was silent. . . .' We are all like Scheherazade's husband, in that we want to know what happened next.

Was ever generalization more neatly and subtly led up to? We could not bring ourselves to disagree, even if we wanted to. The natural and the lazy way of reading a book of criticism is to accord it a moderate measure of attention until one reaches a definite judgment about an author one knows. If one agrees, the critic is right, probably right about everything; if not, he is wrong. The partisan reader, who sets out bristling with preconceived loyalties and animosities, may find himself at first disappointed in 'Aspects of the Novel,' because Mr. Forster seldom gives utterance to an absolute judgment—his strictures and commendations are delivered by the way, in the process of finding categories and furnishing them with appropriate novelists. He does not adopt an historical method; he imagines all the novelists of the last two hundred years writing busily in one large room; and tries to peep over their shoulders and peep into their minds. This is a great relief—to have the static quality of art reaffirmed. The fashion of imprisoning a work of art in the pigeon-hole of its period takes all the zest from criticism.

The novelists, then, meet on equal terms. But where is Balzac, where is Stendhal, where is Turgenev? Mr. Forster does not mention them; perhaps they do not fall within his categories. That is the difficulty of having a plan, even a plan as elastic as Mr. Forster's; it has to be exclusive and as it were plan-proud. In the category of 'Prophecy' are included Dostoevsky, D. H. Lawrence, Herman Melville and Emily Brontë. Some of these also find their way into 'Fantasy,' along with Peacock, Max Beerbohm, Virginia Woolf, Walter de la Mare, Beckford, James Joyce, Sterne and Swift. Most of the others are accounted for under the headings of 'The Story,' 'People' and 'The Plot.' To justify the composition of these groups,

Mr. Forster gives extracts; his eye for essential resemblances, hidden under a wide dissimilarity of subject and manner, is most remarkable. He succeeds in cutting several royal roads through his subject and persuading us that novelists who seemed to have little in common, Virginia Woolf and Sterne, for instance, lived in the same street and are near neighbours. Indeed, he rather points to roads that are already in existence than makes them himself.

Of course, one cannot always (happily) agree with him. Of Scott he says: 'Think how all Scott's laborious mountains and scooped out glens and carefully ruined abbeys call out for passion, passion, and how it is never there!' But surely it is wrong to deny Scott passion; the scene of the Laird of Dumbiedikes's death, for instance, has the quality in a high degree. 'Hawthorne,' he says, 'potters too anxiously round the problem of individual salvation' to have the true freedom of the fantasist. But a writer must have something to be fantastic *on*: and Hawthorne's foundation seems to me a very adequate one. Again, I refuse to be humble in the presence of Mr. D. H. Lawrence, though Mr. Forster urges humility upon me; and I cannot see in the work of Mr. Norman Matson a tithe of the interest he sees.

THE ETERNAL MOMENT

1928

140. Edith Sitwell, letter to E. M. Forster

30 March 1928

Edith Sitwell (1887–1964), elder sister of Osbert and Sacheverell Sitwell. She published *Wheels* in 1916, *Façade* in 1922 and *Gold Coast Customs*, an attack on social frivolity and corruption, in 1929.

Published by permission of David Higham Associates Ltd.

I can't tell you what a delight and happiness *The Eternal Moment* has been to me, and I can't even thank you enough for your very great kindness in sending it to me. Even though I was undergoing the horrors of a bad attack of influenza, I realised what a wonderful book it is. Well, all I know is that 'The Machine Stops' made me feel as though I had come out of a dark tunnel in which I had always lived, into an immense open space, and were seeing things living for the first time. I believe it is the most tremendous short story of our generation. But then the whole book has got every quality of beauty and truth and illumination. I do think 'The Point of It' is such a wonderful story too, and *The Eternal Moment* is enough to frighten one out of one's wits,—but not to frighten one only. It is in a way, the most terrifying ghost story I have ever read.

[. . . . .]

141. Cyril Connolly, notice, *New Statesman*

xxx, 31 March 1928, 797

Cyril Connolly (1903–), influential reviewer and critic since the 'twenties. In 1939 he founded *Horizon* and edited it until its demise in 1950. His publications include *The Rock Pool* (1935); a book of essays, *Enemies of Promise* (1938); and, under the pen-name Palinurus, *The Unquiet Grave* (1944).

The Eternal Moment is a collection of Mr. Forster's early stories, mostly supernatural, and only in the last does the familiar spinster emerge. The other stories are visions of judgment or of the machine age, they are tenderly earthy and full of that demure malice with which the author delights to punish the *bonne élève*. Though slight, they are all of merit, pagan, supernatural, youthful—in the best senses of those maltreated words. *The Eternal Moment* itself is weaker though revealing the full Forster world. There is the Italian hotel, the English spinster, the love scene, the muffled crisis, the packing up in anger and tears. It is curious that Mr. Forster has never been able to describe a woman so as to make her appearance attractive, even when it is intended to be so, or a crisis so as to make it seem real. The central moments in Mr. Forster's books come out like those blurred interludes in certain films when the picture has got upside down, and a little later we are back among the wild, shy, wandering, maiden ladies, the clergymen, schoolmasters, retired soldiers, and cabmen who form the limpid Utopia of Baedeker and Berlitz and whom only Mr. Forster is now able to describe.

142. Unsigned review, *The Times Literary Supplement*

no. 133, 5 April 1928, 256

There is a slight suggestion of warning to be found in the note that precedes Mr. E. M. Forster's little volume, *The Eternal Moment and Other Stories*. They were written, we are told, 'at various dates previous to 1914, and represent, with those in the Celestial Omnibus volume, all that the writer is likely to attempt in a particular line'. That announcement has, indeed, an effect of closing a phase of development; and any judgement of the various items must take account of the fact that for more than fourteen years Mr. Forster has had no further impulse to express himself in this form or, what is still more important, in this mood.

For it is the mood rather than the method that deserves attention in this collection. Mr. Forster, the artist, reached a high level of achievement early in his career, and has maintained it ever since. He found a mode that satisfied him; and his own pronouncement, made in his lectures on 'Aspects of the Novel', that 'the novelist who betrays too much interest in his own method can never be more than interesting', ranks him with those who regard with impatience the late Charles Doughty's boast of valuing his style far more than his matter. But Mr. Forster, the philosopher, must be judged for our present purpose solely as a pilgrim in a certain stage of his journey—a familiar stage, that of *Howards End*, with the slightly pathetic cry of that book's keynote, 'Only connect', still faintly audible. In his first, and terrible, picture of humanity become the slaves of one vast machine that controlled the comfort of the whole earth, the individual is presented as almost finally isolated. He communicates with the rest of the world by telephone and television. The son who calls to his mother from the antipodes, expressing his desire to see her again in the flesh, is a freak in that society, representative of a type that the 'Central Committee' does not wish to perpetuate. And when the machine stops, this slightly didactic little fancy closes with a frank moral.

They wept for humanity, those two, not for themselves. . . Ere silence was completed their hearts were opened, and they knew what had been important on the earth. Man, the flower of all flesh, the noblest of all creatures visible . . . beautiful naked man was dying, strangled in the garments that he had woven . . . Truly the garment had seemed heavenly at first, shot with the colours of culture, sewn with the threads of self-denial. And heavenly it had been so long as it was a garment and no more, so long as man could shed it at will and live by the essence that is his soul, and the essence, equally divine, that is his body.

Here the cry is clearly audible; in the other five items that make up the collection it sounds less easily recognizable as the motive of the fugue. Sir Michael, the Civil servant, who begot three children, died and went to a hell that he tried hard to persuade himself was truly heaven until a spirit crossed the river and taught him desire: Mr. Andrews, who truly went to a heaven after the manner of Captain Stormfield's and left it dissatisfied to enter again into the 'world soul'; Miss Haddon, the schoolmistress whose futile scheme of co-ordination was upset by a spirit intrusion that taught her pupils to co-ordinate 'through the central sources of Melody and Victory'—all these fail to 'connect' in the wider sense that Mr. Forster seeks, or perhaps sought, to expound. In the two remaining stories the aid of the spirit-world is not invoked, or if invoked in the case of the Italian fisherman who heard the Song of the Siren, has left us to infer its message. Lastly, *The Eternal Moment* keeps very near to earth in its account of the revisiting of Vorta in Italian Switzerland by Miss Raby, who had written a successful novel on the place in her youth, thereby making Vorta's fortune as well as her own; returned to it after twenty years; and found the young guide who had once in a mad moment of passion proclaimed his love for her transformed into a stout, complacent *concierge*.

Because it was Mr. Forster who wrote these six stories they are all interesting, have each of them some effect of penetrating below the appearance, of seeking, if now and again a trifle impatiently, the true essence of life. But the phase, the mood, seems to be of dissatisfaction. It is as if Mr. Forster were at that time almost painfully aware of the fatuity of existence and sought something too uneasily to explain it.

143. Rachel Annand Taylor, notice, *Spectator*

7 April 1928, 543–4

Rachel Annand Taylor (1876–1960), Scottish poet and biographer, was one of the first women to study at Aberdeen University. Her *Poems* were published in 1904. She had a strong interest in the Renaissance, publishing *Leonardo the Florentine* in 1927. She was admired by G. K. Chesterton and Hilaire Belloc.

Rachel Annand Taylor spoke similarly of Forster in her article 'The Post-War English Novel' (*Sociological Review* xx, no. 3, July 1928, 192):

> He regards his characters, not with active malevolence or mockery, but with a cool disinterestedness which often leaves them hard to understand. The truth is that his heart is with the carven rock and lucid pool, and holy asphodel of Greece, or with bronze sailors by the siren sea. That lovely book, *The Celestial Omnibus*, contains far more beauty and tenderness than any of his long novels, the *Passage to India* even, remarkable as that may be for its cool felicity of style.

In the first of Mr. E. M. Forster's stories, the Machine Stops, or is destined to stop when Kuno, the one creature in a mechanized civilization who can hear the call of Orion among the unheeded stars, crawls out to the deserted surface of Earth in a hollow of Wessex, where the mist is like pearl. This is a satire of dreadful gentleness which nearly dissolves one's conviction that the revolt against the Machine has already begun. But it just fails to convince, because one knows that the genius for rebellion is much stronger in most people than in Mr. E. M. Forster's conscious and uncertain characters, whom he himself often regards with so little enthusiasm. This distinguished, disillusioned book, with all its cool graces of style, is bound as a companion volume to *The Celestial Omnibus*. If it does not captivate like that lovely group of fantasies it is because the author is less fortunate with his themes. Forecasts of existence after death cannot but fail in aesthetic effect since the imagery of immortality became so nebulous, though Mr. Forster's ethic is definite and penetrative. Nor does the name-story, *The Eternal Moment*, seem psychologically true. The behaviour of Miss Raby leaves the reader incredulous. It is characteristic of Mr. Forster that so many of his heroines retain their conventional 'Miss' to the end. An imaginary lady who persists in being 'Miss' may do any wild spinsterish thing—and does. The truth is that Mr. Forster prefers to any 'Miss,' the 'siren who will rise up from the sea, and sing.' The tale of the Siren, with its mingling of Latin brutality, sharp scepticism, and wild sea-magic, is a wonderful thing. Not often enough in this volume does Mr. Forster catch that glimpse of classic asphodel and lucid spring which moves him to his rarest speech; but, whatever his subject, the style has an astringent beauty, and, if his human beings are slightly irritating, his comments on humanity are profound.

144. 'C. M.', review, *Manchester Guardian*

20 April 1928, 7

On page 27 Mr. E. M. Forster gives a convenient standard for suggesting, if not estimating, the merits and the defects of the six stories, all written before 1914, reprinted from various periodicals, in this collection. Escaped from 'the machine' that rules the world, the hero of the first story says: 'Man is the measure. That was my first lesson. Man's feet are the measure for distance, his hands are the measure for ownership, his body is the measure for all that is lovable and desirable and strong'. So we might add that man's nature is the measure of all that is profitable in fiction. By this standard the title story, which is placed last in the volume, comes first in esteem, because everything in it is relative to the behaviour of men and women, without mechanical or supernatural interference. It might be rash to describe the people in it as 'ordinary', though Miss Raby, the heroine, is extraordinary only by being more practical than is common. On her way out to an Alpine resort in the company of Colonel Leyland, with Elizabeth, her maid, for propriety, Miss Raby recalls that twenty years before a young man had made a declaration of love to her in the place they are approaching. He was a porter, not even a certificated guide, 'a male person who was hired to carry the luggage, which he dropped'. At the time she did what a young lady should, screamed and ran; but she now recognises two things: that the incident had been one of the great moments, and the most enduring, of her life, and that the novel, inspired by it, which had made her reputation, had also vulgarised the place where it occurred. The young man is now the concierge of the hotel, fat, prosaic, and obsequious. Not because she is in love with him, but from the sheer necessity for her of getting at reality, Miss Raby reminds him of their previous encounter—and his scared behaviour and the embarrassment of the listening Colonel will be comic or tragic to the reader according to the point of view. For us Miss Raby is the belated discoverer of what really counts in life, compared with which external circumstances are the dream; to her companions she is an old maid, slightly 'touched'. Her unflinching quest for reality brings the Colonel—who has mild expectations—and the quaking concierge to the same level.

The other stories are less well adapted to the human scale, though they all deal in one way or another with the contrast between the reality which is human and the dream—or the nightmare—which is mechanical. All are good in idea, but most of them fail, comparatively, in execution, being, or seeming, calculated rather than conceived. 'The Machine Stops' fails to convince us that a machine so inefficient ever began—much less obtained mastery of the world—since it is still at the stage of telephone receivers and pneumatic posts. The result is that we cannot get very excited about anybody who contrives to escape from the machine—even though it is into the death which is life, under the 'untainted sky'. Next to 'The Eternal Moment' we should place 'Mr. Andrews', who went to heaven on a loving thought—and came out again when he found that heaven fulfilled his expectations but not his hopes. But the chief interest of these stories is as showing the inventive stage, intelligent but crude and stiff in adjustment, of a writer who has passed on to creation. In writing them—and he says that he is not likely to attempt others in their particular line—Mr. Forster was learning his first lesson, that man is the measure.

145. Mary Ross, review, *New York Herald Tribune*

22 April 1928 (books, 3–4)

By amusing coincidence the week that this volume of stories is published in America the American newspapers are blaring the beauties of a machine which sells you cigarettes automatically, making change, offering the appropriate change and certificate, and even its mechanical 'thank you' and the advertising slogan of the brand you select. This machine, its promoters say in effect, releases human beings from the mere mechanical (can they mean human?) aspects of salesmanship, reserving their energies for unspecified and finer phases of the art. And Mr. Forster, in his opening story, amuses himself with picturing the end of a world in which such a process has gone to its ridiculously logical conclusion, in which people, no longer able to bear the light or air of day, spend their lives in hexagonal cells underground, pressing buttons for compressed food tablets, or mechanical medical service, or the sight of a friend by television, or music, or whatnot, but never descending to the grossness of muscular exertion or contacts with nature or people, ever adoring and subservient to the Machine. In time that Machine ran down, and a world of people with faces as white as mushrooms were forced up through the tunnels and vomitories to the hills and plains that once had been Wessex, or Cathay, or Iowa. These they knew dimly from the unceasing flow of lectures that had been provided when one pressed the appropriate button, but the air they had never breathed except through respirators, and they perished miserably like eyeless creatures from a subterranean cavern thrown up to rot in the sun.

Through all the half dozen stories of the volume there runs a rich vein of fantasy, catching its glint now from a sophisticated revision of heaven and hell, again from the shades of Napoleon and Beethoven, or the siren of Capri, and ending in the tragic comedy of an English lady novelist seeing again, after many years, the Alpine village made prosperous and popular by a story of her own, and the plump concierge, once a lean romantic porter, who had ventured to love her in her youth. In this last there is a clear foreshadowing of the subtle and ironic clash of class and race and individuality which, in bolder colors and more magnificent form, gave its character to *A Passage to India*. It is as though a sensitive and intelligent mind, after speculatively playing with ideas and personalities that passed his way, turned there to some straighter path that led ahead.

For, though but one of these stories has previously been published in this country, they were all written prior to 1914, and, as Mr. Forster declares in a foreword, represent, with *The Celestial Omnibus*, a path in his literary career which he probably will not take again. 'Much has happened since,' he continues. 'Transport has been disorganized, frontiers rectified on the map and in the spirit, and under the mass-shock of facts Fantasy has tended to retreat, or, at all events, to dig herself in.'

As a general statement, that assumption is open to question. Surely, once the first shock of disaster was past, fantasy flowered again on the ruins of the old world, in such diverse and delicate creations as have been offered, among others, by Aldous Huxley, David Garnett, Sylvia Warner and Elinor Wylie. The heartier romantic flavor of the pre-war H. G. Wells has been accepted again with acclaim in such a novel as 'The Deluge.' But, general tendencies aside, it would seem unlikely that Mr. Forster should go back to the mood or the manner of his earlier volumes. Indeed, without disparagement, one might consider such a return from his richer and more considered work undesirable. Yet now, fourteen years since the last of them was written, the stories of *The Eternal Moment* are still fresh and provocative, amusing in themselves and interesting in the light of the work they presaged.

146. L. P. Hartley, review, *Saturday Review*

28 April 1928, 530–1

Mr. Forster is surely the most unreviewable of contemporary novelists. He knows so well what he is about, he succeeds so perfectly in what he sets out to do, that criticism, which delights to elucidate the obscure or to discover a discrepancy between intention and performance, is silenced. There is another quality in Mr. Forster's work which forestalls criticism: the exquisite finish of every detail—the joy given by sentences, single words, punctuation; the eloquent transitions between paragraphs. The very spacing of the lines, the waste places of the page, have grace and significance, reminding us of those Chinese pictures in which, so we are told, the things the artist has left out have an equal importance with those he has put in. Beauty of detail is as rare in the modern novel as it is in the modern world; and the critic, recognizing it, is disposed to close his eyes and let himself go in a luxury of praise.

But unfortunately, literature being such a very mixed art, he has to look further. Whether or not in painting the subject makes a difference, in literature it certainly does: the writer, like the reader, has his temperament, his private preferences and preoccupations to contend with, and do what he may to subdue himself to the austere impersonality of art, these personal predilections will out, and send their partisan challenge rumbling through his pages. And the reader is forced to take the challenge up: he can no longer abandon himself to the 'pure, æsthetic emotion': he must confirm and applaud, or deny or murmur.

All the stories in *The Eternal Moment* were written before 1914, so that consideration of them is in the nature of an exhumation rather than a vivisection. Some are concerned with ordinary, sublunary life; some with the future; some with Heaven and Hell. One, 'The Story of the Siren,' has been printed separately and there must be, I imagine, many lovers of English prose who know its first paragraph by heart. To me, the ironic fantastic tales are the least satisfactory. They are conceived in a mood of dissatisfaction, that never rises into moral indignation but that does, on the other hand, sometimes degenerate into querulousness and into a gesture less generous and wholehearted than kicking against the pricks. Mr. Forster seems to believe in a Golden Age, an age of youth, in which golden lads and lasses disported themselves, free from the repressive influence of their Elders. Nowadays (one seems to conclude from his pages) the 'lovely brutality' of youth is at the mercy of the old, the hide-bound, the stupid, the respectable and the philistine. More than once he has emphasized the contrast between youthful and ingenuous natures, full of animal grace and beauty, and the stern pedagogic persons, armed with ferrules and breathing the unenterprising maxims of middle-age, who crush the life out of them. The letter killeth, the spirit giveth life; with this few would disagree: but Mr. Forster seems to identify the spirit with a certain definite race of beings—amiable, animal natures akin to Pan; and at times he writes as though he were trying to organize a Society for the Prevention of Cruelty to Children of Nature. But he will never quite declare himself. The darts fly and the victims fall: but exactly who is defeated, and who victorious, I am unable to say. What one can say is, how much one enjoyed 'The Story of the Siren' and what marvellous passages there are in *The Eternal Moment* itself:

[Quotation follows.]

One looks back wistfully to the year 1914, since when Mr. Forster has written all too little.

147. Unsigned review, *Bookman* (London)

lxxiv, no. 440, May 1928, 138

Our pleasure in the exquisite talent of these short stories, their precise approach to life, their individual comment on character, is rather chastened by Mr. Forster's introductory note that he does not expect to produce any more work in this particular line. There are too few writers of sensitive and imaginative short stories for Mr. Forster to stop working at them. His peculiar gift is an acute sense of idiosyncrasy in human character combined with a firm belief in a spiritual background, in a power which sustains, feeds, as it were, both the good and bad qualities in his people. All these stories were written before 1914, and it is remarkable how little they seem to 'date'. No doubt if he were to write it to-day the story called 'The Machine Stops' would be given a rather different form by Mr. Forster; but in its deep and wise attack on the growing fear of personal relationship, of intimate human contact, it has a poignant meaning for a world which has rushed more and more into the refuge of the machine, and abandoned the search for meaning to wallow in the shallow comforts of ingenuity. The human appetite for device, for invention, the human admiration for the merely cunning were never more in evidence than now; and in his superbly uncomfortable parable, Mr. Forster exposes the logical end of these evasions from life. The title story, in a different way, is occupied with the same theme. Miss Raby, the novelist, revisiting the village in Italia Irredenta, the village her novel made famous ten years before, discovers the old simple life, the exquisite verities overwhelmed by international conventions, covered by the designs of convenience. In a way the best story is perhaps 'The Story of the Siren', published some years ago by the Hogarth Press. Here Mr. Forster gives us once more his vision of beauty, beauty misunderstood and slain by men unready to take risks, nervous of the depths, however clear and silver-reflecting, where the siren lives but cannot sing. The book is a treasure of lovely things, low-toned no doubt, and only not despairing because of the author's evident belief in the validity, if not in the temporal triumph, of splendid and eternal things.

148. Edwin Muir, review, *Nation & Athenaeum*

12 May 1928, 184

'These stories,' Mr. Forster informs us, 'were written at various dates previous to 1914, and represent, with those in the Celestial Omnibus volume, all that the writer is likely to attempt in a particular line.' There is nothing for it but to accept this fact; Mr. Forster is the only judge of the matter; but the reader cannot but regret that an imagination so just and so original should cease to express itself in the form where its justice and originality are most incontestably evinced. When, *apropos* such novels as *A Passage to India*, critics speak of Mr. Forster's genius, one has a feeling of doubt; talent, a talent so accomplished as to attain exquisiteness, one may allow the book; but there is something missing, and that, one imagines, is precisely genius. But if genius be the power to do what nobody else can, it cannot be denied to certain stories in this volume. The best are the deliberately symbolical, the stories about Heaven and Hell, and the supernatural in general. Of these, 'The Point of It' and 'The Siren's Story' are perhaps the most remarkable. The first is the tale of an amiable, sympathetic, cultured man before and after death. He is received into Hell. 'He had seen good in everything, and this is itself a sign of decay. Whatever occurred he had been appreciative, tolerant, pliant. . . . He had mistaken self-criticism for self discipline, he had muffled in himself and others the keen, heroic edge. Yet the luxury of repentance was denied him. The fault was his, but the fate humanity's, for everyone grows hard or soft as he grows old.' This passage is rather too flatly elucidatory, it may be complained; the best thing in the story, and indeed in the book, is the evocation of Hell, a Hell which breathes the atmosphere of humanity's hidden frustrations and shames, and is effective because it is psychologically profound. 'The Story of the Siren' is about an Italian sailor who sees the Siren and afterwards has no desire for action, and no interest in human affairs. He finds a woman who like him has seen the Siren, but when their child is about to be born, she is killed by a superstitious priest. The man's brother tells the story:

'Never in my life will there be both a man and woman from whom that child can be born, who will fetch up the Siren from the sea, and destroy silence, and save the world.' That is all the tale says, but there is such a wealth of suggested meaning throughout, conveyed so certainly and yet with such an absence of direct insistence, that it stands out from all the others. It is pure imagination.

Except for these two stories, however, and 'Mr. Andrews,' a charming trifle, the volume is rather disappointing. 'The Eternal Moment,' though witty and profound in flashes, is unconvincing psychologically. 'The Machine Stops,' which takes up a third of the whole book, and stands at the beginning, is also unconvincing. When Mr. Forster is writing of Heaven and Hell he may let his imagination range freely, so long as it is in pursuit of symbolical truth. But in 'The Machine Stops' he is writing of the future; and that future, as it is ours, must be conceivable in terms of the world we know. Mr. Forster's picture of the future is quite inconceivable, however. In its last stages, he tells us, humanity will live in cells under the ground, shut off from the outer air, the surface of the earth, the sea, the sky, and one another; and everything will be done for them by pressing a button. But we immediately want to know why they should live under the ground, and as we cannot imagine why, the story becomes unreal. Perhaps Mr. Forster's imagination is rather clogged here with sociological notions.

149. 'J. F. S.', review, *Boston Evening Transcript*

12 May 1928

With many a greater and lesser genius, Mr. Forster takes a strange standpoint regarding the place of his own work in the literary movement of the time. 'These stories,' he declares in the foreword to his most recently published collection of tales, 'were written at various dates previous to 1914 and represent, together with those in the *Celestial Omnibus* volume, all that I am likely to accomplish in a particular line. Much has happened since then . . . and under the mass shock of facts Fantasy has tended to retreat or at all events to dig herself in.'

Now it may very well be that the author of *Howard's End* and *A Passage to India* is no longer in the mood for those extravagant essays; irony which he terms fantasy; but to imply that fantasy has retreated since the war is surprising, for do not all the Martin Armstrongs, Sylvia Warners, and David Garnetts of the moment suggest that this genre has bloomed again in the furrows of war almost as prolifically as the poppies in Flanders Field? Five of Mr. Forster's six tales (the title story is scarcely Fantasy) are not only not dead matter; they are peculiarly in the spirit of the day, although they were written fifteen years ago, and even reflect a prevailing irritable discontent with modern civilization. And far from being mere literary curiosities of an author who has not followed up a great success with a new novel, they are exceptionally good of their kind. Mr. Forster need not explain or apologize for *The Eternal Moment*.

The kind, however, is out of the usual run of Fantasy, for the burden of irony, though gracefully carried, remains the impressive feature of the stories contained in *The Eternal Moment*. Particularly is this true of the longish 'The Machine Stops,' looking backward from the Future and subtly scorning the Utopias of Edward Bellamy and H. G. Wells. The prophetic notion with which Mr. Forster plays is that of physical effeteness developed to absurdity; his mankind dwell underground, their jelly-like bodies swaddled in hygienic clothes, their daily needs brought mechanically to their rooms wherein they loaf and listen to lectures and exchange 'ideas' with their friends by telephone, rarely stirring their flabby bodies save when need compels an airplane trip from one part of the world to another. Vashti, mother of Kuno, travels in such wise to see her son, and spellbound by the machine during the trip, shuts from her gaze the swiftly disappearing sites of Simla or Greece because 'there are no ideas' to be had therefrom. Thus is the sense of a lost glory ironically suggested; so also is it suggested by the narrative of her son, an adventurous-minded weakling who had pushed his way to the surface of the Earth, where once was Wessex, and had known the bite of real air and tasted the aesthetic delights of a real Sun and real clouds, yielding them only with an actual physical struggle.

As in the case of 'The Machine Stops,' the peculiar beauty and force of 'The Point of It' lies in the author's implied regret from the passing of Greek ideals of bodily and mental vigor, the tale is the imagined life story of a sedentary scholar who, awakening in the hereafter is justly punished not for his sins, but for his softness and lack of will. It is in part a second, and rather less joyous trip in the celestial omnibus, a gayer excursion in the same vehicle being made in 'Mr. Andrews,' brief but delightful, in which the souls of a Nonconformist Englishman and a Moslem Turk are wafted to a heaven where they find their expectations, but not their hopes, fulfilled. They are puzzled to discover that the only spiritual satisfaction they have had was at the moment of entrance into heaven, when each had prayed that his unbelieving brother might be admitted to paradise. In 'Co-ordination,' also toying fancifully with the unknown, the shades of Beethoven and Napoleon, hoodwinked by flattering clerks, play at benevolent destiny with the pupils and teachers of a girls' school.

The other two stories are of slightly different character. 'The Story of the Siren' handled a fairly familiar Mediterranean legend, but seems inferior; and 'The Eternal Moment' is not fantasy at all. This last tale, a firm and acid piece of work in the best style of the author of *Howard's End*, tells of the return of an English spinster author to the Swiss village she has made famous by her popular novel, only to find that prosperity has corrupted a decent peasantry beyond all hope of mending. Outwardly in marked contrast with the other tales, it yet partakes of the same pervading disgust with the vitiating influences of what we call progress. One is not altogether sorry if Mr. Forster has rid himself of this particular obsession. But if it is true that his celestial omnibus has been taken off the route for good, it is indeed a pity.

150. Dorothy Bacon Woolsey, notice, *New Republic*

lvi, 29 August 1928, 54

Recalling Forster's characterization of Lawrence in *Aspects of the Novel* as a master in the prophetic school of fiction and in a 'bardic quality' of utterance, it is interesting to turn to that sensitive critic's own essay in the line of prophetic fantasy. *The Eternal Moment* is a collection of lively and imaginative tales, all dealing with the preternatural, and tinged with an irony which is sometimes grim, sometimes merely rueful. This writer likewise adopts the prophetic strain, but more delicately and more precisely than his brother seer. Where Lawrence lowers in sultry and oppressive gloom, Forster flashes illuminating fancies across outlandish vistas—slight flickering revelations of disillusionment or pity that betray a philosophic bewilderment equal to Lawrence's own. In successive tales, the teller's irony shifts from the sentimental, as in the title-story, to the mystical—'The Point of It'—or the starkly terrible—'The Machine Stops'—wherein a mechanical civilization is carried to its logical conclusion. 'The Siren' is barbaric and weird—'Mr. Andrews' amiably satirical. The deft lightness of Mr. Forster's method in no way weakens the effect of his auguries—nebulous as they are. There is as tragic an implication in the established skepticism of an imaginative idealist as in the passionate paradox of a prophet of Tantalus. Forster's accents are those of unearthly comedy—and to readers accessible to ironic pity the 'bardic quality' in his mirth is no less apparent than in the thunderous mutterings of D. H. Lawrence.

151. Howard N. Doughty, Jr, 'The novels of E. M. Forster', *Bookman* (New York)

lxxv, October 1932, 542–9

This is the first important general article on Forster by an American critic.

I

E. M. Forster is a novelist of whom Mr. I. A. Richards has said that 'at the heart of his work there is less satisfaction with human existence as he sees it than in the work of any living writer'. Yet, though often mentioned with respect, and, indeed, having, it is said, a special coterie of admirers, he has received on the whole very little serious attention from critics of modern English literature. There are reasons for this comparative neglect. The principal one can be expressed in a simple fact of chronology: there is a gap of fourteen years between his latest novel, *A Passage to India*, published in 1924, and its predecessor, *Howards End*, published in 1910. As a consequence of this fourteen years' silence, *A Passage to India*, though it had considerable popular success, was read and reviewed almost entirely without relation to its author's earlier work and was generally set down as simply a book on India. Mr. Middleton Murry was almost alone in calling attention to its real significance.

It can also be seen that the particular term of years which intervenes between Mr. Forster's latest novel and the bulk of his work (three novels precede *Howards End*) might mean more as far as the critical estimation of a writer is concerned than almost any two dates that one could have chosen. They do indicate in fact what happened to Mr. Forster—he fell, critically speaking, between two worlds. Most of his work was done when writers like Shaw, Bennett, and Wells were representative of the main tendency of English literature and were the writers about whom criticism polarized; when he re-emerged in 1924 that world had disappeared; its great men were discredited; literature and criticism had taken a new direction. Just as Mr. Forster had shared little in the *éclat* of the former age, so he was greeted without obloquy on his reappearance in the later—indeed, as I have said, he has always commanded respect. It is significant, however, that when two of his most ardent admirers of this later age, I. A. Richards and Virginia Woolf, write about him, they should both be mainly concerned with trying to answer the question why he is, comparatively speaking, a failure as a novelist.

That his novels do not 'come off' as wholes is true. As Mrs. Woolf says, there is a lack of integration in his work. The three rather diverse strains of fantasy, of realism, and of sociology that compose his talent do not coalesce satisfactorily; on putting down one of his books one is not left with the feeling of a total experience. Sociology breaks the surface of realism, fantasy gets in the way of both. His books, in spite of a thousand careful, perhaps too careful, linkings, are disrupted. They are not, in short, taken individually, complete works of art. But when Mrs. Woolf goes on to suggest that, in effect, Mr. Forster would be a better writer if he devoted himself to unmixed comedy of manners (and a very genuine talent for comedy of manners is a part of his equipment as a realist) one demurs. 'Directly he ceases to feel responsible for his characters' behaviour and forgets he should solve the problem of the universe', she says, 'he is the most diverting of novelists', and singles out for praise Tibby Schlegel, an indeed diverting but minor character in *Howards End* (for whose actions, anyway, Mr. Forster does not disclaim the responsibility). Solving the 'problem of the universe' is Mrs. Woolf's way of phrasing what Mr. Richards calls '[lack of] satisfaction with human existence as he sees it'. Her sentence may suggest what I mean when I say that Mr. Forster has fallen between two critical worlds. It may also suggest why he is, on the whole, a more interesting novelist than Mrs. Woolf.

One needs to trace a little further Mr. Forster's weaknesses. The lack of integration that Mrs. Woolf indicates is really a failure in technique. Mr. Forster has not succeeded in evolving a formula of technique that would fuse into a single whole his varying approaches. Like most failures in technique, I think this one can be referred to the defect of some quality in the writer's mind. The fault of temperament in Mr. Forster's case is perhaps best illustrated by what he says himself in *Aspects of the Novel* about his own methods as a novelist. He is speaking of what he calls 'prophecy'—the quality that makes a book like *Moby Dick*:

> Another prophet, Blake, had no doubt that it [the double vision of prophecy] was right.

'. . . May God us keep
From single vision and Newton's sleep. . . .'

Few will agree with Blake. Fewer still will agree with Blake's Newton. Most of us will be eclectics to this side or that according to our temperament. The human mind is not a dignified organ, and I do not see how we can exercise it sincerely except through eclecticism. And the only advice I would offer my fellow eclectics is: 'Do not be proud of your inconsistency. It is a pity, it is a pity that we should be equipped like this. It is a pity that Man cannot be at the same time impressive and truthful'.

This is not a valid generalization. It sums up, however, Mr. Forster's own experience.

Having had to choose between truth and impressiveness, having, like Mr. Fielding in *A Passage to India*, sacrificed passion to clarity, Mr. Forster has paid the penalty—of not having been very impressive. Clarity and truthfulness have, however, their compensations and they have enabled him to make a sociological analysis which is at once a valuable document and in its development through his novels as a whole an admirable work of art. Though of an utterly different temperament, he has a striking similarity of outlook with another writer of sociological tendencies, D. H. Lawrence. Lawrence is a writer who is sometimes both impressive and truthful—it is significant that of all his contemporaries Mr. Forster seems to admire Lawrence most—but he is also often simply impressive. He sacrifices clarity to passion and needs Mr. Forster to complement him. Together, they make a last stand for an individualism, the social and economic conditions necessary to the healthy existence of which they are forced to watch disappear.

II

Mr. Forster starts with the common observation that modern civilization distorts and deforms the life of the individual in all its range. Industrialism, by driving man from the soil, has spoiled his capacity for the naïve life of the body that flourishes in contact with the earth, and the regimentation of democracy has substituted in him a set of automatic responses for the idiosyncrasies of real personality. Pledged as he is to an archaic individualism, Mr. Forster displays, as one might expect, a profound distrust of the machine and of all forms of organization.

The life of the body is fundamental in Mr. Forster's scheme. A recognition of it is the necessary basis for any healthy self-conscious development of personality (the 'life of the spirit', the 'inner' life), and it is better to have this alone than any unhealthy or distorted form of the 'inner' life. Out of its manifestations in sex and mating, Mr. Forster builds the concept of generation and of continuity of raec that has such an important place in his work. As for the life of the spirit, as I have said, Mr. Forster disallows it if it involves a rejection of the life of the body. Furthermore, it is not genuine if it is based on any retreat from reality, a shutting of the eyes, a shrugging of the shoulders. The pursuit of culture as an end in itself, for instance, is for him one of the worst of perversions. Finally, as a real 'inner' life, it postulates an 'outer' life, that is, a world of action, a society of which it must not only be aware but in which it must have some stake, from which, to be healthy, it must not feel itself totally cut off. One can see that Mr. Forster's demands on the life of the spirit are to the last degree exigent. He will accept no substitutes for what he regards as the real thing—and the keenness of his ability to detect substitutes is uncanny.

Thus in his first novel, *Where Angels Fear to Tread*, he displays in the progress of Philip Herriton two of the most common false attitudes to which an attempt to lead the life of the spirit in the modern world can bring one—aestheticism and indifference. The book is patterned round the relations of Philip and Miss Abbott—Miss Abbott, who had been the travelling companion in Italy of Philip's widowed sister-in-law, Lilia, at the time of Lilia's marriage to the son of a small-town Italian dentist. This fiasco in the Herriton clan has had the effect on Philip of consolidating further the disillusion that usually follows on the petering out of a bright boy's adolescent revolt: his militancy turns to cynicism and he takes refuge in the ivory tower. Thus he explains matters one day to Miss Abbott, whose unreliable conduct in Italy was caused, he finds, by the fact that she too had had a moment of revolt against Sawston (the Herriton suburb), a moment which she now bitterly regrets. Sawston she feels was right; Lilia's marriage is turning out very badly indeed. She shouldn't be discouraged, Philip tells her:—

'Society *is* invincible—to a certain degree. But your real life is your own and nothing can prevent your criticizing and despising mediocrity—nothing can stop your retreating into splendour and beauty—into the thoughts and beliefs that make the real life—the real you.'

'I have never had that experience yet. Surely I and my life must be where I live.'

Evidently she had the usual feminine incapacity for grasping philosophy. . . .

Similarly, when the parties re-assemble in Monteriano in a mass attack on Gino for the possession of the child he has had by Lilia, now dead, Miss Abbott is again a step ahead of Philip. They both have succumbed once more to Monteriano—but with a difference. Philip has become the disinterested spectator, amusedly watching himself carrying on the futile negotiations that his fanatic, fighting sister Harriet keeps him to. Miss Abbott, however, has taken sides.

'. . . To fail honourably! To come out of the thing as well as you can! Is that all you are after? . . . Do you want the child to stop with his father, who loves him and will bring him up badly, or do you want him to come to Sawston, where no one loves him, but where he will be brought up well? There is the question put dispassionately enough even for you. Settle it. Settle which side you'll fight on. But don't go talking about an "honourable failure". . . .'

'Because I understand the position of Signor Carella and of you, it's no reason that—'

'None at all. Fight as if you think us wrong. Oh, what's the use of your fair-mindedness if you can't decide for yourself? Anyone gets hold of you and makes you do what they want. And you see through them and laugh at them and do it. . . .'

'You are wonderful!' he said gravely.

'Oh, you appreciate me!' she burst out again. 'I wish you didn't. You appreciate us all—see good in all of us. And all the time you are dead—dead—dead.'

After the catastrophe precipitated by fighting Harriet's attempt to kidnap the baby, the bonds of Philip's spirit break. In his remorse he sees something portentous in Miss Abbott's rightness. Her magnificence to himself and to Gino makes her seem to him an ideal, a goddess-like incarnation of pity and courage. He undergoes a sort of conversion and his life is re-oriented. But good as this is for Philip, it is based on a fundamental unreality, and going home on the train he has to learn a final lesson. Miss Abbott is not the incarnation of an abstract pity and courage. His misunderstanding forces her at last to a recognition and revelation of what has been unconsciously the mainspring of all her actions—that she too, like Lilia, had loved Gino, had desired him physically.

In his next book, *The Longest Journey*, Mr. Forster has studied another type of unhealthiness in personality. He here deals with one of Philip's states of mind, his moment of idealization, as a fixed trait of character: Rickie Elliot, the hero of *The Longest Journey*, is a chronic, a hopeless idealist; just as physically he is congenitally lame, so morally he is essentially tainted—he cannot see things as they are without adding to them. That Mr. Forster has drawn Rickie as an exceedingly attractive and likable character and has made of his story a pathetic one, only gives added impressiveness to the climax of the book, the judgement pronounced upon Rickie and all his kind by the voice of his mother in a dream the night of his first disillusionment: 'Let them die out—let them die out'. Rickie's mother, whom he has idolized, is long since dead and he does not know the import of her words, but because of her peculiar importance in the book, she speaks as a prophetess. She is the first of the mystic mothers that haunt Mr. Forster's work—earth-mothers, portentous, half-mythical figures, who embody his concept of continuity, of an essential race-life. Just as she turned away to a farmer-lover from Rickie's father, an egotistical dilettante, the worst of the Elliot kind, so in the dream she rejects Rickie, the gentle idealist, the best of the Elliot kind. Her bastard, Stephen Wonham, is her true issue; it is to him that the words Rickie hears are spoken, 'Come away—never mind—let them die out—let them die out'.

Stephen is the earth-mother's choice for the basic type that shall replace the tainted Elliots and inherit the world from which they sprang. It is this that makes him the most interesting of the foils or antitypes that appear in Mr. Forster's early novels. Gino, the Italian, belongs to the past; the Emerson pair, in *A Room with a View*, are escaped refugees from Sawston; Stephen on the other hand is a new creation, a pure type belonging literally to another world. In one sense he is unreal because, in order to have a free hand in drawing him, Mr. Forster has put him in as complete a social vacuum as possible. As Mrs. Elliot's son, however, as the substance of things hoped for, he has strange verisimilitude. His traits—his health and physicality, his lack of false sentiment, his directness of thought and action, his complete realism, the whole make-up of his character even to the atheistic materialism (from the pamphlets of Colonel Ingersoll and others) that he adopts out of hand as his philosophy—are prophetic. One thinks of that post-War parody of him, the Hemingway 'hard guy'; one thinks also of certain types adumbrated in Soviet literature.

With Stephen's personality Mr. Forster's divining stops. It is significant that Stephen finally settles down to farming, the most individualistic and isolated of all occupations. In the right kind of a world he is not, as Mr. Forster has drawn him, unimaginable in a factory as well as on a farm. The construction of such a world, however, is beyond Mr. Forster's scope. He put his trust in the earth-mother. She, apparently some day will suddenly begin to 'throw' a new race, Stephens will come by some unpredictable spontaneous twist in generation like the mutation of sports to species in biology. Mr. Forster has further dealings with the earth-mother in *Howards End* and *A Passage to India*.

In *A Room with a View*, Mr. Forster returns to the theme that he had treated in the story of Miss Abbott. *A Room with a View* is the simplest and least complicated of his novels. Yet in spite of the smallness of its scale he has so arranged its pattern that it probably gives a truer estimate of the social forces in play about the issue it translates into terms of character and situation than any novel of its time dealing with that issue—the 'emancipation' of women. One has but to compare it, for instance, with H. G. Wells's *Ann Veronica*, which was published a year later, resembles it in theme, and, in fact, duplicates (badly) one of its characters. Mr. Forster is aware of the reach of his problem; Mr. Wells sees only the immediate foreground. Mr. Forster has a philosophy; Mr. Wells lives, philosophically speaking, from hand to mouth. Though one is conscious on every page of *Ann Veronica* of the controversy that gave it birth, and, after twenty-three years one realizes only with a start that *A Room with a View* was born of the same controversy, the difference between them is exactly the difference between a good sociological novel and a bad one.

III

By the exigence and sureness of what one might call his taste in personality, Mr. Forster has avoided accepting any of the false attitudes or unhealthy states of mind that masquerade as personality in modern society. On the other hand his insight into the essentials of personality has kept him from the mistake of regarding it as a free, autochthonous growth. He feels with an extraordinary sensitivity the multiform and complex ways in which society tends to mould the individual, and so can gauge to the last decimal its force and pressure at any given point. This awareness of Mr. Forster's to the dual nature of personality forces him to confront a question which has been making itself more and more insistently felt through his earlier books—the question of whether there is any possibility at all of a healthy individual life in modern society. Personality is enfeebled by withdrawals or escapes from society, yet what can it feed on in contemporary society that will not poison it?

In his fourth novel, *Howards End*, Mr. Forster gathers the threads of his work together and faces this question directly. In order to do so he has had to make a grouping in the persons of his characters of the central forces that make up capitalist society; in his particular arrangement and manipulation of these forces he has summed up accurately their position and direction during the period before the War, when the novel was written. It is this that gives *Howards End* its documentary value. It is, however, a true interpretation, not a hit-or-miss exploitation of current issues to make a timely book. Its genuine insight and the skill with which Mr. Forster has distilled a whole society into the lives and situations of his characters are what give it its value as a work of art.

The two heroines of *Howards End*, Helen and Margaret Schlegel, are characteristic products of the pre-War bourgeois intelligentsia. One finds them in their late twenties, the flower of an upper middle-class background of comfort, enlightenment, and culture; interested in 'causes', socially sensitive, believing intensely in the 'inner life', and yet, in spite of the vitality and responsiveness—so important in his scheme of things—that Mr. Forster attempts to endow them with, they already display symptoms of the futility that was to become more and more the hall-mark of their class and type.

Their search for reality brings them in contact with the Wilcoxes, with Mr. Henry Wilcox, in whose person is distilled the race of imperialist business men, super-Babbitts, effective in action but incapable in thought of any mental connections beyond the necessities of the immediate job to be done. Helen, the more impulsive of the two sisters, rejects the Wilcoxes *in toto* after one experience. Their imperviousness to the order of ideas which she and Margaret represent, she instinctively feels, is absolute. Margaret herself is not so sure. She is conscious of an inadequacy in the 'inner' life she has so sedulously cultivated. She feels that there is a reality about the Wilcoxes lacking in her own world. She cannot dismiss as irrelevant their practicality, their ability to get things done, the Empire that they have built. 'More and more do I refuse to draw my income and sneer at those who guarantee it', she says to the expostulating Helen. So, since she likes Mr. Wilcox as a man, Margaret accepts him when, tired of his widowerhood and in a muddled way genuinely fond of her, he asks her to marry him. She knows what she is taking on. She has had proofs enough that the concept of personality and its implications for living mean nothing to him. She has also learned in another connection—in the affair of Leonard Bast—that the blindness of which this blindness to personality is a part has implications and consequences reaching far beyond the field of personal relationships. She hopes, however, by patience and by playing the game according to his rules, to succeed at last in making him see and understand. Confident in her knowledge of him and of herself, she goes ahead. 'If insight were sufficient, if the inner life were the whole of life their happiness had been assured.' It would mar the reality of Mr. Forster's analysis to follow Margaret's attempt to its final shipwreck. In this picture of a hopeful member of the intelligentsia taking up with a representative of Capital and trying to make it over, he has given in essence the history of pre-War 'reform'.

It is over the city clerk, Leonard Bast, symbol to Mr. Forster of what democracy and the machine have done to a once upstanding yeomanry, that the shipwreck occurs. Leonard has the same rôle in *Howards End* as Gino and Stephen Wonham and the Emersons in the earlier books, with the difference that he is not separated from modern society in various ways as they are, but is a part of it, bone of its bone, a cog in the machine, what Stephen Wonham might be if Society were allowed to claim him. The Wilcox world, having given him the vote, has washed its hands of him. The Schlegel world, more conscious of his plight, have felt that his soul at least must be free and have tried to redeem him with education, *their* education. The result, of course, is a mock-culture, the double dilution of a spiritual stream already running thin itself. Experience soon teaches Leonard the unreality for him of this class-culture. 'Miss Schlegel, the real thing's money and all the rest is a dream.' Helen (and Mr. Forster) can only play with a dubious metaphysics for answer.

Under the wash of half-digested books, under the lineaments and complexes of the city-clerk, the basic Stephen has not been altogether crushed out of Leonard. Helen and Margaret perceive this, and, appalled at what they and the Wilcoxes have unconsciously collaborated to make of him, they try to set things straight. Their efforts drive Leonard himself from bad to worse and finally to his death.

But in the pessimism that creeps up through *Howards End* there is one earnest for the future. It is to the impulsive, revolutionary Helen that the care of Leonard particularly falls—Margaret is preoccupied with Mr. Wilcox—and through her Leonard begets a child, a child over whose destiny presides the genius of Mrs. Wilcox. One will have guessed the rôle of Mrs. Wilcox: she is the earth-mother again, an amplified and more portentous version of Mrs. Elliot. She dies early in the story, but it is for her that Helen and Leonard have begotten their child and it is to Howards End (her place) that Helen finally comes with it. Through her, Leonard, the third generation from country forbears, sucked into the city, will in his issue be redeemed from that Hell and cleansed to the essential Stephen. It is on this note the book closes: 'The field's out!' Helen cried excitedly—'the big meadow. We've seen to the very end, and it'll be such a crop of hay as never!' Hay is a crop antipathetic to the Wilcoxes; they can't go near it, it gives them hay-fever. The Howards have ended, the earth-mother has been bearing Wilcoxes; but some sudden turn in generation will come and a new crop will dominate.

Mr. Forster's confidence in the untutored workings of the earth-mother is not so sure, however, as the ending of the book would indicate. There is another passage on the same theme in a significantly different key:

> 'All the same, London's creeping. . . . And London is only a part of something else, I'm afraid. Life's going to be melted down all over the world.'
>
> Margaret knew that her sister spoke truly. Howards End, Oniton, the Purbeck Downs, the Oderberge, were all survivals, and the melting pot was being prepared for them. Logically they had no right to be alive. One's hope was in the weakness of logic. Were they possibly the earth beating time?
>
> 'Because a thing is going strong now, it need not go strong for ever,' she said. '. . . All the signs are against it now but I can't help hoping, and very early in the morning in the garden I feel that our house is the future as well as the past.'

One does not feel much confidence in any hopes for the future nourished by this feeble nostalgia. The idea on which Mr. Forster lavishes all his gifts of poetic evocation, to embody which he creates with considerable travail of the imagination symbolical figures like Mrs. Wilcox, is an idea that fundamentally can give him no more compelling assurance than one finds in Margaret's words. He wishes to make convincing a sentiment which his heart sets great store by, but his honesty forces him to set down how unconvincing it is to his intelligence. It is this not very forcible conflict of heart and head over one of its central ideas that is the flaw in *Howards End* as a novel. It explains why the note sounds forced in the purple passages, why the book in spite of its finish seems artistically incomplete. As I have said, it was of himself that Mr. Forster was speaking, when he said that 'Man cannot at the same time be impressive and truthful'.

A Passage to India, published in 1924, whatever it may be as an interpretation of India, is in essence an epilogue to *Howards End*. In the disillusion of Mrs. Moore and Mr. Fielding, Mr. Forster has written a finis to everything Mrs. Wilcox and the Schlegels stood for. Mr. Fielding's reflections as he watches the Marabar hills at sunset are a quiet epitaph on the Schlegels' 'inner life'.

> . . . He felt dubious and discontented suddenly, and wondered whether he was really and truly successful as a human being. After forty years' experience, he had learned to manage his life on advanced European lines, had developed his personality, explored his limitations, controlled his passions—and had done it all without becoming either pedantic or worldly. A creditable achievement, but as the moment passed, he felt he ought to have been working at something else the whole time—he didn't know what. . . .

Similarly Mrs. Moore's experience in the heart of the same Marabar hills that Mr. Fielding watches from a distance sums up what has happened during the momentous fourteen years since *Howards End* was written to the earth-mother and the hopes Mr. Forster centered in her. One must consult the book for all he says of the echo in the Marabar caves and its effect on Mrs. Moore. The import is clear. She (and Mr. Forster with her) pass into 'the twilight of the double vision', the limbo where 'everything exists and nothing has value', where 'we can neither act nor refrain from action, . . . neither ignore nor respect infinity'—into Mr. Bloom's Dublin and the Waste Land, in short. The frail dyke of 'Howards End, Oniton, the Purbeck Downs, the Oderberge' has crumbled away. The earth-mother's milk is soured and her womb diseased.

I have spoken of the similar tenor of ideas in Mr. Forster and in D. H. Lawrence. If Mr. Forster is the weaker writer, he is also more clear-headed; if *Lady Chatterley's Lover* is distorted in emphasis and hysterical, the sum of Mr. Forster's work rounds out its statement with a quiet finality. The ideas and feelings with which both writers deal are not uncommon ones. They run the gamut of every protest that outraged individualism makes against the society which Frankenstein-like it has created. Their insight into what genuine personality is, however, and their refusal to put up with make-shifts, to accept any attempt at a reintegration of personality of which health and wholeness are not the fundamental conditions, is not common and is what gives point to the despair, quiet or frenzied, on which their work finally abuts. They would seem to have demonstrated the impossibility of any restoration of the individual along the classic lines of anarchic individualism; it is beyond the individual's power to adjust solely from within the balance between himself and society on which unwarped personality depends.

152. E. H. W. Meyerstein, letter to Professor R. M. Dawkins

14 August 1933

E. H. W. Meyerstein (1889–1952), F.R.S.L., published poetry, novels, music criticism, a Life of Chatterton, and translated the Elegies of Propertius. He had failed, when at Oxford, to obtain a First and a Fellowship, and spent his later years in London and finally, again, in Oxford. John Wain, in his autobiography, *Sprightly Running*, gives a sympathetic portrait of him, describing him as a 'disappointed man'.

Reprinted from *Some Letters of E. H. W. Meyerstein* (selected, edited and introduced by Rowland Watson, 1959), 155, by permission of the publishers, Neville Spearman Ltd.

What you tell me about meeting E. M. Forster interests me extremely. There is no writer of fiction today whom I admire so whole-heartedly as I do him, and whose kind word for any work of mine (perhaps I shouldn't say this) would mean more to me. . . I know no modern short book . . . that so completely satisfies me as a work of art as Forster's early *Where Angels Fear to Tread*, and the prose in *A Passage to India*—read, or read again the trial, especially the description of the court and the punkah wallah!—it is almost classical! Years ago I expressed this zeal of mine to Middleton Murry and all he said was 'If you want to see that sort of thing really properly done read *The*

Voyage Out—was it that? A novel by Mrs. Woolf anyway! But I don't see Forster in that galley at all. He has almost a poet's mind, and a very sensitive warm heart. Of course I see Forster's limitations. The warder in *Howard's End* is not realized at all; and his issues don't always seem to me to be vital—e.g. whether Miss Quested was raped, or, if so, by whom. But you have to grant all that—like the twilight background in so much of de la Mare's poetry. Forster is somebody, I am quite sure of that, and he will be remembered when honest gentlemen like Martin Armstrong[1] and R. H. Mottram[2] are still collected but unread. . . .

[1] Martin Armstrong (1882–), novelist and poet, published his *Collected Poems* in 1931.

[2] R. H. Mottram (1883–), a prolific novelist, encouraged by Galsworthy. His best-known novel is *The Spanish Farm* (1924), which won the Hawthornden Prize.

153. E. K. Brown, 'E. M. Forster and the contemplative novel'

April 1934

From the *University of Toronto Quarterly* iii, no. 3, 349–61, reprinted by permission of the University of Toronto Press.

E. K. Brown (1905–51) was born in Toronto, where he was later Professor of English from 1938 to 1941. He was appointed Head of the English Department, Cornell University, in 1941, and moved to Chicago University in 1944. He published books on Edith Wharton, Matthew Arnold, and Canadian poetry, but is best known for *Rhythm in the Novel* (1951).

In a later article, 'The Revival of E. M. Forster' (*Yale Review*, June 1944), Brown quoted Forster's reaction to the essay reprinted here: 'It is a great novelty to be written about like that. I have been praised for my character drawing, sense of social distinctions etc., but seldom for the things which really interest me, and which I have tried to express through the medium of fiction'.

Nobody but a maker of dictionaries cares to rush in with a definition of the novel. Most of us would agree, however, that in a novel things happen. Perhaps an empire collapses,—perhaps a reputation is made for broiling chicken. At all events something happens. Broad as its confines are, the novel appears to belong to the world of actions. The pure contemplative eschews action and would say—if he could be so false to his aim and discipline as to bother with explanation—that he has risen beyond the world of actions:

> He has outsoared the shadow of our night;
> Envy and calumny and hate and pain,
> And that unrest which men miscall delight,
> Can touch him not and torture not again.

The novel may, of course, record a man's quest of the contemplative ideal, the process of his transformation into a contemplative spirit. That is a happening just as his transformation into an air-pilot or a Marxist would be a happening. The struggle to become a contemplative, to repudiate the world of actions, is a part of that world. It is a subject readily amenable to the novelist; and in *The Fountain* Mr. Charles Morgan[1] has recently shown how admirable a subject it is.

The central character in *The Fountain*, Lewis Alison, is an inexpert contemplative. He is diverted from the contemplative discipline first by a plea that he should captain the project of escape conceived by his fellow prisoners of war. Subsequently he is far more perilously distracted by his passion and love for Julie von Narwitz, into whose intimate company he has been almost involuntarily thrown. Far more perilously, for Alison distinguishes between two kinds of sexual love, one of the flesh only and 'spiritually valueless,' the other, such as Julie arouses in him, 'spiritually contributory.' After an evening spent in the study of the *Phaedo*, Alison lies sleepless for hours, revolving the problem, and rests in the conviction that 'a man's love for a woman, though one of the expressions of it be carnal, may be the very air in which his soul grows.' Doubtless it may; but the soul is not thus to be disengaged from the world of actions. The dramatic force of *The Fountain*—and it is abundant—is generated by the impacts of Alison's love for Julie and the theory he evolves in its defence upon his resolution to ascend to the contemplative plane of being. At moments he does pass onto this plane, but the record of these moments is obscure. He is, however, never long away from the world of actions, and to the end of the novel he remains essentially a part of it.

In the Graf von Narwitz, Julie's husband, Mr. Morgan does present an expert, a very nearly pure, contemplative. At Narwitz's entrance into the novel but one 'illusion' intervenes between him and the state to which he aspires. In his first conversation with his wife's lover he says: 'Birth and death are solitary; thought and growth are solitary; every final reality of a man's life is his alone, incommunicable; as soon as he ceases to be alone, he moves away from realities.' In a moment he adds, 'falling into the tone of personal confession,' that love, 'like every other supposed sharing is an unreality, but it is the supreme unreality—the last that we recognize as unreal.' Narwitz cannot in this

[1] Charles Morgan (1894–1958) was a novelist once fashionable (especially in France) and later neglected. He published *The Fountain* in 1932, winning the Hawthornden Prize for it the following year.

first stage concede with his whole being the unreality of his love for Julie; and just as long as he remains unable to concede it he remains a part of the world of actions and a dynamic character. But, without being told, he comes to apprehend the love of Julie for Alison and surrenders his desire to win her love for himself. In a sharp brief crisis he experiences the absolute of carnal desire, renounces it, and, the last impediment removed, disengages himself from the world of actions.

Narwitz, it should be said, enters the story, a disabled man, his wounds so grievous that only his desire for 'the supreme unreality,' love, maintains him alive. Free of this desire, his wife 'become a shadow' and his love for her 'a story that was told long ago,' he passes into a phase of philosophic wonder, a phase 'in which pardon and pity and condemnation and all the judgments of philosophy are fused in wonder.' In this phase, expectant of death, he talks with Alison of the contemplative way in language which Alison himself, let alone the reader, cannot comprehend. And then he performs the only action of which he is now capable—he dies.

As a secondary character Narwitz is one of the glories of the novel, and the last phase, in which he is purely contemplative, is deeply moving. The reader's impulse is to protest that the novel should have been about Narwitz, not about his fumbling imitator. On reflection, however, one asks whether a novel about Narwitz in his last phase, in his ascent into the serene contemplative sphere, is conceivable. Can one transpose the qualities of a state of rest into the terms of narrative?

And pursuing this query one turns to the greatest master of the contemplative novel in our time, to Mr. E. M. Forster. From *Where Angels Fear to Tread* (1905) to *A Passage to India* (1924), all Mr. Forster's novels are illustrations of a single idea—the chasm between the world of actions and the world of being. *Only connect* . . . is the epigraph of *Howards End* (1910); and the typical situation in Mr. Forster's fiction is that of the dweller in the world of being who tries to conduct himself in the world of actions according to his inner light, the light of contemplation.

The world of actions appears in his several novels in extremely varied guises: in *A Room with a View* (1908) it is a group of conventional women and clergymen; in *The Longest Journey* (1907) it is the family of a public-school master; in *A Passage to India* it is an Anglo-Indian station; only in *Howards End* is it a group of genuinely active people, city-men and their women-folk. Whether looking out over the muddy Arno to San Miniato and the enclosing hills, or from Chandrapore into the vivid squalor of an Indian town, or over the slopes and valleys of Wiltshire towards the grey spire of Salisbury, the dwellers in the world of actions are torpid, and inadequate to the subtlety of nature. No matter with what persons they have to do, whether with members of another race and religion and culture, or with members of their own family living under the same roof, they are obtuse and unshakeably complacent. To their honesty, cleanliness, sporting spirit, essential decency and justice, Mr. Forster pays his homage frigidly and reluctantly—but he pays it. He cannot, however, believe in their ultimate reality; and he cannot for more than a moment consider them with unrelieved seriousness. For him those who dwell in the world of actions are always trivial or ludicrous or both. Ronnie Heaslip may be caught in an immense misfortune: he remains throughout *A Passage to India* the 'red nosed boy' at whom the Moslems gibe in the first chapters. Mr. Pembroke, in *The Longest Journey*, is transparently conscientious, generous, and active, but the images which encircle his name are those of 'the hierarchy of jerseys and blazers and the many-tinted bathing-drawers that showed how far a boy could swim.' They are all of the stamp of Mr. Wilcox in *Howards End*, who 'lived for the five minutes that have passed and the five to come: he had the business mind.' They may succeed in seeing life steadily; they do not even try to see it whole.

Over against the contented prisoners in the world of actions are set the persons whose device is *Only connect*. Margaret Schlegel, the heroine of *Howards End*, is their representative as she reflects: 'The business man who assumes that this life is everything and the mystic who asserts that it is nothing, fail, on this side and on that, to hit the truth. . . . It was only to be found by continuous excursions into either realm.' Margaret means to keep the ideals of the Schlegels and yet adapt herself to the facts, to the 'life of telegrams and anger,' of the Wilcoxes. She proposes to ally herself both with those who have made England exist and with those who have made the existence of England a value to the world of being. Looking out over the south coast, Margaret asks herself whether England 'belongs to those who have moulded her and made her feared by other lands, or to those who have added nothing to her power but have somehow seen her, seen the whole island at once, lying as a jewel in a silver sea, sailing as a ship of souls, with all the brave world's fleet accompanying her towards eternity?'

On this note of interrogation, the sign of a muddled mind, a chapter ends; and Margaret's misfortunes, her marriage to Mr. Wilcox and her fruitless struggles to let air into his mind and give him, so to speak, a room with a view, flow from her inability to perceive, instinctively and at once, that the Wilcox way of life, the way of telegrams and anger, is an illusion, something which has only a pragmatic existence. It is the same story with Adela Quested in *A Passage to India*, a girl who resembles Margaret like a sister. The mental muddle which allows her to believe that she can ally herself at once with India and with Anglo-India is the source of her misfortunes. The same story again with Rickie Elliot in *The Longest Journey*. In the first chapter he introduces to his genuinely, if inexpertly, contemplative friend Ansell the girl whom he is later to marry: 'Ansell remained absolutely motionless, moving neither hand nor head —and absolutely silent.' When he is next alone with Ansell, Rickie curses Ansell for his silly rudeness. Ansell's reply is this:

> Did it never strike you that phenomena may be of two kinds: *one*, those which have a real existence, such as the cow; *two*, those which are the subjective product of a diseased imagination, and which, to our destruction, we invest with the semblance of reality? If this never struck you, let it strike you now.

If Rickie had only let it! He would have moved along his life on his own line, he would have remained clear and sound in his judgments and, above all, he would have been saved the long fool's errand which led him to the school of the three kinds of caning and the many-tinted bathing-drawers.

Margaret and Adela and Rickie and a dozen others of their sort are the Lewis Alisons of Mr. Forster's fiction. What of his Narwitzes? Old Mr. Emerson, in *A Room with a View*, and Stewart Ansell, whose wise rudeness has just been illustrated, are the most elaborate portraits of the true contemplative. The most elaborate—not the most successful. For there are moments in which the wisdom of Mr. Emerson is no more than an echo of old Polonius and in which Ansell seems no more than the sort of don who should have outwatched the Bear with Robert Burton. In the portraits of these awesomely learned men, he does not succeed as fully as Mr. Morgan with the Graf von Narwitz.

Mr. Forster has, however, another way of dealing with the intractable problem of presenting a profoundly contemplative mind, a way as subtle as the subject itself. He employs it with Mr. Failing in *The Longest Journey*, with Mrs. Moore in *A Passage to India*, with Mrs.

Wilcox in *Howards End*. It is his great addition to the technique of the novel, the element in his work which makes him irreplaceable.

With Mr. Failing he is less successful than with the two women; but then Mr. Failing was an unpromising subject, scarcely richer than Mr. Emerson. What is striking is Mr. Forster's achievement in making Mr. Failing so much more impressive than Mr. Emerson. It is purely a triumph of method. Not only does he refuse to let Mr. Failing act a main part in the novel, he refuses to let him act at all: he has Mr. Failing's body safe in the grave before the novel opens. Mr. Failing is an influence, now strong, now weak, but, in an unsteady way, gaining ground as the novel proceeds. Near the beginning we say, with some surprise: 'But Mr. Failing is wiser and deeper than Rickie!'; towards the middle we go further and say 'wiser than Ansell!' who, we had thought, was to be the incarnation of wisdom; in the last chapters we perceive that Mr. Failing's wisdom was of a kind not to be compared with Rickie's, not even with Ansell's pedantic insight, that it was wisdom flowing easily and continuously from 'the life whose fountains are within.' It was wisdom strangely similar to Edward Carpenter's as Mr. Forster describes this in his essay *Some Memories*: a hatred of restlessness and of the mentally fidgety, and a disposition to break in upon someone's 'intelligent if useless remarks' with a gentle 'Oh, do sit quiet.'

To Mrs. Wilcox and Mrs. Moore a small part is allowed in the action of the novels in which they appear. Let us note Mrs. Wilcox's first entrance upon the stage. Her two sons are quarrelling noisily on the doorstep of Howards End:

'I didn't—I don't—'

'Yes or no, man; plain question, plain answer. Did or didn't Miss Schlegel—'

'Charles dear,' said a voice from the garden. 'Charles, dear Charles, one doesn't ask plain questions. There aren't such things.'

They were all silent. It was Mrs. Wilcox.

She approached just as Helen's letter had described her, trailing noiselessly over the lawn, and there was actually a wisp of hay in her hands. She seemed to belong not to the young people and their motor but to the house, and to the tree that overshadowed it. One knew that she worshipped the past, and that the instinctive wisdom the past can alone bestow had descended upon her. . . . She did not ask questions. Still less did she pretend that nothing had happened, as a competent society hostess would have done. She said, 'Miss Schlegel, would you take your aunt up to your room or to my room whichever you think best . . .?'

Alone of the characters in *Howards End*, Mrs. Wilcox is always adequate to the subtlety of nature, is always able to ride the whirlwind as serenely as she presides at the tea-urn of Howards End. 'She was not intellectual, nor even alert, and it was odd that all the same, she should give the idea of greatness.' Very odd indeed, and very daring of Mr. Forster to attempt to validate the idea without allowing to his character any action more dramatic than the episode cited. Without demur we nod assent to Margaret Schlegel's tribute, uttered when Mrs. Wilcox is in her grave:

> I feel that you and I and Henry are only fragments of that woman's mind. She knows everything. She is everything. . . . I cannot believe that knowledge such as hers will perish with knowledge such as mine. She knew about realities. She knew when people were in love, though she was not in the room.

As Mr. Failing, but far more powerfully, Mrs. Wilcox communicates an impression of a spirit differing in quality from her associates, of a wisdom incommensurable with their clearest perceptions and strictest reasonings.

I have said that Mrs. Wilcox does not reveal her greatness by any acts of remarkable significance. Nor does she speak with the tongue of a prophet or a sibyl: 'Clever talk alarmed her and withered her delicate imaginings; it was the social counterpart of a motor-car, all jerks, and she was a wisp of hay, a flower.' Without a shade of irony she remarks to the heedless incoherent Margaret: 'Indeed you have put the difficulties of life splendidly. . . . It is just what I should have liked to say about them myself.' Mrs. Wilcox does not put the difficulties of life splendidly: she perceives them too acutely to care to put them at all. She is content with solving them unobtrusively and effectively. Brilliance of speech, like energy of action, belongs to that life of telegrams and anger which Mrs. Wilcox transcends. Doing little, saying less, Mrs. Wilcox left no strong impression upon anyone except Margaret Schlegel, but Margaret's seeing eye 'saw a little more clearly than hitherto what a human being is and to what he may aspire.' For all the rest the death of Mrs. Wilcox was not the irreparable loss of a sage but merely the disappearance of a kind, good woman, deplorably slack and somewhat colourless.

No more than Mrs. Wilcox was Mrs. Moore 'the dear old lady that outsiders supposed.' No sooner had she arrived in her son's house at Chandrapore than 'India brought her out into the open.' In the narrow confines of the club, the bungalows, and the official relationships between Anglo-Indians and natives, she felt stifled. 'While we talk about seeing the real India,' says Adela Quested, who stands in the same relation to Mrs. Moore as Margaret Schlegel to Mrs. Wilcox, 'she goes and sees it and then forgets she's seen it.' Alone late in the evening, Mrs. Moore leaves the station—the station with its bridge-games, its amateur theatricals, its trickle of small talk—and enters a mosque. Not as a sightseer. To her India is not a frieze, but a complex reality, alive and appealing. Before she leaves the mosque Mrs. Moore knows more of India than her son has learned in years of civil service. Not that Dr. Aziz—a characteristic Mohammedan whom she meets there—can tell her the facts or the principles of Indian temperament and action. Not that Mrs. Moore does or says anything that could lead him on to theoretic disquisition. It is merely that this red-faced and white-haired old lady, by virtue of being what she is, lights in his supersensitive spirit 'the flame that not even beauty can nourish.' Mrs. Moore lives on a plane where racial and national traits are irrelevant; and with delighted surprise Dr. Aziz exclaims: 'Then, you are an Oriental!' She is out in the open, and consequently India lies open to her.

The mind of Mrs. Moore, although blurred at the edges, is more lucid than the mind of Mrs. Wilcox. At the time of her arrival in India Mrs. Moore is a Christian mystic. The impact of India—and specifically of the charge of attempted rape of Miss Quested preferred against Dr. Aziz—unsettles Mrs. Moore's serene conviction. Mrs. Moore's original frame of mind is easily intelligible: she resents the responsibilities that link her firmly to the world of actions; she is distressed by the inadequacy of the earthly loves and friendships she has experienced or observed; she is indignant at the Anglo-Indian attitude towards the Indian as at any fact which goes counter to her deep conviction of the omnipresence of the Divine. So far Mr. Forster's task has been no more difficult than the realization of Mrs. Wilcox in *Howards End*.

The triumph in *A Passage to India* is the presentation of the spiritual crisis through which Mrs. Moore passes just before her death. So close to the Incommunicable is this crisis that when Mrs. Moore speaks of her spiritual state, her language is as elusive and broken as that of an oracle. No single speech of hers can produce its designed effect if extracted from its context but—this warning given—I shall quote one:

Oh, why is everything still my duty? When shall I be free from your fuss? Was he in the cave and were you in the cave and on and on . . . and Unto us a Son is born, unto us a Child is given . . . and am I good and is he bad and are we saved . . . and ending everything the echo.

These are the rhythms of Melville; and the mood of Mrs. Moore, in this crisis, is analogous to the mood in which Melville wrote *Moby Dick*, full of tortured questionings and hopeless of escape from the darkness of doubt. In this mood, as Mr. Forster observes, 'a spiritual muddledom is set up for which no high-sounding words can be found; we can neither act nor refrain from action, we can neither ignore nor respect Infinity.' In this black mood Mrs. Moore dies.

And yet Mrs. Moore lives on. 'I cannot believe that knowledge such as hers,' says Margaret Schlegel of Mrs. Wilcox, 'will perish with knowledge such as mine.' The strange insight of Mrs. Moore survives, obscured and attenuated, in her daughter and her second son. Her immediate comprehension of India issues in her elevation among the Hindus to the status of a minor deity—a metamorphosis displeasing to her elder son in whose hierarchy of values a British matron stood far above a heathen goddess. Most intensely of all, she lives on in the mind of Dr. Aziz. To her younger son he says: 'Your mother was my best friend in all the world.' And after uttering this munificent eulogy he reflects, 'puzzled by his own great gratitude: What did this eternal goodness of Mrs. Moore amount to? To nothing if brought to the test of thought—she had not borne witness in his favour, nor visited him in the prison, yet she had stolen to the depths of his heart, and he always adored her.'

To define Mrs. Moore more closely would be to weaken her reality: it is enough to indicate that with her as with Mrs. Wilcox we enter the world of the Karamazovs and Myshkin and Raskolnikov. Mr. Forster, in his *Aspects of the Novel*, has suggested the impact that world produces upon us: 'a sensation that is partly physical—the sensation of sinking into a translucent globe and seeing our experience floating far above us on its surface, tiny, remote, yet ours.' 'Prophecy' is the title of the chapter in which this remark comes; and at its outset Mr. Forster explains the peculiar sense in which he uses the word by drawing a contrast between George Eliot, whom he calls a preacher, and Dostoievsky, whom he calls a prophet. In a word, he says that while for George Eliot God is on the same plane as the very chairs and tables, in the novels of Dostoievsky one must change the focus when one passes from chairs and tables and all the other paraphernalia of the world of actions to that other plane to which all the great Dostoievsky characters at some time ascend. Significantly, in speaking of Mrs. Wilcox, Mr. Forster remarks: 'Yet she and daily life were out of focus: one or the other must show blurred. And at lunch she seemed more out of focus than usual, and nearer the line that divides daily life from a life that may be of greater importance.' As the spirit of Mrs. Wilcox or of Mrs. Moore diffuses itself, the world of actions does indeed become blurred. Ronnie Heaslip and Mr. Wilcox, who had seemed to be chunks of the most solid reality, become unsubstantial fragments of the mind of Mrs. Wilcox or Mrs. Moore. Unlike the cow they are no longer there.

We are now able to answer the question with which we approached the novels of Mr. Forster. By applying his formula of a 'change in focus' he generates the disquieting but convincing sense that more real than the world of actions is the dim and but partly comprehensible world in which Mrs. Moore and Mrs. Wilcox have their being. He starts his novel safely and quietly on its course; the plot and the protagonists are securely keeled in the world of actions; ordinary things are happening—there is love and talk and even marmalade and tea. Suddenly an island uncharted by dwellers in the world of actions looms up, alien and puzzling. The novel is momentarily thrown off its course amid general confusion and doubt whether the methods and standards of this world of actions are quite so valid as we had supposed. We are made sharers in the wonder which was the last experience of the Graf von Narwitz—the experience of which he could not communicate the essence even to Lewis Alison. And Mr. Forster leaves us before a door ajar and leading into a room with a view.

ABINGER HARVEST

1936

154. Basil de Sèlincourt, review, *Manchester Guardian*

20 March 1936, 7

Basil de Selincourt, essayist and critic, author of studies of Blake and Whitman and of *Towards Peace and Other Essays* (1932).

[. . .] the main impression left by the volume is that a conservative of the sweetest kind is looking conscientiously around him and recognising in the world, a little ruefully but quite resignedly, the use and value of other influences.

Mr. Forster is, of course, primarily a novelist, and perhaps on that account more interested in recognising what people are than in deciding why or how they are what they are. His many delicious observations leave no doubt about his taste and perception, and may lead to an overestimate of his power. His opening remarks on the English character have much that is pretty and pointed, but nothing that is original.

[. . . . .]

The truth is that on the fundamental issues Mr. Forster remains tentative and fumbling. His book will be read for its wide and gracious sympathies, its happy delicacy of style, its occasional illumination, rather than for any creative or constructive grasp.

155. Elizabeth Bowen, review, *Spectator*

clvi, 20 March 1936, 521

Elizabeth Bowen (1899–1973), the most distinguished woman novelist of the post-Virginia Woolf generation. In 1936 she published her best pre-war novel, *The Death of the Heart*. Her recollections of her earliest reactions to Forster's work are recounted in her essay reprinted in *Aspects of E. M. Forster*, ed. Oliver Stallybrass (1969).

In an age when novelists hum like factories, keeping up to date with themselves, Mr. E. M. Forster's output has been, in bulk, small. The novels which, with their 'new standard of truth,' create an absolute world are five, only, in number. It is over thirty years now since the first: *Where Angels Fear to Tread* was short, and contained in embryo all the other books. The authority with which the novels are written, the power they have to expand inside the mind account, perhaps, for the patience with which his silences are received—he has never been mistrusted and never declined. An artist does not rank somewhere between entertainer and tradesman for nothing; he is expected to ring up the curtain again promptly, punctually to deliver the goods. Silence is undue, and makes the public suspicious. But a quality in all Mr. Forster's work makes peremptoriness of this kind impossible. The books are so clearly more than efforts of his intelligence; when they do come they have so clearly imposed themselves that it is impossible to demand them when they do not come.

Actually, he has not been so silent. Two collections of stories, *Pharos and Pharillon*, *Anonymity*, *Aspects of the Novel*, the Lowes Dickinson biography have been landmarks down the last twenty years. And the eighty or so 'articles, essays, reviews, poems, &c.,' reprinted in *Abinger Harvest* have been appearing since 1904. If they were nothing more—and they are much more—they would be notes on his so-called silences: the absorption and rapture of travel, the exploration of books. That he has been prevailed upon to assemble and republish them is a matter for gratitude.

Too often, collections are to be dreaded. They are the severest test a writer can face. Tricks of mind, prejudices, an overworking of privilege, an iota too much of accomplishment in the writing stick out in the short essay, the *tour de force*: cumulatively, the effect may be desolating, show up unsuspected weakness in other work. Too many collections are scrapheaps from well-known workshops—shavings, filings no doubt of excellent wood or metal, but the dismal topicality of decades ago sits on them like dust, or a journalistic smartness tarnishes them. Too few writers are right in throwing nothing away. Mr. Forster is one great exception: *Abinger Harvest* comes with harvest richness and timeliness.

The essays have been assembled in four groups—The Present, Books, The Past, The East—and the scenario, which is beautiful, of the Abinger Pageant stands alone at the end. The order is vital and should, I feel, be followed—though it is tempting to keep darting backwards and forwards, attracted by titles or opening paragraphs. The collector's desire to be read in this order is more than a whim; it gives the book a form, unity and intention rare in its kind. The dates, startlingly various, of the essays play no part in their arrangement, and should not: there has never been any question of Mr. Forster's *development*; there never seems to have been any early work. The age factor with him must have stayed outside and arbitrary; his maturity is innate. That so many of the essays should be so short, too short, seems less a fault in them than in circumstance. (Many appeared in weeklies.) This tantalising briefness, whatever its first object, is the one trying element in the book—the Greek beauty-box, the physician Cardan, the Doll Souse, the Emperor Babur, the rational Indian wedding, Cnidus in the rain, the Jodhpur dragon, the Scallies pass for moments into the light and disappear too soon. But, for all one's own regrets and disruptions, the book has its own, an extraordinary continuousness. Perhaps because Mr. Forster has changed so little, perhaps because his mind does not flick on and off—it must impregnate not only his writing but all his conscious moments; its abeyances, even, must have their colour. What is remarkable, in these essays as in the novels, is his power of having access to the whole of himself, to what he has called 'the lower personality': the obscure, the involuntary, the general that is in us all the stuff of dreams and art, the source of perception, the arbiter of memory. Few intellects so active are less isolated from the whole of the being. Mr. Forster does not make a doctrine of spontaneity; 'intuition,' he even says, 'makes dancing dervishes of us.' He must have come to terms with his intuition: happen to him what may, he remains, or appears to remain, at once the most active and the governing factor in his own experience. If the perfectly adjusted person does not suffer, Mr. Forster is not the perfectly adjusted person: the perfectly adjusted writer I feel he is. With him, intellect not so much controls susceptibility as balances it; many of us have not the wits to feel. Given this highly sensitive equanimity, the effect of this quick succession of essays is, his not so much pitching upon a series of subjects as momentarily enclosing and then releasing them, added to.

To criticism he brings the make-up of the artist. He perceives in another man's work what he himself knows—which accords with his theory of the deep down, giant part of us being general. In his own novels the sense of conscious life's being built up over a somewhat august vault of horror, that rings under the foot, that exhales coldly through cracks, is constantly palpable. Of *The Waste Land* he says: 'the horror is so intense that the poet has an inhibition and cannot state it openly.' And, later in the same essay: 'In respect of the horror that they find in life men may be divided into three classes' . . . He finds the romantic in Ibsen, in Proust the adventurer. If he is hard on a writer it is in the manner of one accustomed to being hard on himself; he has none of the critic's godlike non-participation. He detects the finest fatal crack in the bowl. He sees Conrad's 'central obscurity.' 'The secret casket of his genius contains a vapour rather than a jewel.' Love for Jane Austen steels him against Miss Austen, who forgot the nobility of Anne, the wise wit of Elizabeth, when she wrote letters. In some of the critical essays his own image more nearly appears than elsewhere; they are the least, in his own sense, anonymous of his work.

The prose throughout *Abinger Harvest* is the prose of the novels; not a word he uses ever obstructs the mind—prose which makes objects appear brighter than themselves, as in very clear morning light, instead of darkening behind a mesh of words. Like Flaubert's, though so unlike, here is a style made perfect by being subject to purpose, and beautiful with vitality. Its rhythm is so inherent in its content that one cannot detect it without analysis. The least frigid of writing, it is the most impersonal; he is enemy to all those lovable little tricks. 'Literature,' he says elsewhere, 'tries to be unsigned,' and as far as manner goes he approaches anonymity. But in prose the point of view is inevitable; every sentence must bear, however lightly, the stamp of the mind, its governing quality. Behind his irony, his impersonality, his gentleness, Mr. Forster is passionately civilised. The novels are manifestos, these essays ring with a note that is startling because it is rare. Passion will out, however much, however wisely irony may temper it. Beliefs that root in the nature cannot be silenced: his give him an unmistakable touch on a page. That he has written little that could be wrongly attributed is not as he would wish, but too few people are like him.

156. David Garnett, review, *New Statesman & Nation*

xi, 21 March 1936, 459

David Garnett (1892–) is perhaps best known for his novel *Lady into Fox* (1922), which won the Hawthornden and Tait Black Prizes in 1923. In that year he became a publisher, and was associated with the Nonesuch Press and with Rupert Hart Davis.

When things go badly with us, when illness and death come near, we find an exaggerated comfort in our friends; the tongue-tied visitor in the ridiculous surroundings of the sick room represents the world outside, a harbinger of the living and the normal, precious because we are sick and he is well. When public affairs go badly, as they do now, and there seems no future for the world but suffering, more suffering and bloody fluxes, then a visitor who speaks to us of the old values and of sanity is invested with a special value which is derived from our desperate need. E. M. Forster tells us that during the war he found some comfort in T. S. Eliot's *Prufrock*.

> Here was a protest, and a feeble one and the more congenial for being feeble. For what, in that world of gigantic horror, was tolerable but the slightest gestures of dissent? He who measured himself against the war, who drew himself to his full height, as it were, and said to Armadillo-Armageddon 'Avaunt!' collapsed at once into a pinch of dust. But he who could turn aside to complain of ladies and drawing rooms preserved a tiny drop of our self-respect, he carried on the human heritage.

And now that the Armadillo has come rumbling out and thrown his shadow over us again, E. M. Forster has brought the most well-timed precious comfort in *Abinger Harvest*. To me, at all events, no one else, now living, could bring quite the same message. Lowes Dickinson, Roger Fry, or Lytton Strachey might have done. If one drew a triangle connecting their three points of view, Forster would be somewhere within it, or very close outside. It is difficult to define exactly what there was in common. It was certainly not simply that all four came from Cambridge and had reached intellectual maturity before the war: but rather that unlike all the pitifully worried elderly people round us, their minds were not propped-up and so did not feel the loss of their props when these were knocked away. They grew unsupported, from their own roots, and what E. M. Forster says of Roger Fry was true of all four: they believed in reason and mistrusted intuition.

Is not belief in reason based upon a misconception of human nature which we should correct? Since the war an increasing number of people have come to feel this, and are taking refuge instead in authority or in intuition. Authority attracts our dictators and our serfs because it seems to promise a stable society. Intuition attracts those who wish to be spiritual without any bother, because it promises a heaven where the intuitions of others can be ignored. Roger Fry rejected authority absolutely. . . . Intuition he did not reject. But he knew that . . . the man who believes a thing is true because he feels it in his bones, is not really very far removed from the man who believes it on the authority of a policeman's truncheon. So he was suspicious of intuition, subjecting it, as it were, to a fumigating process, and not allowing it into his life until it was well aired.

A fumigating process! Yes, it was the practice of ceaselessly fumigating every subject that gave something of the same flavour to minds that were so essentially unlike, and it is this power that seems to be disappearing. There are still many, even among the young, who reject authority and mistrust intuition, but one feels they are children of the age of violence; they hanker after makeshift courses and cannot stay to fumigate.

Abinger Harvest consists of reprinted essays, articles, reviews and poems gathered into a book: the feast of scraps offered when the cook is too lazy to provide a fresh roast. Yet these scraps define Forster more exactly than any of the novels, the last of which was published—as he must be tired of being reminded—a dozen years ago, while its predecessors appeared in the decade before the war. In the novels we are aware of a vein of emotionalism in their author which makes him out of touch with the simple people and things that move him most deeply. In this he seems to illustrate what he says in an excellent criticism of Proust.

Thus Proust's general theory of human intercourse is that the fonder we are of people the less we understand them—the theory of the complete pessimist. Dante took a different view. Dante believed that the fonder we are of people—the better we understand them—the theory of the complete optimist. To him knowledge was love, love knowledge, and Beatrice not Beatrice until he could meet her in heaven. . . . To myself, a child of unbelief, Proust seems more likely to be right.

This perhaps is the explanation of the more baffling passages in the novels—the moments when the Goat-footed God appears. The disturbing hoof-prints are rarely to be found in these pages, which are the work of a middle-aged, detached Forster with all his wits about him, and his company is the more fascinating because he remains cool. His next remark on Proust shows his unlikeness and his wider outlook:

Does he make enough allowance for a certain good sense that persists in the human organism even when it is heated by passion? Does he not lay too much stress on jealousy? He regards it as the very food of love. . . . He and life are not identical here, life being the more amiable of the two, and future historians will find that his epic of curiosity almost sums up you and me, but not quite.

Several of the essays show Forster's political point of view, which he defines as that of:

A bourgeois who adheres to the British constitution, adheres to it rather than supports it, and the fact that this isn't dignified doesn't worry me. I do care about the past. I do care about the preservation and extension of freedom.

Our danger from the Fascism of Mosley he thinks negligible; the real danger is what he calls Fabio-fascism. He thinks it will work in the traditional method known in England since the days of Charles I, that is to say by departmental tyranny and the dictator spirit working behind forms of law. This danger is just as great (in my opinion) from Socialists as from the propertied classes. Forster sees a danger in the Government control of broadcasting, which may certainly grow greater at any moment. And when he has discussed the encroachments that power is always making upon the freedom of the individual, he turns to notice the encroachments that the ownership of property would make on him, if he did not guard against them. At Abinger he bought a wood with a footpath running through it, and soon found that it was a breeding ground of jealousy and selfishness. Ladies of education would grub for botanical specimens, 'other ladies, less educated, roll down the bracken in the arms of their gentlemen friends,' and when he sees a bird, he feels: 'My bird!' and is aggrieved when it flies over the boundary fence as though it belonged to itself. There is something delightful in thinking of Forster feeling such emotions stirring in his heart. And for Abinger he wrote what at Hollywood they would call the Continuity of a pageant which began and ended with a flock of sheep being driven across under the tree; one of the prettiest and simplest of pageants.

Most people crack jokes about things; we see the thing and are grateful for the joke. Forster's humour is in seeing a new truth; in revealing the thing itself. Anyone could have made jokes about the Queen's Dolls' House, with its roof and its exterior walls raised like an extinguisher above it. Any of us might have felt on looking at this miniature Hindenburg statuette into which every creative artist has driven a pin: 'How differently I should feel—how differently must those feel who have been permitted to throw themselves into the Queen's Dolls' House heart and soul!' But only Forster, having paid his sixpence and waited in the queue, would ask:

> What is it like? Why is it so difficult to apprehend? A blot forms on the vision every time the effort is made. Everything must be like something, so what is this like? The carcase of a bullock? . . . These are lungs, those veins, that hole might fit over the horns.

Abinger Harvest is one of the most delightful collections of occasional writings I have read. The description of Babur, of Mr. and Mrs. Abbey, of Voltaire and Madame du Châtelet, of Trooper Comberbacke, give fresh, surprising, living pictures. Must we wait another dozen years for the next novel?

157. Derek Traversi, 'The novels of E. M. Forster', *Arena*

i, no. 1, April 1937, 28–40

Derek Antona Traversi (1912–) is the author of a number of important books on Shakespeare, including *An Approach to Shakespeare* (1938). He has represented The British Council in a number of countries and has contributed to *The Pelican History of English Literature*. He is at present Professor of English at Swarthmore College, Pennsylvania.

F. R. Leavis, in his article 'E. M. Forster' (*Scrutiny* vii, September 1938, 185–202) added an interesting footnote to the effect that if he had 're-read' Traversi's essay 'before writing my own note instead of after, I might perhaps have decided that Mr. Traversi, with his admirable economy, had made my observations superfluous. As it is, I offer my particular limited approach, with its attendant stresses, with the less misgiving because there is his essay to refer the reader to'.

I

There is an increasing tendency in modern literature to take sides, to refashion the stuff of experience in terms of a position independently and dogmatically assumed. Mr. Forster's attitude to this tendency, expressed in some of the best papers of *Abinger Harvest*, springs from a critical balance, from a continual concern for the wholeness and harmony of life. His answer to it, which may be commended both to Catholic and 'proletarian' novelists, may be put in the form of a searching question: 'What does this imposed attitude leave out? What unbalance does it involve, what destruction of possibilities of living?' Questions which only occur to the genuine novelist, but which, if asked, would help any writer who is great enough to produce a truly artistic justification of his philosophy. The root of great art is an honesty by the side of which works like *Murder in the Cathedral* and Auden's plays are seen to be marred by something partial and parochial in them. Their acceptance of their respective dogmas is felt to be, not at once the climax of their experience and the root of further vitality, but an attempt to shelter themselves from their own poverty of life. How far Mr. Forster succeeds in criticizing this poverty, and how far he transcends it by his own qualities, are the proposed aims of this essay.

In the early part of *Howard's End*, Mr. Forster distinguishes his heroine in that book by a 'continual and sincere response to all that she encountered in her path through life.' The novels are a continual attempt to express and justify this ideal in terms of the life with which he is familiar. The boundaries imposed on him by society and upbringing are always obvious, and there is no attempt to avoid them; if Mr. Forster's roots were in anything but leisured middle-class life, he would be a different novelist. The characters of *A Room with a View* are all drawn from that pre-war society which had the means and leisure to tour Italy; they are only distinguished from the mass of that society by the ability of some of them to pierce the comfortable conventions of polite touring and to be affected by the life with which all, consciously or otherwise, are surrounded. The Schlegels, in *Howard's End*, represent the best of established middle-class idealism and integrity; only the daughters show, in addition, Mr. Forster's concern that these qualities should be enriched by contact with actuality.

It is precisely this insistence on actuality that gives the novels a wider validity. Common to them all is a shock, a crisis which interrupts the even flow of social life. In *A Room with a View*, the shock is provided by the excursion in Florence, in which the visitors lose their way and their Baedekers, and meet Mr. Emerson, who upsets their lukewarm, conventional reactions in Santa Croce, just as he later disturbs the thinness of their lives by bringing new suggestions of vitality and richness which break up an inadequate engagement. In *Howard's End*, the Schlegels are taken by Mrs. Wilcox out of the peaceful 'backwater' (so Mr. Forster describes it) of their comfortable London home to 'Howard's End', another kind of house, whose roots are deeper and whose vitality is based on wider and more permanent contacts. It is not unnatural here to speak of the 'vitality' of a house, for it is just this continual living influence of Howard's End which is the central feature of the novel; the house is the dominating environment which embraces all the partial and contrasted characters in its own completeness. In *A Passage to India*, Adela, also on the point of a conventional marriage, enters the Marabar cave with Aziz, and so causes a crisis which starts a series of expanding echoes covering the whole book. As a result of it, Adela sees the inadequacy of her reaction to love and life and declines to marry the Anglo-Indianized Ronny, Aziz is shaken out of his flimsy attachment to Islamic tradition and sentimental happiness, and Mrs. Moore's intuitions about the universe are given at once greater honesty and a new despair.

In all the novels, then, the established middle-class order is faced with a crisis, a premonition of insufficiency. Under the guise of that crisis, Mr. Forster is reflecting his own in each of his recurrent sets of characters. Into each novel he introduces a young heroine, a woman with dormant possibilities, bound in, attractively but inadequately, by the conventions of her society; and he shows us how these possibilities (in the Schlegels, for example) are brought into play by the central 'shock', of whose nature and extent they become only gradually aware. He shows us, too, in Mrs. Wilcox and Mrs. Moore, in Mr. Emerson and his son in *A Room with a View*, other characters, comparatively free *within* their conventional limitations; they are more directly aware of the crisis which faces them, but still unable to discover its significance. These, perhaps, represent most adequately Mr. Forster's own position, and show most clearly the outstanding discrepancy in all his work: the discrepancy between his insistence on awareness, on intensity of experience, and the corresponding sense of vacancy and futility which so unexpectedly meets it.

The root of this profound split in Mr. Forster's emotional make-up is well expressed in the concluding pages of *Howard's End:*—'One's hope was in the weakness of logic.' The opposition of 'hope' and 'logic' is essential, and the connecting 'weakness' describes admirably the kind of feeling, which we might call 'nostalgic', with which the author tries to bridge the gap. 'Logic' is for Mr. Forster the balanced awareness of contemporary tendencies which is so important in his work. His frequent references to the growth of a new England, vulgar and flimsily suburban, his consciousness of the dominating influence of money unaccompanied by responsibility, his sense of the weakening and cheapening of values in the unmanageable masses—all these lead to a deep and engrained pessimism, which comes out well in various remarks in *Howard's End:*—

'Life's going to be melted down all over the world. . . .'
'Again and again must the drums tap, and the goblins stalk over the universe, before joy can be purged of the superficial. . . . Death destroys a man, but the idea of death saves him.'

Only when we are in a position to relate this pessimism to the central impulses in Mr. Forster's work shall we be able to assess its value. For the moment, it is enough to say that it is a critical and sensitive pessimism, awake to the most significant developments of life, and judging them with passion and integrity.

If 'logic' leads Mr. Forster to pessimism, however, the profound interest of that passion is due to the fact that it springs from 'hope.' It is precisely out of his conviction of the value of human feelings and relations that he derives his continual sense of their frustration and vanity; the two attitudes are subtly fused, in a tense and delicate complexity. The peculiar quality of his 'hope' can be seen in *Howard's End:*—

> 'It was the presence of sadness at all that surprised Margaret, and ended by giving her a feeling of completeness. In these English farms, if anywhere, one might see life steadily and see it whole, group in one vision its transitoriness and its eternal youth, connect—connect without bitterness until all men are brothers.'

Whenever Mr. Forster discusses England, we are reminded that it is at once his strength and his weakness to look to the past rather than to the present or the future. His 'hope', in fact, is closely allied to a keen sense of tradition. He sees human relationships as the source of a rich and steady emotional life—that is the vision, gentle yet intensely alive, behind the emphasis on 'connect'—and he sees them as part of an organic continuity with nature. The English village and the country-side are not, for him, mere showpieces to be fenced off from a hostile present. They are rather the moulding influences of a way of life, a unity in which human life may be rooted, and from which it may spring. That, for Mr. Forster, is the ideal, the 'hope' of tradition. But always in his work we are aware that the ideal and the tradition are wearing a little thin, and it is this that gives to his prose its characteristic note of 'sadness', of nostalgia. For Mr. Forster, as we suggested in stressing his leisured and middle-class affinities, is not a writer established in a strong tradition. His references to rural life have not, for example, the sense of directness, the supple thread of continuity which we find in T. F. Powys. His sympathy for 'English farms' is a conscious, critical sympathy; he admires and loves a world from which he does not spring. That explains the need of 'sadness' to complete this vision of the country. Mr. Forster's mansions and farms are survivals, backwaters in a world less happy and more actual than themselves. He can, indeed, suggest that the spirit of Howard's End belongs to the future as well as to the past, that its eclipse is only temporary; but his assurance lacks the essential artistic verification from experience. It remains the aspiration of a sensitive personality for the life from which it feels divorced.

It is significant that Mr. Forster should have given us Mrs. Wilcox as a kind of symbol of the 'connected' life, a character who cannot be said to have any noticeable connection with 'England', who rather fails to come to life at all. We are told that—

> she worshipped the past, and that the instinctive wisdom the past can alone bestow had descended upon her—that wisdom to which we give the clumsy name of aristocracy.

But this 'aristocracy' is not a social attribute, springing from some definite order of society, and strengthened by contact with the life of England. Mrs. Wilcox, in so far as she is more than a shadowy 'symbol', is essentially middle-class and almost Victorian. She shows an important tendency in Mr. Forster, the inability to realize a living 'tradition', to give his characters a setting that at once transcends the personal and gives it life. The author of *Howard's End* is a *social* novelist who is aware of the sterility of his society, but is unable to find a way of living in which the contact of personalities shall be given a wider, impersonal context, and so, by ceasing to be isolated in their self-importance, may cease to be trivial. It is his awareness of triviality in a baseless social life that makes Mr. Forster describe Mrs. Wilcox as 'out of focus', and it is this also that makes her (and Mrs. Moore, her successor in *Passage to India*) so 'apt to brood'. The novels are the product of a society which is rootless precisely because it has nothing to take seriously but itself: a society without a background, which is driven to scrutinize itself so self-consciously that its sensitivity can express itself *only in irony*. In Mr. Forster's case, to irony is added nostalgia, as we have seen; and this nostalgia is merely the revolt of self-consciousness against sterility. The strange sentimentalizing of the business instinct in Mr. Wilcox, which is carried out in the face of a full awareness of its inadequacy, is another product of the same dilemma. The Schlegel sisters have too much of Mr. Forster's sensitive intelligence not to feel the need of a closer contact with something beyond their own idealistic, but enclosed, world; and so Margaret, in marrying the business man Mr. Wilcox, tries to build upon a union with a world totally unlike her own.

'Look at the Wilcoxes. . . . With all their defects of temper and understanding such men give me more pleasure than many who are better equipped, and I think it is because they have worked regularly and honestly.'

But, in spite of himself, Mr. Forster knows that it is not to insensitivity and big business that intelligence needs to be wedded. He provides an adequate estimate of Mr. Wilcox simply by recording his carelessness and callousness to the unfortunate bank-clerk; and he allows Margaret Schlegel to show him up more than once. The sentimental justification in terms of work and honesty scarcely succeeds in affecting the novel. The movement of the plot to final success is not accompanied by a corresponding emotional consent, and remains a mere indication of how the writer planned things to be. The nostalgic references to Howard's End, suggesting that the house might provide a wider context of life in which social intercourse might take its proper and natural place, show the true way in which Mr. Forster would have liked to see the virtues of the Schlegels integrated; and the nostalgic note is due to the obstructions he meets in this effort.

Mr. Forster, then, is keenly and sensitively attached to the elements of experience, and expresses them in clear, supple, and passionate prose. He has the great writer's gift of direct contact with the exterior occasions of his feelings, unblunted by any purely 'literary' distraction; his prose is disciplined by contact with undiluted experience. When Fielding, at the moment when he is divided by opposing loyalties after the arrest of his Indian friend, looks out towards the Marabar caves: when the Schlegels listen to Beethoven, and their emotions shift with the movement of the music, we feel Mr. Forster's astonishing grasp of the emotional moment and its significance to the whole personality. But he shares also the malady of the modern critical intelligence—an inability to bring the intense separate moments of feeling into a continuous, personal unity. Each feeling is in itself intimately related to the man who feels; but, despite all his efforts, he fails to relate it to any other experience. So he clings to these separate moments and elaborates them in spite of their known insufficiency, until they become first poignant, then nostalgic, and even sentimental. The cause of this over-insistence is suggested in *Howard's End:*—

'Margaret realized the chaotic nature of our daily life, and its difference from the orderly sequence that has been fabricated by historians. Actual life is full of false clues and sign-posts that lead nowhere. With infinite effort we nerve ourselves for a crisis that never occurs.'

The last sentence, as we shall see, is a perfect description of the effect of *A Passage to India*. It also throws light upon the social attitude in *Howard's End* and the earlier novels. Lawrence once complained that Forster was occupied too exclusively with 'persons.' He seems to have meant that his critical scepticism made him unable to rely upon the importance and continuity of emotional experience, so that he had to fall back upon the accidental surfaces of personality, the comforting certainties of society. Much of his work is a kind of Comedy of Manners, in which, however, the bottom is knocked out of the comedy by the serious, almost desperate anxiety to justify what he feels to be triviality. As he says in *A Room with a View*: 'Society has this disadvantage: we lose the sense of proportion; we cannot tell whether our secret is serious or not.'

These difficulties appear in Mr. Forster's diffidence about the sexes. There is an interesting statement in *A Room with a View*:—

'Passion should *believe itself* irresistible. It should forget civility and consideration and all the other curses of a refined nature. Above all, it should never ask for leave when there is a right of way. Why could not he do as any labourer or navvy . . .?'

Once more we note the odd shift from wistful naivety to acutely conscious irony. Mr. Forster feels that passion, which is so central to human personality, is the most likely of all human relations to justify itself in terms of value. He tells us that we shall enter the Garden of Eden in the future, 'when we no longer despise our bodies.' But at once the cultured and sceptical consciousness steps in, and he withdraws from his own aspiration by the hint of disillusion and ridicule in 'believe itself.' To act, he implies, as though passion were of value, one must delude oneself, one must forget 'all the other curses of a refined nature.' But Mr. Forster's own nature is, in the true sense, 'refined', and he realizes, even as he writes, that 'civility and consideration' are among these 'curses'. Unable to associate passion with civilization, and too critical not to see the futility of the cave-man ideal, he tends inevitably to scepticism. Now we see why Margaret's relations to Mr. Wilcox are so unsatisfactory, why Mr. Forster does not see the inadequacy of—'she would use her love to make him a better man.' Only a vital sense of the value of deep personal relations could have made *Howard's End* fully alive, and have given its author the power to overcome his nostalgic pessimism. Without it, there is an air of wistful failure about Mr. Forster's 'connect'; the ideal is attractive by its personal integrity, and given point by the intelligence behind it, but it remains emotionally inadequate.

II

I have so far discussed only Mr. Forster's earlier novels—or rather, *Howard's End* as the most inclusive and significant of them. It seems clear that, to write a great novel, he would need a subject in which his critical pessimism should not be sentimentalized, in which his desire for a complete and balanced life should be expressed without blurring the expression. That subject he found in *A Passage to India*. The theme itself reminds us of the particular problems with which Mr. Forster is always concerned. Adela is a heroine of the usual Forsterian type, limited by her English middle-class outlook, but with latent possibilities of honesty and freedom. She is brought out to India by Mrs. Moore to marry Ronnie, a young man of her own type, whose possibilities, however, have been largely submerged in the difficulties and insensibilities of Indian administration. She outrages Anglo-Indian opinion by a rather sentimental desire to make contact with the native population, and accompanies Dr. Aziz to the Marabar caves. In these caves, she is subject to an hallucination (so, at least, Mr. Forster suggests, and he weaves the uncertainty very skilfully into Adela's wavering, half-aware mind) which causes a crisis in her outlook and in Anglo-Indian relations at Chandrapore; at the end of it, she declines to marry Ronnie, and Fielding, the schoolmaster, is bound by his desire to 'connect' and live honestly to defend Aziz and become estranged from his countrymen. The points of similarity between this and Mr. Forster's earlier plots are sufficiently obvious.

The advance represented by *Passage to India* is immediately reflected by a new quality in its prose. This is clear on the first page:—

'The very wood seems made of mud, the inhabitants of mud moving. So abased, so monotonous is everything that meets the eye, that when the Ganges comes down it might be expected to wash the excrescence back into the soil. Houses do fall, people are drowned and left rotting, but the general outline of the town persists, swelling here, shrinking there, like some low but indestructible form of life.'

The relation of man to his environment is still, as in *Howard's End*, one of Mr. Forster's preoccupations, but the nature of that relation is very different. His England was always half an awareness of what had been, and half a desire for what never was; his keen sense of culture and continuity, acutely conscious of adversity, tended to cling to a country that was small and orderly, moulded by a civilization that was at home in it. In the same way, he makes his character Fielding, on his way back from India, find at Venice—'the harmony between the works of man and the earth that upholds them, the civilization that has escaped muddle, the spirit in a reasonable form, with flesh and blood subsisting.' Mr. Forster has never expressed better the values that make him an important writer, but in *Passage to India* they are offset by something exterior to themselves and disturbing. India is frightening and unmanageable, and these qualities impose themselves upon its life; crises come, but in the wrong places and in the wrong way, with ecstacies that seem faint and ridiculous to the startled consciousness. In India, too, there is a unity between man and nature, but a different unity, suggesting an impersonal identity and assuming the unimportance of the spirit. The unimportance, be it noted, rather than the non-existence of it: for unimportance robs us even of the drama, the comforting crisis of despair, and leaves only void and uncertainty. The rhythms of the prose, so different from those of the earlier novels, are cut bare to give prominence to the uncompromising word. 'Mud moving', 'excrescence', 'rotting' and so on—there is no literary cadence to shelter us from a vivid sensation of the oppressive fact. India becomes the solvent by which Forster analyses that faith in causality, in the spirit, in the significance of events, which he has inherited from Europe.

This examination leads to undisguised pessimism. Consider Mrs. Moore's experience on the visit to the caves—an experience which serves as commentary to the central episode of the book:—

> . . . the echo began, in some indescribable way, *to undermine her hold on life*. Coming at a moment when she chanced to be fatigued, it had managed to murmur, 'Pathos, piety, courage—they exist, but are identical, and so is filth. Everything exists, *nothing has value*.' If one had spoken vileness in that place, or quoted lofty poetry, the result would have been the same—'ou-boum'.

One is struck at once by the phrasing. Mrs. Moore 'chanced' to be fatigued; Mr. Forster has even denied any cause to her illness, has blurred the physical and spiritual maladies in a common *malaise*, has implied that neither has real significance. This association of a certain drooping, a lack of vitality, with Mr. Forster's usual almost unnatural sharpness of sensitive perception, is what we should expect of a keen intuition working in a void and fundamentally uncertain of itself; and it fits in with our account of his attitude to society in *Howard's End*. Again, the echo 'managed' to murmur; one gets an impression of the hostile spiritual climate of India creeping into the interstices and unguarded crannies of the European consciousness, making it dead, null, void. All this suggests the difference between Mrs. Moore and the corresponding figure of Mrs. Wilcox in *Howard's End*. It lies in the fact that Mrs. Moore makes no attempt to wrap herself in a vague 'aristocracy'; she is above all transplanted, uprooted from her environment, and the dissatisfaction which was only implicit in Mrs. Wilcox's tendency to 'brood' now becomes a full part of the character. The whole passage shows us why 'everything exists, nothing had value' is an interesting and valuable statement. There is nothing unusual in the idea. What gives this pessimism an unusual quality is precisely the intensity of Mr. Forster's concern for 'values', and the keenness with which he apprehends them. Set this against the corresponding depth of his sense of vacancy, and you have the mood of *Passage to India*.

The incompatibility of these two aspects of life, which so exercises Mr. Forster, is more particularly expressed in the central image of the book—I mean, of course, the cave and the echo. The method by which this image is given a significance beyond that of its place in the plot, the way it relates itself to the whole impression of Mr. Forster's India, the grip it establishes upon Adela's mind and its continual presence on the fringe of Fielding's consciousness—all these are technical devices which suggest the most mature work of Mrs. Woolf, and are not inferior to them in effect. The function of the cave in the book is dominated by a 'metaphysical' contrast between the sense of infinity and the ignobility and smallness of the actual and the finite. Mr. Forster at once emphasizes his sense of the difference of these concepts, and makes them identical. The cave is circular, uniform, and constricted, but its round uniformity suggests infinity within the limits of its smallness; it gives no hold, no point of departure for experience in its effort to achieve coherence. It 'robs infinity and eternity of their vastness, the only quality that accommodates them to mankind,' just as we have seen man's desire for infinite values turn to pettiness before the scrutiny of a highly-developed self-consciousness. The cave, in fact, is simply an outstanding example of the way in which crises fail to develop in any formal or artistic manner. The European visitors expect holiness or beauty; they find only a uniformity like that of India, at once too small to accommodate their spirit and too vast and impersonal to comfort them. This feeling is fundamental in Mr. Forster's attitude to India. It is seen in Professor Godbole's explanation of the Hindu chant:—

'I say to Shri Krishna, "Come! come to me only." The god refuses to come. I grow humble and say, "Do not come to me only. Multiply yourself into a hundred Krishnas, and let one go to each of my hundred companions, but one, O Lord of the Universe, come to me." . . . He neglects to come.'

'He *neglects* to come.' The verb expresses perfectly the inability of the Western mind to grasp what it regards as the casualness, the lack of dependence, in the Hindu universe. This casualness relates itself to Mrs. Moore's discouraging speculations about God, which are themselves recorded in terms that suggest the constricted infinity of the cave: 'Outside the arch there seemed always an arch, beyond the remotest echo a silence.' And this in turn suggests more than one of Mr. Forster's descriptions of the Indian sky:—

Some kites hovered overhead, impartial, over the kites passed the mass of a vulture, and with an impartiality exceeding all, the sky, not deeply coloured, but translucent, pouring light from its whole circumference. It *seemed unlikely* that the series stopped there. Beyond the sky must there not be something that overarches all the skies, more impartial even than they? Beyond which again . . .?

The image of the cave has expanded itself into the universe, and they are the same. As the desire for infinity reaches out through arch after arch of sky, so does the emphasis on 'impartiality' (which means 'indifference') grow. Always there is the same sense of the infinite possibilities of experience, and always the same feeling that they are all unimportant. The unfathomable arch of the sky becomes constricted into a small, perfectly regular cave, the decisive human act becomes, together with its endless consequences, an unending echo. It is all the same thing. Mrs. Moore becomes more and more concerned with the name of God, 'yet she had never found it less efficacious.' And if religion, though vital to a full humanity, is felt to be vain and unimportant, so is love.

This brings us to the particular emotion which Mr. Forster has chosen to involve in these 'metaphysical' contradictions, in the cave. His attitude to love is indicated by the odd mixture of delusion and social convention which leads to the central tragedy. Once more, he is concerned with his own mixture of tragic irony and comedy of manners. The claims of passion to be a central and serious emotion are transformed by his civilized consciousness into Adela's sentimental fixation which leads to collapse and tragedy. To this cultured criticism Mr. Forster adds a sense of the 'metaphysical' dilemma, the same as that which lies behind the cave-image, and behind the contrast between the infinite and the restricted:—

> 'In space things touch, in time things part'—her brain was so weak that she could not decide whether the phrase was a philosophy or a pun.

The essence of passion is seen by Forster to involve belief in its own value, in its ability to achieve a union that breaks down the walls of the single personality in order to enrich them. But in the cave his civilized consciousness finds a symbol of its inability to accept this union: 'The two flames approach and strive to meet, but cannot, because one of them breathes air, the other stone.' There is a double symbolism suggested here. The more obvious one expresses the inability of two civilized persons to escape their own self-consciousness which seems to condemn them to isolation and futility. The other implies a clash in Forster himself between an ideal, which 'breathes air', in which love is seen as a valuable and self-transcending union, and the incapacity of his self-awareness, which 'breathes stone', to accept that ideal in terms of fact. And, lastly, the futility of the whole thing is embraced by the inhumanity of the cave, so that love is given its place as a reverberation in the universal hollowness.

Now we understand the tone of so many of Mr. Forster's references to love: 'There was esteem and animal contact at dusk, but the emotion that links them was absent.' We understand, too, why the experience in the cave gave Mrs. Moore so sharp a resentment against these vain ideals:—

> The human race would have become a single person centuries ago if marriage was any use. And all this rubbish about love, love in a church, love in a cave, as if there is the least difference.

And we can see why her increasing pessimism is bound up with a growing weariness and lack of vitality, a bitter distaste for her body and its functions: 'My body, my miserable body. . . . Why do I get headaches and puff when I walk?' Mrs. Wilcox's 'aristocracy' has succumbed in Mrs. Moore, and, by the contrast between its virtues and its inadequacy, has produced a great book.

Having isolated Mr. Forster's position, it seems unnecessary to dwell upon the wisdom and subtlety of its application to the many particular problems raised in the book. Above all, the world of *Passage to India* is one of divisions and disunities, across which men of goodwill strive, on the whole with small success, to 'connect.' There is the division between Fielding, the product of Western culture at its most sympathetic and intelligent, and his friend Aziz. Fielding, in his own words, travelled light, and was bound by no ties ('Other people can have children. No obligation, with England getting so chock-a-block, and over-running India for jobs'); but he, and Mr. Forster in him, envied Aziz, who 'was rooted in society and Islam, and had brought children into the world, the society of the future.' Then, among the Indians themselves, we find a cleft between Aziz, the sentimental enthusiast living largely on a tradition which still gives him life, but to which he does not really contribute, and the negative, incomprehensible Hinduism of Godbole. Lastly, there is the study of the declining, but still indispensable, British Raj. Popular attention has been almost wholly focussed on this, perhaps the most superficial of all the interests of the book. Mr. Forster criticizes in the British the failure to 'connect', and no doubt, when all reservations in favour of justice and conscientiousness have been made, he is right. But the book is a great book, not because of its political and social acuteness, but because it springs from a sensitive and intelligent attitude, and a consciousness of values with which we are all concerned.

158. Desmond MacCarthy on E. M. Forster, *Sunday Times*

15 May 1938

A review of Rose Macaulay's *The Writings of E. M. Forster*.

Desmond MacCarthy (1887–1952) was knighted in 1951. He was a writer and journalist, making weekly contributions to the *Sunday Times* and, in the 'twenties, serving as Literary Editor of the *New Statesman*. Educated at Eton and Trinity College, Cambridge, he was associated with the 'Bloomsbury Group', and a brilliant future was predicted for him. In his autobiography, Leonard Woolf describes him at some length, giving the distinct impression that his great gifts were never fully used.

Arnold Bennett used to speak of him sometimes with a kind of exasperated astonishment. That was after *Howard's End* had been out a year or so. 'What's 'ee— doing? Why doesn't 'ee—follow it up? He's on the map.' And the invariable excellence of Mr. Forster's occasional essays and reviews (Bennett was a good judge of what was thoroughly 'done') would reawake that astonishment in him. Why had E. M. Forster had no sense of success? Why did he show no wish to be one of 'the big four' or 'the big five'—I forget their exact number—of the superior novelists who also held the public? *Howard's End* was published in 1911; his next novel, *A Passage to India*, in 1924. A gap of fourteen years! And broken only by a collection of earlier short stories (*The Celestial Omnibus*, 1911) and two small books: a guide-book (one of the most delightful of its kind) to Alexandria, and *Pharos and Pharillon* (witty studies in ancient history); these the fruit of his war-work as a non-combatant in Egypt. It may be that it will be proved some day that his inventive imagination was not as dormant from 1911 to 1924 as it seems to have been; but in any case it is for the critic one significant 'point' about him that a writer with so fine a gift for creating characters should not have been more obsessed by concepts clamouring to be embodied.

Another fourteen years have passed since *A Passage to India*, and, though Mr. Forster published during those years another volume of old short stories, *The Eternal Moment*, a notable biography *Goldsworthy Lowes Dickinson*, *Aspects of the Novel* (delightful and most penetrating criticism), and a collection of his finest commentaries on life in *Abinger Harvest* (Arnold), he has not again sat down to write a novel. Why? The answer is to be found partly in a temperament which is discernible in the fiction which he has written. It is the work of one to whom the private life is most important, and of one moreover who might be expected to be also the author of his pamphlet on 'anonymity' in art (Hogarth Press). But besides this temperamental indifference to success and a distrust of ambition visible in his fiction (he dislikes the characters in his stories who want to get on), there is another explanation which incidentally Miss Rose Macaulay's study of his work reveals—namely, the concentration of his interest upon a few aspects of experience. The themes which excite his creative impulse are few. He has none of that miscellaneous avidity for experience which the great prolific novelists have possessed. Already by 1924 he had repeatedly treated the themes in relation to which his characters interested him most. Hence the comparative smallness, for a novelist with his gifts, of his output in fiction.

'The pattern in the carpet' was easy to discern in his work, and Miss Macaulay's book, though animated and acute, is too long—considering especially the nature of her approach. That approach is through enthusiastic admiration. This is no defect in itself. There is room here for the most delicate appreciation. But when the discussion of any author's limitations or faults is reduced to a minimum, and when the critical problem he presents is not of unusual complexity, brevity is an advantage. She could have said, I think, all she wanted most to say in a long essay one third of the length of this book. When she goes through Mr. Forster's books seriatim, and gives an account of each with ample quotation, her analysis is apt to yield similar results, while her praise is only seldom qualified. This results in a certain monotony, in spite of the author's vivacity. But this can be said of her book, and it is much, that she has proved her points and justified her praise. My criticism is that she need not have assembled so much mutually corroborative evidence to do so. Her description of his 'setting' is excellent, so also that of his mental and moral inheritance:—

A young Englishman of the professional classes, whose forbears had for some generations lived cultured, humane, philanthropic, comfortable, liberal, nineteenth-century kind of lives, of the sort lived by the ancestors of so many of us, and by so few, if any, of ourselves. Gentle, intelligent, high-minded, high-browed, these ancestors of ours look down on us from drawings and paintings on our walls, faintly coloured in their gold frames, their minds set on freeing West Indian slaves, on lightening child labour, on attending Evangelical conferences, on reading good books; whatsoever things are pure, lovely, of good intent, they think, we may be sure, on these things. . . . It is all serene, humane and good, and a bad preparation for the savagery and storms of this age; that is to say, it *looks* serene, humane, and good, for we know that really our ancestors led lives of the greatest inner turbulence, the fiercest spiritual and intellectual conflict, the wildest mental adventure and chaos. . . . E. M. Forster, then, is a product of this kind of liberal bourgeois culture, is also a product of an upper-middle-class school and university, and conditioned more precisely by the fact that his college was King's College, Cambridge, and his Triposes classical and historical. It is apparent that he fell in love with Cambridge.

It was clever of her to perceive the importance of Cambridge in forming his mind and standards. I was aware of that, but then I knew Mr. Forster when he was at Cambridge, and I can measure his debt by my own. His pervasive theme is, as she says, the conflict between Reality and Sham 'embroidered with amusing human detail.'

His main theme is the conflict between 'real' people and sham people. Speaking of his short stories, and it applies to the novels, not excepting *A Passage to India*, she writes:—

In them Reality, Life, Truth, Passion, Gaiety, Nature, Youth, call the thing what you will, fights for its life, in various garbs and with various weapons, against Unreality, Death, Sham, Conventionalism, Dullness, Pompousness, Age. Mr. Forster had a message, and the message was about this eternal battle, in which victory ebbed and flowed, now to one side, now to the other. All life gave him news of the battle. Music gave it to him, as Beethoven gave it to Helen Schlegel.

But it is not by any means always, however, that the two sides are merely good or evil. The subtlety with which he reveals 'culture' sometimes fighting on the side of darkness, or crudity on the side of reality, is one of the most remarkable things about his picture of life.

Still, on the whole, the battle is between the right and the wrong *sort of person.*

As Helen Schlegel put it, 'There are two kinds of people—our kind, who live straight from the middle of their heads, and the other kind who can't, because their heads have no middles. They can't say "I". They *aren't* in fact. . . . No superman ever said, "I want," because "I want" must lead to the question, "Who am I?" and so to Pity and to Justice. He only says "want." "Want Europe," if he's Napoleon; "want wives," if he's Bluebeard; "want Botticelli," if he's Pierpont Morgan. Never the "I"; and if you could pierce through him you'd find panic and emptiness in the middle.'

Mr. Forster's peculiar balance of qualities is more often found in woman than in man; and if I could be confident of not being misunderstood by those who are pleased to consider intellect a masculine speciality, I would add that his point of view, both as a critic and creator, is feminine rather than masculine.

In fiction he has often shown an uncanny insight into the shot-silk complexity of feminine reactions. He can render and suggest, better than any novelist I know, woman's amused protest and her sometimes dazed dismay at the simplifications and peremptory conclusions of the male. This is a man-made world. The bewildered acquiescence and resistance of women in it and to it (I am not thinking merely of their economic disadvantages) is a theme on which he invariably shows the subtlest insight. I am aware that he has something most important to teach me: you must *connect*, connect what you have felt, what you have read, what you have thought with your practical judgments; your judgments must be based on total experience. Absurdities and tragedies, he seems to be saying, are due to the failure to link experiences together—to *connect*. That is Mr. Forster's moral 'message.' Now, the essentially masculine way of taking life is to handle it departmentally. A man says to himself: Here is my home and my private life of personal relation; here is my business, my work; here is my life as a citizen. In each department he has principles according to which situations can be handled as they arise. But in each department these are different. His art of life is to *disconnect* in order to simplify problems. How it would complicate, say, his decisions as a politician, to weigh the consequences of his actions in the scales of individual happiness, such as he undoubtedly would employ in his private life! And how much better the world would run if he did so! The feminine impulse, on the other hand, whether on account of woman's education or her fundamental nature, is to see life more as a continuum. That is part of what I meant by saying that Mr. Forster, both as a creative writer and as a critic, takes the feminine side in life.

Miss Macaulay says of his style that it is too unobtrusively personal to have proved infectious; but she adds, and it is true, that if it could be copied it would be a model. No one's written words reflect more subtlety than his, the inflections of a voice, quick turns of mood, afterthoughts, or the gleam of reflection in advance. His style is unrivalled for loquitive precision. His weakness as a novelist is that crucial events are apt to occur off stage, especially if passion is concerned in them; and it sometimes happens that they are of a nature which must be witnessed if they are to be believed. Helen Schlegel's throwing herself out of sympathy into the arms of the almost entirely unattractive little clerk is the most glaring instance. It might have happened, but seeing is believing in such a case, and we are asked to take it on trust (*Howard's End*). Again, the wooing of Ricky, in *The Longest Journey*, by the unattractive Agnes, is suggested by a phrase: a bird flies in a bird flies out of the dell to which the lovers have retired. Again, the death of her first and real love is inadequately imagined.

159. John Crowe Ransom, 'E. M. Forster', *Kenyon Review*

v (1943), 618–23

John Crowe Ransom (1888–), one of the most important American poets and critics of this century, was born in Tennessee. He was at Oxford as a Rhodes Scholar and has spent his life teaching English, first at Vanderbilt University, Tennessee, then at Kenyon College, Ohio. He was at the centre of the 'Southern Agrarians' and of the group of poets who published their work in *The Fugitive*. He edited the *Kenyon Review* from 1939 to 1959, much of his work being associated with the 'New Criticism'.

The Forster revival is good for us, especially in a time when everybody is planning a new world. The only one of the five novels that was sufficiently known to American readers was *Passage to India*; it remains accessible in the Modern Library edition. The earlier four now receive American editions, two from Alfred Knopf and two from New Directions. From the latter firm comes also a suitable critique, the first of book length to be written about this author, by Lionel Trilling.

All these books should be of the staple of our reading. We need not mind if Forster's matter is extremely English; or if he does not advance any well-considered plan for human society, neither prescribing right political institutions for it nor yet laying down the mores and conventions. The point is that five separate times he has taken a set of characters, indisputably alive, at least middling in virtue, and studied them, head and heart, with uncanny and merciless intelligence. They are we; the translation cannot be escaped. As for the powers of intellect, he finds us wanting in imagination, perceptiveness, the sense of beauty. (We remark that other fine powers in us are operative enough, but probably they are taken for granted by Forster, and do not satisfy him.) As for our affections of the heart, he does not in the least report us as abounding in tolerance, fair play, and gentleness. On the strength of these five exercises—and it has been well argued that a novel by an author of scrupulous realism is a sort of laboratory test—we must concede to Forster the right to have little faith in social establishments such as we have yet realized or even projected.

The novels are 'exposures,' they bear destructively upon our habits and institutions, and wit is their fighting instrument. Forster belongs in the literary tradition which is represented by Samuel Butler II, and by Shaw. Mr. Trilling calls it the Liberal tradition. But Forster elects to fall short of it in one respect, and he transcends it in another.

He falls short because this tradition, while it is destructive, has an obverse side also, quite visible, which is Positive, that is, shows a Plan, and is therefore constructive and hopeful; and Forster scarcely troubles to show this side, as if he were indifferent to its advantages, Plan and all. The Liberal tradition has this side with Butler, if I am not mistaken; has it with Shaw, who says that, if only we will have equality of incomes, all good things will be added unto us; and seems to have it with Mr. Trilling, who does not consider that his personal doctrines belong in the present account and therefore may not name a Positive to his own liking, but registers disappointment with Mr. Forster for indicating almost no worthwhile Positive at all. Liberalism to Forster, when at an early age he espoused it, seems mainly to have meant attacking the bad policies of Joe Chamberlain, the imperialism included, and appealing, comparatively, 'from the left.' But I think, and it would appear from the Trilling book, that he put very few of his eggs in any specific political basket; they would be too easily smashed or spilled out. I am sure that as time went on his thinking had less and less of the political cast, and it grew upon him that politics does indeed touch wide and vital surfaces of life, but scarcely reaches to the heart. As for the total efficacy of social and political formulas, or even as to their necessarily having much or any efficacy, his scepticism is profound. Experience only tempered the iron in this man of an age beset with facile professions of faith. It occurs to us inescapably that the program really acceptable to a scepticism of the depth of Forster's is no program at all, but Benevolent Anarchism: the community of good persons, of whom none would be capable of taking advantage of his superior strength, even in order to impose his superior illumination upon the others. For Forster would like to see men recovering their natural goodness, which may be thought of as subsisting for most of them there under the social institutions, waiting to take back its own responsibilities; and his good commune would be distinct technically from the Christian Community in that it did not take its text out of the natural badness of men. But a natural goodness is an individual goodness, that is, a set of aptitudes and attitudes suitable to the individual who possesses it; consequently, for your social outlook, you need chiefly to respect him, and to leave him alone; but if you must be of use to him you may help him to do what, in God's will, he pleases. To live naturally and let live, and, with the utmost discretion, to help live—that would be Forster's idea of our vocation. As for his pattern for a society, that would be the one which interfered with it the least.

To impute this reasoning to Forster is to read the philosophy and the theology that are only between the lines, and to give him a grand strategy which he never authorized exactly. Yet we catch him in many remarks as droll as such an overt profession would be, and for instance the one about Democracy, in 1939:

So two cheers for Democracy; one because it admits variety, and two because it permits criticism. Two cheers are quite enough: there is no occasion to give three. Only Love the Beloved Republic deserves that.

This was said in the shadow of a war with which Forster has concurred wholly: a war for Democracy, which some were to fight and the rest were to cheer. A little douche of cold water down the necks of the cheerers.

Since this is the Henry James Number, let me say that no novel of Forster's five has the fine ideological texture of the Jamesian stories, which record the fastidious transactions of the opulent, the dedicated, the finished and Olympian society. James had the audacity—which with every passing year seems to us the more brazen—to precipitate his Olympians without apology, as having their blessed existence actually and even being assured in it by some divine right. They are unreal to us now, in the sense that the society of his fiction, though postulated so recently and so coolly, is already gone, or at best is busy fighting for what existence it still has, instead of engaging in its charming arts and functions. Once this society existed, or something like it, for it was not all a fiction. Being aristocratic, and therefore exclusive, it used to exercise its becoming privileges with magnificent disdain for the expense, which was borne—it might be placidly—by the excluded: the faithful servants and artisans who made its domains beautiful and secure. Much of our old fiction took this very line;

it was about properties, and consequent personal tones and stances, too fine to be within the reach of common means; whereas now the earth has quaked beneath them, and they have passed as finally as the perfect courtiers of the Elizabethan stage. James came to this stock fiction with an improved technical facility, wonderfully specialized and modern, but for us the modernity of his methods and the obsolescence of his materials are ironically at odds. He arrived at Olympus late, with rumor of his having had difficulty in obtaining the address. But in Forster's books there is just a trace of the old sumptuary splendors, and as a rule it is only modest possessions that enter into his definition of the good life. In his picture society has been fairly immaterialized; the time falls after its Disestablishment. But it is alive enough to be kicking. The issues fought over in the big scenes of Forster sound blatant and vulgar after a reading of James, but Forster did not impress that character upon them; he received it there. We shall not have in fiction another exquisite like James, to be sure; he would repel us before he could win us by flattery. But I think, I am afraid, that we shall not have many other Forsters; writers with wit enough to dissociate themselves, and their educable readers, from the grimness of those who pursue the spoils, and imagination enough to see that the mansions of beauty were not involved in the fall of kingdoms, but are intact, and commodious as ever.

For so we come to that 'aspect of fiction' in which Forster transcends the others of his modern or Liberal school: the beauty and purity of his English style; and his fertility in ascribing aesthetic vision to the consciousness of his pet characters; or for that matter the reception of the vision into his own consciousness, whenever the occasion rises, which is eternally. I admire Mr. Trilling's critique greatly, for he allows for everything, but what I miss principally is the long and loving labor that might have witnessed worthily to Forster's achievement in this kind.

Without venturing to undertake the labor, I will try a remark or two. I feel confident that it is Meredith to whom, of all his literary exemplars, Forster owes the most. That is comforting because I had almost felt, independently, that the chief greatness of Meredith was to have been the cause that greatness might be in other writers. It was Meredith who conceived of a fiction that might have such a scope, such a pyrotechnic, as drama had in the hands of Shakespeare. From Meredith, then, Forster derives his refreshing collocation of wit and poetry in the first place; as for the wit in particular, the exuberance of it, the tendency to carry things to the point of farce (which Forster resisted far better than Meredith), and the innocence, the absence of venom, for there is no meanness in either man's way of spreading his magnanimous gospel; and, as for the poetry, the daring of it, the ubiquitousness, and I should even add the Greek mythologizing, but that Forster is a better Greek than Meredith, and a Greek in his own right, even beyond other English men of letters with his education. I should take it as a fresh bill of health for Forster if I could establish in his letters a filial relation to Meredith. Nevertheless he is a purified Meredithian, like the second and improved generation of a stock. Forster has a grace where Meredith has an excess, and is surely the wiser for Meredith's lumbering. But perhaps not consciously; Forster may have absorbed his Meredith and then in perfect good faith forgotten him.

Everywhere in Forster there suggests itself an aesthetic dogma which is old and probably cardinal. Like many another novelist, but rather more so, Forster is agrarian in his economic dispositions: he fancies the effect of scene for the right stimulation of his characters, and of his own style. The dogma would have to do with the primacy of scene in developing out sensibility, as in gentling our hearts. Actually, if we are sensitive and if we are happy, we either have our own scene continually spread out before us or we are making a pilgrimage to find one. Forster expects his society to be rooted in its sense of soil, and the best moments of his characters involve their social relations no more than they involve their landscape. He is old style, writing from and about the love of nature. More narrowly, since nature is infinitely versatile, and always local, he writes about English landscape, along with those houses and human 'improvements' which incorporate themselves into that landscape. (But of course, once, there is that brilliant collection of pictures from India.) It sounds very elementary, and it is. But I imagine Forster's landscapes are about the best in English fiction; they are rendered the most distinctly, so that even the subtle ones are conveyed; and they are not often rendered too rapturously though it is plain that they count for everything.

I go a little further with this because the dogmas emerge so patly. There appears in Forster almost a kind of claustrophobia as he seeks his landscapes, and values his houses according to the terms they make with their out-of-doors, and especially as he puts forward the merits of a literal 'untidiness' in both interior an exterior scene. The untidiness looks like a new principle in the aesthetics of landscape, but let us not be too sure about that. Certainly it has distressed some of Forster's readers, and Mr. Trilling looks a little quizzically upon it. But the claustrophobia, the reconciliation with nature's untidiness, would be on the pathological side a flight from the closed, antiseptic, Positive modes of thought and action, and it is not so remarkable in Forster as to seem morbid. And note now the difference between the rich positive quality of an actual object and the neat Positive utility that we make of it,—between the big positive and the little Positive. On the philosophical side, where we give a behavior all its dignity, the claustrophobia must represent an ontological scruple, or even a deep ontological bias: the embrace of the big positive of nature, that crowdedness of material content which never can be really whipped into tidiness, and which is a radical and eternal aspect of the real world. The way in which an artistic representation differs from a Positive one, the way for example in which poetry differs from prose or a poetic prose from a plain prose, is just by embodying this untidiness decisively.

Very likely, it sounds shocking. But many indignant persons who deny it will cheerfully repeat an alternative version: Poetry differs from prose by its 'sweet excess.' Or there are other versions. I conclude with a small qualification to the principle of untidiness. It does not mean to say that the work of the artist or aesthetic man who makes the untidiness beautiful by embracing it is to be identified with the vision of the morbid man, the man of low vitality, to whom it remains ugly and hateful. Love and loathing may be said to result from different visions of reality. But with equal truth it may be said that love and loathing produce different visions, even if the realities which they observe are juridically one and the same. When we say Love or when we say Beauty, we are talking upon a radical orientation of the spirit towards the tangle of things as they are; we are talking about an ontological principle.

TWO CHEERS FOR DEMOCRACY

1951

160. Norman Shrapnel, review, *Manchester Guardian*

6 November 1951, 4

Norman Shrapnel (1912–), journalist, on the staff of the *Manchester Guardian* since 1947, becoming Parliamentary Correspondent in 1958.

. . . He appears to regard civilisation as something that scampers out of holes, like mice, and gets busy while violence sleeps. He finds consolation in the fact—a fact terrifying to most intellectuals—that 'the strong are so stupid'. His attitude is firmer than it pretends to be, and it would surely be desirable to pursue those unfashionable thoughts about tolerance, even at the risk of moulding them into a Belief.

But Mr. Forster pursues nothing. The diversity of these wise bits and pieces is a part of their charm, but it leads to the depressing feeling that Mr. Forster is getting far more nourishment out of it all than we. It is like watching a rare bird—so rare, perhaps, as to be virtually extinct—pecking away at the stony ground and finding all kinds of private succulent things where others find only grit. No wonder he rejects despair; though that, no doubt, is more because it is excessive than through any specific hopefulness. Despair, too, in its way, is an act of faith.

. . . Too often in this book Mr. Forster goes in for the deplorable sort of over-jauntiness that puts one in mind of the popular parson who turns out to be a bit more popular than his flock. He remarks somewhere that when Mr. Eliot is addressing a popular audience, and seeking to instruct, his prose is at its best. This is not true of Mr. Forster.

[. . . . .]

THE HILL OF DEVI

1953

161. Richard Hughes, 'Mr. Forster's quandary', *Spectator*

cxc, 16 October 1953, 432

Richard Hughes (1900–), playwright and novelist. As a novelist he is even more reticent than was Forster; his best-known novel is the brilliant *A High Wind in Jamaica* (1929).

[The review begins with a sequence of quotations to give the flavour of the book.]

What quality, what class of book then is this that Mr. Forster has given us at long last? A major work, or a delicate trifle? When an author so eminent as Mr. Forster has published so little for so long both he and his public are put into a quandary. That next book, when at last it comes—if it has any pretensions to being a major work at all, surely will have to be something stupendous! It has to do much more than just to emulate past works already grown to exemplary status, it has as well (he and we may feel) to outface the accusing decades of virtual silence piled up and still piling up in the scales against him. Consequently we shall open it with jealous suspicion. The more indefatigable kind of author, the book-a-year man, is allowed his occasional licence to publish something inferior now and then, even a blatant pot-boiler masquerading: we permit him to be a little below par in 1953 in the hope that he will be his old self again quite early in 1954. But we can't extend any licence of this sort to the Forsters. That at least is one side of the quandary—Mr. Forster's quandary and ours. Here is a great reputation to enhance, a long period of silence to justify by its fruits. To put it as brutally as possible: if Mr. Forster cannot after all this time give us an even better book than the ones which long ago made him famous, surely he is ill-advised now to break his Trappist vows at all? Better, that in due course he should go down still dumb into the tomb?

But fortunately the quandary has quite another and gentler aspect, another way out (as in India, where every hole you get yourself into is said to have two ends). When an author so eminent as Mr. Forster has written so little for so long, ought we not rather to be grateful for anything—anything at all from his golden pen? A volume of his school essays, his lecture notes, even his laundry lists? In short, for *anything* graceful, provided it makes no masquerade of being a work of the imagination, the awaited masterpiece . . . yes, that is the essential point, it must be something patently unassuming, with no pretence of being a major work.

A bundle of old travel-letters (containing interesting source-material for *A Passage to India*), for example, worked up with a few pages of commentary into a biographical sketch of an unimportant Indian princeling . . . what could be more unassuming, and what, in the quandary, more suitable?

We con the blurb, then, on the wrapper of the new book, and the slightly apologetic preface: we glance at the faintly 'period' frontispiece photograph of H.H. Sir Tukoji Rao III, K.C.I.E., and then—confident that we have guessed right about Mr. Forster and his famous quandary and the way out of it he has chosen—we begin to read in a totally disarmed frame of mind: with a sigh perhaps, because we know we must not expect too much, but prepared to enjoy anything enjoyable however slight. This notion that in *The Hill of Devi* we shall be faced with deliberate triviality, will, indeed, be enhanced by some of the first letters we read, those written during the brief 1912 visit to Dewas State: they are readable, they are intelligent, but for the most part quite undistinguished, and it is only in a passage of commentary that we get our first clear glimpse of the young Maharajah himself: 'His clever, merry little face peeped out of an enormous turban: he was charming, he was lovable, it was impossible to resist him or India.'

But after a brief interlude of descriptive narrative, designed to fill the gap between this fleeting early visit and the months in 1921 when the author returned to Dewas as the Maharajah's temporary private secretary, come the 1921 letters themselves and the narrative passages which link them. This was the period when the two men became really intimate, and this is the backbone of the book. The letters are varied in mood and they are vivid: the serious ones are as vividly serious as the first batch of letters quoted at the head of this review are vividly farcical and somewhere in the course of reading them the entranced reader finds growing in him an uneasy feeling—has he been hoodwinked? Is this after all literature, masquerading as something trivial?

For all the book's brevity and unassuming airs, is it the awaited major work? It would need a critic a good deal more cocksure than the present reviewer, and a longer period of cogitation than any reviewer can hope for, to give an unequivocal answer to that question—especially with so much double-bluffing in the air. For the present a few pointers must suffice, and the reader must decide at his leisure.

It was suggested in these columns a little while ago that a proper description of literature is to call it the self-consciousness of society. From that point of view at any rate this book is certainly literature; for it brings into our consciousness a way of living and feeling and thinking and worshipping that were not there already. The Maharajah, 'certainly a genius, possibly a saint, and he had to be a King': the canvas is small, but as a character he is more vivid and more valuable than any character in *A Passage to India*, for example: he is a person, whereas those (no doubt deliberately) were types. An exceptional person, and the catastrophe of his bankruptcy, his flight to Pondicherry and his death have an imaginative as well as a historical truth which exceeds the more contrived catastrophe of the novel.

Again, *ars est celare artem*—how is the effect produced? It is no belittlement of *A Passage to India* to say that it is always possible to see 'how it is done' (which is a far cry, of course, from pretending one could do it oneself): but the literary machinery of *The Hill of Devi* is subtler: after reading it twice, it is still not easy to see 'how it is done.' There is either consummate conjuring here, or else true magic.

One could continue quoting interminably, and yet the *effect* of the book would somehow continue to slip between one's fingers. For this effect is an effect of the whole, and not to be found in any of the parts, nor can the eye see quite *how* the parts combine to create it. Thus we are brought back to the earlier question: has an unwary reviewer allowed himself to succumb to a particularly skilful double bluff—or is this in fact a piece of *literature*, a major work of its author, something that perhaps will live in the minds of readers of a generation which shall label *A Passage to India* as no more than a skilful political tract?

162. L. P. Hartley, 'Life with the Maharajah', *Time and Tide*

24 October 1953, 1392

It is a platitude to say it, but one of the saddest gaps in the bookshelves of contemporary literature is the space that should be occupied by the unwritten works of Mr E. M. Forster. Here is a novelist with almost all the gifts, and yet it is nearly thirty years since he exercised them on the grand scale of *A Passage to India*. Mr Lionel Trilling has said that he 'declined greatness'; he made the *gran rifiuto*. It is true that Mr Forster has always carefully weeded from his work qualities which are sometimes found in company with greatness—self-assurance, an orotund manner, sententiousness, priggishness, all the signs that an author is taking himself seriously. He abhors what Sir Walter Scott called 'the big bow-wow'. But we have it on Scriptural authority that the most important messages are not delivered in the loudest voice.

And may it not also be true that greatness has itself declined in another sense, declined almost to vanishing point, and that though Mr Forster may have declined it, it is no longer there for him to decline? How many writers of today have taken up the challenge that Mr Forster is said to have refused? Greatness is no longer esteemed and sought after as it used to be. The title of Lytton Strachey's famous book not only poked fun at the Victorians, it poked fun at eminence itself. Democracy may come to include a levelling even of letters.

But great or not great, Mr Forster is one of the most enchanting writers of our time. Opposed as I am to every form of physical compulsion I should look with veneration on a heavy chain that had kept him bound to his writing table for six days out of seven. But putting aside vain regrets let me welcome his new book.

The Hill of Devi is an account of Mr Forster's experiences in the Indian State of Dewas Senior. He was there in 1912 and 1913 and again in 1921, first as a visitor and then as private secretary to the Maharajah, HH Sir Tukoji Rao III, KCIE, known more familiarly as Bapu Sahib; and the book is composed of the letters he wrote home, with a commentary connecting and expanding them. Of the letters in their original form he says:

> Most of my letters were addressed to my mother and other relatives. They are unfortunately none the better on that account. I was writing to people of whom I was fond and whom I wanted to amuse, with the result that I became too humorous and conciliating, and too prone to turn remote and rare matters into suburban jokes. . . . I hope that the fineness of Dewas Senior as well as its strangeness may occasionally shine through. It was the great opportunity of my life.

Here in a nutshell is Mr Forster's own criticism of his book; I don't think the reader will subscribe to it. Perhaps Mr Forster's alleged refusal to be great arises from a disinclination to reconcile two things notoriously hard to reconcile: a serious intention and an 'amusing surface'. For it is not only his friends and relations that Mr Forster has always wished to entertain, it is his public too. Few writers can have felt more strongly than he the obligation to be amusing; few more deeply than he the serious nature of what he is being amusing about.

Mr Forster's dislike of 'telling a story' is well known; a story, he says, is the highest factor common to all novels, but he wishes he could substitute for it something different, 'melody, or perception of the truth'. One might say that in *The Hill of Devi* we get melody and a perception of the truth, and a story as well.

The Maharajah is the hero of it: 'Certainly a genius and possibly a saint, and he had to be a king.' Born in 1888, he was nine years younger than his secretary-to-be. Civilized himself and setting great store by civilization, interested in ideas and widely read, he was at the same time a child of Nature whose moods were incalculable. But though you could not understand him you could rely on him. Mr Forster remarks:

> It was possible with him to reach a platform where calculations were unnecessary. It would not be possible with an Englishman.

For the camera he sat with oriental calm; but for a word portrait he was most elusive; and in spite of the many lights thrown on him he remains to the end an enigma, with enigma variations. 'He is generous, enthusiastic, touchy', reports one observer, and Mr Forster writes of his 'nobility, unselfishness, introspectiveness'. Two things are certain: he had a genius for friendship and a genius for religion. Mr Forster quotes some of his remarks.

It is only for the sake of those who love us that we do things. (A dangerous doctrine, Mr Forster comments.)

And again,

I am always hypnotizing myself into the belief that a situation is bearable.

Friendship, religion ('I am going to be holy for two hours'), intrigue—these are three of the aspects in which he appears most consistently; the third was to help to bring about his ruin.

Mr Forster enjoyed and valued the friendship and, as readers of *A Passage to India* will expect, he was intensely interested in the religion. The description of the eight days' ceremony leading up to the birth of Krishna is one of the highlights of this book. Some of its manifestations were silly, many were funny, few, to the European eye, were beautiful; and yet beauty and spirituality shine through the whole experience, as Mr Forster means they should.

The book is not obviously sign-posted: one has to pick things up as one can, following Mr Forster's quick eye and nimble mind. Putting on Indian dress he also, to some extent, took on Indian ideas; these were not necessarily critical of the British Raj, far from it, but they reflect the waywardness, playfulness and inconclusiveness of the Indian mind, and its awareness of mystery. As Indians would be, he is made touchy by 'the Insult'. Small, mirth-provoking happenings feed his delight in the ironical and the absurd. He tells us much about the relations of Indians and Englishmen, but indirectly and allusively. Page by page the effect of the book is piecemeal; but its dates give it a shape and a frame, and the Maharajah's tragic end rounds it off with aesthetic completeness. Only when we see him suffering do we realize how much, in the earlier stages, he has engaged our affections.

MARIANNE THORNTON

1956

163. Graham Hough, 'Bachelor aunt', *Spectator*

cxcvi, 11 May 1956, 663

Graham Hough (1908–), formerly Professor of English at the University of Malaya, has been Professor of English at Cambridge since 1966. He has published a number of important critical books, including *The Last Romantics* (1949) and his sensible study of D. H. Lawrence, *The Dark Sun* (1957).

Marianne Thornton was Mr. Forster's great-aunt, and she lived from 1797 to 1887. She was a managing young woman and she grew to be a more managing old one; her career was not markedly different from that of many wealthy Evangelical ladies in the nineteenth century. Since she was born in the bosom of the Clapham sect her early life affords many intimate glimpses of Wilberforces, Macaulays and other members of the circle; and since, with her handsome masculine face and her autocratic ways she was a predestinate bachelor aunt, her story resolves itself into the story of the Thornton family. Not even Mr. Forster's charming piety can cast much of a glow on this particularly uncharming clan. Good works, money and a dense family conceit form their principal preoccupations. Those who marry into the family, unless they are rich and pious, are disapproved of, or patronised, or suppressed. Those who marry out of the group, unless they marry the rich and pious, are harassed and cut off, or visited just often enough to mark the communal distaste. One of the few moments of exhilaration occurs when Henry Thornton, that pillar of banking respectability, in the teeth of the law and family condemnation, marries his deceased wife's sister, and lives happily with her in the family house till the end of his days.

The latter part of Marianne Thornton's life was occupied with that oppressive elevation of the poor that would have excused a more than Russian revolution; though I suppose one must admit that in fact it helped to prevent one. Much of the story is told by selection from the oceanic flood of correspondence in which the members of this family continually, as the century majestically unrolls, exhort, advise, discuss, reprove and sometimes commend each other—everything except leave each other alone. Mr. Forster is careful to condemn what evidently demands condemnation, and he praises temperately what merits praise. But, for once, his tone is less than impeccable; it seems to suggest a partial reconciliation with that high-minded commual bullying which it was formerly his main business to reject.

164. Ronald Bryden, review, *Cambridge Review*

12 May 1956, 536

Henry Thornton, the Evangelical banker and M.P. for Southwark, died in 1815, leaving three sons and six daughters, the eldest named Marianne, the second youngest Laura. Laura Thornton married a Welsh clergyman, the Rev. Charles Forster, and had a son, Edward, who in turn married and produced, in 1879, a son who was christened Edward Morgan. Eight years later, Marianne Thornton died at the age of ninety, bequeathing to this great-nephew of hers a legacy which enabled him to go to Cambridge, travel to Italy and India, and become the finest English novelist, so far, of this century. This book is E. M. Forster's memorial to his benefactress: a work of piety and affection, and also of extraordinary fascination and art.

A good deal of its fascination is historical. Mr Forster sub-titles it 'a domestic biography'; but the domestic life of the Thorntons at Battersea Rise, their vast old house on Clapham Common, was led only just behind some of the more stirring scenes of the early nineteenth century. Henry Thornton was a leading member of the 'Clapham Sect', and his house became a meeting place for its elders—the Venns, Grants, Macaulays and Stephens. Hannah More and Wilberforce were intimate friends, with whom he worked closely in the cause of Abolition and popular education. The Thornton children used to visit the More sisters down in Somerset, where they lived with two old servants and a couple of cats named Non-Resistance and Passive Obedience, and be regaled with country fare and tales of Hannah's early friendships with Burke, Dr Johnson and Horace Walpole. Marianne became, after her father's death, the Sect's chief correspondent with Hannah, bed-ridden now, and had to describe for her the triumphant May Meeting of 1824, when Tom Macaulay burst to fame with a blazing speech against slavery. Wilberforce, so oddly child-like himself, often played with them in Battersea Rise garden; there, after one painful afternoon trying, with a parliamentary deputation, to persuade a half-drunken Queen Caroline to renounce her coronation for an allowance from George IV, he came to solace his spirit among the flowers, and was overheard murmuring praises to a tranquil, splendid moss-rose, ending 'And Oh how unlike the Queen's countenance!'

Other windows open more generally on the past. Marianne visits Waterloo with her guardians in 1817, and boys offer her bones, buttons and hair for sale. She attends a meeting of Edward Irving's apocalyptic 'church', and compares the shouts of its spirit-taken witnesses, shuddering, to the unforgettable screams of a cousin operated on at Battersea Rise some years earlier, for cancer perhaps, without anaesthetics. And the central incident of her life opens a particularly curious window upon a dead world of conscience. The Thornton clan were broken, exiled from the family home they loved almost better than bridegrooms, by the decision of Marianne's brother, Henry Thornton the younger, to marry his deceased wife's sister. To us, the old prohibition is a footnote to *Culture and Anarchy*, a joke in *Major Barbara*. To them, it is tragedy and ruin. Wounding letters fly. Angry sisters, vicious with the shame, shut their doors forever on their brother and the wanton sister-in-law. Defiant, the outcast pair flee abroad to perform the incestuous rite. Battersea Rise stands empty, dishonoured. Only Marianne, homeless after fifty years at her brother's side, bewildered between love and revulsion, struggles to save something from the wreck: a suspicious truce, a melancholy amity.

But inevitably, the light Mr Forster sheds on his family and the past cannot interest us as much as the light he allows them to shed on him. In form, the book is a proper Victorian memoir, told mainly by the letters and diaries of the subject; but in format, it is a companion to *The Hill of Devi*, and like that volume, lets biography shade into autobiography. Unobtrusively, Mr Forster is always at the reader's elbow, pointing and appraising, delighted by Marianne's kindly practicality where it is a question of family or baby-schools, depressed by her heavy little jibes at Jews and governesses, her Victorian fascination with deathbeds. And he reveals himself not only in judging her. He places her, finally, in family mythology: the family mythology in which he himself grew up, a precocious and didactic small boy. Battersea Rise was its lost Eden, the sin of his great-uncle Henry and poor Emily Dealtry its Fall. Marianne becomes the Moses who guides the tribe through the wilderness, the custodian of the family covenant and laws. We leave her as the small boy saw her: the last great trunk proclaiming where the fallen oak-circle of the older Thorntons stood, asserting their order with a majesty his rebellious young mother and aunts, Darwinians and bluestockings, may resent, but never deny. We are allowed to see the tradition from which he escaped, by which he is still held.

The mythology gives the book its structure, as subtle as any of the novels. Gradually we realise that it entails a theme, as profound as any of theirs. We stumble on it with Mr Forster's comment upon one of the foolish cruelties which rose out of the family smash. Marianne had invited Henry's children to stay with her during their father's and their aunt's honeymoon. Their coming was agreed, a day and hour promised. At the last minute, vindictive with jealousy and fear, the step-mother changes her mind without writing. The hours pass, they do not arrive.

> Anyone who has waited in vain for a beloved person will understand what she felt. A wound has been inflicted which no subsequent reunion quite heals. The insecurity against which we all struggle has taken charge of us for a moment—for the moment which is eternity. The moment passes, and perhaps the beloved face is seen after all and the form embraced, but the watcher has become aware of the grave.

We recognise that insecurity. The universe of the novels is built upon it. It is the formless, terrifying inanity which Ansell detected at the heart of Agnes Pembroke's character, in *The Longest Journey*: the hollowness Margaret Schlegel knew to reside at the heart of Napoleons and Pierpont Morgans, the men without identity who cannot say 'I', but only 'Want this, want that'. It is the Thing which confronts Adela Quested and Mrs Moore in the booming blackness of the Marabar Caves, reducing heroism to filth, friends to unpredictable enemies. Against it, men struggle to build order: to bridge its abysses with love and trust, to combat its meaningless chaos with art and understanding. Our weapon is connection—'Only connect . . .' —and Marianne, for all her limitations, knows how to wield it, turning love and memory to the task of holding together her family. She emerges as a heroine of the war against panic and emptiness, to stand besides Mrs Wilcox and Mrs Moore.

The last letters fall into place like stones of an arch. Suddenly and graciously, she writes asking her ostracised sister-in-law for some milk from Battersea Rise. To her five-year-old nephew she relates how at his age, almost a century before, she was taken by her father to the opening of Parliament, and heard mad old George III address the crowd as 'My Lords and Peacocks.' Her longest bridges are completed, the huge wastes of time she has come through forced into pattern and significance. Mr Forster, who has built so enduringly upon the foundation his great-aunt gave him, has repaid her in this book with the currency she taught her descendants to value—bricks against oblivion.

165. Naomi Lewis, 'A cri-de-cœur', *New Statesman & Nation*

li, no. 1313, 12 May 1956, 536

A fragment from a review.

[. . . . .] The old lady doted on him. Alas, in those early, arrogant years, the affection was not entirely returned.

And we, as readers, may share this reserve. What Aunt Marianne lacks for us is the quality of fiction, Mr. Forster's fiction. If only he had invented her!

166. Pete Hamill, 'The totemization of E. M. Forster'

27 June 1965

'Totem is Taboo', review of the Harvest Books (USA) edition of *Two Cheers for Democracy* in the *Washington Post*, reprinted by permission of the Washington Post Company.

Pete Hamill, journalist and novelist, was born in Brooklyn in 1905. He joined the staff of the *New York Post* in 1960 and was a columnist for that newspaper for two years.

For some time now I have had an increasingly nauseous reaction to the totemization of E. M. Forster. A writer of light entertainments in the distant past, he is increasingly being put forth as the greatest living novelist, apparently on the peculiar grounds that he had the courage to abandon the novel in 1924, after publication of *A Passage to India*.

Because of his age (he is now 86), Forster has also become a kind of Bertrand Russell or Pablo Casals of literature; his utterances, presumably based on a long and civilized life, are supposed to be more important than anything said by, say, John Osborne. Unlike Russell, whose political pronouncements have become increasingly silly, Forster has never been idiotic in public. But like all totems these days, it seems impossible to escape his presence; one dreads picking up book reviews, literary gazettes or books of criticism, knowing that it must be time again for still another birthday, another fawning appraisal, another essay entitled 'A Passage to India After Twenty-Five Years.' Again this prim nanny of the novel will be brought forth as a vigorous champion. Again the insiders will speculate on the quality of the homosexual novel Forster will not allow to be published until after his death.

One receives visions of Forster in a glass case in the Antiquities Department at Cambridge, scholars grouped about him singing reverently from hymnals (with titles like *A Room With a View*, *The Longest*

Journey and *Howards End* engraved in Old English on the backs), all to the muted strains of Gregorian Chant. Occasionally in this vision, the case would be opened, and Forster would be dusted off for an interview with the guys from The Paris Review, or a visit from some Midwestern Romantic who is getting his jollies in a term paper entitled 'Echoes and Cave Images in 19th and 20th Century Literature Produced by the Bloomsbury Group: Identity and Paradox.'

In short, I have felt about E. M. Forster the way I feel when I see still another tearful photo of good old Judy Garland in still more personal difficulties across the front page of still another edition of the *New York Post.* On those mornings I feel like running through the streets screaming Enough Already! I don't want to know any more about her, and for the love of Almighty God, let's get on with something else! If E. M. Forster is a great novelist, Cardinal Spellman is Thomas Aquinas.

But after a week with Forster's essays, I do have to cop out a bit. I still don't think he is much of a novelist (he might have been in 1924, but even *A Passage to India* seems frail today). But the essays and radio broadcasts published in *Two Cheers For Democracy* are excellent, finely-boned and shot through with the civilizing qualities which his novels are supposed to possess. In a way, these essays are another example of Norman Podhoretz's theory that many novelists produce much better discursive writing than novels, because they are allowed the freedom to come out and say what they want to say, without the hampering effect of the novel's essentially limiting form.

'I do not believe in Belief' Forster begins, in the central essay of the collection and goes on to outline the principles by which he has lived his life, principles which he implies others might well follow. Forster feels that in our time, the worst sins have been caused by the True Believers, and that the only way for civilized man to continue living his life is through withdrawal from anything that smells of dogma. 'Faith, to my mind, is a stiffening process,' he writes, 'a sort of mental starch, which ought to be applied as sparingly as possible.'

A man who feels that way can never become some lay Calvinist, or a James Baldwin whining his threats at a presumably impressed world. Instead, he makes friendship—that poor, abused state which has been derided nearly to death by the psychiatrists, the political charlatans, and the hipsters—he makes friendship the basic structure of a life. This is not much to hope for, perhaps, but it is at least something.

Forster is, of course, an Englishman, one of the most English writers I have ever read, and it is not surprising that he makes reliability a corollary of friendship. For Forster it is impossible to maintain friendship without reliability. 'But reliability is not a matter of contract—that is the main difference between the world of personal relationships and the world of business relationships,' he writes. 'It is a matter of the heart, which signs no documents.'

He is, of course, a liberal, an example of the liberal intelligence at its best. But he is not the kind of liberal who runs for office; the last thing he would do is read John Stuart Mill to a kid jammed-up on a rape charge. But he does believe in tolerance and in freedom and is against any encroachment of that freedom by the State. 'I realize that all society rests upon force,' he says, 'but all the great creative actions, all the decent human relations occur during the intervals when force has not managed to come to the front. These intervals are what matter. I want them to be as frequent and as lengthy as possible, and I call them "civilization".'

It occurred to me that Forster, like Lord Acton, might eventually be remembered by a small remark that is really marginal to his major work. Acton talked about Power. Forster wrote a sentence that is one of the most quoted of our time, because in a time of inhuman abstractions, it was the most human. It is in this book.

'I hate the idea of causes,' he wrote, 'and if I had to choose between betraying my country and betraying my friend, I hope I should have the guts to betray my country.'

The man who wrote that would probably be the first to object to his totemization. Anyway, I like to think so.

MAURICE

1914 version

167. Edward Carpenter, letter to E. M. Forster

23 August [?1914]

Edward Carpenter's important essay on the homosexual temperament, 'The Intermediate Sex', was published in 1908. Forster was attracted by Carpenter's ideas and, in September 1913, he visited him at his farm near Sheffield. There he received (as he recounts in his 'Terminal Note' of 1960 to *Maurice*) the direct inspiration for his novel. *Maurice* was finished, in its first form, in July 1914.

I *have* read your *Maurice* after all, and am very much pleased with it. I don't always like your rather hesitating tantalising impressionist style —though it has subtleties—but I think the story has many fine points. You succeed in giving the atmosphere round the various characters, and there are plenty of happenings which is a good thing. Maurice's love affairs are all interesting, and I have a mind to read them again, if I can find time—so I won't send the ms. back for a day or two. I am so glad you end up with a major chord. I was so afraid you were going to let Scudder go at the last—but you saved him and saved the story, because the end though improbable is not impossible and is the one bit of real romance—which those who understand will love.

168. Lytton Strachey, letter to E. M. Forster

12 March 1915

Lytton Strachey (1880–1932), the author of *Eminent Victorians* (1918), was educated at Liverpool University and at Cambridge, where he was influenced by the ideas of G. E. Moore and met the people—John Maynard Keynes, Forster, Desmond MacCarthy, Leonard Woolf, Clive Bell—who were later to form, along with Virginia Woolf and others, the 'Bloomsbury Group'. Strachey worked for the *Spectator* and in 1912 published *Landmarks in French Literature*. During the First World War he was a Conscientious Objector and lived near Marlborough, from where this letter was written.

The 'morbid and unnatural' concern which Strachey criticises in Forster's attitude to sexual contact may be contrasted with Strachey's own fresher approach to such matters, as revealed in his short epistolary novel *Ermyntrude and Esmeralda*, completed in 1914 and much enjoyed by his Bloomsbury friends. Like *Maurice*, however, it had to wait for publication until much later, in 1969 (by Anthony Blond).

I should have written before, but I have been laid up with some horror or other—the Dr. says influenza—I think a chill—but anyhow it's been very unpleasant, and I'm only just beginning to feel that I exist again, after about a week in bed. Your novel was an agreeable surprise in the middle of it. I enjoyed it very much indeed—I think really more than the others. The absence of the suburb-culture question was a relief. I wish I could talk to you about it—the difficulty and boredom of epistolary explanations is rather great.

Qua story, first.—I thought it seemed to go off at the end to some extent. The beginning—especially up to the successful combination of Maurice and Clive—I liked very much: it appeared solid and advanced properly from point to point. The psychology of both excellent. The Maurice–Alec affair didn't strike me as so successful. For one thing, the Class question is rather a red herring, I think. One suddenly learns that Maurice is exaggeratedly upper-classish—one wouldn't at all have expected it in the face of things—and then when the change comes, it seems to need more explanation. No doubt his falling in love with Alec was possible, but it's certainly queer as it happens—perhaps because the ground isn't enough prepared: and Alec's feelings I don't quite seize. As you describe it, I should be inclined to diagnose Maurice's state as simply lust and sentiment—a very wobbly affair; I should have prophecied a rupture after 6 months—chiefly as a result of lack of common interests owing to class differences—I believe even such a simple-minded fellow as Maurice would have felt this—and so your Sherwood Forest ending appears to me slightly mythical. Perhaps it simply is that the position isn't elaborated enough. The writing gets staccato (for the first time) at the end of Ch. xliv—just at the crisis. 'Adamantine', too, can't be right.

This is my main criticism of the story—I wonder if you'll see anything in it. A minor point is that I find it *very* difficult to believe that Maurice would have remained chaste during those 2 years with Clive. He was a strong healthy youth, and you say that, unless Clive had restrained him 'he would have surfeited passion' (Ch. xv). But how the Dickens could Clive restrain him? How could he have failed to have erections? Et après ça—? Well! I suppose it's just conceivable, but I must say I think you seem to take it rather too much as a matter of course.

I admire the cleverness very much. The opening scene with Mr. Ducie is very good, and his reappearance 10 years later. The upper class conversations and that awful household in the country—how can you do it? Then the ingenuity of the machinery—e.g. the piano-moving incident—seems to me . . . 'supreme'! I like enormously Alec's letters. Is it true that the lower classes use 'share' in that sense?—I must find out.

There remains the general conception—about which I don't feel at all certain. I don't understand why the copulation question should be given so much importance. It's difficult to distinguish clearly your views from Maurice's sometimes, but so far as I can see, you go much too far in your disapproval of it. For instance, you apparently regard the Dickie incident with grave disapproval. Why? Then, à propos of Maurice tossing himself off (you call it a 'malpractice') (Ch. xxxii), you say—'He knew what the price would be—a creeping apathy towards all things.' How did Maurice know that? And how do you? Surely the truth is that as often as not the effects are simply nil. Also (Ch. xxxi) you describe Maurice's thoughts in the railway carriage as 'ill-conditioned'—which appears to me the sort of word Mr. Herbert Pembroke would have used.

It almost seems that you mean to indicate that Maurice's copulating with Alec is somehow *justified* by his falling in love with him. This alarms me considerably. I find the fatal sentence inserted (Ch. xliii—British Museum)—'he loved Alec, loved him not as a second Dickie Barry, but deeply, tenderly, for his own sake, etc.' More distressing still, there is never a hint afterwards that Maurice's self-reproaches during that period were exaggerated. I think he had still a great deal to learn, and that the très-très-noble Alec could never teach it him. What was wanted was a brief honeymoon with that charming young Frenchman who would have shown Mr. Eel that it was possible to take the divagations of a prick too seriously.

Another thing is—perhaps even more important—that you really do make a difference between affairs between men and men and those between men and women. The chastity between Maurice and Clive for the 2 years during which they were in effect married you consider (a) as a very good thing and (b) as nothing *very* remarkable. You then make Clive marry (without any change in his high-falutin' views) and promptly, quite as a matter of course, have his wife. (So that when he said to Maurice 'I love you as if you were a woman', he was telling a lie.) I really think the whole conception of male copulation in the book rather diseased—in fact morbid and unnatural. The speechification by which Maurice refuses to lie with Alec on the last night—no!—That is a sort of self-consciousness which would *only* arise when people were *not* being natural. It is surely beastly to think of copulation on such an occasion—shall we copulate? shall we not? ought we to? etc.—All one can think of is that one must embrace.

I could write a great deal more—especially about 'the triviality of contact for contact's sake'—but it's too difficult, and I feel half the time that you have satisfactory answers. I wish we could talk. I hope to be in London before very long. I hope this critique isn't too much of a good thing, and will fit in nicely along with those of Bob Trey,[1] Waterloo,[2] and Hilton Young.[3]

[1] Bob Trey was Robert Calverley Trevelyan (1872–1951), son of Sir George Otto Trevelyan, Bt, O.M., who held various important public offices between 1868 and

Footnotes continued overleaf.

1892. Robert Trevelyan, like Strachey, was educated at Trinity College, Cambridge; he published numerous books of verse (including *Mallow and Asphodel*, 1898) and translations from the classics.

[2] Waterloo was Sidney (later Sir Sidney) Waterlow (1878–1944), educated at Trinity College, Cambridge, and later employed in the Diplomatic Service. He published translations of the *Medea* and *Hippolytus* in 1906, and a study of Shelley in 1912.

[3] Edward Hilton Young (1879–1960) was also educated at Trinity College, Cambridge, and was called to the Bar in 1904. In the First World War he served with distinction in the Navy (also publishing *A Muse at Sea* in 1919), and in 1922 he married the widow of Captain Scott (of the Antarctic). He was a Liberal M.P. from 1915 to 1935, spending the last four years as Minister of Health. He was created Lord Kennet in 1935.

The comments on *Maurice* by these three, which Strachey refers to, have unfortunately not come to light among Forster's papers.

MAURICE

1971

169. C. P. Snow, 'Open windows', *Financial Times*

7 October 1971

C. P. Snow (Lord Snow) was born in Leicester in 1905. He has had a varied career as a scientist, academic, senior civil servant, and novelist. He is best known to the general public for his sequence of novels entitled *Strangers and Brothers*.

It was known for many years that E. M. Forster had written an explicity homosexual novel. At one time, everyone in certain literary circles seemed to have read it in manuscript. One used to hear the question whispering round: ought he to publish it? He didn't, in his own lifetime. The book, it now appears from Mr. P. N. Furbank's introduction, was largely written in 1913–14, that is after *Howard's End* (1910) and before the final novel, *A Passage to India* (1924). Now, in 1971, Forster's literary executors have decided to let it free. In my view, they hadn't any choice.

I will give the reasons later. They are not the merits of the work itself. Although it exhibits some of Forster's good qualities, it makes even more clear his major weaknesses.

The novel is very short, and the story simple. Maurice is a good-looking athletic youth, without distinguished intelligence or insight. He comes from what Forster calls a 'suburban' family, but the usage has changed. Maurice is more than comfortably off, belongs to the moneyed upper middle-class, goes to a public school and Cambridge, where he has social contacts with young men recognisably in the Lytton Strachey circle. All through his school-days Maurice has been vaguely disturbed about his sexual make-up. At Cambridge, in his own college, he meets another young man, Clive, who has from the age of 15 been certain about his own sexual make-up. Clive is a 'county gentleman,' high-principled, clever: he recognises at once that he is in love with Maurice, who after various false starts, tentatives, quarrels decides that he returns the love. In fact, after walking through the court in distress one night, he climbs through Clive's window and gets into bed with him. Although Clive isn't in doubt about his homosexuality or Maurice's, he imposes the rule that the relation must be kept chaste: and this Maurice cheerfully and happily accepts.

The relation continues in this sublimated Edward Carpenter-like fiction (the book was begun under the influence of Carpenter) for several years: and then, almost overnight, Clive realises that his tastes have been transmogrified. He is now exclusively heterosexual. This happens in his mind, without the physical intervention of a woman. Maurice can't believe it. But in time, after much grief, he has to believe it, for Clive gets married and sets up as a respectable landowner (and prospective Tory M.P.) on his ancestral estate. There Maurice visits him, still hankering after a return of love. He is totally abandoned. He even visits a hypnotist, to see if he too can become heterosexual. But on Clive's land is employed a young gamekeeper. He catches sight of Maurice and falls in love with him.

Once more, in the most casual of meetings, Maurice realises that something unexplained has happened to himself. One night, staying in Clive's house, he calls out of his bedroom window yearningly into the dark. Once more some window climbing, this time by Alec the gamekeeper. He duly gets into bed.

The book ends with Maurice explaining to Clive that he and Alec propose to live together like 'outlaws.' Clive is horrified. We are left to assume that he won't meet Maurice again but that Maurice and Alec are going to enjoy a fully sexual and satisfactory life.

About a piece of advice by Maurice's grandfather, Forster remarks that 'it was sincere, it came from a living heart.' Almost exactly the same could be said about this novel. It is sincere, desperately so. First, and least significant, it is an expression of sexual guilt. Most of this guilt Clive and Maurice (not the gamekeeper, who is represented as an example of working class pagan innocence, that curious creation of the bourgeois early 20th century mind) would believe to be caused by the social and legal climate in which they were living. But compare Proust. There is a weight of sexual guilt in *Sodome et Gomorrhe* although Proust's characters and Proust himself were living in an appreciably more tolerant society, and one where Charlus and Morel at least weren't in danger of any kind of legal prosecution. Of course, the Wolfenden Report did good: it would have banished fears from these decent and honourable people of 50 years before; but it wouldn't have removed everything.

However, that isn't the main point of the book. It is a novel with a purpose, and the purpose is to proclaim that homosexual love, in its fullest sense, can be happy and enduring. Hence the ecstatic ending. It rings artistically quite wrong, as a wish-fulfilment: and yet anyone who reads it will hope, without any knowledge of the biography, that for the writer the wish ultimately came true.

In literary terms, though, the purpose—as with most explicit purposes in art—cripples the novel. It brings out, and exaggerates, all Forster's lack of feeling for people different from those he mixed with. The Wilcoxes in *Howard's End* are pretty fair cardboard: here we have the same dismissal, only more contemptuous—'throughout life he had been the ordinary business man.' Except in the writer's mind, what in God's name is the ordinary businessman? It is only very spasmodically in *Maurice* that the characters exist in their own freedom. Maurice himself is well done, and it wasn't easy for a very clever and subtle man to create convincingly a dull one: but, aside from his sexual predicament, the rest of his life is shadowy. So—and again this is an exaggeration of a common Forster weakness—is the grip on the physical world. This applies to illness as much as to sex: Edwardian medicine wasn't so highly developed as our own, but writers like Bennett dealt far less vaguely with physical sickness than Forster does. There is even—shades of Dean Farrar, who is not far away from other passages in the novel—a reference to *brainfever*.

As for the ordinary avocations which these young men must have had, and the games which Maurice is reported as enjoying, Forster is as remote as a rather miffish observer from Japan, and frequently gets the most commonplace idioms wrong. His ear lets him down with a dull thud. The cricket match at Clive's country house is the most absurd and incomprehensible since Dingley Dell. None of this would matter so much if he weren't writing about supposedly hearty young men. There it shows, more nakedly than in his other novels, the blinkering of his interest and vision.

In that case, should the book have been published at all? As I said before, his executors really had no choice. If a writer of Forster's reputation leaves unpublished manuscripts, they are going to be produced some time or other, and it might as well be now as later. Forster himself seems to have attached—understandably enough—great value to the book, and probably wanted it published. If he didn't, he was experienced enough to have destroyed it.

Will it affect his reputation? Very little I fancy. With committed Forsterians, and there are plenty, not at all. With those like myself, who have always had doubts, those doubts won't be strengthened, because this book merely underlines what has been felt for a long time: that there is a weakening ambiguity in his novels which is not the result of art but a kind of equivocation. For instance, 'personal relations' often didn't mean what persons outside his private world took them to mean. Reticences are usually not damaging to high art, but evasions sometimes can be.

Anyway, many of us passionately devoted or more qualified, have made up our minds. The interesting question remains, how this book will affect readers under say 30. To a good many, even among the most intelligent and imaginative, I suspect it will seem utterly distant, possibly without meaning. They ought to realise, though, that in a sense, not so much literally as historical, this book was true, not of many people, but of a section of a small class, for a short period. They may have been unlucky in their temperaments and sexually diffident: but it did happen, and just for once, we can say that things are somewhat better now.

170. Walter Allen, 'The least of Forster', *Daily Telegraph*

7 October 1971

Walter Allen (1911–), novelist (*All in a Lifetime*) and critic, is the author of two of the best guides to the novel, *The English Novel* (1954) and *Tradition and Dream* (1964). He is at present Professor of English at the New University of Ulster.

This posthumous novel of E. M. Forster's, which comes with an introduction by his biographer, P. N. Furbank, and a postscript by Forster himself, dated 1960, was written in 1913–14, worked on at intervals over the years and, according to Mr. Furbank, 'revised once more, fairly drastically, in 1959–60.' On the cover of the 1960 typescript, Mr. Furbank tells us, Forster wrote, 'Publishable—but worth it?'

Worth it? Of course. Anything by a novelist of Forster's distinction is worth publishing. We did not have it during his life because it is a novel about homosexuality written at a time when the subject was taboo in fiction. As Forster makes plain, its origin lay in the acceptance of his own homosexuality. It is a thesis novel, a plea for the public recognition of the homosexual and his right to express his love.

The plot is simple. Maurice Hall discovers his condition at Cambridge when he and Clive Durham, another undergraduate, fall in love with each other. But Clive, in Greece, realises that for him homosexuality is merely a stage in growing pains when he falls in love with a girl, whom he marries. Maurice as lover is cast aside and he is forced to face his condition—'congenital homosexuality'—and its consequences. Staying in the country with Clive and his wife, he meets a young gamekeeper, spontaneous, uninhibited, a kind of Noble Savage, with whom, I think we are expected to believe, he settles down for life.

The novel will not, I think, cause anyone to change his notions of Forster as a man or of his stature as a novelist. If it had come to us anonymously, it would have been recognisably Forster's. Yet I am bound to say that of all his novels it seems to me the least in literary value. He himself realised it was dated. Dated, I think, in a way in which the earlier novel, *The Longest Journey*, over which, if I read it right, the shadow of homosexuality hovers, is not. Simply, *The Longest Journey* contains more of Forster.

In *Maurice* Forster was writing a thesis novel. It was a brave thing to do and would have been a braver one if he had striven to publish it. But the faults are those of the thesis novel, the over-concentration on a single issue. And reading *Maurice*, one can't fail to be struck by the difference 60 years have made in our attitude towards homosexuality. The novel, of course, has its interest for this very reason, but the interest, it seems to me, must be mainly historical.

And there is something else. In his 'terminal note' Forster says: 'In *Maurice* I tried to create a character who was completely unlike myself . . .; someone handsome, healthy, bodily attractive, mentally torpid, not a bad business man and rather a snob.' Maurice becomes a stock-broker interested in the Territorial Army. He is a near relation to the Wilcoxes of *Howards End*, the novel that preceded *Maurice*. I must say I found him a bore, as Rickie in *The Longest Journey*, who seems to me a version of Forster himself, is not.

In 1913 or thereabouts something happened to Forster. Whatever it was, having read *Maurice*, I can only wish Forster had written about it autobiographically, whether directly or in fiction. He was as a man more interesting than Maurice and too fine a novelist to waste himself on the thesis novel, however worthy the thesis may have seemed to him.

171. Julian Mitchell, 'Fairy tale', *Guardian*

7 October 1971

Julian Mitchell (1935–) was educated at Winchester and Oxford. He is the author of a number of novels, including *Imaginary Toys* (1961) and *The Undiscovered Country* (1968).

E. M. Forster wrote *Maurice*, a homosexual novel, in 1913 and 1914. He went on tinkering with it until 1960. He thought that because of its happy ending it couldn't be published until the Wolfenden recommendations were made law; and they never would be. He was wrong about that, and wrong, I think, not to have published *Maurice* in however doubtful a foreign edition during his lifetime. It could conceivably have helped to get the law changed sooner. Now, instead of shocking or making people think, it seems sadly tame and sloppy, a painful demonstration of his limitations as a novelist. The academics who depend so much on Forster for 'value' will have a terrible time, I am afraid, justifying an ending which in any other context would be called woman's magazine. The failure to connect fantasy to recognisable life seriously mars the other novels: here it's utterly destructive. And a vital character, a pre-Lawrentian gamekeeper, remains little more than a masculine blur in spite of attempts to re-write him into credibility.

That said, there are redeeming features. *Maurice* began when Forster was touched gently and just above the buttocks by George Merrill, the 'Comrade' of Edward Carpenter. The sensation 'seemed to go straight through the small of my back into my ideas, without involving my thoughts,' and he found himself with the novel ready formed in his head. It is written in short, urgent chapters which convey much of that original excitement,

Maurice himself is a suburban public schoolboy who falls in love, to his initial horror, with Clive Durham, a socially grander fellow undergraduate at Cambridge. Their affair is absolutely chaste, absolutely loving and lasts for three or four years. Then Clive discovers that he's really normal after all. Maurice almost goes mad; he nearly assaults a youth; he consults a doctor, then a hypnotist. At last, staying with the now married Clive in his dilapidated country house, he groans his need into the night, and Alec the game-keeper comes up a convenient ladder and into his bed. (If this scene sounds ludicrous, it is.) Finally, after a good deal of agonising on both sides, Maurice and Alec go off into the 'for ever and ever' of the conventional couple.

Until Alec appears there is much to admire. People may scoff at chastity but that doesn't stop it being practised now as then, and Forster's account of undergraduate romance rings true. Harder to take is Maurice's slowness to rebel against the appalling suburbia in which chivalrous values were so hideously twisted. Forster's point is that Maurice *isn't* clever, *isn't* a natural rebel. He genuinely believes that 'the feeling that can impel a gentleman towards a person of lower class stands condemned'—so he suppresses it and manages as best he can with guilt and masturbation. This is a perceptive and credible study of an all but ordinary middle-class Edwardian. From an early age he dreams of a perfect friend.

Alec is the dream's sexual reality. Forster's fantasy, though, wants dream and reality. It's to be Alec and Maurice against the world—'they must show that when two are gathered together majorities shall not triumph.' He wrote an epilogue, wisely repressed in which the two roamed the greenwood as woodcutters, in what I can only imagine as a Home Counties version of 'The Song of the Loon.'

All this seems terribly silly. Edwardian attitudes to homosexuality were harsh, of course, and if you got caught, you suffered grotesquely. But there's no evidence to show that there were less queers then than now, and very few can have dreamed such a romantic defiance of society. Social acceptance has always been and still is the only possible serious objective for homosexuals. Forster seems to have shied away from its possibility. His last 1960 note says that Clive on the bench would go on sending Alec to prison while Maurice got off. This sounds like impure pre-Wolfenden excitement, the thrill of being against the law. Thank God we are spared that childishness now. Unfortunately Forster never takes his characters into adulthood, never deals with homosexuals in society. *Maurice* ends like a fairy tale in the worst possible sense.

172. Michael Ratcliffe, review, *The Times*

7 October 1971

Maurice was E. M. Forster's penultimate novel and was written, with uncharacteristic speed, after his first visit to India in 1912 and his first meetings with Edward Carpenter and George Merrill, the simple-lifer and the slum boy who lived together for thirty years and came, in part, to exemplify that brotherhood of lovers whose high civic role so exercised certain German and English writers of the late nineteenth century. Forster must have been familiar with the writings of at least Walt Whitman, John Addington Symonds and Carpenter himself—we shall have to wait for P. N. Furbank's biography for verification of this as of so many other Forsterian mysteries—but with the bulk of his own fiction complete, something was still missing and the visits to Millthorpe suggested it.

George Merrill also touched my backside—gently, and just above the buttocks. I believe he touched most people's. The sensation was unusual and I still remember it, as I remember the position of a long-vanished tooth. It was as much psychological as physical. It seemed to go straight through the small of my back into my ideas, without involving my thoughts (Terminal Note, 1960).

He rejoined his mother in Harrogate and wrote *Maurice* in a matter of months. It was not intended for publication in his lifetime and remained an exceptionally unpublicized secret until the day he died; even the opinion of those friends who had read it—Lytton Strachey and, presumably, Virginia Woolf—and predeceased him, never surfaced into print. For all Carpenter's courageous eccentricity, it was only 14 years since Wilde's death and the act of sodomy, for example, carried a *minimum* penalty of 10 years' penal servitude. It is as essential to keep such a context in mind when looking at Forster's reticence now as it is to remember the muscular and soppy rhetoric of the earlier 'Uranian' apologists when one reacts with some disappointment at the mildness of *Maurice*. Forster took a deliberately circumspect approach.

Certainly he wrote better novels—five, to be precise—but even at its least effective *Maurice* deals, like them, with what Lionel Trilling called 'the profound pathology' of the undeveloped heart, and so can take its place in the canon without further question.

There are three main characters: Maurice, Clive and Alec. Clive loves, and is slowly loved by, Maurice; Clive ceases to love Maurice and, assuming his place as Wiltshire squire, marries Anne; Maurice despairs, seeks 'normality' in vain; Maurice goes to bed with, then loves, and is loved by, Alec. They go off together. 'A happy ending was imperative. I shouldn't have bothered to write otherwise. I was determined that in fiction anyway two men should fall in love and remain in it for the ever and ever that fiction allows.' A happy ending?

Lytton Strachey gave them about six weeks, and he was right—not because Alec is an under-gamekeeper and Maurice a stockbroker, but because, as fictional lovers, they do not come alive. Alec is introduced too late and hovers like an unrealized shade between Forster's earlier earth-man Stephen Wonham and Lady Chatterley's lover (still a decade off). He remains a fantasy of fulfilment entertained for the sake of the central cause. So too does Maurice himself in so far as he becomes that somewhat emblematic figure of the Edwardian age, the Stockbroker. Forster is at immense pains to establish the ordinariness of his hero. Disciplined, Anglican, philistine, commuting, motor-cycling and slow to take on: the points are regularly tapped into place as if *Maurice* were a dummy-run for the 'Notes on the English Character' (1920). Indeed there are many points in common: 'an undeveloped heart, not a cold one. The difference is important.' Maurice is too typical for words.

Maurice and Clive together is another matter. Their love-conflict inhabits the territory of Forster's own first 30 years; public school, matriarchy, Greece, Italy, Cambridge: the landscape of passion and compromise so dazzlingly illuminated in *The Longest Journey* (1907). The idea that love moves in when religious belief declines, that the fruitless search for God becomes the hopeful search for the one true Friend, was much in the air (Carpenter himself was disingenuous in this vein: 'I now realize', the former man of God once declared after a particularly satisfying encounter at the age of 80, 'that this is a much more intimate communion, for is not man made in the image of God?'). It is an exchange of faiths fundamental to *Maurice* and to all Forster's fiction from 'The Story of a Panic' onwards.

Thus Clive the loving hellenist rejects his inherited orthodoxy and sets to work on his friend. When he sports his oak, it is not to declare his love for Maurice, but in order first to demolish, in utter privacy, his feeble acceptance of the Trinity. That done, the door is reopened and nothing more physically alarming has taken place than shameful blushes and the trembling of a coffee cup. Once discovered to be quite hollow Maurice's religious beliefs crackle like tinder long stacked for the fire. By such constructive truths do the boys come slowly together.

For Forster India had already offered both God *and* the Friend and indicated in neat and charming symbols how the two could be made one. Almost as much as the inspirational visits to Millthorpe, Forster's first experience of the sub-continent casts its allusive power over *Maurice*. The most important single word in the book is 'Come!', the soft call to Krishna by his aspiring milkmaid, the voice of sensual instinct which also recurs in the later masterpiece. Clive detects it in Maurice's face after the crash of his Trinity; it is torn out of Maurice himself in two great cries when he is barely aware of his ability to utter it. The old hellenist has become a coward and a prig, but the second of the cries is answered. Krishna climbs the ladder to the Russet Room: the under-gamekeeper is more than ready to play God.

It doesn't work. Forster was a superb contriver and we have long accepted the contrivances of the novels for the wit and majesty of their setting, the essential elements of which are a transcending command of melodrama and a comic genius of Austenite magnitude. Both are almost excluded here and in their exclusion poor contrivance stands exposed. *Maurice* is the least poetic, the least witty, the least dense and the most immediately realistic of the six novels. Two of Forster's strongest cards—the spirit of place and the fringe of emasculating women—are scarcely played at all, though he holds them in his hand and needs them to win this particular game like no other. Passion is smothered by the killing hand of care, yet there is evidence enough of hasty composition—subsequent revisions seem merely to have added rather than improved. But then he was not writing an ordinary —or even an extraordinary—novel. He was avowedly writing about and in some way to further the cause of, homosexual love. How fares he there, then?

Whitman had thrilled his songs of Democracy and Comradeship; and Athletic Love, in his hazily noble sense, had figured in much of Forster's fiction before *Maurice*, though always shaded to an infinitely subtle and private thing when compared to its Western Unionised original. There is no need to go as far as one Forster scholar who has seriously suggested that Lucy Honeychurch in *A Room with a View* is a boy *en travesti*; in Stewart Ansell (*The Longest Journey*) Forster drew one of subtlest portraits of a homosexual in English literature—without, of course, ever saying that was what he was doing or, for that matter, getting much credit for it since. Ansell's attraction to Rickie (the Clive-figure) and Rickie's to the absurdly doomed Gerald ('Just where he began to be beautiful the clothes started') is expressed with greater tension and physical tenderness than any of the love scenes in *Maurice*. No, when facing the thing head on, Forster seems to have turned off.

In 1914 he had insufficient facts to hand: it was another 10 years, so his friends have told us, before he really began to enjoy a sexual life and then, when he was nearly 50 and had just completed *A Passage to India*, would have been the time to write *Maurice*: it was, in fact, the precise moment when he chose to give up fiction for good. But there is a direct line from *Maurice* to 'What I Believe' (1939) and even here, there are moments of steadfast simplicity, of fearlessness and darkness lightening, which are entirely characteristic, momentarily take one's breath away and give a hint of what this too hasty record of discovery might have been.

173. Paddy Kitchen, review, *The Times Educational Supplement*

8 October 1971

Most of us, from time to time, need a moral tutor; and in my view E. M. Forster, through his writings, is the ideal person. In K. W. Gransden's words, he has 'indicated those areas of the human heart where he thinks further research should be done' and 'has upheld the ethical and the aesthetic good though fashion has derided them'.

That his books are being read even more widely now is heartening, since there did seem a time when his reputation threatened to fade away under the maiden-aunt image some critics tried to give him. I hope young people respond to the anti-authoritarian sound of his very personal voice as enthusiastically today as Elizabeth Bowen did when she was a schoolgirl in 1915. She and her friends had never heard of Forster before, but the contents of *The Celestial Omnibus* 'set up not only an instant enthusiasm but an *engouement*: we were ready to go to any lengths, any expenditure of pocket money, to get hold of more from the same pen'.

But although it is good to see Forster's name on so many reading lists, my heart sinks at anyone being forced to read him against their will. He would so have hated that. On the flyleaf of his guide to Alexandria, he quotes Plotinus: 'To any vision must be brought an eye adapted to what is to be seen.' Equally, he would have disliked young people having to spend pointless hours dissecting his novels in order to exhibit their contents in the form of academic criticism. As he himself said: 'If critics could only have a course on writers *not* thinking things out . . .'

Certainly, critics love batting orders, and insist on singling out *A Passage to India* (or, occasionally, *Howards End*) as Forster's 'best' novel. He preferred to refer to his 'favourite', which was *The Longest Journey*. It is mine too, and the one with the closest emotional links to *Maurice*, now published posthumously.

In comparison with the other works *Maurice* is schematic, but this is not surprising when one considers that it was written to delineate a specific moral theme. This theme is expressed, in P. N. Furbank's introduction, as the affirmation 'without possibility of retreat, that love of this kind [ie between two men] could be an ennobling and not a degrading thing and that if there were any "perversion" in the matter it was the perversity of a society which insanely denied an essential part of the human inheritance'.

To do this, Forster intentionally brought in as many aspects of the 'problem' as he thought relevant, and made no attempt to flesh out minor characters in order to create the connecting fabric of a large-scale novel. The book needs to be taken on the terms in which it was conceived and not as some contender to *War and Peace* or even *Howards End*.

Within that context, is it still relevant? It was, after all, written in 1913–14, at which time there was no possibility that a novel treating homosexuality in such a liberal way could ever be published. I think the answer is certainly 'yes'.

In the opening chapter, when Maurice is given a sex lesson by a kindly preparatory schoolmaster, we are reminded that all the instruction in the world will not prepare the unawakened heart. Yet Forster is not against the lesson. He merely points the dilemma. The realization that he was homosexual would perhaps have dawned on Maurice rather earlier today, but it could still be just as bewildering. We may have changed our laws but on the whole we have not changed our opinions. How many parents even now could sympathetically accept their child's homosexuality? *Maurice* treats sternly with society's habit of turning a blind eye: the doctor who said 'Rubbish, rubbish!' when Maurice sought help; the friend, his first love, who married and then pretended there was no reason why Maurice should not do likewise. Above all, these confrontations and soliloquies are expressed in Forster's inimitable voice, carrying as it does that tension between thought and feeling that never fails to set up vibrations that linger long after the initial reading.

Forster undoubtedly suffered from not being able to make his homosexuality explicit in his published writings during his lifetime, but did the writing suffer? It is, of course, impossible to give a real answer. But I am certain that in one way it did not. In England, particularly, male homosexuality tends to be a very romantic business. It is impossible for individuals to maintain romance throughout their lives. Hence the drabness, the betrayals, the loneliness, that are the obverse side of the coin. But initially, the incandescent side is foremost. And it was this that Forster illuminated so well in *Maurice* and *The Longest Journey*.

The latter is not, of course, a book about homosexuality. But it carries all the intellectual fervour and excitement of young male closeness. Certainly Stephen Wonham is Forster's supreme romantic creation—not a real person at all, but an idealization of some suburban-bred Englishman's yearnings and aspirations. It is significant that in the first excesses of creation he was called Siegfried rather than Stephen, and that one chapter omitted from the novel was what Forster described as 'extremely romantic'.

In his terminal note to *Maurice* Forster quotes Lytton Strachey's comment on the relationship between Maurice and Alec in which he said that it 'rested on curiosity and lust and would only last six weeks'. However, Forster goes on to say that both Alec and Maurice were capable of loyalty whereas another character, Risley, 'the clever Trinity undergraduate, wasn't, and Risley, as Lytton gleefully detected, was based upon Lytton'.

Which is, I think, the crux of it. The final style of homosexuality expressed in *Maurice* is more idealistic than realistic. But Forster was dedicated to moral evolution, and since homosexuality exists, he would wish it to exist on the best level possible. The Forsters of this world are more scarce than the Stracheys, and all the more valuable.

174. V. S. Pritchett, 'The upholstered prison', *New Statesman*

8 October 1971, 479–80

V. S. Pritchett (1900–), novelist, short story writer and critic, author of *Nothing Like Leather* (1935), *Dead Man Leading* (1938) and *You Make Your Own Life* (1938).

Embarrassment has been the note among those who had been allowed to read Forster's secret novel, the apologia for homosexuality which has lain unpublished, but frequently revised, since 1912. One's expectations have consequently been too low. To have set a burning topic in what is now an Edwardian period piece is awkward. It puts the fire out and leaves one with the uncomfortable impression that Forster complained of in Meredith: that he thought the Home Counties were the universe. Although the book has been many times revised in the course of 50 years, it must be said that the first 100 pages of *Maurice* are fossilised. After that, when he begins to tussle with his hero's homosexuality, the book comes to life. It has a good deal of Forster's tart gift for moral puncture, all his talent for not forgiving and for not shedding tears. It has always been engaging to see him using the stiff upper lip of pre-1914 manners, in order to loosen it in others and to persuade them of the vital necessity of losing it altogether. The grey, unconsoling sentences, so curtly dismissive, have the humanist's courage. Of Maurice, at the moment when he goes down into the hell of sexual crisis, he writes:

He hadn't a God, he hadn't a lover—the two usual incentives to virtue. But on he struggled with his back to ease, because dignity demanded it. There was

> no one to watch him, nor did he watch himself, but struggles like his are the supreme achievement of humanity, and surpass any legends about Heaven. No reward awaited him. This work, like too much that had gone before, was to fall ruining. But he did not fall with it, and the muscle it had developed remained for another use.

That is the classic Forster voice.

The story is simply that of an able young Edwardian of the well-off suburban and conventional kind who discovers he is homosexual at Cambridge. Maurice is caught up, first of all, in a romantic and platonic friendship with the son and heir of country gentry, but is thrown over when the lover decides to marry. Not before he realises that his desires are physical, however. This appals him. He tries to be cured. Eventually he falls physically in love with a servant and gamekeeper at his friend's country house. Social disaster: he is forced to see that his homosexuality is, in a sense, political; he will become an outcast and indeed, under the English law of the time, a criminal. He risks this role, gives up his respectable business as a stockbroker and opts for sexual love as a rebellion against the social values of the moneyed Edwardian middle class.

Maurice is the male version of *Lady Chatterley's Lover*, written in 1913, long before D. H. Lawrence's book, and a similar criticism of English life, as Forster says himself, in a few pages of comment on the book, written some 10 years ago. There is the same preoccupation with snobbery and class-consciousness, the same allegory of the stagnant condition of English life. Lawrence's tutelary sexual games are missing, and this is as well; for the early novelists of the sexual revolution had so strong a sense of sex as 'the Cause' that they lost the stalking, primitive gaiety of the hunt, and the natural good humour of love. If Forster's own sense of Cause gives an unusual dry harshness and something very wooden to the book, it is to his credit that he shows Maurice emerging recklessly on the side of instinct.

The happy ending of the book was, it seems, criticised by his friends. Lytton Strachey said the affair would last only six weeks. But I don't think 'lasting' was ever Forster's interest: in all his novels the life of the heart is precarious; the scene in the Marabar caves tells us that the puritan of measure and reason was open to the guess of the mystic. As in Lawrence, one grins at the figure of the gamekeeper—Forster's Alec Scudder is a good deal better drawn. Why these young rural Housmanites? The symbolism is not random. Scudder is a figure from 'greenwood England'; the outcast heir of Robin Hood, that old social protest. 1914 killed greenwood England. Forster wrote afterwards:

There is no forest or fell to escape to today, no cave in which to curl up, no deserted valley for those who wish neither to reform nor corrupt society, but to be left alone. People do still escape, one can see them any night at it in the films. But they are gangsters, not outlaws, they can dodge civilisation because they are part of it.

If Maurice, the stockbroker, has opted out, so has Alec Scudder, surly and unsure though he is. He is a gamekeeper and servant by chance, for he is the son of a small shopkeeper.

Forster wrote that comment on the book in 1960, uneasily defending the end from the charge of sentimentality: the Cause does, I'm afraid, show its exalted head here. I prefer his droll account of the genesis of the book, which shows the irreverent glove on the iron hand of social comedy. The book was started by a visit to Edward Carpenter, who certainly believed in the greenwood:

Carpenter had a prestige which cannot be understood today. He was a rebel appropriate to his age. He was sentimental and a little sacramental, for he had begun life as a clergyman. He was a socialist who ignored industrialism and a simple-lifer with an independent income and a Whitmanic poet whose nobility exceeded his strength, and, finally, he was a believer in the Love of comrades, whom he sometimes called Uranians. It was this last aspect of him that attracted me to him in my loneliness.

At Carpenter's Forster met George Merrill, who made a profound impression and touched a creative spring—literally:

[Encounter with Merrill described.]

The difficulty was Maurice, the hero, for a story that was to spring from an intimate conflict in the novelist's own life, because the book was one that had to be written, even if it were not published. To make Maurice a man totally unlike himself was a sensible idea; but why choose an able, handsome, young suburban stockbroker, totally conventional? Good for illustrating the Cause, of course; but he has to be endowed with Forster's intelligence and sensibility. Forster was writing before novelists had learned to let people give themselves away. One hardly believes in Maurice at all. For one who does not like playing cricket with people outside his own class, he is altogether too perceptive about society. The social observations are marvellously in

Forster's small but deadly drawing-room style, as for example when Maurice is out of his depth socially at a country house:

> It seems strange that Maurice should have won any respect from the Durham family, but they did not dislike him. They only disliked people who wanted to know them well—it was a positive mania—and the rumour that a man wanted to enter county society was a sufficient reason for excluding him from it . . . The Durhams felt they were conferring a favour on him by treating him as one of themselves, yet were pleased he should take it as a matter of course, gratitude being mysteriously connected in their minds with ill-breeding.

But a real Maurice does come to life when he wakes up to the facts of his sexual case. It is very good that he is endowed with the faculty of instant, unspoken recognition, terrifying in its certainty, which—to heterosexuals—is one of the mysteries of homosexual love. It is less the *coup de foudre* than the scarcely audible click of the released safety-catch. The blackmailing scene in the British Museum, with its lies, its collapse and abrupt reconciliation, is excellent; and it makes one realise with what expert craftsmanship the emotional scenes have been managed throughout the book. One is apt to overlook this because the Edwardian scene and the slang of Edwardian bickering are totally unrecognisable to us; but in fact the changes of heart and the break-downs are thoroughly domesticated in a setting of unbelievable dullness. To present passion in a society so trivial, in which people settle for continuous irritability and nerves as the most convenient way of not knowing the volcano they are living on socially, is an achievement. And this society is not there for its own faded sake as mere background; it is there to show that it is itself an upholstered prison—just as much a prison as the one it would send Maurice to, if they found out about him.

One cannot put *Maurice* beside Forster's other novels, for the story is a case; it is not his fault that the 1914 war pulled the carpet from under the feet of his characters, or that today, after Wolfenden, if homosexuality is still a subject on its own, he would be able to write the same book without corseting it, like some 19th-century tract on the risks of adultery or the right to be a teetotaller in a society of hard-drinkers.

175. Alan Hunter, 'Novel that haunted Forster'

8 October 1971

Review in *Eastern Daily Press* (Norwich), reprinted by permission of *Eastern Daily Press*.

Alan Hunter (1922–), journalist and writer of crime novels (*Gently Does It*, 1955; *Landed Gently*, 1957; etc.), regular contributor to the *Eastern Daily Press*.

In 1914, when Proust, in a cork-lined bedroom in the Boulevard Haussmann, was filling notebook after notebook with his vast exploration of homosexualism, E. M. Forster began his own very English tilt at the devil. But Proust was assured of publication and acceptance; E. M. Forster despaired of either. Proust finished his great work, and died; E. M. Forster lingered on, and so did his novel. *A Passage to India* had yet to be written, but after that began the long silence; and it may be that the frustration he experienced with *Maurice* was at the root of Forster's complete creative eclipse. The novel haunted him. He worked it over continually, but could not bring himself to publish it in his lifetime.

Maurice, now published for the first time, tells the story of an upper-middle class young man who discovers he is a congenital homosexual. The discovery is forced on him by Clive, a fellow-undergraduate at Cambridge, and the two enjoy a tender, 'Platonic' relationship. Then tragedy occurs. Clive changes sexual polarity. He marries and withdraws his affection from Maurice. Maurice, trapped helplessly by his middle class background, experiences the agony and loneliness of his condition. He makes attempts to cure himself by hypnotic treatment and by trying to nerve himself to marriage, but has to realise he is only toying with these remedies; at last he finds physical and spiritual relief with a young gamekeeper on Clive's estate, and joyfully accepts this solution, though it means the abandonment of society and affluence.

The ending was critical. If Maurice had hanged himself, Forster felt he might have published, and it is a nice point whether he was bold in his ending or whether he built into it this excuse. Certainly the excuse ceased to be valid towards the end of Forster's lifetime, and there is nothing in the subdued, meticulous tone of his narration to offend the most prejudiced.

Considered as a novel, the book suffers from an inconsistency in the principal character. Forster chose deliberately to make Maurice a person as unlike himself as possible. Thus he produced a hybrid of an uncultivated athlete and a man of intense sensibility, and the dichotomy worries us throughout the narrative. The vexed ending, often re-written, is also an uneasy performance, and we are left with little belief that Maurice's euphoria is a solution to anything; but against these flaws one must set the immense Forster-virtues of observation and precise expression. *Maurice* may not be the best book in the canon, but it belongs, and is perhaps the most interesting.

176. Colin Wilson, 'A man's man', *Spectator*

9 October 1971

Colin Henry Wilson, born in Leicester in 1931, came to prominence in 1956 with his book *The Outsider*. Since then he has published prolifically in various fields, including the novel. In 1969 he published *Bernard Shaw: A Reassessment*.

E. M. Forster's career is one of the mysteries of modern literature. In the five years between 1905 and 1910, he produced four important novels, including *Howard's End*. Then there was a silence for fourteen years, followed by *A Passage to India*. After which, he dried up for good, although he lived for almost another half-century. The only parallel case that comes to mind is Sibelius; but at least his output *during* his productive years was tremendous. Forster seemed to have the capacity, but to have preferred not to use it.

Most of Forster's friends knew he had written a homosexual novel, and many of them had read it. I never met Forster, but I was told about *Maurice*—by one of his friends—several years ago. Unlike Lytton Strachey—whom he portrays in *Maurice*—Forster believed in being extremely discreet about his homosexuality. Strachey's Cambridge circle thought him altogether too discreet and colourless—Strachey described him as 'a mediocre man,' the kind to whom waiters are naturally rude. All this certainly explains the non-publication of *Maurice* in Forster's lifetime. What I had not expected was that *Maurice* should prove to be the key to the whole of Forster's work, and the vital clue to his artistic tragedy.

Those early novels—*Where Angels Fear to Tread, The Longest Journey, Room with a View*—are brilliant, but oddly frustrating. Forster seems to see himself as a kind of English Ibsen. He loathes and detests the middle classes, with their snobbery and prejudice; he also hates clergymen, schoolteachers, and authority in general. Like D. H. Lawrence, he feels that all this needs to be blown up. Without ever losing his temper—as Lawrence and Aldous Huxley are inclined to—he impales them like butterflies. But obviously, he needs a standard of happiness and vitality to oppose to all this deadness—and this is where he comes unstuck. He is never quite sure what to oppose to middle-class deadness. In *Where Angels Fear to Tread* there is the magnificent Italian youth Gino, who adores his baby son. But he is rather stupid, and in the main scene of the book, he tortures a man by twisting his broken arm. This sneaking admiration for violence appears in several of the early novels.

And neither violence nor sensuality seem all that much preferable to the things Forster hates—money, corruption, 'withered hearts.' Of course, there's also honesty and decency; but in Forster, these also tend to become rather negative virtues, symbolised by nice but frustrated spinsters who long to go to bed with the magnificent Italians, but never do. In *Howard's End* the ambiguity becomes maddening. At first you think he's contrasting the decent and cultured Schlegels with the stupid, narrow middle-class Wilcoxes, but by the end of the novel it's all been qualified so much you don't know where you are.

The answer now sticks out a mile, and I'm ashamed that I didn't spot it earlier. Forster certainly wasn't sparing with the clues—all that admiration for Greece and Italy and healthy male bodies. In the story 'Albergo Emperdocle,' the young Englishman Harold remarks about his past incarnation as a Greek: 'I loved very differently . . . Yes, I also loved better too.'

It was not simply a matter of being homosexual, like Strachey, Keynes and the rest. He was a Platonic homosexual, obsessed by the notion of friendship, the feeling that two men can be closer together —spiritually—than a man and woman can ever be. There was also the amusing complication that, as a shy, subtle, withdrawn man, he had a sexual preference for stupid and extroverted males. (This later developed into a preference for policemen, says my informant—a taste he shared with Hugh Walpole and James Agate.) *Howard's End* is all about women—there is not an interesting male in the book. Forster dried up for four years. Then he decided he would try to unstop the creative springs with the novel he had always wanted to write.

Maurice is a very fine novel, if much simpler in structure than *Howard's End* or *A Passage to India*. The hero is, inevitably, a healthy, cheerful, rather stupid young chap. With his intellectual inferiority complex, he becomes fascinated by a clever young man called Clive Durham; when Clive confesses to being in love with him, Maurice is shocked, then slowly realises that he is a homosexual, and always has been. ('At the bottom of their hearts, [girls] disliked him entirely, but they were too confused mentally to know this.') A love affair follows, although Forster implies they never actually have sex; they confine their activities to kisses and stroking one another's hair. Then, abruptly, Clive turns 'normal.' (I found this the one unconvincing touch in the novel; I suppose it does happen, but I have never come across a case.) Maurice, left high and dry, goes through a long period of misery, and even tries to get 'cured' by a psychiatrist. Then, staying at Clive's house (after Clive's marriage), he ends up in bed with the gamekeeper (this was years before *Lady Chatterley*, as Forster points out). The gamekeeper originally intends to blackmail him, but they end by falling in love and going off together—to live happily ever after, Forster implies. I found this ending unsatisfactory; not because I am not homosexual, but because I feel that Forster has allowed himself to be blinded by sentimentality. He is always bright enough to see that a marriage between a sensitive man and a stupid woman won't work; but he is too involved in his own wish-fulfillment fantasy to see that the relation between Maurice and Alec Scudder could not last for long.

Maurice was finished in 1914, and Forster felt much better. He launched into another novel, *Arctic Summer*, which would again concern the relationship between two men—one 'intellectual,' the other a simple soldier. But he now knew what he was writing about; he really wanted to get them into bed together, but he wasn't allowed to—at least, if he hoped to publish the novel. So it was abandoned after a few chapters. And the problem remained, and haunted *A Passage to India*. The relation between Fielding and Aziz in that novel ought to be homosexual; but this was out of the question. The whole story—as everyone knows—turns on the delusion of a frustrated virgin that Aziz has tried to rape her. It all peters out, leaving you oddly up in the air. Inevitably, because the frustrated virgin theme needed the counterpoint of a fulfilled homosexual relation theme.

And Forster knew it. So he stopped writing novels. The really brave alternative would have been to publish *Maurice* (which would have been quite feasible after *The Well of Loneliness*), and possibly jeopardise his job as a don. It would probably have allowed him to develop into a great writer. As it was, his work was virtually superseded by Lawrence, who treated all Forster's themes, but treated them better because he could be frank about sex.

No one has the right to blame Forster for the choice he made. But one can't help wishing that he'd been a little less cautious and discreet . . .

177. John Cronin, 'Publishable—but worth it?', *Irish Press* (Dublin)

9 October 1971

John Cronin, formerly of the University of the Witwatersrand, Johannesburg, is now Senior Lecturer in English at Queen's University, Belfast.

E. M. Forster is, among novelists, the apostle of the possible. He is the one who teaches us that it is better to travel hopefully even when we know we are not going to arrive. The novels by which we have hitherto known him are full of images of the unattainable and equally full of warnings against the despair which is always so very close. Stewart Ansell, in *The Longest Journey*, draws a square with a circle within it and a square within that again and, as he continues to draw, Rickie Elliott asks him 'Are they real?' The answer his friend gives him is 'The inside one is—the one in the middle of everything, that there's never room enough to draw.' But you must go on drawing. Mr. Emerson instructs Lucy Honeychurch in *A Room With a View* that 'Life is a public performance on the violin, in which you must learn the instrument as you go along.' In Forster's novels a select few are tutored in the 'holiness of the heart's affections,' are taught to strip themselves of the restraints of convention and learn the great lesson that 'passion is sanity.' It is inevitable that even the best of the novels should contain a fair share of prosing. Forster intrudes, he bores, he sermonizes and tea-tables, he can never resist the mantic philosophic generalisation even when his point has been more than adequately made in the action of the novel. But, at his best, all that does not matter. At his best, his novels blossom into great, genially humourous scenes observed with compelling accuracy and informed by a wise and genial irony. One thinks of the Beethoven concert in *Howard's End* or Gino playing with his baby son in *Where Angels Fear to Tread*, of the never-to-be-forgotten satiric power of the jingo-scene in the Club in *A Passage to India* in which Mrs. Blakiston is so marvellously mocked. Again and again Forster makes us laugh delightedly, again and again the cosy-seeming tabby-cat flicks out a delicately dangerous paw. So great an ironist is he, so amusing a narrator, that we might easily forget the pain and terror which are everywhere in his work: the dead baby in *Where Angels Fear to Tread*, Rickie Elliott's death under the train—such scenes are, on reflection, almost as numerous as the others.

In *Maurice* there is a great deal of pain and almost no humour at all. This is the novel which he suppressed because of its homosexual theme and its intimate personal overtones. It belongs to the period just after *Howard's End* when Forster feared that he was drying up and losing his creative power. For a time, apparently, he despaired but a visit to his friend, Edward Carpenter, inspired him to begin the new book in 1913 and finish it the following year. It will, inevitably, be read for its associations with the other novels and for its biographical overtones. Among the other books, it will be *The Longest Journey* which will be brought most to our minds by *Maurice* and much of the painful morbidity of the earlier book falls into place in the light of the torments explored in its successor. *Maurice* is a tense and painful book and perhaps the least artful of all of Forster's novels. Though he worked over it for many years, the narrative method of the opening section of the book is thin, almost in the C. P. Snow manner, and there is a fragility in the style which recalls the work of Forster's friend and contemporary, Forrest Reid. What a gulf of maturity and discipline lies between the tenuousness of this book and the expansive wisdom of the great work which was to follow it a decade later and crown the writer's achievement! Forster is too close to his material in *Maurice* and the result is that, while he conveys the dreadful loneliness of the name character, he never manages to give him his proper fictional distance. Now and again the familiar Forster peeps out, in a brief flash of wit or irony which rouses our hopes that subject will allow itself to be properly clothed in treatment but the fictional effort is not sustained. The fabric of the novel never really grows into symbolic support of its theme. As always, Forster is before us, in his own judgment on the novel. His energetic and interesting 'Terminal Note' makes clear his impish and wilful determination to attach a happy ending to his novel, come what may, and his final comment on the 1960 typescript was 'Publishable—but worth it?' To that question, it would be churlish to answer 'No.' All Forster enthusiasts will read *Maurice* with great interest. It will in no way diminish his deservedly high reputation. After I had read it, I went back to *The Longest Journey* and found, along with many other things both old and new, the following passage in which a kindly publisher comments to Rickie Elliott on his stories:

> 'Your story does not convince.' He tapped it. 'I have read it—with very great pleasure. It convinces in parts, but it does not convince as a whole; and stories, don't you think, ought to convince as a whole?'
>
> 'They ought indeed,' said Rickie . . .

178. Cyril Connolly, 'Corydon in Croydon', *Sunday Times*

10 October 1971

At last, E. M. Forster's 'unpublishable' homosexual novel, about which we have been hearing for some forty years.

It was written in 1913–14, the period was 1912. It could not, of course, have been published then, a mere twenty years after the Oscar Wilde affair, or in the Twenties when Radclyffe Hall's Lesbian novel, *The Well of Loneliness*, got into such trouble, or in the Thirties—except abroad; and there would seem something rather underhand about publishing abroad a book that is so gloriously English, as if it had something in common with Proust or Gide or Joyce—or Lady Chatterley. And in the Forties? That would have been doing Goebbels' work—and after that, when Forster had become the Sacred Maiden Aunt of English letters, Keeper of the Bloomsbury Conscience, it might have damaged his image.

Even in 1960 he was writing:

Happiness is its keynote—which by the way has had an unexpected result: it has made the book more difficult to publish. Unless the Wolfenden Report becomes law, it will probably have to remain in manuscript.

The Wolfenden Report, he surmised, would be indefinitely rejected, police prosecutions would continue. It might have struck him that the lot of the consenting adult could well have been improved and legislation even been undertaken much earlier if he had published his idyll when it was written or at least in the Twenties or Thirties. Public opinion would have had to take note of it and Forster, though he might have suffered some obloquy, had nothing to lose, being, like Gide and Proust, of independent means. Was it a failure of nerve? It looks like it. He continued to work on the novel all his life.

Forster is closer to Gide than is any other English writer (see his remarks on *Les Faux Monnayeurs*) and even Gide had been shocked by the outspokenness of Proust; his *Corydon* (written in 1911, published in 1923), a Socratic dialogue, is merely a biological defence of homosexuality, and a student would have had difficulty in finding a novel which told us what homosexuals actually do.

Maurice, however, is not true to Forster's principle of introducing key-events in an off-hand way at the breakfast-table. It is a direct narrative, written with sustained lyricism, and shows the quality of a novelist at the height of his powers: it would have been well able to take its place between *Howard's End* and *A Passage to India* as a long short story or short novel in a vein of comedy absent from the others.

But by now the element of dating is fatal, like foxing on a book. It's not all that important, but one can't ignore it. We can make allowances for what dates if it was once contemporary, even as the foxed pages were once immaculate, but there's something artificial when a book is born dated.

Two things date: the language, especially the language of love, and the platonic ragging and romping of those two splendid fellows—Maurice Hall, the suburban hearty, and Clive Durham, the sensitive young squire, both 'varsity' men as Maurice puts it. Fellows romp in *Look Back in Anger* you might say—or in the Embassies of Maurice Baring, the consulates of Graham Greene, or in the 'well-directed pillow hit the ebullient baronet' school of fiction. Proust wrestled with Albertine. Perhaps it's what they say:

> 'Waou that hurts!' cried the other joyously. . . . 'Waou! Ee! Shut up. I'm going.' He fell between Maurice's knees. 'Well, why don't you go if you're going?' 'Because I can't go.'
>
> It was the first time he had dared to play with Durham. . . .
>
> There was nothing but ragging for many days after that. . . .

Sexual terminology, once dated, is often very odd. 'Spending' and 'swiving' are cases in point, even 'pleasuring' and 'yarding'—but what about 'sharing,' apparently a working-class word since it is first used by the amorous young gamekeeper who replaces the stuffed-shirt young squire as the lover of suburban Maurice? 'I do long to talk with one of my arms round you then place both arms round you and share with you,' he writes, and Maurice asks his hypnotist doctor (who would have been his analyst ten years later).

> 'You mean that a Frenchman could share with a friend and yet not go to prison?' 'Share? Do you mean unite?' replied the Physician. 'If both are of age and avoid public indecency certainly.'

Maurice's mother lived near London, in a comfortable villa, among some pines. His father is dead, he has two sisters, he will go into the family business (stockbroking). He is a hearty who plays rugger at a dull public school and goes up to a dull college; it is never made clear why he is homosexual and when he falls in love with Clive Durham, the brilliant senior fastidious 'apostle-type' of undergraduate, friend of the sinister Risley (Lytton Strachey), it is Durham who would seem the true homosexual, Maurice the temporary one, like many an easy-going athlete who falls in with the homosexual mores of a university before going on to marry his best friend's sister.

It is part of Forster's art that it is not Clive but Maurice who turns out to be the incurable—with considerable irony.

> Durham could not wait. People were all around them, but with eyes that had gone intensively blue he whispered 'I love you.' Maurice was scandalised, horrified. He was shocked to the bottom of his suburban soul and exclaimed, 'Oh rot! Durham, you're an Englishman. I'm another. Don't talk nonsense. I'm not offended, because I know you don't mean it, but it's the only subject absolutely beyond the limit as you know, it's the worst crime in the calendar. . . .'

But two years later Durham is writing to him 'Against my will I have become normal. I cannot help it' while Maurice is blurting out to his family doctor 'I'm an unspeakable of the Oscar Wilde sort' and Dr Barry replies 'never let that evil hallucination, that temptation from the devil, occur to you again.' Clive marries (can it be unintentional when the Master makes him say 'Anne's dear little hole may grow in the night'?) and Maurice finds physical satisfaction for the first time, aged 24, with Clive's uninhibited young gamekeeper, Alec Scudder, with whom he resolves to live happily ever after.

Forster mentions that Lytton Strachey (the real one) wrote to him that this affair was based only on lust and curiosity and could not last more than six weeks, but Forster, who had met Edward Carpenter and listened to his Whitmanesque theories, was convinced that his ending must be happy and that the two friends must affront society and go into exile together.

Since Forster kept on revising his book and has left us some notes on his characters, who belonged 'to an England where it was still possible to get lost, to the last moment of the greenwood' one must give him the benefit of the doubt for every moment when we are tempted to scoff. Platonic love between men was for long the backbone of empire, it was bred with responsibility, honesty, and leadership in the public schools, and it is bad luck on Forster if Freud has taken the whole latency period (which could last a lifetime) out of cold storage since those Cambridge summers which he describes so nostalgically.

Much more dates, too—the serene class-consciousness of the 'Varsity men,' their dreadful mothers and sisters patronising the servants, even the poor.

'They haven't our feelings. They don't suffer as we should in their place.' Anne looked disapproval but she felt she had entrusted her hundred pounds to the right kind of stockbroker.

The story opens with a brilliant vignette of Maurice among ushers, at his prep school, being instructed in the facts of life. It closes in his duel for the soul of the gamekeeper with Clive's newly appointed rector, the Reverend Mr Borenius, who proclaims that:

Where there is heresy immorality will sooner or later ensue. Until all sexual irregularities and not some of them are penal the Church will never reconquer England.

Happy days! 'It was a dinner jacket evening—not tails because they would only be three.'

179. Philip Toynbee, 'Forster's love story', *Observer*

10 October 1971, 32

Philip Toynbee (1916–), son of the historian Arnold Toynbee, was educated at Rugby and Oxford. He has been foreign correspondent and reviewer for the *Observer* since 1950. His novels include *The Savage Days* (1937) and *Pantaloon* (1961).

It was no secret among his friends that E. M. Forster had once written a homosexual novel, which was not to be published until after his death. Now that the whole topic is so much, and so properly, in the open there is no conceivable point in trying to conceal that Forster was himself a homosexual and for many years a fully practising one.

But nor should this ever allow us to forget that in the Edwardian years—the years of all Forster's previously published novels except *A Passage to India*—male homosexuality was an unmentionable subject except in the most sophisticated circles, and homosexuals—I take this from *Maurice*—were commonly described as 'Unspeakables.' The Wilde case was still reverberating and English homosexuals were living in greater fear, shame and distress than they had done even in the middle years of the nineteenth century.

If one adds that Forster came from a thoroughly conventional middle-class home and attended a profoundly philistine public school, the anguish that he suffered must have been very acute. It is little wonder that Cambridge came to him as an almost miraculous revelation: he made several homosexual friends there and quickly learned that his condition was neither rare nor universally regarded as shameful. How natural, then, that this very intelligent and sensitive young man should have wished to express his true feelings, by some means or other, and that he should have felt a crusading zeal in doing so. *Maurice* is a *roman à thèse* with a vengeance; a defiant declaration that 'the love which dares not speak its name' *ought* to dare to speak both frankly and proudly.

Though Forster first wrote *Maurice* in 1914 he continued to revise it until 1970: he showed it to several friends at different times and received at least enough encouragement to persuade him that the book might be publishable after his death. Yet he was also full of doubt, and by the end of his life he suspected that the book was both 'dated' and 'a fake.' His final comment, inscribed on the cover of the 1960 typescript, was 'Publishable—but worth it?'

I fear that Forster's literary executors have given the wrong answer to that question.

In all Forster's writings, except his masterpiece, *A Passage to India*, there was a disturbing element of Victorian fine writing, whimsicality and high-minded gush. But this flaw was controlled and counter-balanced by a splendid litheness, even toughness of mind: above all by a pervasive humour which was by no means always good-humoured. The reason why *Maurice* should never have been published is that this depressing work isolates and concentrates the worst of Forster's faults, and is almost totally devoid of his great virtues.

Maurice tells the story of a young, upper-middle-class Englishman growing to manhood at the turn of the century, through prep school, public school, university, and the City. The point is heavily made that Maurice Hall is a very ordinary, rather philistine boy and man—after Cambridge he takes over his dead father's partnership in a firm of London stockbrokers—whose single peculiarity lies in the fact that he happens to have been born a homosexual. After a long platonic affair with a Cambridge friend and a brief, dazzled infatuation with a Woolwich cadet, he falls in love with a gamekeeper (pre-Mellors vintage) and enjoys a complete physical relationship for the first time.

As in so many of Forster's other books the point comes when the hero is put dramatically to the test. Will this conventional young stockbroker choose 'life,' 'the heart,' 'real' reality; or will he choose the fake, conventional and heartless values of suburb and city? (It required a novelist of Thomas Mann's stature to do equal justice to both sides in this traditional romantic argument.) Anyway, unlike several of Forster's other heroes, this one makes the right choice, and the book ends with Maurice and Alec vaguely making off into 'the Greenwood,' there to live happily ever after as lovers and manual workers.

I shall forbear to quote: it must be enough to say that *Maurice* is novelettish, ill-written, humourless and deeply embarrassing. And with the wisdom of hindsight I think I can see why it was almost inevitable that this should be so. To begin with, much of the worst in the other novels came from the general thesis that Forster was constantly propounding. It is the thesis which Lionel Trilling has described as an assault on 'the underdeveloped heart'; a defence of all naturally loving, innocent and fearless human beings against the prevailing deadness and cruelty of that society which Forster epigrammatised as 'the world of telegrams and anger.' Yet I think this novelist's real talent was for seeing, understanding and describing, rather than for making a moral point. In *A Passage to India*, in *Howard's End* to a lesser extent, he made a true novelist's attempt to show the tensions and conflicts of human reality, without drawing any explicit lessons from his demonstration. In *Maurice*, where the lesson is all-important, everything else is perfunctory to the point of painful incompetence.

But there is something else here as well. However much Forster may have fretted at the taboos of his time it is the case that every good writer needs his own system of prohibitions and restraints—and it sometimes seems hardly to matter whether these are imposed from within or from without. The notion of total self-expression, an opening of the floodgates to their fullest extent, is a modern absurdity which has led to some of the worst writing ever seen in print.

It now seems that one of the special restraints which Forster needed was precisely that he should *not* express his homosexual feelings directly: that they should be sublimated, transmuted and confined within the banks of that millrace which proved, in so many of his books, to be such an effective driving-force.

A further question, of course, is whether there really is such a thing as a specifically homosexual sensibility, or vision, or mode of apprehension. In the course of the present novel Forster suggests that a homosexual has two distinct approaches to, for example, a drawing of a young man by Michelangelo, whereas the heterosexual has only one. (Correspondingly the heterosexual has the advantage of two approaches to, let's say, one of Renoir's *jeunes filles en fleur*.) But this is surely too simple, for we all, mercifully, have enough sexual ambiguity to enable us to *lend* a bit of our minority impulse whenever the occasion demands it.

Certainly I can detect nothing particularly homosexual about *Maurice* except that it happens to be about homosexuals. There is plenty of 'hellenic' talk, several rather febrile descriptions of male beauty and one lively passage of anti-female disgust. But all the high sentiments—both of love and of passion—could just as easily have been inspired by the most heterosexual of romances. As, indeed, dozens of contemporary romancers were demonstrating at the time when *Maurice* was first written.

180. Nigel Dennis, 'The love that levels', *Sunday Telegraph*

10 October 1971

Nigel Dennis (1912–), journalist and dramatist, was educated in Southern Rhodesia and Germany. From 1938 to 1958 he was a journalist in America. He became staff book-reviewer for the *Sunday Telegraph* in 1961, and was Joint Editor of *Encounter* from 1967 to 1970. Two of his best-known plays are *Cards of Identity* (1955) and *The Making of Moo* (1957).

A posthumous novel by E. M. Forster—can we open it without fear of disappointment? In all the English literature of this century, no voice is more familiar to the ear than Forster's, no attitude to life more part and parcel of our liberal education. How dreadful to find that he had laid an egg!

We worry the more because *Maurice* was written in 1914, so that instead of growing up with it we must step back into its 'period.' Finally, it is published only now because its theme is homosexuality —too taboo for words when it was written, but perhaps too dated for words when it is read today.

We are relieved pretty quickly of most of our worries—helped, certainly, by the fact that Forster shared them and touched up *Maurice* from time to time until as late as 1960. He confessed then that he could do nothing about the 'endless anachronisms' such as 'half sovereign tips, pianola records, norfolk jackets, Police Court News,

Hague Conferences, Libs and Rads and Terriers . . .', still less about the English background itself—an unregimented world 'where it was still possible to get lost . . . the last moment of the greenwood.'

But he had little to say about the 'dating' of his treatment of the theme itself—which is what we notice most. Homosexuality once had its sublimities—its Greek ideals, its rejection of actual sexual intimacy, its dream of unsullied comradeship. Forster began *Maurice* with this sort of homosexuality in mind, but he ended it with the sort we know today. So we discover that we are reading a sort of history—how the sensitive plant grew into the hardy shrub that flourishes nowadays not only in the public parks but in many private gardens.

We discover, too, that in Forster's mind, class—that favourite English subject even of recent generations—is woven in tightly with the sexual theme and that it made Forster a very angry young man—much angrier than he is in any of his other novels. Perhaps one reason for this is that homosexuality has always defied distinctions of class.

When queer meets queer, there is no question of Norman blood. Forster strongly approved of this—which is why *Maurice* gives one the feeling that he saw homosexuality as a condition that worked strongly in the direction of social equality. This, in turn, implies that when society sends the practising queer to prison, it is not only to punish him for his bad morals but for his addiction to levelling.

It is the twinning together of the two themes that makes *Maurice* (which appears with an introduction by P. N. Furbank) most recognisably a Forster work. There are long moments in it, one may say, when the class theme is so strong that the homosexual subject almost vanishes. And because it is an angry book, centred on a personal struggle, it is unique among Forster's works—sharper, bolder, more belligerent, more indignant. The wit is often very acid, especially when suburban life is the target:

'Church was the only place Mrs. Hall had to go to—the shops delivered.'

'They would come to him and ask for a safe six per cent. security. He would reply, "You can't combine high interest with safety—it isn't to be done;" and in the end they would say, "How would it be if I invested most of my money at four per cent., and play about with an odd hundred?" Even so did they speculate in a little vice.'

When it is said of one of the characters: 'He liked the atmosphere of the North, whose gospel is not truth, but compromise,' we hear the Forster voice we know so well. But the character of whom it is said is not Forster himself this time, it is a young gentleman with a large estate, and his 'compromise' with the North is to start off queer and then turn normal in order to go on being a little gentleman, to have an heir, to keep the classes in their places.

He is not the villain of the book: there are no villains in Forster. But he is the nearest thing to one. For this book is also about the country gentry, and the young gentleman's refusal to be his natural self is seen by Forster as part of the suicide of the ruling class. The decayed condition of the young gentleman's estate is presented both as an omen of the future and a fatal flaw in the owner's character: what it means is summed up drily in a sentence about the young squire's bride:

Miss Woods had brought no money to Penge. She was accomplished and delightful, but she belonged to the same class . . . and every year England grew less inclined to pay her highly.

No, Forster's faith—insofar as he ever had a faith—was always with the 'middle middle-class,' the unbending backbone of the country. The gentry was decaying too fast to be resurrected, but the respectable commuters might still be saved—if only because they were so totally dead that only resurrection could bring them to life.

Maurice, the hero of *Maurice*, is such a type. Suburban to the core, he makes it hard for us to believe that he will ever struggle to the heights of classless, homosexual rhapsody that Forster demands of him. But with one of the best novelists in the world to supply the horse-power, to manipulate the mind, to inject the inspiration, to provide the anger, what character could hope to remain safe in the bosom of Welwyn Garden City?

It is here that a certain unintentional comedy comes into the novel. Forster chose Maurice as his hero precisely because he was such a challenge to an author's powers—and so entirely unlike the author himself. Dull, stolid, orthodox, brainless, alive only to the peril of asking more interest than four per cent., poor Maurice must struggle to realise that to be true to one's own nature is the only thing in life that matters. Where the country gentleman surrenders, suburban Maurice fights on, eschewing all he holds dear in order to be wholly queer. One cannot help feeling that the remorseless author, driving this poor lamb up Lord Hill and down Mrs. Dale, rather loses his head in the thrill of it all:

There was no one to watch him, nor did he watch himself, but struggles like his are the supreme achievements of humanity, and surpass any legends about Heaven.

Maurice winds up triumphantly in the arms of—a gamekeeper. Forster, nursing his novel in a locked drawer, had to watch his ace being trumped by D. H. Lawrence, which can't have pleased him very much. Luckily, he must have had the consolation of knowing that the difference between *Maurice* and *Chatterley* was the difference between writing and rubbish.

One thing we miss in *Maurice* is an explanation of the homosexual condition. There is no awesome, blue-rinsed Mum in the background, no physical or environmental influences. Forster argued that the condition was innate, like red hair or large noses. However, having determined to make his hero as average and typical as possible, he may have deliberately suppressed all circumstantial evidence to the contrary—following the character who says: 'As long as they talk of the unspeakable vice of the Greeks they can't expect fair play.'

Only the first half of the novel 'dates'—school, university, Platonic ideals. When we read lines like: 'Maurice is a rip really—Waow, you're hurting my head,' our minds cannot easily recapture the day when Bunter and Socrates paced the old quad together.

Certainly, a novel to be read. It is full of aphorisms, interesting disquisitions, and effective characters, and the writing is what we would expect from Forster. Its theme is still a very important one, and, for this reason, likely to upset the nerves. But, as one of the characters remarks very truly: 'Landscape is the only safe subject. . . .'

181. David Craig, 'A faulty but brave attempt at candour'

15 October 1971

From *The Times Higher Educational Supplement* i, 21.

David Craig (1932–) was educated at Aberdeen University and Downing College, Cambridge. He taught for a time at the University of Ceylon, and is now Senior Lecturer in English at Lancaster University. His publications include *Scottish Literature and the Scottish People 1680–1830* (1961).

For the first two parts of this novel it seemed as though Forster had failed to write himself into a position beyond those very taboos which have prevented this novel, about homosexual love, from being published till 57 years after its completion. For years Maurice and Clive adore each other but never have it off together—or is it, the reader wonders (remembering the unhappy gaps in *Middlemarch* and *Tess of the D'Urbervilles* and many other Victorian novels), that Forster could not bring himself to present the veritable fleshly act? Maurice (the main character throughout) and Clive (his first love) are at Cambridge together. The one makes lame, half-blind advances to the other. Clive, the submissive but more aware of the two, sits against Maurice's chair while he, the more dominant and less self-aware, strokes Clive's hair. They set off on an idyllic motor-bike ride to Ely—presented with a characteristic immediacy and sense of the unexpected zig-zags of human action:

They became a cloud of dust, a stench, and a road to the world, but the air they breathed was pure, and all the noise they heard was the long drawn cheer of the wind . . . A tower, a town—it had been Ely—were behind them, in front the same sky, paling at last as though heralding the sea. 'Right turn,' again, then 'left', 'right,' until all sense of direction was gone. There was a rip, a grate. Maurice took no notice. A noise arose as though of a thousand pebbles being shaken together between his legs. No accident occurred, but the machine came to a standstill among the dark black fields. The song of the lark was heard, the trail of dust began to settle behind them. They were alone.

I can think of no other fictional prose of 1913 which was anything like as supple with the very point-to-point movement of life. Yet, psychologically, these sections are skimped. There is a not credible lack of introspection on the part of the young men, who would have been at their most introverted age. Do Maurice's genitals not stir as he caresses Clive or lies cheek to cheek with him among ferns? The manner of the novel here, with its resort to Forsterian epigrams and whimsies, ducks out from under this question. It is not till chapters and years later that we are told (rather baldly) that Clive and Maurice had kept their relationship platonic. This is not incredible. Victorian sex could be buried deep indeed. A comparison between the 'dirty books' quoted in Steven Marcus's *The Other Victorians* and Dickens's coy substitutes shows how wide and carefully defended a no-man's-land lay between how people pretended they behaved and how they wanted to and often actually did.

A psychiatrist told me once that Victorian middle-class girls, with their unreal upbringing and heavily chaperoned courtship, only got through the ordeal of the wedding night by getting drunk. But these cultural factors cannot fully account for the evasive thinness of the writing in the first stages of *Maurice*, since the realism becomes more complete later on. Forster was possibly let down by his idolization of Cambridge, which gives rise to unrealities in the early part of *The Longest Journey* and seems similarly to blur that part of *Maurice*: the two young men can apparently fondle and caress in company without a hint of the gossip and knowing grins which would surely have happened actually.

Once the characters are in London, this under-written quality changes quite abruptly into the masterly dramatic treatment which has long been familiar from sequences such as Gerald's death in *The Longest Journey* or Fielding's expulsion from the Club at Chandrapore in *A Passage to India* or Lucy's first, involuntary embrace with George early in *A Room With a View*. Time after time Forster gets just the nuance he needs by unexpected cuts, by stress laid on 'small' incidents and by epitomizing large changes with ironical or dismaying speed. One of these, unfortunately, makes a hiatus at a crucial stage; but to do the novel justice one has first to note the skill with which Forster presents Maurice in young manhood.

In summary this may sound like Forster's immediately previous version of the type, Mr. Wilcox in *Howards End*, with his 'thick moustache and the eyes that Helen had compared to brandy balls [which] had an agreeable menace in them, whether they were turned towards the slums or the stars.' But there are two important differences. Maurice, homosexual as he is, is an outcast disguised as a normal citizen, which begins to be the essence of his plight; and it is made to happen, in terms of pages, so quickly that it stings us into a fresh realization of how soon the free wheeling student can become the man with the umbrella, cheque-book, watch-chain, smoking room, insurance policy, *Daily Telegraph*, investments, clients, servants, opinions—in short, Pozzo.

To discuss the rest of the novel, the strongest part of it, forces me to give away some plot, which is scarcely forgivable in a reviewer. The crux is when Clive, touring Greece, ceases to be homosexual, and this comes out in sentences as sparse as this: 'There had been no warning—just a blind alteration of the life spirit, just an announcement, "you, who loved men, will henceforward love women"'. This development is not incredible. But it is not shown. Such oversights may have got by because Forster more or less knew he was writing for the drawer and for a few associates, like Lytton Strachey, who were homosexual and could easily understand and identify with the emotional crises and raptures of this particular kind. That is, Forster was not pressed—as he would have been if he had had to think of the novel as a self-sufficient work of art—to articulate the thing as fully as for a normal public.

The remainder of the novel can hardly be faulted. Maurice's sexuality hounds him hither and yon, snobbery only just holding him back from the 'abyss' of picking up 'lower-class' lads from the London streets. The power of this part is not great compared with Daniel's self-hating indulgences in Sartre's *Roads to Freedom*, yet this is one of the points where we have to honour Forster for writing the thing at all two and a half generations ago. And one is not honouring him for a kind of tract supporting Homosexuals' Lib. The point here is that a novelist, which means in part a dramatist, has put his super-alert sense of the flow and recoil between persons at the service of a punitively taboo theme. It is not freedom about sex but the supple freedom of the prose that one admires page after page.

Moving the novel towards some kind of ending must have been extremely difficult. Forster's own Terminal Notes and P. N. Furbank's

Introduction give us some of the long-needed evidence of what was blocking and troubling Forster's talent for all those years. The ending he finally achieved—as late as 1960—will be much argued about and probably accused of forcing things towards an unlikely happiness. It strikes me as being done with the utmost finesse. A homosexual love begins anew and is felt to be affirmed, although the technique of the last four pages is the novelistic equivalent of a dissolve, neither a 'happily ever after' nor a stage littered with corpses. Here again Forster is pioneering, modern, in opening out the structure of the novel so that it can present the unpredictability of our lives from one phase to the next. It is a Lawrence ending and if the whole book had been written by a Lawrence (that is, by Lawrence), it would have been stronger and less evasive. In the extraordinarily interesting Terminal Notes Forster writes of one character that reworking him made him 'livelier and *heavier*' (my italics), and that is what this novel lacks, heaviness, a consistent density of evoked life. The triangle of the three main characters in *Maurice* joins the triangle of Jude, Sue, and Phillotson in *Jude the Obscure* as another of those faulty, brave attempts at the total candour Lawrence was shortly to achieve in *The Rainbow* and *Women in Love* and *Lady Chatterley's Lover*.

182. David Lodge, 'Before the deluge', *Tablet*

23 October 1971, 1024

David Lodge (1935–) was educated at London University and is now Senior Lecturer in English at Birmingham University. He has published an influential critical work, *Language of Fiction* (1966), and a number of novels, including *Ginger, You're Barmy* (1962), an interesting adaptation of authentic National Service experience, and *The British Museum is Falling Down* (1965).

Maurice is not a very good novel, but even if it were a very bad novel (which it is not) its publication would still be a major literary event. Most judges, after all, would rank E. M. Forster second or third among native English novelists of this century—below Lawrence, though not necessarily below Virginia Woolf—but this reputation has rested on only five published novels. The last and greatest of these, *A Passage to India*, was published as long ago as 1924, while Forster lived on until 1970. In his later years it was an increasingly open secret that there was another novel, about homosexuality, which was to be published posthumously, and *Maurice* (written in 1913–14, and revised from time to time up until 1960) is that novel. It will not enhance Forster's reputation, but it should not be allowed to damage it either.

Structurally, *Maurice* is less complex than any of Forster's other novels. It is a *bildungsroman* which follows the hero's fortunes in a straightforward and often summary way. Maurice Hall is a product of Suburbia and a minor public school from which he passes to the University with all the usual prejudices of his age and class, 'conventional, petty, treacherous to others, because to himself.' At Cambridge he meets Clive Durham and, after initial shock and recoil, recognises the nature of the attraction that draws them together. For several years, extending beyond their undergraduate careers, the two young men enjoy a fervent but Platonic relationship. Then, abruptly (and a little implausibly) Clive becomes 'normal' and marries. Maurice, diagnosed as 'congenitally homosexual' is desolated. Still bound by habit and conviction to respectability, he struggles to sublimate his instinctual drives, and even tries to cure himself through hypnotism. Then he meets Alec Scudder, Clive's gamekeeper, who performs much the same service for Maurice as Lawrence's Mellors for Connie Chatterley (though, as one might expect, Forster is far less explicit). After a struggle, on both sides, against the divisive power of Class and the stock notions attached to it, the two men are romantically re-united and allowed to escape society's disapproval—now represented by Clive—into an indeterminate but promising future with vaguely pastoral overtones. 'A happy ending was imperative' E. M. Forster wrote in a fascinating Terminal Note dated 1960. 'I shouldn't have bothered to write otherwise. I was determined that in fiction anyway two men should fall in love and remain in it for the ever and ever that fiction allows.' This candid admission of the wish-fulfilment inherent in the whole conception of *Maurice* is an obvious clue to its weakness as a work of art.

I do not mean to imply that the novel is without value, or entirely unworthy of its author. There are some finely managed scenes, occasional flashes of Forster's special brand of compassionate irony in contemplating the undeveloped heart, and deft management of the fictional technique he called 'rhythm' in, for instance, the use of rain and windows as leitmotifs. But, remembering that *Maurice* was written between his two most mature and ambitious novels, *Howard's End* and *A Passage to India*, one must be struck forcibly by the extent to which it falls short of them in complexity, interest, humour and rhetorical skill. To say it was the fault of the subject would be far too crude, but it had, one must feel, *something* to do with the subject. An interesting paradox is involved. *Maurice* deals with the kind of love that (we now know) Forster himself knew inwardly—indeed it was written as a direct response to his full acceptance of this aspect of his selfhood; yet it is significantly less powerful than the novels where Forster, because of the taboos of his time, was forced to express himself deviously or indirectly through heterosexual themes. The reason, I believe, is that because he knew that he could not publish *Maurice* for an indefinite period of time, Forster wrote it for himself and his own coterie, losing the sense of that ideal audience—austere, discriminating, yet catholic—for whom, like all good writers, he wrote his other books. *Maurice* is one more proof that in literary matters artistry is more important than sincerity.

TWO VALEDICTORY REVIEWS

183. George Steiner, 'Under the Greenwood Tree', *New Yorker*

9 October 1971, 158–69

George Steiner (1929–) was educated at Paris, Chicago, Harvard and Oxford. From 1952 to 1956 he worked on the staff of the *Economist*, then spent the years 1956 to 1960 at the Institute for Advanced Studies, Princeton University. He has been a Fellow of Churchill College, Cambridge, since 1961, and was made a Fellow of the Royal Society of Literature in 1964. One of the most influential critics of recent years, Steiner has published *Tolstoy or Dostoevsky* (1958), *The Death of Tragedy* (1960), and *Language and Silence* (1967).

Nothing would be easier than to patronize E. M. Forster's posthumous novel, *Maurice*. Begun in 1913, completed the year after, and, one gathers, scarcely touched since, the book dates. 'Not only,' as Forster observes in a delightful terminal note, 'because of its endless anachronisms—its half-sovereign tips, pianola-records, norfolk jackets, Police Court News, Hague Conferences, Libs and Rads and Terriers, uniformed doctors and undergraduates walking arm in arm, but for a more vital reason: it belongs to an England where it was still possible to get lost. It belongs to the last moment of the greenwood.' *Maurice* is a tale of homosexuality which, as legend had widely broadcast, Forster did not wish to publish during the lifetime of a cherished aunt and which, more surprisingly, he chose to keep from all but a few near friends and younger admirers until after his own death, a year ago. Inevitably, the conception and handling of the theme are almost risibly hedged and dated. There is, moreover, a curious incompletion, a forced artifice of happiness at the close. 'I was determined that in fiction anyway two men should fall in love and remain in it for the ever and ever that fiction allows.' So far as the material involved Morgan Forster's own life at its most guarded and vital pulse, the motive is understandable. Yet the wish nevertheless makes for fleeting sentimentality.

But whereas the defects of the book are obvious, the interest of the case lies in the several strengths of *Maurice* and in its place in Forster's work. Written immediately after *Howards End* and in a confident rush of creation, *Maurice* says things that obviously meant the world to the novelist and that he excised from his public and—in that sense—less engaged, less than perfectly honest writings.

The opening vignette is brilliant. Maurice and his prep-school master are walking on a beach. Mr. Ducie enlightens his charge on the mystery of sex. He draws diagrams in the sand. As in a drowse, Maurice takes in these occult and shadowy specifications. Liberated, the man and the boy stroll on by the colorless sea. They are followed by promenaders. Mr. Ducie realizes that he has not obliterated the infernal diagrams. He turns back, sweating with fear. Luckily, the tide is rising and the waters will wash away the perilous truths. Maurice is obscurely outraged: 'Liar,' he thought. 'Liar, coward, he's told me nothing.' So far the little scene is that of a master. Then comes the impairing note of period rhetoric, the nervous sonority of the late Victorian: 'Darkness rolled up again, the darkness that is primeval but not eternal, and yields to its own painful dawn.'

We follow Maurice through family life—a widowed mother, two sisters, turnip tops in a villa outside London—and school. Dr. Barry's lecture to him on the need for man 'that is born of woman to go with woman' is not a success. But soon there is Cambridge, with its gray stone full of spun light and the slow music of the river. The university chapters are the heart of the book. They show the impatient ease, the compression of autobiography. Durham is a small man with simple manners and a fair face. He plays the march from the 'Pathétique' on the pianola, confesses to agnosticism, and has read Plato's 'Symposium.' When he tells Maurice that he loves him, his eyes go intensely blue. At first, Maurice recoils. Forster precisely mimics the style of muscular Christianity: 'Durham, you're an Englishman. I'm another . . . a rotten notion really.' But soon he is in anguish. The instant of revelation crystallizes the anachronism of the novel and its integrity:

Then savage, reckless, drenched with the rain, he saw in the first glimmer of dawn the window of Durham's room, and his heart leapt alive and shook him to pieces. It cried 'You love and are loved.' He looked round the court. It cried 'You are strong, he weak and alone,' won over his will. Terrified at what he must do, he caught hold of the mullion and sprang.

'Maurice—'

As he alighted his name had been called out of dreams. The violence went out of his heart, and a purity that he had never imagined dwelt there instead. His friend had called him. He stood for a moment entranced, then the new emotion found him words, and laying his hand very gently upon the pillows he answered, 'Clive!'

How easy it is to pick apart, to exhibit for irony and boredom the flushed loftiness of Forster's manner. Our current economies are Hemingway's. They come of understatement and carry a physical punch. Forster's abstractions are at once prepotent and hollow. They have behind them a genteel code of values and a psychology that is flat because it is reticent. Our hearts no longer declaim in the vocative; if we take hold of the mullion and spring, it is in order to rifle the dean's files for incriminating dossiers from the F.B.I. A fair number of us, one supposes, are still called Clive, but we would hardly admit to the fact on a pillow. Yet how unembarrassed a truth there is in the passage, and how obvious is the hand of a master in the contracted, clouded syntax of the phrase 'the new emotion found him words.'

Maurice visits Durham at Penge, a rundown property on the Somerset border. Both house and estate are marked not by decay but by the immobility that precedes it. 'There is no forest or fell to escape to today,' complained Forster in 1960, 'no cave in which to curl up, no deserted valley for those who wish neither to reform nor corrupt society but to be left alone.' The occurrences at Penge make for a doomed pastoral. Private corruption darkens the glade and the larger insanity of world war is near. The very short eighteenth chapter is, structurally, the center of *Maurice* and a stylistic disaster. Ecstasy 'carves channels.' Maurice 'makes' love, and Clive 'preserves' it, causing 'its rivers to water the garden.' The lovers tread a 'narrow and beautiful path,' distilling 'to their utmost the nobility and sweetness of the world.' They have their last year at Cambridge and travel in Italy. Then 'the prison house' of adult life closes on them. By comparison, *Love Story* is marmoreal prose. It looks as if Forster were under extreme pressure here, as if he did not elect to 'write well' of a remembrance so vital. The saccharine intensity he produces is almost destructive of credibility. Perhaps it was a private code, meant to put off the uninitiate. But why did he leave such pages vulnerable, why did he not revise obvious weaknesses during the long years he kept the manuscript and even gave occasional readings from it to a circle of Cambridge friends? This, as one reads *Maurice*, becomes an insistent question.

During a trip to Greece—the location is an ironic reversal of the symbolic pattern, for Greece would in the usual convention of fiction be the place of homoerotic experience—Clive Durham 'becomes normal.' 'The love of women would rise as certainly as the sun, scorching up immaturity and ushering the full human day.' Again, this is the kind of sentence one finds awkward to place seriously. At one level, it is pompous bathos. But inflect it otherwise, imagine a fiercer context, and the idiom takes on something of the hammering urgency of D. H. Lawrence now so greatly admired.

Maurice's existence turns to ash. He works in the City, joins the Territorials, and gives up Saturday golf to play football with the youths of the College Settlement, in South London. But abrupt attacks of physical lust leave him sickened and afraid. He seeks medical advice, only to be told that he must banish forever such evil hallucinations and temptations by the Devil. The scene of the consultation is one of the sparsest, bitterest in the whole of Forster. Maurice is invited to Penge, where Clive is now a married man, playing cricket with the villagers and seeking election to Parliament. There is a gamekeeper, Alec Scudder, a vaguely coarse, insinuating fellow bent on emigrating to the Argentine. Despite the cold, the scents are everywhere that night. The laborers repairing the tiles on the roof have left their ladder resting against a windowsill. Maurice hears a noise so intimate that it might have arisen inside his own body. The top of the ladder quivers against the moonlit air. The head and shoulders of a man rise up, a gun is leant carefully against the window, 'and someone he scarcely knew moved towards him and knelt beside him and whispered, "Sir, was you calling out for me? . . . Sir, I know. . . . I know," and touched him.'

The scene was written in 1913–14, but Forster looked at it again in 1960 and knew that it would be published even later. Why, in the name of *Lady Chatterley*, stick to the gamekeeper? Surely a gardener would do as well. I feel that if one had a convincing answer to this unavoidable question, much of the novel, or, rather, of Forster's attitude to it, would fall into place. Indifference to a rival reputation? A biographical touch so exact and precious that it could not be elided? Or is Scudder's profession a stroke of feline malice (not wholly uncharacteristic of Forster's late years), a wink to the informed reader that Lawrence's heterosexual posturing might be suspect? In any event, one flinches from future theses on 'the nocturnal role of the gamekeeper in the twentieth-century novel.' In French fiction, the face at the window is that of a poacher. By which thread great differences may be said to hang.

The concluding chapters of *Maurice* are by far the trimmest. After a faintly comical attempt to 'cure himself' by means of hypnosis, Maurice returns to Alec's arms. Alec threatens blackmail. Master and man meet in the British Museum. It is a duel of two worlds, of two systems of speech and perception, narrated with an incisive delicacy that will lead directly to *A Passage to India*. The lovers pace among the statues of heroes 'perfect but bloodless.' Each in turn moves from solicitude to savagery. The razor edge of caste cuts between them. Alec's blackmail is bluff; the police will always back a gentleman against a menial. But despite his shallow greed, the gamekeeper knows more than does his patron of the anarchic equality of love. The barriers of class and fear break down; they go out together into the rain and seek a hotel for the night. In a closing scene, Maurice confronts Clive Durham with the quiet announcement that he is in love with Scudder, that they are proposing to share their lives. There can be no twilight henceforth, no compromise with the world. Maurice literally disappears from the room: 'To the end of his life Clive was not sure of the exact moment of departure, and with the approach of old age he grew uncertain whether the moment had yet occurred.' All that is left is a little pile of the petals of the evening primrose, 'which mourned from the ground like an expiring fire.' Epilogues, says E. M. Forster, are for Tolstoy. Or for critics.

Gide's *Immoralist* had appeared in 1902. By the time Forster was at work on *Maurice*, Gide was preparing, though for private circulation only, his ascetic but unabashed apologia for pederasty in *Corydon*. Proust was immersed in his social and psychological anatomy of Sodom and Gomorrah. Conditions in England were, obviously, thornier. As we know from the life of A. E. Housman, which at certain precise points uncannily resembles that of Forster's hero, the impact of the Oscar Wilde scandal had been felt throughout English sensibility. Homoerotic passions had to be kept clandestine, under peril of ostracism. Nonetheless, Forster's ambivalence, particularly in a text not intended for publication, remains puzzling and, ultimately, damaging. In the very instant of mutual acceptance, when Maurice and Alec go to seek out a hotel for the night, Maurice's tone is 'affectionate yet dejected.' That sadness dims the entire novel. Forster tells us that *Maurice* springs directly from a visit to Edward Carpenter at his 'Uranian Shrine' in Millthorpe, near Sheffield. (Curiously, Forster's postscript of 1960 distorts the name to 'Milthorpe.') Now almost forgotten, Carpenter was at the time an influential guru, and he provides a further odd link between Forster and D. H. Lawrence. Carpenter saw in Whitman's conception of the love of comrades the highest ideal of eros, the true and democratizing coming of age of love. But, besides being colored by elaborate, inane theories of astral influence, Carpenter's sexual creed was, in fact, evasive. Homosexuality was itself only a stage on the road to perfect 'intermediacy.' The 'Child of Uranus' would possess a

> Woman-soul within a Man's form dwelling . . .
> So gentle, gracious, dignified, complete,
> With man's strength to perform, and pride to suffer
> without sign,
> And feminine sensitiveness to the last fibre of being.

Thus, whereas 'Maurice' is clearsighted and aroused about class relations—'Clive on the bench will continue to sentence Alec in the dock. Maurice may get off'—it articulates its central sexual theme with duplicity. It is as if Morgan Forster lived in a measure of self-condemnation, or, more exactly, as if he could never shake off the secrecies, the aura of shame that a prudish, vengeful society had sought to instill in him. When he speaks of Clive Durham's 'cure,' of his 'normality,' he does it without irony and in pained defeat.

This defensive pathos diminishes the book. *Maurice* is not anywhere near Forster's best. But because Forster is an important writer with a coherent *œuvre*, this posthumous novel forces one to rethink his achievement as a whole. It throws particular light on the genius of *A Passage to India*. The choice of theme and treatment in Forster's masterpiece, it now seems likely, represents an act of sublimation, a 'second go' at commitments and insights he had been forced to suppress in their original form. Fourteen years intervened between *Howard's End* and its great successor. The creative nerve of the novelist may have been inhibited by the ambivalence of *Maurice* and by the fact that the book had to remain hidden. But clearly his consciousness was seeking ways of imagining openly, of stating in daylight concerns that were vital to his self-respect, to his restless sense of human justice. Notice the masterly surrogates. By translating his locale to India and to the social discriminations between raj and native, Forster can now express the full gamut of his protest against snobbery, against the shallow cruelty of status and inherited privilege that almost destroyed the love of Maurice and Alec. Half a century before the New Left, E. M. Forster saw that sexual eccentricity could be isolated in racial or caste terms. The encounters between white and native, between emancipated rulers and 'advanced' Indians, in *A Passage to India* are a brilliant projection of the confrontations between society and the homosexual in *Maurice*. Subtlest of all is Forster's solution of the problem of 'physical realization.' In *Maurice*, this basic difficulty had lamed him. Unlike Gide or Lawrence, he had found no sensuous enactment adequate to his vision of sex. Gesture recedes in a cloying mist. The mysterious outrage in the Marabar caves is a perfect solution. Though, as the rest of the novel will show, 'nothing has happened' in that dark and echoing place, the force of sexual suggestion is uncompromising. As only a true writer can, Forster had found his way to a symbolic action richer, more precise than any single concrete occurrence. The non-event in the hills of Marabar comprises values that we can now confidently recognize as being both heterosexual and homosexual. Both are facets, momentary and—it may be—contingent, of the unbounded unity of love. Finally, one can conjecture that it was the happy ending of *Maurice*, its clandestine statement of the consummation achieved between two human beings of different castes, that enabled Forster to close *A Passage to India* on a precarious, ironic note.

At the same time, it would be silly to deny that the very centrality of *Maurice* in Forster's private life and work (*A Passage to India* was his last novel and last book of any real stature) may narrow or specialize the sum of his achievement. In the light of an intensely spiritualized yet nervous and partly embittered homosexuality, a number of Forster's most famous dicta—it is better to betray one's country than a friend, 'only connect'—take on a more restricted, shriller ambience. His 'two cheers for democracy' and lifelong defense of the rights of private conduct lose nothing of their humane fineness, but we cannot help being aware henceforth of the personal hurt from which they derive. Inevitably, *Maurice* will strengthen one's feeling that E. M. Forster is a minor master who produced one major novel, and that his gifts are less representative of modern English literature than some critics have argued. The physical truth, the philosophical energy of John Cowper Powys's handling of 'normal' and homosexual passion offer a revealing contrast.

But it is not the weaknesses in *Maurice* that bring a sense of sadness. It is the simple fact that there will never again be an autumn book list with a new novel by that late and most eminent Fellow of King's College, Cambridge.

184. 'A chalice for youth', *The Times Literary Supplement*

mccxvi, 8 October 1971

An unsigned review.

In February, 1915, Forster visited D. H. Lawrence at Greatham, and while he was there Lawrence wrote his impressions of his guest in a letter to a friend: 'He is very nice. I wonder if the grip has gone out of him. I get a feeling of acute misery from him—not that he does anything—but you know the acute, exquisite pain of cramp.' We may take that intuitive diagnosis as essentially accurate: what Forster was suffering from was homosexual cramp, the spiritual and imaginative restraints of a suppressed and guilty sexuality. At the same time that he visited the Lawrences he had accepted his sexual nature, and had even written a novel about it, but he had no thought of publishing the book or of revealing his condition to the world; and so, when Lawrence and Frieda began to analyse his problems he responded first with reticence and finally with anger. His cramp might have been painful, but it was none the less necessary: it made his literary and social existence possible.

For Lawrence, Forster's cramp was a pain that could be cured; 'Why can't he take a woman', Lawrence wondered, 'and fight clear to his own basic, primal being?' But post-Freudians know better than that, not only about the persistency of sexual drives, but also about the creative consequences of psychic wounds. The impulse that suppresses and distorts the sexual life may liberate the imagination, though at a price which only the artist can reckon. Forster may have disliked and resented his condition—it seems clear that he did—but it was as central to his art as to his sexual being; to say that he was homosexual is to define not only his private nature, but the nature of his imagination.

With the private nature the critic has no proper business, and it is easy to respect and continue Forster's life-long reticence. But the homosexuality of his imagination is a critical matter, for it explains both the qualities and the limitations of his work. It informs the essential properties of his novels, the voyeuristic distancing of the narration, the ironic tone, the self-deprecating humour, and it imposes the most serious limitations—the blind spots and imaginative failures.

Most obviously, Forster could not imagine any aspect of the range of experience between men and women—heterosexual attraction, heterosexual relations, marriage were mysterious to him. No wonder he resented having to write 'marriage novels'—the subject was quite beyond his range. If we consider the crucial marriages in his books—Lucy Honeychurch and George Emerson, Lilia and Gino, Margaret Schlegel and Mr. Wilcox, Rickie and Agnes—they seem equally unreal and unrealized; and the one irregular union that he attempted—the one-night affair of Helen and Leonard Bast—is even worse, a case of conception as an Edwardian schoolboy might have imagined it, out of a few facts and a large ignorance.

No doubt this is why one feels in so many of Forster's novels a kind of transference at work, as though one were reading a different sort of story, but translated into socially acceptable terms. *The Longest Journey*, Forster's most personal novel, and the one he himself liked best, is a case in point. It is a 'marriage novel', but not in any ordinary sense; rather, it seems a kind of homosexual nightmare, in which the condition of marriage is imagined—cold, loveless, and degrading. The central relation is not that between husband and wife, Rickie and Agnes, at all, but that between Rickie and Stephen Wonham. Forster confessed in an interview that he had 'had trouble with the junction of Rickie and Stephen. How to make them intimate . . .'—and the difficulty is surely that he was writing a crypto-homosexual story, in which his protagonist is 'saved' by his intimacy with a young man of humble station (Forster himself favoured young men of the lower classes). Forster made the relationship acceptable by basing it on kinship, and by marrying Rickie to Agnes (his abnormality is transferred to his crippled foot), but the curious dissonance remains that all the heat of the novel is concentrated on the one-man scenes, and the man-woman scenes have a chill repugnancy. Agnes, we are told, had a child, but the statement is incredible: how could a child possibly have been conceived in such a union?

In other novels there are other signs. In *A Room with a View*, for instance, no physical scene between the lovers is treated as vividly as the all-male bathing scene, so reminiscent of the pederastic bathing of Victorian homosexual writing and photography. In it, male nakedness liberates George and Mr Beebe from their conventionality, and the women, when they appear, are a confining and depressing end to the affair. Over the whole episode a vague spiritual-mythological presence hovers which is evoked in the purplish prose that Forster characteristically employed on such occasions: 'It had been a call to the blood and to the relaxed will, a passing benediction whose influence did not pass, a holiness, a spell, a momentary chalice for youth.' As an account of the effect of pond-bathing this seems rather fruity; but it works better if we take it as a veiled description of sexual feeling—physical and urgent, beneficial but temporary, an event out of the ordinary range of society's possibilities.

Pan is not quite present in that scene, though one can sense him elsewhere in the novels when feeling is released; he is Forster's presiding deity, the spirit of liberation from convention, the god of boys and bumpkins. He appears most overtly in the short stories, but he is also present in Stephen Wonham, and in most of Forster's passionate Italians. Pan may be identified with the force of Nature in Forster, but one must qualify that remark somewhat; for Forster was never really interested in Nature as such, and what Pan really represents is an idea of natural human behaviour—a complete life without conventional restraints, a life that acknowledges 'bestiality'. Which is to say that Forster's Pan is the deity of a homosexual world, or a world in which homosexuality is natural. He is necessary to the stories and novels simply because, in Forster's Sawston-and-Cambridge world, homosexual love could not be a force in itself; it was only by supernatural intervention that direct emotion could find expression.

Looking back over the novels and stories, one must conclude that Forster was incapable of recording deep currents of feeling—sexual feeling most obviously, but other deep feeling as well. The occasions when feeling should flow—sexual love, birth, death—are treated distantly, with a cold casualness; we remember 'Gerald died that afternoon', in *The Longest Journey*, but forget from the same novel 'while he was out his brother died', and 'by the time they arrived Robert had been drowned'—three throw-away deaths of loved persons.

Ordinary emotional states were beyond Forster, and perhaps the moments of melodrama so often remarked in the novels are there because they offered him his only means of indicating strong feeling; but how gross it always seems—the stabbed man in the piazza, the baby hurled from the carriage, death under a train; extreme stimuli for the feelings they express. And when the emotion is explicitly sexual, the failure is complete. *Howards End* is the weak novel it is because it has heterosexual relationships at its centre—an engagement, a marriage, and a fornication move the plot—and Forster could not handle any of them convincingly. And so the events that should be fully treated are either shuffled off-stage, or are brought on so wrapped in rhetoric as to be quite meaningless (all that embarrassing stuff about 'rainbow bridges', for instance). *Where Angels Fear to Tread* is a better novel than *Howards End* partly because it does not attempt sexuality, or only indirectly: what it is really about is the difficulties a homosexual has in understanding the behaviour of heterosexuals, and Forster knew a good deal about that.

The exception to these strictures is, of course, *A Passage to India*, which is more and more clearly Forster's one achievement. Perhaps Forster learnt about love in India, or perhaps race did what sexual difference didn't do; at any rate, the relation between Fielding and Aziz is the one deeply moving intimacy in the novels, far more intimate than any marriage Forster attempted, or any love affair. It is the principal evidence that he did have a developed heart, for all his donnish reticence.

'How much time does love take?' Forster asks in *Aspects of the Novel*, and he concludes that two hours a day is a handsome allowance. And indeed in Forster's world that is more than enough; setting aside Aziz, one can scarcely find a character in the novels who spends as much time loving as he does in being ridiculous or nasty. This is in part a circumstance of the curious Forsterian tribe that inhabits his world, a tribe that seems designed to make loving, and especially sexual loving, unnecessary, or even impossible. Typically it has at its centre a fatherless family: a widowed mother, some daughters, and one—always just one—rather inadequate son. There are some variations (no daughters in *The Longest Journey*, Mrs Wilcox for the mother-figure in *Howards End*), but the tribal pattern is strikingly uniform through the novels up to *Passage to India*. The tribe represents restraints: convention, propriety, suburbanism, and the sexual restraints of widowhood and virginity. To escape the tribe is to free the imagination, to move from suburbs to country, from the rule of the C of E God to the rule of Pan, from control to freedom, from no-sex to sex. It is also, in the most personal books, to escape from the world of women to a world of men; woman is the Mother, but man is the Comrade, the brother Rickie wanted but did not have.

In each of Forster's tribes there is a Forster-like character, a boy or young man, ascetic and detached, imperfectly involved in life, and slightly ridiculous. These characters differ a good deal in particulars, and in the roles they play in the actions, but they are always in evidence—in Forster every mother has a son to devour, and every son has a slightly chewed look. Seen together—Freddie and Rickie, Tibby and Philip—they seem a common type without a common function. What they provided for Forster was a steady point of reference, a self in the novel, who can view the emotional lives of others with some ironic detachment, but, because he is a character, can also in turn be viewed ironically. If society disapproves of limp-wristed young men, then Forster will put one in each of his novels, and ridicule him. These are Forster's selves, but seen through the world's eyes, and denied and disinherited by their creator.

Though Forster was homosexual, he lived in a world which believed in marriage and in marriage-novels, and his desire to remain in that world was stronger than his desire to tell the truth about himself. Obviously his work was affected by this disharmony, and certainly his gifts were distorted by it, but it would be too simple to say that the repression of his sexual nature crippled his imagination, or was necessarily a factor in his 'drying-up' as a novelist. One could more readily argue that in fact a *creative* tension existed between the impulse and the work, and that the effort to transform homosexuality into socially acceptable forms was an ordering force, which determined both his characteristic vision and his characteristic tone. He saw the world as emptied of absolutes, lonely, and threatening (the truest expression of this vision is in the concert scene in *Howards End*, when Helen hears

'Panic and Emptiness!' in Beethoven's Fifth Symphony); but he expressed this bleak vision with a self-deprecating irony that refuses to be altogether serious, and never reached toward tragedy. If one says that tragedy and homosexuality do not sit well together, but irony and homosexuality do, this is not to be taken as a judgment of a sexual state, but as an observation of social attitudes. Forster was a sensitive judge of such attitudes, and he wrote, one might say defensively, to preserve his place in the society which would ostracize him if it knew. But cunning defensiveness suited his talent, and he made out of self-deprecation, transference, and evasion a personal and functioning style.

One had always heard rumours that there was one exception: that there was an unpublished novel which eschewed evasion, and was too frank to be published. Now at last we have that novel, and some of the circumstances of its composition. It was written in 1913–14, and a 'Terminal Note' Forster explains the initial impulse. He had been visiting Edward Carpenter, the Edwardian guru of sandals, the simple life, and 'homogenic love', and while he was there Carpenter's friend, George Merrill, had touched Forster fondly on the backside:

> The sensation was unusual and I still remember it, as I remember the position of a long vanished tooth. It was as much psychological as physical. It seemed to go straight through the small of my back into my ideas, without involving my thoughts.

He returned to his mother, who was taking a cure at Harrogate, and began to write *Maurice*.

The novel came to him easily—no doubt because he did not have to translate his feelings into other terms—and he seems to have written with a sense of private liberation. But having written, he recovered his instinctive cautiousness, and did not try to publish it (not that publication would have been easy in a decade that suppressed *The Rainbow*). He showed it to friends from time to time, and he went on tinkering with it (most recently in 1960), but he was unwilling to endure the disturbance to his quiet life that publication would cause, and he left the manuscript at his death with the laconic Forsterian comment: 'Publishable—but worth it?'

Maurice is an example of a common twentieth-century kind of novel, the novel of growth and self-discovery; it belongs to the same category as *A Portrait of the Artist*, *Of Human Bondage*, and *The Longest Journey*. But it differs from those novels in what Maurice discovers—

that he is homosexual, and that homosexual love is possible. In his personal circumstances Maurice is Tibby and Rickie and Philip all over again, the Weak Young Man with a widowed mother, sisters, a house in the Surrey suburbs, and a Cambridge education; and though Forster made some effort to make him un-Forsterian by giving him healthy good looks and a rather dull mind, this scarcely matters—he is in essentials true to type.

There is, however, one significant deviation from the tribal pattern; Maurice comes to a happy ending, in fulfilled love with a gamekeeper. Forster mistrusted and disliked happy endings; most novels, he thought, went off at the end as the author huddled resolutions together, and his own instinct was for dissonances. But in this case, he wrote,

> a happy ending was imperative. I shouldn't have bothered to write otherwise. I was determined that in fiction anyway two men should fall in love and remain in it for the ever and ever that fiction allows. . . .

He was writing, this time, for the sake of homosexual love, and was willing to violate his own sensibility to assert that such love was possible. The ending of the novel is clumsy and improbable, and is altogether without the defences of irony that protect the other novels; but it is done that way by intention, to put a human principle above an aesthetic one. This is a very Forsterian thing to do, but it complicates the act of critical judgment, as it complicated the act of creation.

The crucial question about *Maurice* is, what happens when that creative tension between the homosexual imagination and society's restraints which informs Forster's other novels is abandoned for truth-telling? What happens when Forster tries to put 'the private lusts and aches' of his sexuality into fiction? How, in short, does he write without cramp? The answer, alas, is that he has written a novel of such uncharacteristic badness as not to be comparable to any other of his works, a novel almost as good, perhaps, as *The Well of Loneliness*, but certainly no better. He has sacrificed all the qualities that make his work interesting—the ironic tone, the distance, the humour, the touches of shrewd wisdom, the style—and he has gained no commensurate values. The sentimentality that is always close to the surface in Forster (his liberalism was never much more than sentimental humanism) here oozes forth everywhere; indeed both the sentimentality and the prose style are so reminiscent of Edward Carpenter at his worst that one can only regret that trip to Milthorpe, and the pat on the bottom that started it all.

Most serious of all the novel's faults is what can only be described as the incompleteness of the imaginative act. *Maurice* is composed of many short chapters, more of them, and shorter, than in any other Forster novel. This is more than a statistic: it suggests what is indeed the case, that episodes are not fully realized, that the imagination has been imperfectly made verbal. Forster wrote the book rapidly because he was writing from experience, and no doubt for the same reason he did not succeed in turning experience into literary reality. If one examines, for example, the three pages that see Maurice through his public school, one finds a tissue of thin and general statements that might have been written by an Edwardian headmaster: 'Thoughts: he had a dirty little collection. Acts: he desisted from these after the novelty was over, finding that they brought him more fatigue than pleasure'—so much for the adolescent sex life of our protagonist. One is surely not being prurient in suggesting that a novel about the Growth of a Homosexual ought to treat sex more frankly than that.

The heart of the matter is there, in the treatment of sex. Forster may have thought he wrote the book because he had come to terms with his own nature, but the book shows that this is not quite the case; *Maurice* is about homosexuality, but the attitudes it expresses are far from liberated. The language is the language of society—*morbidity*, *perversion* versus *normality*—and the attitude is substantially guilty and regretful. Maurice accepts his condition, but he disapproves of it, and so, one gathers, does Forster, for at the end he turns from the real, social world, and sends his lovers off into a sentimental world of romance, like two Scholar Gypsies; there is to be no assimilation, no contact with society, but rather a sentimentalized form of ostracism.

Nor does Forster give to homosexual love any greater reality than he was able to evoke in his accounts of marriage. One had thought that he was vague and rhetorical with Lucy and George because he did not and could not know anything about their relationship, but he is no better with Maurice and Alec—there is the same poverty of feeling here, the same lack of emotional complexity, the same cramped heart. The language is meticulously decent, but the treatment is as emotionally thin as pornography is. And this, too, must be a consequence of Forster's ambivalence and sense of sordidness; he could not imagine sex that was neither furtive nor repulsive. Love for him may have been a Beloved Republic, but it was never an innocent act.

Maurice is interesting as an Edwardian view of homosexuality, but it does not transcend that historical limit, and so, as a friend told Forster when he had read the manuscript, it can only have a period interest—plus, one might add, that morbid interest one has in the unsuccessful work of a good writer. It adds nothing to his achievement as a novelist, and little to his reckoning as a man. If he had published it when he wrote it, it would have been a courageous act, as Carpenter's was when he published *Homogenic Love* and *The Intermediate Sex*; but now it appears as evidence of his fearful caution—the sort of thing that Sawston would have understood.

Forster would probably not mind; he had a modest opinion of his place in the record, and did not worry about it, and in any case he would rather have had the kind of immortality that he ascribes to Carpenter, the sort that rests, not on words and deeds, but on the constancy and intensity of affections. . . . But the critic can make no estimate of that achievement, and must be content to judge the book. And for that judgment, the words of Mrs Failing, upon reading Rickie's story, are perhaps the best:

> 'It is bad', said Mrs. Failing. 'But. But. But.' Then she escaped, having told the truth, and yet leaving a pleasurable impression behind her.

Select Bibliography

This bibliography contains only items which relate to the growth or state of Forster's literary reputation.

BEEBE, MAURICE AND BROGUNIER, JOSEPH, 'Criticism of E. M. Forster: a selected checklist', *Modern Fiction Studies* vii (Autumn 1961), 284–92.

BRADBURY, MALCOLM (ed.), *Forster: A Collection of Critical Essays* (1966): Professor Bradbury's introduction deals perceptively with Forster's developing reputation from 1927 onwards.

BROWN, E. K., 'The revival of E. M. Forster', *Yale Review* xxxiii (Summer 1944), 668–81: comments on the state of Forster's reputation in America before 1943, and on the reprinting of four of Forster's novels in America in that year.

GERBER, HELMUT (ed.), 'E. M. Forster: an annotated checklist of writings about him', *English Fiction in Transition* ii, 1 (1959), 4–27: gives a useful indication of the extent of Forster's reputation in England and America, and lists a few items on Forster published in Belgium, Holland, Germany and Japan.

KIRKPATRICK, B. J., *A Bibliography of E. M. Forster* (1965): includes full publication details of all Forster's books, and lists the many translations of his novels published between 1927 and 1964.

MACDOWELL, FREDERICK P. W., 'E. M. Forster: an annotated secondary bibliography', *English Literature in Transition* xiii, 2 (E. M. Forster Memorial Volume, 1970): the most comprehensive list of books and articles on Forster, together with some reviews.

ZABEL, MORTON DAUWEN, 'A Forster revival', *Nation* clvii (7 August 1943): comments on Trilling's study (1943) and on the American reissue of four of Forster's novels in that year.

Index

The index is arranged as follows: I. Newspapers and journals; II. Critics and reviewers; III. Writers compared with E. M. Forster; IV. References to E. M. Forster's fiction.

I. NEWSPAPERS AND JOURNALS QUOTED FROM OR REFERRED TO

II. CRITICS AND REVIEWERS QUOTED OR REFERRED TO

III. WRITERS AND WORKS COMPARED WITH FORSTER OR MENTIONED IN CONNECTION WITH HIM

IV. DISCUSSIONS OF FORSTER'S FICTION, INCLUDING INTERESTING REFERENCES TO INDIVIDUAL CHARACTERS

THE CRITICAL HERITAGE SERIES

GENERAL EDITOR: B. C. SOUTHAM

Volumes published and forthcoming

MATTHEW ARNOLD: THE POETRY	Carl Dawson
JANE AUSTEN	B. C. Southam
BROWNING	Boyd Litzinger and Donald Smalley
BURNS	Donald A. Low
BYRON	Andrew Rutherford
THOMAS CARLYLE	Jules Paul Seigel
CLARE	Mark Storey
CLOUGH	Michael Thorpe
COLERIDGE	J. R. de J. Jackson
CONRAD	Norman Sherry
FENIMORE COOPER	George Dekker and John P. McWilliams
CRABBE	Arthur Pollard
STEPHEN CRANE	Richard M. Weatherford
DEFOE	Pat Rogers
DICKENS	Philip Collins
DRYDEN	James and Helen Kinsley
GEORGE ELIOT	David Carroll
HENRY FIELDING	Ronald Paulson and Thomas Lockwood
FORD MADOX FORD	Frank MacShane
GISSING	Pierre Coustillas and Colin Partridge
THOMAS HARDY	R. G. Cox
HAWTHORNE	J. Donald Crowley
IBSEN	Michael Egan
HENRY JAMES	Roger Gard
JOHNSON	James T. Boulton
JAMES JOYCE 1907–1927	Robert H. Deming
JAMES JOYCE 1928–1941	Robert H. Deming

Continued